Potterversity

Potterversity

Essays Exploring the World of Harry Potter

Edited by
KATHRYN N. MCDANIEL *and*
EMILY STRAND

McFarland & Company, Inc., Publishers
Jefferson, North Carolina

This book has undergone peer review.

LIBRARY OF CONGRESS CATALOGUING-IN-PUBLICATION DATA

Names: McDaniel, Kathryn N., editor. | Strand, Emily K. (Emily Katherine), 1976– editor.
Title: Potterversity : essays exploring the world of Harry Potter / edited by Kathryn N. McDaniel, Emily Strand.
Description: Jefferson, North Carolina : McFarland & Company, Inc., Publishers, 2024. | Includes bibliographical references and index.
Identifiers: LCCN 2023046323 | ISBN 9781476690537 (paperback : acid free paper) ♾
ISBN 9781476651279 (ebook)
Subjects: LCSH: Rowling, J. K. Harry Potter series. | BISAC: LITERARY CRITICISM / Children's & Young Adult Literature | PERFORMING ARTS / Film / Genres / Science Fiction & Fantasy | LCGFT: Literary criticism. | Essays.
Classification: LCC PR6068.O93 Z829 2023 | DDC 823/.914—dc23/eng/20231004
LC record available at https://lccn.loc.gov/2023046323

BRITISH LIBRARY CATALOGUING DATA ARE AVAILABLE

ISBN (print) 978-1-4766-9053-7
ISBN (ebook) 978-1-4766-5127-9

© 2024 Kathryn N. McDaniel and Emily Strand. All rights reserved

No part of this book may be reproduced or transmitted in any form or by any means, electronic or mechanical, including photocopying or recording, or by any information storage and retrieval system, without permission in writing from the publisher.

Front cover image by Lacey Villareal

Printed in the United States of America

McFarland & Company, Inc., Publishers
 Box 611, Jefferson, North Carolina 28640
 www.mcfarlandpub.com

With gratitude to our listeners:
You have a place at *Potterversity*.

Acknowledgments

Putting together this collection of essays has been a labor of love.

Katy and Emily would like to thank, most especially, all of the contributors to the *Potterversity* podcast and this book. You maximize the "love" and minimize the "labor" for us as we collaborate to build a scholarly Potter Studies community. We are grateful for all your serious questions, thoughtful answers, diligent and insightful research, good humor, and abiding conviction that conversations about *Harry Potter* can help us understand our own world at a deeper level. We additionally benefited from constructive reviews of the manuscript, and we appreciate very much the support of Layla Milholen and all the folks at McFarland as we made our vision a reality.

We'd also like to thank the educational institutions that supported us in developing this book. Marietta College granted Katy a sabbatical in the spring of 2022 to work on this project, and the staff at the Legacy Library were especially helpful to her in tracking down sources. Emily thanks Mount Carmel College, Signum University, and all the *Potter* scholars who welcomed her into the conversation. Having been accepted into this vibrant and challenging community, particularly via the Harry Potter Academic Conference at Chestnut Hill College, we hope to provide a forum for others to participate in the conversation, too.

And so, finally, many thanks to you, our listeners and readers: we are glad you have joined us.

Table of Contents

Acknowledgments — vi

Introduction: Your Potterversity *Orientation*
KATHRYN N. MCDANIEL *and* EMILY STRAND — 1

Occult Knowledge

Good Men and Monsters: Bram Stoker's *Dracula* and *Harry Potter*
BEATRICE GROVES — 9

Dark Arts and Secret Histories: Investigating Dark Academia
AMY H. STURGIS — 26

Conversation: Occult Knowledge — 43

Ancient Magic

Here Be Dragons and Phoenixes: A Thematic Direction for the *Fantastic Beasts* Series
LANA A. WHITED — 49

The Real Magic of Christmas in *Harry Potter*
EMILY STRAND — 67

Conversation: Ancient Magic — 85

A Question of Character

Padfoot Revelio! The Life and Love of Sirius Black
EMMA NICHOLSON — 89

The Weasley Witches: From Snitches to Stitches to "Not-My-Daughter-You-Bitches"
LOUISE M. FREEMAN — 107

Arthur Weasley and the Misuse of Muggle Artefacts
    Kathryn N. McDaniel   121

Conversation: A Question of Character   136

Self and Others

The Problem with Loving Enemies: Kindness and Oppression in "The Wizard and the Hopping Pot"
    Travis Prinzi   143

Uncle Remus's Shack: Tokenism in the Wizarding World
    Mark-Anthony Lewis   158

Conversation: Self and Others   173

Playing Potter

It's All Fun and Games Until…: Leisurely and Competitive Pursuits in *Harry Potter* and Chivalric Romance
    Laurie Beckoff   179

Gamifying the *Harry Potter* Studies Classroom
    Tison Pugh   193

Conversation: Playing Potter   210

Teaching, the Hogwarts Way

Dumbledorisms: The Idiosyncratic Style of a Hogwarts Headmaster
    M'Balia Thomas   215

Hem Hem… I Take Umbridge with Bigotry: Using the Witch-in-Pink to Counter Oppression
    Brent A. Satterly   230

Conversation: Teaching, the Hogwarts Way   247

Before the Dismissal Bell: Closing Thoughts
    Kathryn N. McDaniel   253

Bibliography   255

About the Contributors   269

Index   273

Introduction

Your Potterversity *Orientation*

KATHRYN N. MCDANIEL *and* EMILY STRAND

Welcome to *Potterversity*! It's time to get sorted.

Whether you're a Hufflepuff, Gryffindor, Ravenclaw, or Slytherin, you're in the right place. We here at *Potterversity* embrace hard work and humanistic values, courage and daring, wit and wisdom, ambition and cleverness. And we like to think that we're more inclusive than those medieval houses, too, in bringing to the conversation a wide range of voices and making sure that our ideas are accessible—to magical folk and Muggles alike. That's what makes *Potterversity*'s virtual campus such a wonderful place to learn: everyone is invited.

We, Katy and Emily, are your guides to the academic side of *Harry Potter* fandom, or "acafandom,"[1] through our *Potterversity* podcast and now in this companion book of scholarly essays. As the "Hermione-approved" *Potter* podcast on the fansite MuggleNet, we aim for the best and most innovative analytic approaches to the universe of the *Harry Potter* novels, ancillary texts, films, and fandom, often referred to as the Potterverse. The field of Potter Studies is robust, provocative, and interdisciplinary, engaging a wide variety of serious scholars from within the academy and also outside of it. Through our conversations we hope to engage not only the mind but the spirit as well—the emotional, personal, and moral responses that the Potterverse has evoked in so many people around the world. Despite its fantasy setting, the wizarding world speaks to us Muggles, showing us our problems as well as provoking questions, wise solutions, and vibrant critique. Fundamentally, we and our guests on the show believe that the characters, stories, and situations of the magical world promote thinking that helps us navigate our more mundane but no less dangerous world. Perhaps even more important, they help us to recognize the magic amid our everyday Muggle realities.

2   Introduction

You'll find all of that in your education at *Potterversity*. We asked *Potter* experts, some of our favorite guests, and memorable conference presenters to contribute their latest scholarship to this volume so that you can read their essays all in one place. We're all about class discussion on our virtual campus, so we wanted to give you a sense of the kinds of interchanges we have at *Potterversity*. To that end, after each set of lessons on a particular topic, we've included a short "conversation": an excerpt from a podcast featuring those authors talking in more depth and sometimes personally about their topics. For the whole conversation, you can listen to those podcasts on our podcast feed and on MuggleNet (we could only fit a few choice bits of those conversations here). The essays and conversations complement each other in the same way academic writing, at its best, represents a multi-layered conversation among scholars.

No one is above criticism, so you'll find that some of these scholars directly engage with the problematic aspects of the series and its author, J.K. Rowling. A recent challenge in the world of Potter Studies is how (and whether) to respond to Rowling's controversial statements about trans people, which began in June 2020 and have continued. Like the *Potter* fandom in general, the scholars participating in our podcast and this book express a range of responses to the controversy. Although some people have left the fan and acafan community, none of the scholars involved in this book have (yet) made that choice. You will, however, find in the essays below that some scholars have adjusted their analytical perspectives to consider Rowling's world in the light of her statements: both in subtle ways and through direct critique. Others have assumed a "death of the author" approach, intentionally focusing on the text itself as opposed to the author's intentions or influences. Still others engage little with the controversy as they focus on issues unrelated to the source of the fandom controversy. Our aim is not to throw out the author's work entirely, nor let her off the hook, nor let her dominate the conversation. At *Potterversity*, in the best academic tradition, we seek to incorporate a variety of viewpoints based on a shared conviction that the wizarding world remains both influential and revelatory—politically, culturally, and psychologically. The best way forward is through encouraging open conversation and providing a forum for diverse voices.

Although you should feel free to approach this book in any order you like (we're betting that some topics will grab your attention right away), we have also been sensitive to creating an instructional arc you can follow throughout the book. You'll start with foundational questions about genre and supernatural dangers in "Occult Knowledge" and then learn about the deeply-rooted literary and religious symbols that convey the properties of "Ancient Magic." Next, we'll discuss some of our favorite magical people with "A Question of Character" and examine what the *Harry Potter* books have to say about contemporary issues of social justice in "Self and Others." Take a recess break for "Playing Potter," in which you'll learn about the serious (and not so serious) business of games in the series. Finally, we investigate the teaching and learning process itself in examining the lives of Hogwarts professors you love and hate in "Teaching, the Hogwarts Way." Throughout, the *Potterversity* faculty in this volume provide both analysis and critique, demonstrating that wizarding world stories remain rich sources of meaning and catalysts for making a better world. From start to finish, you'll uncover new insights about what we know and how we know it that will shape the way you experience the *Harry Potter* stories.

Our first set of lessons focuses on "Occult Knowledge" in the *Harry Potter* books—the dark, disturbing mysteries they contain and why such secrets are not just thrilling but thematically significant. Beatrice Groves's essay "Good Men and Monsters" points to the surprising allusions to Bram Stoker's *Dracula* in the *Harry Potter* series, despite the scarcity of actual vampires in the novels. She examines the Gothic engagement with dark supernatural forces in both and the different choices made by each author to convey the lingering effects of confronting evil. Amy H. Sturgis's essay "Dark Arts and Secret Histories" provides an essential definition of Dark Academia, a genre the *Harry Potter* series popularized and shaped, and explains how *Prisoner of Azkaban* acts as a model of the form. Essential to Dark Academia fiction is real-world critique. In that spirit, post–Rowling Dark Academia novelists often take the opportunity to comment critically on the *Harry Potter* novels and their author via their own troubling, imaginary landscapes. (You'll want to have a notebook handy to record Amy's book recommendations.)

Moving from dark histories to sacred legacies, the authors in our section on "Ancient Magic" look to the religious and mythic symbolism in wizarding world stories. Whether through beast lore or religious traditions, creating a powerful interpretative backstory for the magical realm emphasizes both its depth and its transcendence. Lana A. Whited explores the deeply-rooted understanding of magical beasts in the *Fantastic Beasts* film series in her essay "Here Be Dragons and Phoenixes." Recognizing mythological creatures from a variety of cultures helps us understand the relationship between Albus Dumbledore (associated with the phoenix) and Gellert Grindelwald (who has many dragon-like features) and why Magizoologist Newt Scamander is the chosen hero for this series. Focusing on the religious symbolism in the *Harry Potter* books, podcast co-host Emily Strand examines the Christmases in the series as symbol-laden, magical thresholds that help Harry's development of Christian virtues. Her essay "The Real Magic of Christmas in *Harry Potter*" shows how the rituals of Christmas in each book set the stage for Harry's transcendent experiences in *Deathly Hallows* as he comes to understand the meaning of sacrifice.

In the next set of lessons, "A Question of Character," we focus intensely on some of our favorite—and most challenging—characters from the *Harry Potter* series, with deep dives into the motivation and significance of key members of Harry's "found family." By questioning the character of these characters, we come to an enriched understanding of how they relate to key themes of the novels. *Potterversity*'s technical editor Emma Nicholson unveils the influence of Sirius Black's past traumas on his role as Harry's godfather in "Padfoot Revelio!" Although some have berated Sirius for his shortcomings, a meticulous reconstructing of Sirius's own youth helps us understand why he acts as he does and how he expresses his profound love for his godson. In "The Weasley Witches," Louise M. Freeman explains how Ginny and Molly Weasley fit into feminine versions of Jungian archetypes. As both "Amazon" and "Mother," the two Weasley women who make up Harry's found family show the varied and continuing evolution of nuanced female characters in the series. And what about Harry's stand-in father figure? In "Arthur Weasley and the Misuse of Muggle Artefacts," Kathryn N. McDaniel (a.k.a. podcast co-host Katy) ponders whether Mr. Weasley is culturally appropriating Muggle artefacts, particularly in bewitching the Ford Anglia. Arthur's magical tinkering also elicits questions about how we use technology to extend life beyond ourselves; comparing Mr. Weasley with Voldemort shows how such measures can be positive and life-affirming or corrosive and life-destroying.

Central to the question of cultural appropriation is understanding the power dynamic between wizards, Muggles, and other beings in the series, and this informs the next essays in the volume as well. The section on "Self and Others" considers what the wizarding world tells us about how we relate to marginalized people in our society, particularly in regard to race in the modern United States. Travis Prinzi's essay, "The Problem with Loving Enemies," takes a closer look at the power differentials between Muggles and wizards and how that relates to Black/White relations in contemporary America. A nuanced approach to the moral theme of loving those who've wronged us in Beedle the Bard's "The Wizard and the Hopping Pot" leads to important insights about that message—who delivers it and to what audience—and why we should be careful about how we apply it to marginalized people. In "Uncle Remus's Shack," Mark-Anthony Lewis analyzes the tokenism of characters like Lupin, Hagrid, Firenze, and Dobby to discuss the limitations of token representation as well as the challenges of living as a token inhabiting two worlds. This analysis not only provides greater insight into these key characters but also helps us empathize with those in our own society who bear the burden of a double identity, which disrupts their belonging within either the dominant or the marginalized group.

Our next section, "Playing Potter," explores the thematic and pedagogical importance of games in the wizarding world. *Potterversity* producer Laurie Beckoff points out the similarities between medieval tournaments and other games of Arthurian literature and what we find at Hogwarts in her essay, "It's All Fun and Games Until..." In addition to simply giving a recreational pause to the more serious action of the stories, games serve an important purpose in character development and social commentary, both when applied to medieval and contemporary society. Games reveal not only the pleasures but also the dangers of the world in which the characters live. In the first of our pedagogical essays, "Gamifying the *Harry Potter* Studies Classroom," Tison Pugh explains how including competitive elements to his *Harry Potter* class promotes engagement and learning. From Hogwarts House competitions to individual challenges, he gives students a chance to win points and prizes as they learn about literary analysis, particularly applied to the *Harry Potter* novels. Teachers of the series will find this essay a treasure-trove of useful ideas for their classrooms.

At *Potterversity*, we're all about teaching and learning. This theme continues in our final section, "Teaching, the Hogwarts Way," where our *Potter* scholars combine character analysis with pedagogical insights. M'Balia Thomas's essay "Dumbledorisms," which investigates the Hogwarts Headmaster's use of aphorisms, provides insights into why Albus Dumbledore has trouble communicating more directly with students. To bridge the knowledge asymmetries between himself and others, he invokes wise phrases as part of his pedagogical style. Understanding this practice and its motivation helps us regard him more compassionately as a teacher doing the best he can in his situation. In "Hem Hem... I Take Umbridge with Bigotry," Brent A. Satterly highlights another controversial Hogwarts teacher: Dolores Umbridge. Taking on her personality in drag cosplay in the classroom and other venues, Brent embraces her power but inverts her prejudice, turning Umbridge into a voice that skewers intolerance while supporting and celebrating difference. He shares his own experience reading *Harry Potter* as an LGBTQIA+ social work professor, and he has a special message in his "Call Out" box for series author J.K. Rowling on the issue of trans acceptance.

In addition to these thought-provoking essays, you'll find our author conversations at the end of each section broaden and deepen exploration of their themes. These discussions also allow for more personal connections with the *Harry Potter* themes, which provide powerful insights into the continuing relevance of these characters and stories, even as these interpretations move beyond the author and her intentions. These sections of our book underline the vital role that interchange plays in the field of Potter Studies—we learn from each other by listening, questioning, and making important connections. We hope you'll weigh in yourself through comments at our *Potterversity* sites on social media and at MuggleNet. Unlike Professor Binns, we at *Potterversity* want to engage with our listeners, and unlike Professor Umbridge, we believe that students can be teachers, too.

To matriculate at *Potterversity*, just turn the page. A rich, transfiguring education awaits. Class is in session!

Note

1. Henry Jenkins used the term "acafan" (original plural, "acafen," conjoined by Patricia Gillikin) to emphasize that the scholars who wrote about fan communities also commonly experienced them from within, as members: "We wanted to signal a dual allegiance—to treat our subcultural knowledge as part of what informed the work we were doing as scholars. We were not simply fans and we were not simply academics—we were acafen." Henry Jenkins, "Acafandom and Beyond: Week Two, Part One," June 20, 2011, http://henryjenkins.org/blog/2011/06/acafandom_and_beyond_week_two.html.

Occult Knowledge

Good Men and Monsters
Bram Stoker's Dracula *and* Harry Potter

Beatrice Groves

"The world seems full of good men—even if there are monsters in it."—Bram Stoker, *Dracula*[1]

J.K. Rowling's early plan for a vampire tutor (called Trocar) at Hogwarts came to nothing, and she has written that subsequently vampires ended up playing "no meaningful part in the story."[2] However, Rowling is consciously underselling the importance of vampire lore in general, and Bram Stoker's *Dracula* (1897) in particular, to *Harry Potter*.[3] *Harry Potter* is full of explicitly comic vampiric allusions—from hammy performances of *Voyages with Vampires* and blood-flavored lollipops, to Hagrid's "sligh' disagreement with a vampire in a pub in Minsk."[4] The only explicit vampire that the reader meets is Sanguini at Slughorn's Christmas party, an appearance which is framed in entirely comic terms, from Luna's startling suggestion that this vampire might in fact be Rufus Scrimgeour to the "gaggle of girls" who surround Sanguini at the party "looking curious and excited."[5] The dangerous, erotic allure of the vampire is here alluded to only to be wittily undercut when Sanguini starts edging towards this groups of girls with "a rather hungry look in his eye"[6] but is deflected from his devious purposes by Worple stuffing a pasty into his hand. This comic theme continues into Rowling's *Pottermore* writing when, dismissing a persistent rumor about her Potions Master, she punningly claims that "Snape is not a *revamped* Trocar."[7] But the comedy of these moments effectively obscures the deep influence of Stoker's novel on the conception of evil within the novels. Substantive (although generally overlooked) parallels range from the possession of Harry and Ginny by the Dark Lord and the talismanic power of blood transfusion to the hunting down of the Horcruxes and the scar which links protagonist and enemy—echoes which all position Voldemort as a direct descendant of Stoker's creation.

Far from playing "no meaningful part in the story," vampire lore forms a rich undercurrent to Rowling's world.

Stoker's *Dracula* presents itself as marking clear boundaries between "good men" and "monsters," but since the late-twentieth-century critics have found it a novel marked out by Decadent transgression—a literary movement which celebrated sensuality and the subversion of traditional moral categories—rather than clear boundaries. The current critical consensus, indeed, finds in the miscegenation of the vampiric mode of attack a symbolic queering of *Dracula*'s overt moral binaries.[8] The quintessentially connective Gothic mode is often expressed via shadow-selves and doppelgängers and, as in *Dracula*, through the taint of physical connection between hero and villain.[9] The uncanny mirroring of Voldemort by Harry is one of the most Gothic aspects of *Harry Potter*, and it is a connection expressed through precisely the same symbols—a forehead-scar and shared blood—as we find in *Dracula*. Dracula forcibly takes Mina Harker's blood, and the scar that marks her when the Host (a consecrated Eucharistic wafer) touches her forehead is both an echo of Dracula's own scar (a version of the mark of Cain) and a sign of her internal pollution through this bloody miscegenation.[10] The symbols of infection in *Harry Potter* are remarkably close to *Dracula*: the Dark Lord forcibly takes Harry's blood and gives him a forehead-scar that is a fragment of his own dark soul.

The striking parallelism of these symbols, however, masks the moral clarity that *Harry Potter* reinscribes on the fin-de-siècle decadence of its source material. The shared blood, which mortally endangers Lucy Westenra and Mina, will save Harry. Instead of Harry being infected by his connection with Voldemort, it is Voldemort who keeps Harry alive by taking into his veins the deep magic of Lily Potter's sacrifice. Mina, conversely, is contaminated by her bloody union with Dracula—she declares herself "Unclean! Unclean!" when the Host burns her forehead.[11] Her degeneration is expressed by her desiring enslavement to Dracula: "I did not want to hinder him. I suppose it is a part of the horrible curse that such is, when his touch is on his victim."[12] Mina's love for Jonathan fights against this enslavement, but this love is ultimately the weaker power. Unless Dracula is destroyed, Mina will be lost. Harry is likewise possessed by the Dark Lord, and that possession likewise fights against his true-hearted love. But there is no question in *Harry Potter* which is the stronger force: "You have flitted into Lord Voldemort's mind without damage to yourself, but he cannot possess you without enduring mortal agony, as he discovered in the Ministry."[13] Voldemort cannot possess Harry, and when he attempts it, Harry's love (for Sirius and, later, for Dobby) drives him out.

Mina's scar is the burn-mark left when her forehead is touched by divine love (in the form of the consecrated communion wafer). But in the world of *Harry Potter* the damage of this burning contact between good and evil is reversed. It is Quirrell (possessed, both literally and figuratively, by Voldemort) who cannot touch Harry's skin without his own "blistering before his eyes": "Quirrell, full of hatred, greed, and ambition, sharing his soul with Voldemort, could not touch you for this reason. It was agony to touch a person marked by something so good."[14]

Stoker's novel—"a paradigm of Decadent form and structure predicated on transgression"—seems, like its eponymous protagonist, to be more interested in the transgression of boundaries than in the restoration of order, more attracted by "eroticized infection" than the cleansing power of love.[15] *Dracula*'s Gothic sense of a polluting miasma, in the physical connections forged between Mina and Dracula, are present in the fears that possess Harry for much of *Order of the Phoenix*. But Harry's anxiety of contamination by Voldemort proves to be groundless; in a reversal of the dangers of *Dracula*, the Dark Lord can infect the hero's body but not their soul.

The close parallels which this essay traces between *Harry Potter* and *Dracula* reinscribe the importance of the Gothic as a source for the series, but more importantly they shed light on *Harry Potter*'s striking departure from Stoker's novel. The message of *Dracula* is about the threat posed by external pollution to the purity of an imagined "Englishness." *Harry Potter*, however, both locates this threat in Britain, rather than "othering" it, as Stoker does, and denies it the dangerous allure with which Stoker imbues its exoticism. The dark, erotic appeal of Dracula is transferred in *Harry Potter* to Snape (who fights against Voldemort) rather than in Voldemort himself, and Harry, though sharing in the physical connections of blood and scar with the Dark Lord, never once desires to submit to him.[16] The honoring of goodness which we may suspect to be a mere form of moral display in *Dracula* is, conversely, whole-heartedly celebrated in *Harry Potter*.

Dracula *and Gothic Misdirection*

The vampire mythology that swirls around the *Harry Potter* books—from Quirrell's putatively garlic-filled turban to Sanguini hungrily eying up party guests—led to a persistent fan theory that Snape (the series' Gothic romantic lead) might turn out to be a vampire.[17] Rowling has repeatedly addressed and ostensibly quashed this rumor, while simultaneously stoking the fires by releasing images of her first imaginings of Snape in the high-collared black cloak of a pop-culture Dracula.[18] But there are also strong implications that Snape might have trouble locating himself in a mirror within the novels themselves—and, indeed, once the idea has been mooted a "severed nape" becomes temptingly audible in Severus Snape's moniker. The logical inference to be drawn from Snape's black hair, pale skin and bat-like cloak are first fleshed out in *Prisoner of Azkaban*. Neville and Harry are discussing their vampire essay and Snape suddenly appears, as if conjured by their conversation, and at the end of the novel Dean Thomas hopes that they might get a Defense Against the Dark Arts teacher who is a vampire. The novel in which Snape finally becomes the tutor for the Dark Arts opens with Snape (in arguably the most erotically charged scene of the series) offering Narcissa a goblet of "bloodred wine,"[19] and when the students enter the Dark Arts classroom, they find that Snape has covered all the windows and shrouded the room in darkness. This raises the question as to whether Snape has always taught in an underground classroom because he has an aversion to the light. Throughout the series both Snape's vampiric death-like paleness is stressed, but also (more surprisingly) his hooked nose. Snape's nose is mentioned in every novel of the series, and it is an aspect of his appearance which is not linked to the pop-culture vampire aesthetic. But it is part of Stoker's visualization of Dracula. Snape is described as a "thin man with sallow skin, a hooked nose, and greasy, shoulder-length black hair,"[20] while Dracula is "a tall, thin chap, with a 'ook nose."[21]

The dark echoes that gather around Snape, however, find their fulfilment elsewhere. Snape's secret identity is not, despite these heavy hints, that of a vampire, but that of a double-agent, who is working undercover for Dumbledore. His vampiric appearance is narrative misdirection, both for Snape's ultimate allegiance and for the deep connections between the central villains of Stoker's and Rowling's stories.

The overwhelming majority of vampiric references in *Harry Potter* are comic, from Luna's matter-of-fact assertion that the Minister of Magic is a vampire, to Lockhart's boast about lettuce-eating vampires and the similarly grandiose claim of the Leaky Cauldron dishwasher to be "a Vampire Hunter, I've killed about ninety so far—."[22] Likewise, the romantic wreathes of white garlic flowers in *Dracula* become comically solidified as a "large clove of garlic" in *Harry Potter*.[23] But humor is part of Rowling's narrative misdirection, implying as it does that vampires play no serious role in the story. Indeed, the crucial link between Voldemort and Dracula itself opens in comedy: "[Quirrell's] classroom smelled strongly of garlic, which everyone said was to ward off a vampire he'd met in Romania and was afraid would be coming back to get him one of these days ... they had noticed that a funny smell hung around the turban, and the Weasley twins insisted that it was stuffed full of garlic, as well, so that Quirrell was protected wherever he went."[24] Romania is the modern-day location of Transylvania, and whether Quirrell met the Dark Lord there or in Albania (as

Harry surmises), both the location and the garlic identify Voldemort—the darkness in Quirrell's head from whom he does indeed need protection—as a literal and spiritual vampire.

The connection between vampires and Voldemort is thus made in *Sorcerer's Stone* but only as the series draws to a close does it become clear how strongly Stoker's *Dracula* has inflected *Harry Potter*'s plot. In *Harry Potter and the Half-Blood Prince*, for example, Voldemort is first described in fully vampiric terms with waxy white skin, a black cloak, and red eyes.[25] This is the novel in which the reader learns that Voldemort, like Dracula, hoards external objects as talismans of immortality. In *Dracula* the eponymous protagonist collects fifty boxes of earth, and he is safe while his body sleeps inside them. In *Harry Potter*, Voldemort makes six Horcruxes, and he is safe while his soul remains within them. Both stories climax with the band of friends hunting down these receptacles, one by one, in an attempt to destroy them all before their antagonist realizes what they are doing. In each story, the Lord of Darkness has a dawning recognition about what the "crew of light"[26] is up to. The climax involves some carefully timed negotiations as the band of friends has to decide which Horcruxes/boxes to destroy based on the order in which they think their antagonist will check on them. Dracula, just like Voldemort at the climax of *Deathly Hallows*, checks each of his hiding places in turn: "he is as yet only suspicious; and he went from Carfax first to the place where he would suspect interference least."[27]

The Horcruxes form a double link between *Dracula* and *Harry Potter*, in the parallel inherent in the friends' systematic destruction of these talismans of immortality, but also because the only way in which Horcruxes can be destroyed strongly recalls the primary mode of destroying vampires. The scene in which Harry drives the stake-like fang into the "heart" of Riddle's diary is unmistakably influenced by the staking of vampires. In *Dracula* when the Lucy-vampire is staked: "the Thing in the coffin *writhed*; and a *hideous, blood-curdling screech* came from the opened red lips. The body shook and quivered and *twisted* in wild contortions … the blood from the pierced *heart* welled and *spurted* up around [the stake]."[28] When Harry destroys the diary–Horcrux, the same screaming, writhing, twisting, and spurting from the pierced heart all occur: "Harry seized the Basilisk fang on the floor next to him and plunged it straight into the *heart* of the book. There was a *long, dreadful, piercing scream*. Ink *spurted* out of the diary in torrents, streaming over Harry's hands, flooding the floor. Riddle was *writhing* and *twisting*, screaming and flailing and then…. He had gone."[29] In both, the vanquisher (Arthur and Harry) falls exhausted from the effort, and the loved woman they are attempting to rescue (Lucy and Ginny) is in some sense "saved" by this act of violence.

The horror of the moment in both is mitigated by the sense that the "Thing" the hero destroys is avowedly inhuman, but in both the writer creates a Gothic frisson with the uncanny sense that a living thing is being murdered, rather than an undead object being exorcised. The parallels are even more explicit (in both senses) in the destruction of the third Horcrux, as Ron pierces the locket-Horcrux with the sword in an echo of the perverted sexuality of the staking of the vampire bride. In *Dracula* Van Helsing tells Arthur, Lucy's lover, that he must stake Lucy's femme-fatale corpse, just as Harry tells Ron that he must destroy the locket Horcrux. Lucy's vampire-sexuality unsettles those who have loved her—"the bloodstained voluptuous mouth ... the whole carnal and unspiritual appearance, seeming like a devilish mockery of Lucy's sweet purity"[30]—just as the Riddle-Hermione unmans Ron: "the Riddle-Hermione, who was more beautiful and yet more terrible than the real Hermione: she swayed, cackling, before Ron, who looked horrified yet transfixed, the sword hanging pointlessly at his side."[31] The Riddle-Hermione, like the Vampire-Lucy, is revealed as at once voluptuously appealing and terrifying, imbuing the act of her destruction with disturbingly erotic undertones.[32]

However, the erotic appeal of the vampire, one of his most enduring pop-culture legacies, is hardly alluded to in *Harry Potter* except in this fantastical moment, and (in comedic guise) in the girls who crowd round Sanguini. Voldemort is not sexualized in *Harry Potter*, except by Bellatrix, whose passion for him serves rather to illustrate his lack of appeal for the reader. Rather, the erotic excitement of the vampire myth, central to both *Dracula* and his later (especially filmic) incarnations, is transferred from the arch-villain to the brooding sex appeal of Hogwarts's Potions Master.[33]

Animal Transformation: Werewolves and Barghests

Snape's most emphatically vampiric aspect is the way in which the narrative voice continually reaches for bat similes as he sweeps by. After "swooping around like an overgrown bat"[34] in the opening novel, Snape glides "like a large and malevolent bat"[35] in *Chamber of Secrets*, while in *Half-Blood Prince* he looks "just as much like an overgrown bat as ever."[36] In *Goblet of Fire* we even find Ron muttering about how Snape might be able to "turn himself into a bat."[37] Dracula takes the form of a bat and, just as with Snape, this transformation is intimated by his habitual attire: "his cloak spreading around him like great wings."[38] In *Deathly Hallows* Snape flies out of a window, "a huge, batlike shape flying through the darkness toward the perimeter wall," in imitation of the way in which Dracula is seen flying through the sky as "a big bat, which was flapping its silent and ghostly way to the west."[39]

Dracula's transformation into a bat is the most famous aspect of his therianthropy, but he also takes the form of a great black dog when he lands at Whitby. Stoker chose this form because a monstrous black dog appearing as a death omen—the barghest, barguest, or Grim—was a pre-existing myth, particularly prevalent in the north of England. Sirius's ghostly manifestations as "the Grim," when he appears as a great, black dog, are drawn primarily from folktales of the barghest, but *Dracula* is an additional source for the haunting menace of this large dog. Indeed, when Harry first sees Sirius's image it reminds him of a vampire, which may be a subtle hint that Sirius, just like Dracula, can transform into a black dog.[40] Dracula leaps ashore at Whitby in the form of an "immense dog" while a local man dismisses those who see him as fools who fear "bar-guests an' bogles an' all anent them is only fit to set bairns an' dizzy women a-belderin'. ... They, an' all grims an' signs an' warnin's, be all invented."[41] Sirius's connections with Dracula and the Grim, however, just like the bat similes that surround Snape, are designed to mislead the reader about where his true allegiance lies.

Dracula's therianthropy is an important part of his transgressive myth as it creates a permeable boundary between the categories of human and animal.[42] But in *Harry Potter* the ability to transform into an animal is a morally neutral characteristic. Once again, the only central character whose human-to-animal transformation has a negative moral dimension is Voldemort. And while Dracula transforms into animals with traditionally dark associations, Voldemort takes this one step further as he gradually takes the form of the most explicitly Satanic animal: the serpent.[43]

Satanic Parallels and Christian Gothic

The Christian Gothic aesthetic created in *Dracula* through the use of the Host and crucifixes, in particular, figures the vampire as a Satanic adversary. In 1897 one newspaper suggested that when reading *Dracula* "persons of small courage and weak nerves should confine their reading of these gruesome pages strictly to the hours between dawn and sunset,"[44] and indeed, one of the most famously Satanic aspects of Dracula's nature is his symbolic shunning of the light. Once Tom Riddle has transformed into Voldemort, likewise, the reader encounters him predominantly, if not solely, after sundown.[45] In *Deathly Hallows*, for example, morning has broken for Harry in Shell Cottage but, as he views Voldemort about to rob Dumbledore's tomb, he sees "a vision of the main street in Hogsmeade, still dark, because it was so much further north."[46] Jonathan Harker notes that his host always disappears at cock crow,[47] and the destruction of the cockerels in *Chamber of Secrets* (because their crowing is fatal to the basilisk) draws on the same, traditionally Christian, imagery of the antagonism between the bird who heralds the dawn and a Satanic creature of darkness.[48] Medieval bestiaries state unequivocally that "the basilisk signifies the devil,"[49] a symbolism on which Stoker (like Rowling) draws by having Dracula—with his eyes of "basilisk horror"[50]—fleeing from the sound of cock crow.

One reason for the Satanic basis of Stoker's conception of Dracula is that the character was drawn, in part, from Henry Irving's celebrated performance of Mephistopheles in *Faust*. Irving was a close friend of Stoker's, as well as his employer and artistic collaborator, and the author long cherished the hope that Irving would take the role of Dracula on the stage, completing the circle of influence. Voldemort shares a number of Dracula's Satanic attributes, such as red eyes, connections with occult animals, and a literal, as well as symbolic, shrinking from the light.

Both Stoker and Rowling draw on one of the most famous literary incarnations of evil for their anti-hero. While Stoker is directly influenced by Goethe's Mephistopheles, Rowling draws not only on Dracula but on Milton's Satan. Voldemort's ophidian transformation, for example, seems to be based on that of Satan in *Paradise Lost* who likewise becomes imprisoned within the snaky form which is the physical expression of his sin. Milton's Satan, like Voldemort and Dracula, also has eyes which gleam red.[51] In *Harry Potter* the reddening of Voldemort's eyes expresses his gradual descent into irremediable evil. It moves from the red gleam Harry catches in Riddle's eyes as he is about to kill Hepzibah Smith, to the perpetually blood-stained look ten years later (when Riddle asks Dumbledore for a job) and the final scarlet of his full transformation into Lord Voldemort. Dracula's red eyes, just like Voldemort's, start as an early momentary ruddy gleam (Harker first notices "a red light" in the Count's eyes) before hardening into fully red eyes.[52]

The parallel between Dracula and Mephistopheles underlines the explicitly Christian Gothic of *Dracula*'s aesthetic in which holy symbols illustrate "Christianity's palpable efficacy."[53] In Stoker's novel the consecrated Host in particular has power over Dracula, circumscribing his movement, and at the end of the novel a ring of crumbled consecrated communion wafers forms a protective boundary which no vampire can cross. This holy circle recalls traditional ideas of the talismanic power of the Host,[54] and there is perhaps a faint echo of this vampire-proof boundary in the power of sacred space in *Harry Potter*.

The only explicitly Christian space in *Harry Potter* is the church in Godric's Hollow. Harry visits its churchyard as Midnight Mass is being celebrated and reads biblical verses on the gravestones. It seems possible that this sacred site subtly performs the same talismanic function as the circle of communion wafers Van Helsing makes in *Dracula*. Dracula's vampire brides are unable to cross this holy boundary, and in *Harry Potter* it is intimated that one of the women possessed by Voldemort—Bathilda Bagshot animated by his Horcrux, Nagini—is likewise unable to cross into the churchyard. While Harry and Hermione remain in the churchyard Bathilda cannot approach, though they catch a glimpse of her circling it, watching them, and it seems that a sacred space of protection is created by "the dense black boundary of the graveyard."[55]

The satanic nature of the vampire is underscored by the power of crucifix and Host against him, and the latter also creates one of the most explicit connections between *Dracula* and *Harry Potter*. When Van Helsing places a Host on Mina's forehead, intending to protect her, it "burned into the flesh as though it had been a piece of white-hot metal."[56] Harry's scar burns in a similar way—"burning beneath his fingers as though someone had just pressed a white-hot wire to his skin"[57]—but there is an inversion of the moral meaning of this pain. As Rowling has noted "the pain he feels ... is this piece of soul seeking to rejoin the master soul."[58] It is the evil in the scar, not the goodness of the Host, that causes the pain. In sharp distinction to Mina, Harry's suffering is not a sign that he himself has been morally polluted.

The scar, however, creates a telepathic connection between Harry and Voldemort, which is something that Mina and Dracula likewise share.[59] This telepathy is another close link between the two stories. In both, the connection carries dangers for the "crew of light": Van Helsing fears that through this telepathic bond Dracula will compel Mina's "mind to disclose to him that which she know[s]"[60] about their activities against him, just as Harry fears that through him Voldemort is going to discover the secrets of the Order of the Phoenix (and his failures in Occlumency will, indeed, lead to the death of an Order member). In both texts the Lord of Darkness is slower than his antagonists to realize the potential of this telepathic connection, and in both it is finally used against him, as Van Helsing hypnotizes Mina to track Dracula just as Harry uses the connection to track Voldemort in *Deathly Hallows*.

The transfusion of blood, the telepathic connection, and the scar all place Harry in the position of Mina Harker, the position of a Gothic heroine, and in doing so, form a parallel which inverts some of the gendered expectations of Stoker's novel.[61] Mina famously cries, "Unclean! Unclean!"[62] in response to her own possession by Dracula, a word Harry echoes—"the feeling of being unclean intensified"[63]—when he fears that Voldemort is possessing him. In Stoker's *Dracula* the primary victims of vampiric possession are both women (Lucy and Mina) and one aspect of the quasi-sexual nature of Dracula's bite is that the Count poses no direct danger to Jonathan.[64] But in *Harry Potter* the characters directly possessed by Voldemort—Quirrell, Ginny, and Harry (during the battle at the end of *Order of the Phoenix*)—are predominantly male. Ginny, her spirit drained near to death by Riddle, becomes a version of Mina, the traditional imperiled female who must be saved by the hero.[65]

There is, however, a shift in the conventional gender politics here, because it is Harry—not Ginny—who is figured as Mina throughout the whole series. The male hero shares in, and indeed goes far beyond, the contamination endured by his love-interest. It is Harry, not Ginny, who bears Voldemort's scar—Harry, not Ginny, whose blood is transfused into Voldemort's veins. Ginny may take the role of a traditional Gothic heroine in *Chamber of Secrets*, but Harry inhabits this role for the series as a whole. And there is an aspect of reciprocity in the power of salvation, too. Harry physically frees Ginny from Voldemort in *Chamber*, but she psychologically frees him in *Phoenix*, using her own knowledge gained by suffering to save Harry from the fear that Voldemort might have made him "unclean."

Dracula on Film

As mentioned above, Dracula famously shrinks from the light, shunning the dawn as a symbol of his status as the Lord of Darkness. Dracula's shrinking from the light was to become an infamous part of his pop-culture myth, due in part to the dominance of filmic vampires in the twentieth century. Stoker's *Dracula* has, in fact, been "the subject of more films than any other novel,"[66] and its filmic appeal was immediately recognized, with the original Dracula film appearing in 1922—the German expressionist fairy tale, F.W. Murna's *Nosferatu*. Film is an artform composed of light, but while its medium is light it must (in an inversion of the reading experience) be experienced in the dark. It is, therefore, in keeping with the chiaroscuro medium itself that *Dracula*'s stark symbolism of light and dark should so appeal to filmmakers. Films, indeed, intensify the dichotomy Stoker places on vampiric darkness and the salvific importance of light. While Stoker's *Dracula* is merely weakened by the daylight hours, and unable to shape-shift in them, for example, Count Orlok in *Nosferatu* is the first of the undead to be destroyed by the dawn. Later vampire films followed suit, and in the *Horror of Dracula* (1958), Dracula is likewise killed by the light. Lane Roth notes that with *Nosferatu* "the ritual hour for vampire-killing changed from dusk to dawn," and Roth convincingly links this shift with "the oneiric experience of the film experience itself," as "ending a monster movie story at dawn is metaphoric of the completion of a nightmare."[67]

In *Harry Potter* Voldemort is likewise killed at dawn. While in the books there is a Satanic aspect to the defeat of the Dark Lord at the break of dawn,[68] the filmmakers (scriptwriter Steve Kloves and director David Yates) made Voldemort's dawn death into a specifically vampiric reference. Dracula is "one of the most mediagenic cultural icons of the twentieth century,"[69] and it is therefore unsurprising that the filmic Dracula should have had a particular and distinct influence on the portrayal of the Dark Lord in the *Harry Potter* films. For example, in the film *Deathly Hallows, Part 2* (as distinct from the book), Voldemort turns to dust in the dawn light. This choice to deviate from Voldemort's death as described in the books creates a startlingly close homage both to the vaporization of *Nosferatu*'s Count Orlok in the light and to the famous Hammer Draculas. In the *Horror of Dracula*, the Lord of Darkness likewise turns to dust as the sunlight hits him.

It seems likely that *Nosferatu*, the original and most influential Dracula film, has also influenced the filmic visualization of Voldemort's followers. Peter Pettigrew, the rat Animagus of the *Harry Potter* books, is visualized in Alfonso Cuarón's *Prisoner of Azkaban* in a way that strongly recalls Count Orlok. The anti-hero of *Nosferatu*, unlike all later pop-culture vampires, stays true to Stoker's vision of a visually unappealing vampire, and in keeping with Count Orlok's rodent-like appearance, the film associates him with rats rather than the bats chosen by all later celluloid incarnations.[70] The rats that overrun *Nosferatu*'s visuals are recalled by Pettigrew, who has a "curious affinity" with these "filthy" creatures as well as, of course, being able to become one.[71] When Pettigrew transforms in the film of *Azkaban*, his prominent front teeth, pointed ears, bright eyes, and balding head are strikingly reminiscent of Max Schreck's iconic portrayal of Count Orlok. This connection effectively surrounds one of Voldemort's most important henchmen (the one who will enable him to return to a living body) with a suitably vampiric miasma.

Voyages with Vampires

In the *Harry Potter* books, likewise, there is a filmic link between Voldemort's disciple (Quirrell) and the obsessive devotion of Dracula's most ardent follower (Renfield). Quirrell, like Renfield, believes that drinking animal blood will give him life, and like Renfield (who is murdered by Dracula), Quirrell will die as a result of allowing Voldemort to possess him. In Stoker's *Dracula*, Harker, the hero of the novel, travels to

Transylvania and assists Dracula's journey to England. But in Tod Browning's *Dracula* (1931), probably the most well-known version of Count Dracula's story, it is Dracula's slavish disciple Renfield who travels to Transylvania. Only Browning's film version, therefore, finds a parallel in Quirrell's journey to eastern Europe from whence, like Renfield in the 1931 film, he will bring back the Dark Lord to England.

This idea of the vampire-myth as an embodiment of an anxiety about an "invading occidental monster"[72] polluting Englishness is central to *Dracula* criticism, typified, for example, by Carol A. Senf's influential argument that Jonathan Harker fears in Dracula "a kind of reverse imperialism, the threat of the primitive trying to colonize the civilized world."[73] *Dracula* expresses a xenophobic horror at this contagion reaching England (and it is perhaps a witty sign of Lockhart's lack of judgment that he should celebrate his *Voyages with Vampires* rather than encouraging them to stay put). Rowling has called vampires "a tradition of Eastern Europe,"[74] and (just like *Dracula*) *Harry Potter* seems to imply that vampires are inherently un–British.[75] In addition to the vampire Quirrell is rumored to have met in the Black Forest, Hagrid has a contretemps with a vampire "in a pub in Minsk," and in *Quidditch Through the Ages*, the Transylvanian Captain cheats by releasing "a hundred blood-sucking vampire bats."[76] In *Harry Potter*, however, such apparently xenophobic vampire lore is not only shown to be inaccurate (there must be native vampires around to purchase Honeydukes's blood-flavored lollipops, for example) but also beside the point. The most important "vampire" of the series, the Dark Lord by whom Quirrell was possessed after he travelled to eastern Europe, may have been encountered by him in modern-day Transylvania or Albania, but he is an entirely home-grown embodiment of evil.

Epilogues: Seven (and Nineteen) Years Later

Most of the vampire references in *Harry Potter* have a strikingly literary quality—from the opening reference to the new book on vampires which Quirrell claims to be purchasing in Diagon Alley[77] and Xenophilius Lovegood's "very long article"[78] on Scrimgeour's vampirism, to the appearance of Sanguini with his biographer (author of *Blood Brothers: My Life Amongst the Vampires*).[79] Lockhart's *Voyages with Vampires* is his most frequently mentioned work, and its alliteration recalls the title of the first "penny dreadful" vampire novel—James Malcom Rymer's *Varney the Vampyre* (1845–47), a serialization of John Polidori's trailblazing novella *The Vampyre* (1819). *Harry Potter*'s many literary vampires point up the influence of Stoker's *Dracula,* and a final, emphatic link is created between the two texts in their epilogues. Each story ends with an epilogue in which the larger forces opened up by the narrative are contained in a tidy ending; an imposition of order embodied by a child who bears the name of those who have suffered and died in the earlier story. In *Dracula* Mina and Jonathan have a son who they have named after the whole "crew of light": "his bundle of names links all our little band of men together; but we call him Quincey."[80] This baby was born on the anniversary of the day on which Quincey Morris died saving Mina from Dracula, just as Victoire Weasley was born on the anniversary of the Battle of Hogwarts (and both are named accordingly). Baby Quincey's name is recalled more directly in the naming of Albus Severus Potter, a child whose moniker honors *Harry Potter*'s own "crew of light" and in particular the two men who died in their quest to save Harry from the Dark Lord.[81]

The symbolism of purity returned is also underlined in *Dracula* through the disappearance of Mina's scar, as Van Helsing promises her: "that red scar, the sign of God's knowledge of what has been, shall pass away and leave your forehead as pure as the heart we know."[82] At the very end of *Dracula*, this scar does indeed disappear when Dracula is destroyed, and there is a disappearing scar (of sorts), too, in *Harry Potter*. Rowling had always said in interviews that the final word of the series would be "scar," a symbol of the wounds that time cannot heal.[83] Harry's physical scar remained at the end of the series, but—in a disappearance that recalls Mina's healing—that final "scar" had gone. When readers reached the end of the series for the first time they were primed by Rowling's interviews to expect the word "scar" as the final word, but found instead that this symbol of the connection between Harry and the Dark Lord had disappeared and been replaced by the affirmation that "all was well."

Conclusion

There are numerous distinct parallels between *Harry Potter* and *Dracula* which center both on the embodiment of evil (typified in both by the villain's therianthropy, his hoarding of external talismans of immortality, and a certain preference for nighttime) and its nemesis, the "crew of light." The stories share the idea that, despite all the spiritual insight and pragmatic wisdom of the elder guide (Abraham van Helsing/Albus Dumbledore), it is not given to him alone to triumph over the Lord of Darkness. Gregory A. Waller argues that this is an essential aspect of Stoker's novel "because *Dracula* is, perhaps above all, the story of the formation and growth of a community."[84] This parallel underlines the way in which the growth of communities of "light"—Dumbledore's Army, the Order of the Phoenix, Potterwatch, and Harry's final understanding that Hermione and Ron will not allow him to walk his dark path alone—are central, likewise, to *Harry Potter*. It is an important and powerful part of *Harry Potter*'s modulation of the traditional hero's quest, indeed, that each of the Horcruxes is destroyed by a different person. Overcoming Voldemort is truly a communal act.

In both its formation of a "crew of light" and its depiction of the Dark Lord, *Harry Potter* shares much of its symbolism with Stoker's depiction of "good men" and "monsters." But there is also an important distinction. Some of the closest allusions to *Dracula* in *Harry Potter* are found in the relationship between the Dark Lord and the hero, an uncanny relationship forged, as in *Dracula*, through a scar, miscegenated blood, and a telepathic connection. But Rowling inverts the moral of these associations. The polluting miasma of vampirism is symbolic of the transgressive power of evil in Stoker's novel. Yet while the mirroring of hero and villain creates an explicitly Gothic frisson for the reader in *Harry Potter*, evil has been emptied of its corrupting appeal. The erotic charisma of the vampire has been transferred to Snape, an undercover agent of the Order of the Phoenix, while Harry himself remains resolutely pure of heart throughout. In *Harry Potter*, evil has lost its seductive, contaminating power. The numerous plot parallels between Stoker's and Rowling's novels serve, in the end, to delineate the difference at their heart. They illuminate the way in which *Dracula*'s miscegenation of "good men" and "monsters" is reversed by *Harry Potter*. In *Harry Potter*, the power of the uncanny is overturned, and it is only love which is "more wonderful and more terrible than death."[85]

Notes

1. Bram Stoker, *Dracula* (London: Penguin, 1897/2003), 198.

2. J.K. Rowling, "Vampires," first published on *Pottermore* (now *Wizarding World*), August 10, 2015, wizardingworld.com/writing-by-jk-rowling/vampires.

3. Given the importance of the *Dracula* connection, this is an understudied area of literary and cultural allusion in *Harry Potter*. The most extensive previous treatments of which I am aware are John Granger, *Harry Potter's Bookshelf: The Great Books Behind the Hogwarts Adventures* (New York: Berkley Publishing Group, 2009), 65–104; John Granger, *Harry Potter Meets Hamlet and Scrooge* (Allentown, PA: Methodios Press/Lulu, 2009), 88–121; FinnBV, "Villains in Dracula and Harry Potter," *The Leaky Cauldron*, accessed October 17, 2023, http://www.the-leaky-cauldron.org/features/essays/issue4/villains/.

4. J.K. Rowling, *Harry Potter and the Order of the Phoenix* (New York: Scholastic, 2003), 426.

5. J.K. Rowling, *Harry Potter and the Half-Blood Prince* (New York: Scholastic, 2005), 316.

6. Ibid.

7. Rowling, "Vampires." Italics mine.

8. For two classic examples, see Carol A. Senf, "*Dracula*: The Unseen Face in the Mirror," *The Journal of Narrative Technique* 9, no. 3 (1979): 160–70; Christopher Craft, "'Kiss Me with Those Red Lips': Gender and Inversion in Bram Stoker's Dracula," *Representations*

8 (1984): 107–133. For a more recent treatment, see Jonathan Stone, *Decadence and Modernism in European and Russian Literature and Culture: Aesthetics and Anxiety in the 1890s* (Cham, Switzerland: Palgrave Macmillan, 2019).

9. See, for example, Whitney S. May, "'Powers of Their Own Which Mere "Modernity" Cannot Kill': The Doppelgänger and Temporal Modernist Terror in Dracula," *Gothic Studies* 23, no. 1 (2021): 60–76.

10. Stoker, *Dracula*, 300, 316.

11. Ibid., 316.

12. Ibid., 306.

13. Rowling, *Half-Blood Prince*, 511.

14. J.K. Rowling, *Harry Potter and the Sorcerer's Stone* (New York: Scholastic, 1997), 299.

15. Stone, *Decadence and Modernism in European and Russian Literature and Culture*, 68, 70.

16. See also the way in which *Harry Potter* uses, but inverts, Gothic tropes via comedic echoes of Jane Austen's *Northanger Abbey*: Beatrice Groves, *Literary Allusion in Harry Potter* (London: Routledge, 2017), 111–19.

17. See, for example, "Severus Snape: Vampire (extended thoughts and articles)," *Harry Potter Fan Theories*, Tumblr, accessed February 14, 2023, https://harrypotterfantheories.tumblr.com/post/80720198044/severus-snape-moody-potions-master-forever-in-the.

18. See, for example, World Book Day Chat, March 4, 2004, http://www.accio-quote.org/articles/2004/0304-wbd.htm; Leaky Cauldron and MuggleNet chat, July 16, 2005, http://www.accio-quote.org/articles/2005/0705-tlc_mugglenet-anelli-2.htm; and Rowling, "Vampires."

19. Rowling, *Half-Blood Prince*, 24.

20. J.K. Rowling, *Harry Potter and the Chamber of Secrets* (New York: Scholastic, 1999), 78.

21. Stoker, *Dracula*, 148.

22. J.K. Rowling, *Harry Potter and the Goblet of Fire* (New York: Scholastic, 2000), 126.

23. Rowling, *Chamber of Secrets*, 210.

24. Rowling, *Sorcerer's Stone*, 134.

25. "It was as though his features had been burned and blurred; they were waxy and oddly distorted, and the whites of the eyes now had a permanently bloody look. … He was wearing a long black cloak and his face was as pale as the snow glistening on his shoulders." Rowling, *Half-Blood Prince*, 441.

26. The name "the crew of light"—commonly used in *Dracula* criticism to refer to the vampire hunters (punning on Lucy Westenra's first name)—comes from Craft, "'Kiss Me,'" 109.

27. Stoker, *Dracula*, 324.

28. Ibid., 230. Emphasis added.

29. Rowling, *Chamber of Secrets*, 322. Emphasis added.

30. Stoker, *Dracula*, 228.

31. Rowling, *Deathly Hallows*, 376.

32. For the unmistakably sexualized aspect of staking female vampires—in Stoker's novel it is only Lucy (not Dracula) who is staked, and in the Hammer movies "only female vampires are staked"—see Nina Auerbach, *Our Vampires, Ourselves* (Chicago: University of Chicago Press, 1995), 137.

33. On this topic, see Joyce Millman, "To Sir, with Love," in *Mapping the World of Harry Potter*, ed. Mercedes Lackey (Dallas: BenBella, 2005), 39–52.

34. Rowling, *Sorcerer's Stone*, 288.

35. Rowling, *Chamber of Secrets*, 193.

36. Rowling, *Half-Blood Prince*, 179.

37. Rowling, *Goblet of Fire*, 566.

38. Stoker, *Dracula*, 41.

39. Rowling, *Deathly Hallows*, 599; Stoker, *Dracula*, 119.

40. "Harry had never met a vampire, but he had seen pictures of them in his Defence

24   Occult Knowledge

Against the Dark Arts classes, and Black, with his waxy white skin, looked just like one." Rowling, *Prisoner of Azkaban*, 38. "Waxen," incidentally, is a word frequently used by Stoker for Dracula's pale skin. *Dracula*, 326, 400.

41. Stoker, *Dracula*, 89, 73.

42. For human-to-animal transformation myths see Joyce E. Salisbury, *The Beast Within: Animals in the Middle Ages*, 2nd edition (London: Routledge, 1994/2011).

43. For more on the moral dimensions of snakes in *Harry Potter*, see Beatrice Groves, "The Snake Woman in Harry Potter and Fantastic Beasts," in *Beyond the Ivory Tower: More Essays on the World of J.K. Rowling*, ed. Lana Whited (Columbia: University of Missouri Press, 2023).

44. *The Daily Mail*, quoted in May, "'Powers of Their Own,'" 61.

45. Examples include the night-time scenes in the Riddle House and the climactic fight with Harry in the Little Hangleton graveyard in *Goblet of Fire*; asking Dumbledore for employment in *Half-Blood Prince*; his midnight arrival at Bathilda's house, the wet and windy night on which he kills the Potters, robbing Dumbledore's tomb, and the final night-time confrontation in the Forbidden Forest in *Deathly Hallows*.

46. Rowling, *Deathly Hallows*, 498.

47. Stoker, *Dracula*, 32, 37, 59.

48. For more on this, see Beatrice Groves, "Christmas in *Chamber of Secrets*, or why is the crowing of the rooster fatal to the basilisk?" *The Leaky Cauldron*, December 23, 2019, http://www.the-leaky-cauldron.org/2019/12/23/christmas-in-chamber-of-secrets-or-why-is-the-crowing-of-the-rooster-fatal-to-the-basilisk/; Beatrice Groves, "Christmas in *Chamber of Secrets*, or why is the crowing of the rooster fatal to the basilisk? Part 2," *The Leaky Cauldron*, December 24, 2019, http://www.the-leaky-cauldron.org/2019/12/24/christmas-in-chamber-of-secrets-or-why-is-the-crowing-of-the-rooster-fatal-to-the-basilisk-part-2/.

49. Richard W. Barber, trans., *Bestiary: Being an English Version of the Bodleian Library, Oxford M.S. Bodley 764* (London: Folio Society, 1992), 185.

50. Stoker, *Dracula*, 60.

51. For connections between Voldemort and Milton's Satan, see Groves, *Literary Allusion*, 67–74. Lana Whited also finds links to *Paradise Lost* in *Fantastic Beasts: Secrets of Dumbledore* in her contribution to this volume.

52. Stoker, *Dracula*, 58. See also 104, 108, 148. Irving's Mephistopheles, incidentally, was dressed from head to toe in red.

53. Lucas Kwong, "Dracula's Apologetics of Progress," *Victorian Literature and Culture*, 44 (2016): 116.

54. See for example the medieval story of Melusine, a snake woman who disappears at the point of the consecration during Mass. Groves, "The Snake Woman."

55. Rowling, *Deathly Hallows*, 330. For a reading of this scene in the context of the series' depiction of Christmas, see Emily Strand's essay in this volume.

56. Stoker, *Dracula*, 316.

57. Rowling, *Goblet of Fire*, 16. See also Rowling, *Order of the Phoenix*, 463, 474, 752.

58. Melissa Anelli, "Transcript of Part I of PotterCast's J.K. Rowling Interview," *The Leaky Cauldron*, December 23, 2007, http://www.the-leaky-cauldron.org/2007/12/23/transcript-of-part-1-of-pottercast-s-jk-rowling-interview/.

59. In the latter case, however, the psychic bond occurs not through the scar but through the mixing of their blood.

60. Stoker, *Dracula*, 344.

61. For Harry as a traditional Gothic heroine, see Granger, *Harry Potter's Bookshelf*, 85–87.

62. Stoker, *Dracula*, 316.

63. Rowling, *Order of the Phoenix*, 497.

64. Like the fact that staking is reserved for female vampires, Jonathan's safety from Dracula's bite means that, despite the queering aspects of the novel, its dominant presentation of sexuality remains heterosexual. For a classic account of homosexual desire in *Dracula* see Craft, "'Kiss Me with Those Red Lips.'"

65. For more on Ginny Weasley's heroism and development, see Louise Freeman's essay in this volume.

66. Senf, "*Dracula*: The Unseen Face in the Mirror," 161. Rowling has noted the importance of film to the reception of *Dracula*, noting that the vampire myth "has been exploited so many times in literature and on film" (Rowling, "Vampires").

67. Lane Roth, "Film, Society and Ideas: *Nosferatu* and *Horror of Dracula*," in *Planks of Reason: Essays on the Horror Film*, ed. Barry Keith Grant (London: Scarecrow, 1984), 246.

68. For the echo of Christ's Harrowing of Hell, see Groves, *Literary Allusion*, 77.

69. Auerbach, *Our Vampires, Ourselves*, 144. For *Dracula* in more recent multimedia see Simon Bacon, "The Transmedia Vampire: From Bram Stoker's *Dracula* to HBO's *True Blood*," in *Words, Worlds, Narratives: Transmedia and Immersion*, ed. Tawnya Ravy and Eric Forcier (Brill: Leiden, 2014), 55–75.

70. Both animals are associated with Dracula in the novel. He can transform into a bat, as discussed above, but his earth-boxes are surrounded by rats: "The whole place was becoming alive with rat. … The rats were multiplying in thousands." Stoker, Dracula, 268–69.

71. Rowling, *Goblet of Fire*, 655.

72. Stone, *Decadence and Modernism in European and Russian Literature and Culture*, 69.

73. Senf, "*Dracula*: The Unseen Face in the Mirror," 164.

74. Rowling, "Vampires."

75. For more on views of eastern Europe in *Harry Potter* and other fantasy literature, see Marek Oziewicz, "Representations of Eastern Europe in Philip Pullman's *His Dark Materials*, Jonathan Stroud's *The Bartimaeus Trilogy*, and J.K. Rowling's *Harry Potter* Series," *International Research in Children's Literature* 3, no. 1 (July 2010): 1–14.

76. Rowling, *Order of the Phoenix*, 426; J.K. Rowling, *Quidditch Through the Ages* (New York: Arthur A. Levine Books, 2017), 40.

77. Rowling, *Sorcerer's Stone*, 70.

78. Rowling, *Half-Blood Prince*, 314.

79. *Ibid.*, 315.

80. Stoker, *Dracula*, 402.

81. We might also note that Harry's other children—Lily and James—are likewise named after people who died attempting to save (in the case of James) and actually saving (in the case of Lily) Harry from the Dark Lord.

82. Stoker, *Dracula*, 316.

83. Interview with Juan Cruz, *El Pais*, February 8, 2008, http://elpais.com/diario/2008/02/08/cultura/1202425201_850215.html; interview with Meredith Vieira, *Today Show* (NBC), July 26, 2007, http://www.accio-quote.org/articles/2007/0726-today-vieira2.html.

84. Gregory A. Waller, *The Living and the Undead: From Stoker's Dracula to Romero's Dawn of the Dead* (Urbana: University of Illinois Press, 1986), 35.

85. Rowling, *Order of the Phoenix*, 843.

Dark Arts and Secret Histories
Investigating Dark Academia[1]

AMY H. STURGIS

"I've loved Dark Academia since before I even knew it was an official thing," notes Jen Ryland in her book blog, *Jen Ryland Reviews*, as an introduction to her April 17, 2021, post "Exploring Dark Academia: A YA and Adult Book List."[2] In 2021 alone, mainstream English-language publications invited scholars and authors to discuss its appeal, publishing industry professionals and readers posted book recommendation lists, and writers and presses publicly identified their new and forthcoming novels as Dark Academia works. Multiple curated book box subscriptions in the United States and United Kingdom dedicated their monthly or seasonal offerings to the celebration of Dark Academia, including in these boxes both newly-published Dark Academia novels and bookish items inspired by older works in the genre, thus creating a sense of tradition, continuity, and history as context for the latest releases.[3] Publishers and booksellers in the United States and Canada also organized online interactive events in which authors discussed Dark Academia before live, international audiences.[4] By 2021, Dark Academia as a genre of literature clearly had earned "official thing" status.

This groundswell of interest in Dark Academia literature and its use as a label in recommendation lists and reviews, marketing, and promotion suggests that creators and consumers now know Dark Academia when they see it.[5] What that "it" is has yet to be articulated fully, however. For example, in the introduction to the "Dark Academia" episode of the *Shelf-Involved* podcast from August 26, 2020, host and professional librarian Emily acknowledges the lack of a formal definition with a laugh, describing the genre as "mostly boarding-school murders but other stuff too."[6] Vera Kurian, author of the Dark Academia novel *Never Saw Me Coming* (2021), foregoes offering a definition in her September 7, 2021, essay for *CrimeReads*, choosing instead to describe her personal experience of the genre: "To me it's a mood, a strangely welcome feeling of claustrophobia, of being trapped in a single location, but a cozy location with dark nooks to explore."[7] In fact, any search for a systematic definition of Dark Academia leads to the same conclusion reached by Adiba Jaigirdar in "What Is Dark Academia and Why Is It So Popular" from *Book Riot* on September 9, 2021. Jaigirdar writes, "What is Dark Academia? The truth is, nobody seems to have an exact answer here."[8]

A more exact answer will exist, however, if we extrapolate a definition from the very sources that illustrate a consensus about the genre. That definition of Dark Academia will provide clarity about the genre's purpose and patterns as well as its evolution over time. It will also supply a tool for future study and analysis. Furthermore, applying that definition across time will show that many readers engaged with Dark Academia before the term existed via the worldwide sensation of the *Harry Potter* series, an example of the genre with perhaps the widest name recognition globally. Examining the context of the Dark Academia conversation reveals an ongoing and dynamic dialogue that clearly includes the *Harry Potter* books but may increasingly have left their author behind.

Defining Dark Academia

If audiences and authors know Dark Academia when they see it, well, what is it that they see? What do these works have in common? Analyzing novels frequently listed and labeled as Dark Academia, as well as those directly identified by their writers and publishers as Dark Academia, reveals that the genre rests on the foundation of four cornerstones.

1. Academia

As the term suggests, works of Dark Academia connect in some vital way to the project of academia. Main characters are (or were) students or faculty members. The story may be set at or involve a nonresidential school or boarding school, a college or university campus, or a related space such as a private library or laboratory. Dark Academia tales emphasize research and learning; this might include the study of traditional or taboo academic subjects, the investigation of a campus or personal mystery, or simply the discovery of how to navigate the formal and informal—and often problematic—"system" of the institution or culture.

2. The Gothic

In his introduction to *The Cambridge Companion to Gothic Fiction*, Jerrold E. Hogle admits to the difficulties inherent in studying the Gothic tradition, given "how pliable and malleable this type of fiction-making has proven to be, stemming as it does from an uneasy conflation of genres, styles, and conflicted cultural concerns"[9]—a description well suited to Dark Academia itself. Hogle does, however, identify key features of the Gothic, and from his description we may construct a useful checklist to apply to Dark Academia. It seems clear that Dark Academia employs the Gothic imagination, and Dark Academia works generally display at least three if not all four of the chief Gothic characteristics Hogle enumerates.

According to Hogle, Gothic stories are (A) rooted in setting (an "antiquated or seemingly antiquated space," such as a campus with its signature architecture, atmosphere, and claustrophobia); (B) absorbed with the past (either in general as a subject of study or with a recent, personal past); (C) associated with secrets (that are, either physically or psychologically, haunting); and (D) involved with blurring the boundary between the natural and supernatural, "often siding with one of these over the other in the end, but usually raising the possibility that the boundaries between these may have been crossed, at least psychologically but also physically or both."[10] This last ingredient may not appear in all mundane works of Dark Academia, but it applies to many Dark Academia works of science fiction, fantasy, and horror. In short, the same genre-defying tendency that makes the Gothic a parent genre of many others also makes Dark Academia a natural vehicle for cross-genre or multi-genre storytelling.

Furthermore, because the Gothic formula relies on the hidden and the secret, many Gothic protagonists (from whom knowledge has been kept) are by nature outsiders, without the same privilege or power as others around them. Similarly, many Dark Academia protagonists are outsiders, non-elites or the uninitiated who do not belong to—and thus observe all the more keenly—the culture or system in which they find themselves.

3. Mood

Dark Academia earns the "dark" in its name. Its tales emphasize atmosphere and involve tragedy. An otherwise standard impulse—loyalty to a group of friends or mentor, interest in a specific subject of study, or dedication to independent projects—may become obsessive and spiral out of control. Dark Academia stories highlight the theme of death in some way, such as depicting morbid fascination with death, controversial research aimed at thwarting death, the destruction of reputation (social death, or the death of opportunity or dreams), or a school-related disappearance, murder, or suicide.

4. Critique

Dark Academia stories interrogate power dynamics, often shining a spotlight on exclusivity, privilege, inequality, and hypocrisy. Campus-specific problems such as faculty members abusing their power, students bullying their classmates, secret societies acting with impunity, cliques pursuing their own agendas, and institutions resting on morally-dubious foundations represent larger concerns about injustice in society. In other words, Dark Academia uses the intense and atmospheric backdrop of academia to address issues that, while often shown in high relief in that setting, are also universal.

Ashley Winstead, author of the Dark Academia novel *In My Dreams I Hold a Knife* (2021), affirms in her July 31, 2021, *Salon* article, "Dark Academia and Debt: University thrillers are the literary subgenre of the student loan crisis," that "while the dark academic subculture can at times glorify college … critique has also been endemic to the genre, part of its DNA."[11] The critique inherent in Dark Academia is not a recent trend; it appears consistently throughout the history of the genre. That said, creators and critics appear to be taking new notice of how effectively recent works deliver incisive and timely political and social commentary. As Adiba Jaigirdar explains,

> a lot of dark academia published in recent years is speaking back to the romanticisation of academia, and its Euro-centrism. We see this in books like *Ace of Spades* [2021] by Faridah Àbíké-Íyímídé, which is described as *Get Out* meets *Gossip Girl*, and follows the only two Black students in an elite school being targeted by Aces, an anonymous texter who seems to be driven by a racist system. We can also see this with Alexa Donne's latest novel, *The Ivies* [2021], which seemingly draws inspiration from the 2019 college admissions bribery scandal. Books like these are not using academics as a backdrop for the mystery or murder at the heart of the story, but as a way to explore the seedy underbelly of academia itself.[12]

This critique at the heart of the genre sets it apart from the online aesthetic movement also (rather confusingly) known as Dark Academia, a trend involving everything from fashion to home décor, photography to paper dolls. Compared to the literary genre, the Tumblr, Instagram, and TikTok phenomenon is a newcomer, only dating back to the mid–2010s and gaining attention from the mainstream—for example, from *The New York Times*—in 2020.[13] In her *Refinery29* article "Meet Dark Academia, The Bookish Fashion Trend That's All Over Tiktok," Amal Abdi notes that by October 2020 the aesthetic had inspired "93.1 million TikTok views and 200,000 posts on Instagram."[14] Contrary to the timeliness Adiba Jaigirdar notes in Dark Academia fiction, the aesthetic is rooted in the imagined past, a social-media-driven fascination with a seemingly quaint pre-Internet era. The phenomenon draws its inspiration from a select number of Dark Academia genre stories; Abdi explains that "its genesis appears to be a heady mixture of a few key cultural works. Donna Tartt's 1992 novel *The Secret History* is the trend's foundational text but films like *Dead Poets Society* (1989) and *Kill Your Darlings* (2013) also serve as essential influences."[15] These stories are set in the 1980s, 1950s, and 1940s, respectively, distanced from and easily appearing exotic to audiences today.

Although there may be some overlap between readers of the genre and consumers of the aesthetic, there are vital differences in the projects each represents. The aesthetic seems to glamorize some of the same problematic aspects of academia that the genre interrogates, generating nostalgia for a romanticized past time and cozy setting, celebrating and even fetishizing an idealized view of the elitist, exclusionary, and often dangerous world that the genre routinely paints as disturbing and threatening. Perhaps it is understandable that this aesthetic trend exploded during the Covid-19 pandemic, which disrupted many students' normal school experiences worldwide and forced a reliance on the virtual, when many craved an intriguing past or place some steps removed from real peril and made "retro," low-tech, safe, charming, and inspiring. While the aesthetic dwells on the idealized, however, the genre engages with a more challenging reality.

Finding Hogwarts in Dark Academia

In her essay about the Dark Academia aesthetic trend from June 17, 2021, *L'Officiel*'s Lisa Zirngast ends by posing the question "Where Else Can Dark Academia Be Found?" and answering it with books: "More demanding works of literature such as Sophocles' *Antigone* can be read as well as lighter options in the form of J.K. Rowling's *Harry Potter*."[16] While Potterphiles might quibble with the assumption that the *Harry Potter* series represents a light reading option, it is noteworthy that critics identify *Harry Potter* as part of the Dark Academia aesthetic.

As for the Dark Academic literary genre, the *Harry Potter* saga as a whole, as one story told through multiple books, and also as a series of individual book-length tales, fits the criteria well. The stories are so deeply connected to Hogwarts School of Witchcraft and Wizardry—its founding ethos, its recent history, and its houses, ghosts, and grounds—that the school itself serves, one could argue, as a main character in the novels. Each book represents a year of Harry's experience as a student, and other main actors, both protagonists and antagonists, include fellow students, professors, and graduates. Harry's journey of self-discovery unfolds through learning and research, from events in the classroom (both positive and negative)[17] to personal investigations into the mysteries hidden in his past and the dangers posed by his future.

Prisoner of Azkaban, the third book of the series, offers a useful example of the saga as a whole. This volume expands Harry's understanding of his own story through the experiences of the generation who came before him at Hogwarts, namely the experiences of his parents, their schoolmates, and their peers who eventually became Harry's professors, such as Remus Lupin and Severus Snape. Harry progresses as a student; his in-class and extra-class study of the Patronus charm with Professor Lupin yields a result far surpassing his years, one that saves his life and that of his godfather, Sirius Black. Harry also gains knowledge through his own persistent (and frequently advised-against) investigation into Black's story, which ultimately leads him to a new understanding of his parents' deaths. In fact, at the heart of this mystery lies a story of past independent research and forbidden study at school: the fact that three Hogwarts schoolmates—Black, James Potter, and Peter Pettigrew—taught themselves to become secret animagi in solidarity with their werewolf friend Lupin, cementing their bond as self-styled Marauders until that connection was severed by betrayal and murder.

Much has already been written about how J.K. Rowling employs Gothic storytelling in the *Harry Potter* books.[18] The saga offers all four of the ingredients derived from Hogle's discussion of the Gothic, including the blurring of lines between the natural and supernatural worlds thanks to its witchcraft-and-wizardry elements of fantasy, such as magic and prophecies, spells and curses, goblins and giants, and that most Gothic of creatures, the Dementors. That said, it is worth noting that part of what makes the series fit the Gothic tradition also connects the tales to the "academia" facet of Dark Academia: its deep roots in the time-hallowed halls of Hogwarts, a school whose institutional past and secrets not only directly impact Harry, but are also tied to Harry's own family past and secrets in a deeply personal, haunting way.

The *Harry Potter* series captures the mood of Dark Academia as well. Each novel contains its own ominous mystery, and the series as a whole builds dark and dramatic tension until its ultimate resolution in the final installment. The theme of death permeates the series. The title of the first chapter of the first book in the series opens by identifying Harry as "The Boy Who Lived," scarred by the same attack that claimed his parents' lives.[19] Lily and James Potter's murders form the backbone of Harry's story; readers learn that the architect of this tragedy, Lord Voldemort, was and is obsessed with evading death with the support of his aptly-named followers, the Death Eaters. The series does not shy away from depicting real and lasting mortality, either; before the series' end, Harry loses many of those he loves and also embraces his own potential sacrificial death.

Here, again, *Prisoner of Azkaban* as a mid-series case in point is instructive. Harry deals with the threat of death throughout the book, including the haunting omen of the black dog, or Grim, as well as the related suggestion that the escaped Black is on the loose, stalking Harry and planning his demise. Harry hears his mother's final screams when the Dementors draw near, and death recurs in the threatened execution of Buckbeak the hippogriff and the also-threatened fate as dire as death, the Dementor's kiss for Black. The assumed death of Pettigrew, when proven false, offers a chance at another near-murder by once-friends as well as new information about the treachery that made Harry an orphan. Given the sense of dread pervasive in the book, when Professor McGonagall asks mockingly of Professor Trelawny's Divination class, "Tell me, which of you will be dying this year?" the question resonates with both wry humor and truly serious import.[20]

Finally, the *Harry Potter* series also fulfills the last qualification for Dark Academia by interrogating power dynamics. Harry himself is mistreated by his biological family, unimaginative adherents of the status quo; he is tormented by elitist classmates who envy his celebrity and disdain his friend Ron Weasley's lack of material wealth and his friend Hermione Granger's lack of magical family ties; and he is targeted unfairly by adults who abuse their positions of authority such as faculty member Snape, journalist Rita Skeeter, and political opportunist Dolores Umbridge. To return to *Prisoner of Azkaban* as a helpful illustration, the novel seeds critique in multiple scenarios. The novel opens with Harry experiencing the casual cruelty of his prejudiced Aunt Marge. Forbidden from answering her attacks with truth, Harry fears losing his place at Hogwarts due to the unintentional (and underage) use of magic her abuse understandably provokes. His unique susceptibility to the Dementors' presence and the trauma they trigger in him also isolates Harry both en route to Hogwarts and on campus, a situation exacerbated by the fodder his vulnerability provides for his bullying classmates. Those close to Harry are also wronged. Draco Malfoy leverages his family's political influence to attack Hagrid's teaching position and Buckbeak's very life out of malicious spite. For crimes he did not commit, Sirius Black is unjustly imprisoned and later hunted, robbed of his freedom and the opportunity to be a godfather to Harry for years.[21] Furthermore, Hogwarts—and, perhaps more to the point, Harry—loses a dedicated professor and champion, Remus Lupin, because Snape, Lupin's former schooldays enemy and present-day professional colleague, outs him as a werewolf, which renders Lupin essentially an unemployable pariah.[22] The injustices highlighted in the series are not simply personal matters, either. As Susan Hall points out in "School Ties, House Points, and Quidditch: Hogwarts as a British Boarding School," "Harry possesses an ability to draw parallels between evils he has experienced in the Muggle world and their equivalents in the magical one. He rejects both the corrupt Ministry of Magic and the seductive imperialist fantasies of the Death Eaters."[23]

Clearly, then, by addressing the academic project, employing the Gothic imagination, building a dark mood, and offering incisive critique, the *Harry Potter* series qualifies as Dark Academia. This is important for both the genre and the series. This means that the Dark Academia tradition includes the bestselling book series of all time, one that, by virtue of being ubiquitous, has lasting visibility, cultural purchase, and influence on both readers and writers.[24] This also means that the *Harry Potter* series has a place and context in yet another literary tradition beyond those previously recognized by fans and scholars, one that is gaining great popularity and attention and one, significantly, that is older than most critics recognize.

The undeniably influential novel *The Secret History* by Donna Tartt (1992) is a work frequently mentioned in articles about Dark Academia as a foundational text due to its depiction of a murder mystery involving a close-knit group of classics students at an elite liberal arts college.[25] Less commented upon, perhaps because of its status as a classic of fantasy, but arguably equally path-breaking is *Waking the Moon* by Elizabeth Hand (1994), which won both the James Tiptree, Jr., Award and the Mythopoeic Award for Adult Literature. This novel features archeology faculty members, undergraduate students, and shadowy secret societies in its portrayal of the awakening of an ancient and violent goddess at a fictional university. The early 1990s one-two punch of *The Secret History* and *Waking the Moon* clearly set the stage for later developments in the genre, including *Harry Potter*.

That said, these are far from the first works in this tradition. For example, Joan Lindsay's *Picnic at Hanging Rock* (1967) follows the mysterious disappearance of a group of students and the violent aftermath at a girls' boarding school. Shirley Jackson's *Hangsaman* (1951) presents a disturbing study of a traumatized and troubled college freshman's psychological unraveling in the midst of her search for self. Fritz Leiber's *Conjure Wife* (1943), which in 2019 won the "Retro" Hugo Award for 1944 Best Novel, recounts a horror tale of a small-town college professor who discovers witchcraft on his campus and in his home. Each of these novels and others fit the four-part mold of Dark Academia.

In fact, employing the definition of Dark Academia retroactively and consistently shows that the genre stretches back into the nineteenth century, back at least as far as 1818, to Mary Wollstonecraft Shelley's tale of an obsessed student who leaves his university studies to pursue taboo research and the deadly tragedies that mark his failure to take responsibility for the life he creates: *Frankenstein, or the Modern Prometheus*. As ancestor texts for genres go, it is hard to conceive of a more impressive work than *Frankenstein*, which is already considered a classic of Gothic, science fiction, and horror storytelling. Dark Academia has deep and vibrant roots.

Goldy Moldavksy seems to nod to this long tradition in her 2021 contribution to Dark Academia. Following Latina scholarship student and trauma survivor Rachel Chavez as she seeks a new start at a school on Manhattan's wealthy Upper East Side, Goldavsky's novel shares a name with the secret society Rachel joins: *The Mary Shelley Club*. This reference appropriately connects the dots of the genre, which is fitting, given that the latest wave of Dark Academia appears to represent continuity more than rupture, even as diverse voices and perspectives in this dynamic conversation add fresh insights and energy to the genre.

In short, applying the definition of Dark Academia in hindsight allows us to trace the history of the genre and add context to later waves of Dark Academia publication and popularity. This in itself invites further investigation and analysis, of course. It also shows us another place in the history of literature where the *Harry Potter* series belongs. That fit, however, may be an increasingly uncomfortable one for J.K. Rowling, as Dark Academia creators alternately push back against or dismiss her.

Considering the Explosion of Dark Academia

Many possible factors may contribute to the recent explosion of Dark Academia works. Amy Gentry, author of the Dark Academia novel *Bad Habits* (2021), in her February 18, 2021, *CrimeReads* article "Dark Academia: Your Guide to the New Wave of Post–*Secret History* Campus Thrillers," describes this trend as "kicking into high gear in 2017."[26] And it shows all indications of gaining, not losing, momentum. From our vantage point in the midst of this phenomenon, one could argue it is too soon to draw many conclusions, but we may speculate and identify suggestive patterns.

Part of the attraction of Dark Academia is, of course, timeless. Mysteries, for instance, have appealed to audiences for centuries. For that matter, Ashley of *The Infinite Library* notes, "More often than not, DA books are actually coming of age stories, twisted and bleak ones, but learning experiences for characters all the same,"[27] and coming-of-age tales are a time-honored and evergreen form of storytelling. Furthermore, most readers can identify with the general experience of being a student regardless of where or for how long they studied, making these stories uniquely accessible, as Vera Kurian explains: "School is an intriguing environment because we all have some familiarity with it which means that everyone can imagine themselves in the space."[28]

Others see a timeliness to this new enthusiasm for Dark Academia. Ashley Winstead links interest in the critiques implicit in Dark Academia to issues of economics, asserting that the genre is gaining popularity as "America's relationship to higher education is more fraught than ever, our collective dream of education haunted by the specter of debt."[29] In addition, the global Covid-19 pandemic not only has separated many students, faculty, and staff from their experience of campus routine, creating a desire to return to school normalcy at least through fiction, but it also has taken an unfathomable number of human lives worldwide, making newly relevant what Adiba Jaigirdar describes as Dark Academia's "exploration of death and morbidity."[30]

Amy Gentry suggests there may be yet more to the phenomenon:

> Perhaps there's one more way to explain the Dark Academia trend. A generation of Harry Potter–loving children were raised on the idea that a perfect combination of pure heart, ancient birthright, and excellent study skills could dispatch any villain. All grown up and heartbroken by Rowling's anti-trans hate speech and shallow commitment to diversity, they may rightly question whether hallowed halls and sacred traditions can ever be a place for real rebellion.[31]

Some of the authors of contemporary Dark Academia explicitly note how their works push back against aspects of the *Harry Potter* series. Sarah Gailey, author of the "Angst-Ridden Magic School Noir"[32] work *Magic for Liars* (2019), notes that their novel "is obviously in conversation with the *Harry Potter* books in a major way,"[33] explaining that Rowling's series and similar works "always seemed to focus on a chosen-one, someone who was learning to navigate a strange new world and then mastering it. I wanted to write a story that felt truer to the experience of someone who is outside that world of magic—a story that would explore those feelings of exclusion, longing, and isolation."[34] Moreover, many of the social issues Gailey's novel explores, such as sex and reproductive rights, sexuality and identity, drugs and alcohol, relate directly to the topic of "consent and bodily autonomy," a focus Gailey cultivates as an answer to *Harry Potter*:

> For instance, the leg-locker spell in *Harry Potter*—a spell that locks the victim's legs straight and together, so they can't walk. This spell is treated as mild, nonthreatening, and relatively harmless (if inconvenient). In practice, though,

a spell like this would be viscerally harmful. It's a spell that immobilizes and pronates a person without their consent. In much of *Magic for Liars*, I explore the consequences of such casual disregard for bodily autonomy.[35]

Gailey is not alone. Naomi Novik, author of the Dark Academia *Scholomance* trilogy (including 2020's *A Deadly Education*, 2021's *The Last Graduate*, and 2022's *The Golden Enclaves*), admits the novels are "influenced by Harry Potter fandom," in which she has participated "at various points in my life…."[36] But while Novik recognizes that Hogwarts and the Scholomance do have one thing in common—"it's crazy to go to either school"—the world Novik has created is darker by far (and arguably more realistic), based in part on her conviction that the economic basis of Rowling's wizarding world is fatally flawed: "The world, when you start poking at it, doesn't work. Magic doesn't cost anything, right? ... If magic doesn't cost anything except the time it takes to learn and cast it, then the more wizards you have, the richer you are, right?"[37] Novik responds with pointed economic critique in a trilogy in which magic does cost, dearly, and students must confront and survive the reality of scarcity in a harsh and threatening world.[38]

Olivie Blake, fanfiction author and professional author of the Dark Academia *The Atlas* series (including to date *The Atlas Six*, first published in 2020 and re-released in a revised version in 2022, and both the short story "Sacred Hospitality" and the novel *The Atlas Paradox* in 2022), suggests that other authors are choosing to move on from the conversation about J.K. Rowling altogether:

> As a fanfiction author, people naturally want me to reflect on whatever recently came out of JK Rowling's mouth. I urge you to ignore it. Your outrage is justified, of course, because what she wrote informed a collective imagination that defined a generation and beyond…. She has always played into stereotypes and has never accurately reflected the depth of experiences that her audience has. For her, diversity is an aesthetic—the appearance of many threads. But the fabric itself is still what has always been, and this is why she's not important to the conversation right now.[39]

In other words, some authors respond to the legacy of *Harry Potter* (directly or indirectly, intentionally or unintentionally) by producing works in this new wave that do offer something like Gentry's "real rebellion" or, at the very least, that reveal Blake's "fabric itself" by showing genuine diversity in the topics covered and voices represented and thus the critiques offered. In the place of the tendency "to fetishize a nostalgic British culture that never really existed—implicitly fetishizing whiteness, assimilation, and rigid gender norms," Gentry notes that newer Dark Academia stories "reckon frankly with sexual harassment and abuse, class disparities, homophobia, and systemic racism."[40] Certainly the "default settings" of recent Dark Academia works are not, like Rowling's wizarding world, overwhelmingly White, heteronormative, and cisnormative, and as authors of different races and ethnicities, gender identities and sexual orientations, economic backgrounds and nationalities, abilities and experiences join the conversation, they both expand its insights and extend its reach, proving more relevant to the lives of its many and varied readers.

For example, contemporary Dark Academic works include same-sex relationships between main characters (see, for example, Rory Power's *Wilder Girls* from 2019, Micah Nemerever's *These Violent Delights* from 2020, and Lee Mandelo's *Summer Sons* from 2021), nonbinary characters (see Maureen Johnson's *Truly Devious* trilogy from 2018 to 2020 and its stand-alone sequels and Victoria Lee's *A Lesson in Vengeance* from 2021), and characters with disabilities (see Peadar Ó Guilín's *The Call* from 2016 and *The Invasion* from 2018 and Kelly Andrew's *The Whispering Dark* from 2022) as a matter of course, not as the main point of the novels.[41] They also represent the voices of authors from different demographics, including those not writing in English. For instance, *Vita Nostra* by Marina Dyachenko and Sergey Dyachenko (a novel, it is worth noting, described by Bethanne Patrick of *The Washington Post* as "the anti–Harry Potter you didn't know you wanted"[42]) was first published in 2007 in Ukrainian and later translated into English by Julia Meitov Hersey in 2018, and *Four by Four* by Sara Mesa was first published in 2012 in Spanish and later translated into English by Katie Whittemore in 2020. Furthermore, some authors—see Layne Fargo in *They Never Learn* (2020) and Vera Kurian in *Never Saw Me Coming* (2021) as illustrations—subvert the "chosen one" trope, choosing to present their critiques of injustice by spotlighting antiheroes as protagonists, including what Gentry identifies as "vigilantes" and "revenge schemes."[43]

Examples of sophisticated discussions of contemporary issues abound. Take, for example, the 2020 Dark Academia novel *Legendborn* and its 2022 sequel *Bloodmarked* by Tracy Deonn, a two-time graduate of the University of North Carolina at Chapel Hill. Deonn uses that campus as a backdrop for the collision of European Arthurian romance and African root magic in the service of confronting the legacy of power disparity, hypocrisy, and racism in the U.S. South in general and at that institution in particular. Meanwhile, while still a student herself, Faridah Àbíké-Íyímídé wrote *Ace of Spades* to, in her words, discuss "themes that I am very passionate about, such as homophobia in the black community, institutional racism and the diversity of thought among black people."[44] The story involves the only two Black students at an exclusive private academy who become the target of an anonymous antagonist who uses the contemporary, omnipresent technology of the cell phone as a means to threaten them.

Such novels are not outliers. For instance, Katie Zhao's Dark Academia novel *How We Fall Apart* follows Asian-American teens at a preparatory school. Zhao's goal, she says, is to unravel "seemingly high-achieving students to make a point about the toxic, competitive mentality that's found in these school environments … this is even more true for students of color, who face further barriers and are often pitted against each other for limited spots."[45] Author Elisabeth Thomas normalizes differences in race, class, gender, and sexual orientations among characters in *Catherine House*, a Dark Academia novel in which all of the students are on full scholarships—and in great peril, as they are manipulated to fit the mysterious secret agenda of the school's leadership.

While the diversity of contemporary Dark Academia may appear revolutionary when compared to past British schooldays-esque stories, including the *Harry Potter* novels—and yes, much more to the point, when contrasted with the public and political positions taken by author J.K. Rowling—it is important to recognize that the current boom of Dark Academia works represent continuity more than rupture within the genre. After all, Dark Academia works interrogate power dynamics, and that is a difficult task, one could argue, if that interrogation takes place exclusively from positions of power, from dominant perspectives. The Gothic tradition itself originated in the margins and has consistently given voice to underrepresented points of view. The trend at hand appears to be not abrupt change, but rather healthy growth and successful evolution.

It is also worth noting that, in true horror trope fashion, the call of Dark Academia is often coming from inside the metaphorical house. The varied experiences and perspectives these works offer represent informed, knowledgeable critiques, coming as they often do from writers who are themselves students, educators, and/or creators with strong ties to the academy. (For example, Dark Academia authors and critics Amy Gentry, Ashley Winstead, Vera Kurian, Victoria Lee, Emily M. Danforth, and Lauren Nossett all hold doctoral degrees, and R.F. Kuang and Lee Mandelo are currently pursuing theirs.) The problems these works highlight, while universal, are often more visible in the claustrophobic, intense dynamic of a school setting, and some of these authors have experienced and/or witnessed first-hand examples of such wrongs. For all of its darkness and dread, however, Dark Academia is also a product of hope, giving voice to the outsider, pointing out injustice as a call to action. Nina Reyvor, author of the Dark Academia novel *A Student of History*, noted this while a guest speaker at the "Dark Academia: A Panel Discussion" live event on October 7, 2021. Authors interrogate the academy—and in so doing, the larger world it represents—not because its cause is hopeless, she said, but because "It could be so much better than it is."[46]

Such observations add to the genre's ongoing conversation. And the Dark Academia genre *is* a conversation, a tradition of storytelling and inquiry. Applying a definition to the genre offers an opportunity for us to investigate its past and evolution, to put its representative works into a new context, and to engage with recent and forthcoming works as part of this broader dialogue. Dark Academia is not new; it is not going anywhere; and it deserves further study.

Notes

1. This work has benefited from the insights and comments of Jessica O'Brien and Larry M. Hall as well as conversations with graduate students and colleagues during my "Dark Academia" course in the Fall 2022 semester at Signum University. Any errors belong to the author.

2. Jen Ryland, "Exploring Dark Academia: A YA and Adult Book List," *Jen Ryland Reviews*, April 17, 2021, https://www.jenryland.com/exploring-dark-academia-a-ya-and-adult-book-list/.

3. The U.S.-based Owlcrate (young adult fiction) and Fox & Wit (young adult) offered Dark Academia boxes in August 2021, both featuring *A Lesson in Vengeance* by Victoria Lee; that same month, the U.K.-based Illumicrate (young adult and crossover adult fiction) offered a Dark Academia box as well, featuring *The Devil Makes Three* by Tori Bovalino. In October, the U.S.-based Rainbow Crate (LGBTQIA+ fiction) also offered a Dark Academia box featuring *Summer Sons* by Lee Mandelo, while the Unplugged Book Box (young adult and mainstream adult fiction) featured a Dark Academia novel in its Limited Edition Horror Box for Halloween (*Dark Things I Adore* by Katie Lattari).

4. For example, HarperCollins Canada hosted "Campus Crime Night: A Back to School Thriller Event" on September 9, 2021, with Dark Academia authors Ashley Winstead (*In My Dreams I Hold a Knife*, 2021) and Vera Kurian (*Never Saw Me Coming*, 2021) interviewed by Dark Academia author Micah Nemerever (*These Violent Delights*, 2020), and bookseller BookWoman sponsored "Dark Academia: A Virtual Panel Discussion" on October 7, 2021, with Dark Academia authors Ashley Winstead, Amy Gentry (*Bad Habits*, 2021), Layne Fargo (*They Never Learn*, 2020), and Nina Revoyr (*A Student of History*, 2010) interviewed by Molly Odintz of *CrimeReads*.

5. As of October 17, 2021, *Goodreads*—"the world's largest site for readers and book recommendations"—has twenty-two different user-generated, crowdsourced reading lists marked as "Dark Academia," and users have tagged a total of 3,380 books for their virtual bookshelves labeled "Dark Academia." *Goodreads*, accessed October 17, 2021, https://www.goodreads.com/.

6. Kenzie and Emily, hosts, "Dark Academia," *Shelf-Involved* (podcast), August 26, 2020, https://podtail.com/en/podcast/shelf-involved-podcast/dark-academia/.

7. Vera Kurian, "The Dark Pleasures of School-Based Mysteries," *CrimeReads*, September 7, 2021, https://crimereads.com/the-dark-pleasures-of-school-based-mysteries/.

8. Adiba Jaigirdar, "What Is Dark Academia and Why Is It So Popular," *Book Riot*, September 9, 2021, https://bookriot.com/what-is-dark-academia/.

9. Jerrold E. Hogle, "Introduction: The Gothic in Western Culture," in *The Cambridge Companion to Gothic Fiction*, ed. Jarrold E. Hogle (Cambridge: Cambridge University Press, 2002), 2. Although Hogle identifies the Gothic as first originating and evolving in western culture, he also recognizes that creators and audiences from other places, backgrounds, and experiences continue to join the tradition/conversation.

10. Ibid., 2–3.

11. Ashley Winstead, "Dark Academia and Debt: University thrillers are the literary subgenre of the student loan crisis," *Salon*, July 31, 2021, https://www.salon.com/2021/07/31/dark-academia-and-debt-university-thrillers-are-the-literary-subgenre-of-the-student-loan-crisis/.

12. Jaigirdar, "What Is Dark Academia and Why Is It So Popular."

13. Lisa Zirngast, "Everything you need to know about the 'Dark Academia Aesthetic' Trend," *L'Officiel*, June 17, 2021, https://www.lofficiel.at/en/pop-culture/dark-academia-aesthetic and Kristen Bateman, "Academia Lives—On TikTok," *The New York Times*, June 30, 2020, https://www.nytimes.com/2020/06/30/style/dark-academia-tiktok.html.

14. Amal Abdi, "Meet Dark Academia, The Bookish Fashion Trend That's All Over Tiktok," *Refinery29*, October 7, 2020, https://www.refinery29.com/en-us/2020/10/10079305/dark-academia-aesthetic-tiktok-trend.

15. *Ibid*. It is worth noting that *Kill Your Darlings* stars Daniel Radcliffe (as poet and writer Allen Ginsberg), the same actor who portrayed Harry Potter in the eight original *Harry Potter* films.

16. Zirngast, "Everything you need to know about the 'Dark Academia Aesthetic' Trend."

17. M'Balia Thomas, Alisa LaDean Russell, and Hannah V. Warren note how the "tales of the good, the bad, and the ugly of teachers and teaching" at Hogwarts parallel those that "haunt the halls of real-world schools." Thomas, Russell, and Warren, "The Good, the Bad, and the Ugly of Pedagogy in Harry Potter: An Inquiry Into the Personal Practical Knowledge of Remus Lupin, Rubeus Hagrid, and Severus Snape," *The Clearing House* 91, no. 4–5 (2018), 186.

18. See, for example, John Granger, "Gothic Romance: The Spooky Atmosphere Formula from Transylvania," in *Harry Potter's Bookshelf: The Great Books Behind the Hogwarts Adventures* (New York: Berkley Books, 2009), 65–104 and Amy H. Sturgis, James Thomas, Travis Prinzi, and John Granger, "Gothic Schoolboy (1)" and "Gothic Schoolboy (2)," in *Harry Potter Smart Talk*, eds. James Thomas, Travis Prinzi, and John Granger (Constantia: Unlocking Press, 2010), 31–61, as well as Travis Prinzi's discussion of supernatural horror in Prinzi, "Hogwarts, A (Haunted) History: Fear and Supernatural Horror in Harry Potter," in *Harry Potter & Imagination: The Way Between Two Worlds* (Hambden: Zossima Press, 2009), 43–69.

19. J.K. Rowling, *Harry Potter and the Sorcerer's Stone* (New York: Scholastic, 1998), 1.

20. J.K. Rowling, *Harry Potter and the Prisoner of Azkaban* (New York: Scholastic, 1999), 109.

21. For more on Sirius Black's troubled life, see Emma Nicholson's essay in this volume.

22. Mark-Anthony Lewis discusses Remus Lupin's "token" status in his essay in this volume.

23. Susan Hall, "School Ties, House Points, and Quidditch: Hogwarts as a British Boarding School," in *Harry Potter and History*, ed. Nancy R. Reagin (Hoboken: John Wiley & Sons, 2011), 198. For more discussions of how the Harry Potter series offers moral dilemmas, teachable moments, and critical storytelling as a multi-book British schooldays story, see James Gunn, "Harry Potter as Schooldays Novel," in *Mapping the World of Harry Potter*, ed. Mercedes Lackey (Dallas: BenBella, 2005), 145–155 and Emily Strand, "The Second War was Won On the Quidditch Pitch of Hogwarts," in *Harry Potter for Nerds II*, eds. Kathryn N. McDaniel and Travis Prinzi (Oklahoma City: Unlocking Press, 2015), 115–138.

24. Aaron Radford-Watley, "This book has sold the most copies," *Fox Business*, June 24, 2020, https://www.foxbusiness.com/lifestyle/this-book-sold-the-most-copies.

25. J.K. Rowling read *The Secret History*. In her words, "If you ask me, the book would have benefited from the attention of a scissor-happy editor, but it is an undeniable page-turner and I doubt whether *Unzeitgemässe Betrachtungen* is half as informative on the subject of hallucinogenic drugs." J.K. Rowling, "What Was the Name of That Nymph Again? or Greek and Roman Studies Recalled," *Pegasus: Journal of the University of Exeter Department of Classics and Ancient History* 41 (April 1988), 25.

26. Amy Gentry, "Dark Academia: Your Guide to The New Wave of Post-*Secret History* Campus Thrillers," *CrimeReads*, February 18, 2021, https://crimereads.

com/dark-academia-your-guide-to-the-new-wave-of-post-secret-history-campus-thrillers/.

27. Ashley, "The Dark Academia Reading List: 49 Books of Tragedy, Elitism, Secrets, Violence and the Pursuit of Knowledge," *The Infinite Library*, August 18, 2021, https://ashsinfinitelibrary.wordpress.com/2021/08/18/the-dark-academia-reading-list/.

28. Kurian, "The Dark Pleasures of School-Based Mysteries."

29. Winstead, "Dark Academia and Debt."

30. Jaigirdar, "What Is Dark Academia and Why Is It So Popular."

31. Gentry, "Dark Academia."

32. Quoted in "Interview with Sarah Gailey, Author of Magic for Liars," *The Qwillery*, June 3, 2019, https://www.theqwillery.com/2019/06/interview-with-sarah-gailey-author-of.html.

33. Quoted in Paul Semel, "Exclusive Interview: Magic for Liars Author Sarah Gailey," *paulsemel.com*, July 15, 2019, https://paulsemel.com/exclusive-interview-magic-for-liars-author-sarah-gailey/.

34. Quoted in Daryl M. (Maxwell), "Interview With an Author: Sarah Gailey," July 11, 2019, https://www.lapl.org/collections-resources/blogs/lapl/interview-author-sarah-gailey.

35. Quoted in "Interview with Sarah Gailey," *The Qwillery*.

36. Quoted in Tasha Robinson, "The Last Graduate fills the Harry Potter void, and so much more," *Polygon*, September 28, 2021, https://www.polygon.com/22697256/the-last-graduate-naomi-novik-scholomance-series.

37. Ibid.

38. Novik is not the only Dark Academia creator to have made the leap from *Harry Potter* fandom—or to be motivated to answer the limitations of J.K. Rowling's vision. Victoria Lee explains that writing and reading *Harry Potter* fanfiction provided not only training as an author, but also the opportunity to explore sexuality and identity. Lee writes, "Harry Potter fandom took a set of books that were almost aggressively straight and cisgender and colored them in with rainbow ink." Lee's Dark Academia novel *A Lesson in Vengeance* (2021) features queer characters and romance. Victoria Lee, "Harry Potter and the Conspiracy of Queers," *Tor.com*, October 14, 2019, https://www.tor.com/2019/10/14/harry-potter-and-the-conspiracy-of-queers-discovering-myself-in-fandom-and-roleplay/. R.F. Kuang is the author of the 2022 Dark Academia novel *Babel: Or the Necessity of Violence: An Arcane History of the Oxford Translators Revolution*, described by publisher Harper Voyager as a work "that grapples with student revolutions, colonial resistance, and the use of language and translation as the dominating tool of the British empire." *Harper Voyager*, accessed March 23, 2022, https://www.harpervoyagerbooks.com/book/9780063021440/babel/. When asked about the books that influenced her and how her opinion of them has changed over time, Kuang responded, "This is a good question to ask when we're all grappling with what to do with our Harry Potter memorabilia now that J.K. Rowling insists on being a TERF, isn't it?" Arley Sorg, "Diagram and Story: A Conversation with R.F. Kuang," *Clarkesworld Science Fiction & Fantasy Magazine* 170 (November 2020), https://clarkesworldmagazine.com/kuang_interview/.

39. Olivie Blake, "Olivie Blake *Is Writing," *Olivie Blake*, June 8, 2020, https://www.olivieblake.com/post/olivie-blake-is-writing.

40. Gentry, "Dark Academia." For more on how such critiques are coming from within the Harry Potter acafan community, see Brent Satterly's essay in this volume.

41. The success of this trend—and related, supporting evidence, such as the appearance of reader-generated, crowdsourced recommendation lists for topics like "Queer Dark Academia" and "YA Diverse Dark Academia" at *Goodreads*—suggests that many readers and critics find value in this new and diverse wave of Dark Academia.

42. Bethanne Patrick, "The 10 books to read in November," *The Washington Post*, October 30, 2018, https://www.washingtonpost.com/entertainment/books/the-10-books-to-read-in-november/2018/10/30/34d15356-dba3-11e8-b3f0-62607289efee_story.html.

43. Gentry, "Dark Academia."

44. Quoted in Alison Flood, "Faridah Àbíké-Íyímídé: the 21-year-old British

student with a million-dollar book deal," *The Guardian*, September 8, 2020, https://www.theguardian.com/books/2020/sep/08/faridah-abike-iyimide-british-student-million-dollar-book-deal-ace-of-spades.

    45. Quoted in Jen, "Interview: Katie Zhao, Author of How We Fall Apart," *Pop! Goes the Reader,* August 17, 2021, https://popgoesthereader.com/interview/interview-katie-zhao-author-of-how-we-fall-apart/.

    46. Nina Reyvor, "Dark Academia: A Panel Discussion" moderated by Molly Odintz of *CrimeReads* and hosted by BookWoman, live event online, October 7, 2021.

Conversation
Occult Knowledge

Beatrice Groves (BG) and Amy H. Sturgis (AHS) talk with Katy McDaniel (KM) and Emily Strand (ES) about their essays.

KM: Bea and Amy, in your [essay]s, each of you is explaining how Rowling is working within a certain set of genre or allusory expectations—you know, how she's building a Dark Academia setting, or she's playing off of these motifs from *Dracula*. But to what extent does she break with these expectations, and what's the effect of those choices she's making?

BG: So with the *Dracula* connection, there are a number of very close connections with *Dracula*, which I discuss in my essay. But I did feel that what she was doing by setting up these extensive connections with the scar, the blood, and the Horcruxes are forming a link with the way in which *Dracula* worries about the miscegenation of evil.

So these good characters—you know, Mina Harker's entirely, morally good, but when Dracula drinks her blood, she then turns into a vampire. And you can see her saying, "I wanted him (you know) to violate me," basically—that she becomes desirable, and the erotics of evil is something that she succumbs to powerlessly, because he has physically attacked her. So the physical attack is something that changes your moral being.

I felt that *Harry Potter* was intent on overturning that completely in that Harry is physically attacked by Voldemort, he is given this scar, he becomes a Horcrux, in fact. He has a part of the Dark Lord's soul lodged within him, but his essential self is never changed by that. He is pure of heart—in the beginning when he sees the Philosopher's Stone and sees only how to overcome Voldemort in the Mirror of Erised. Dumbledore says to him, the Dark Lord should have realized then that he was never going to be able to possess—never going to be able to beat you, because you have a purity of heart that he does not understand. Your ability to love can push him out. So, Mina Harker loves her husband, but that love is clearly going to be completely subsumed by her vampirism if they don't manage to kill Dracula. Whereas Harry is not—you know, when he feels his love for Dobby and for Sirius as grief, it pushes out the power of the Dark Lord. When the Dark Lord tries to possess him in the fight in the Ministry, when Quirrell touches him at the beginning, that causes the *Dark Lord* pain, not Harry.

Whereas that's the inverse of what happens to Mina—Dracula never suffers from the fact that he's in contact with goodness; it's goodness that suffers from contact with him. I felt that Stoker is interested in the decadent; he's interested in the erotics of evil. He's basically trying to undermine a certain Victorian morality, whereas Rowling is doing the opposite. She's trying to emphasize the importance and the power of good in a culture which is more interested in a sort of Stoker decadence. Both of them are counter-cultural, just in their completely different cultures, as it were. It's an interesting overturning of actually what *Dracula*'s about. She's exploring the links.

KM: Right. And your title, "Good Men and Monsters," I think speaks to that argument you're making. One of the elements, too, that is a really cool addition is that you talked about Mina's powerlessness, and over and over again, Rowling tells us—the *Harry Potter* series tells us—that Harry has choices, and that he's able to choose the good.

BG: Exactly. That phrase "a power the Dark Lord knows not," and Harry's like, "oh, it's just love again, isn't it?" And it's like, "yes, it's just love again!" This *is* a power! John Granger points this out in *Harry Potter's Bookshelf*, that Harry is linked to Gothic heroines. You know, throughout Gothic we have characters like Mina Harker, but also Jane Eyre, to an extent, going back to Cinderella—they're sort of oppressed and abused by men. So we think of Jane Eyre locked in the Red Room and Harry locked in the cupboard under the stairs—that he takes on this position that has been a feminine position in literature of fighting against this powerlessness. So I think it's interesting, what Rowling wants to say about the strength of the good that is oppressed in changing over the gender expectations there.

KM: Amy, what do you think about this question about the breaking with Dark Academia? Do you see [Rowling] breaking it at all, or is she setting the definition in some important ways?

AHS: Well, first of all, I think it's important to point out that Dark Academia is, by its very nature, sort of a flavor that can be added with other flavors. And so the fact that *Harry Potter*, each individual novel and the novels as a whole as one big story, represents multiple genres—that's not a breaking with, that's actually a consistency with Dark Academia. You see that *Harry Potter* is doing fantasy, and it's doing mystery, and it's doing multiple things—that's part of Dark Academia. She's not breaking with it by involving other genres in her storytelling. I think it's important that *Harry Potter* does qualify as Dark Academia, and that we recognize that, because it means then that this tradition, this genre on its own, includes the best-selling book series of all time. And by virtue of being ubiquitous, it has lasting cultural cache, right? It's got visibility, purchase, it has lasting influence on readers and writers in the culture. It gives us, also as *Potter* scholars, another way to look at *Harry Potter* by recognizing that it is part of Dark Academia.

But to be perfectly honest, as far as breaking away is concerned, I think looking at what's happening now, and particularly in the explosion of Dark Academia that's happened since 2017, it's a bit more like Dark Academia has broken away from *Harry Potter* and not the other way around....

I think a lot of the works we see in this new explosion, post–2017, show that offering something like real rebellion, as Amy Gentry calls it, is possible—or at least ... the authors of these works are trying to push back against things they are dissatisfied with in the *Harry Potter* series. So that means showing genuine diversity in the topics covered, in the voices represented, and that also means the critiques offered are different, or more diverse than we see in the *Harry Potter* series.

Ancient Magic

Here Be Dragons and Phoenixes
A Thematic Direction for the Fantastic Beasts *Series*[1]

Lana A. Whited

> "Beware the sleeping dragon, for when she awakes the Earth will shake."—frequently misattributed to Winston Churchill[2]

In *Fantastic Beasts: Secrets of Dumbledore,* Gellert Grindelwald employs a bewitched qilin (pronounced *ch'i-lin*), sometimes called the Chinese unicorn, for nefarious purposes: the qilin has a long history of identifying righteous leaders,[3] and Grindelwald wants to ensure that the creature chooses him as Supreme Mugwump-elect of the International Confederation of Wizards. Discussing Grindelwald's plan on *Potterversity* in May 2022, Beatrice Groves contends that the critical role played by the qilin explains Newt Scamander's prominence in the film series.[4] Groves is right, but the reason Albus Dumbledore recruited a magizoologist to help him fight Grindelwald was already clear well before *Secrets of Dumbledore.* The Hogwarts headmaster needs his former pupil for the same reason that Beowulf needs Wiglaf: there is a dragon to be conquered. Knowing Scamander's talents for managing beasts, his role is unlikely to involve literal violence against any creature, even the one suggested in the final scenes of *Crimes of Grindelwald*. In that film's climax, Grindelwald emerges as the beast typically cast in Asian mythology as the only worthy companion (and sometimes adversary) for the phoenix, which is, of course, the Dumbledore family herald. The phoenix-dragon pairing overlays the two Über-wizards' confrontation with the status of instant myth.

J.K. Rowling's interest in monsters is famous, and the *Harry Potter* series is rife with both human and nonhuman creatures. Rowling first uses the term *monster* in Chapter Nine of the first book, after Harry, Ron, and Hermione see the three-headed dog, Fluffy. But over twenty years later, in an interview just before the release of the *Fantastic Beasts: The Crimes of*

Grindelwald film, she pointed out that her first allusion to a beast comes in Chapter Three, when his name appears on Albus Dumbledore's Chocolate Frog card: Gellert Grindelwald. In 2018, Rowling called the character "the *beast* that was in the back of my mind for nearly ten years" before the author wrote of his confrontation with Dumbledore over the Elder Wand in *Deathly Hallows*.[5] As Travis Prinzi has suggested, "it might be argued that Grindelwald represents a more sinister evil than Voldemort, for Grindelwald thought he was working for the good of wizardkind, whereas Voldemort was working out of pure self-interest."[6] Grindelwald does not receive full characterization in the *Harry Potter* series, but by the second *Fantastic Beasts* film, set primarily in 1927 Paris, he emerges as that series' antagonist, a realistic monster of dangerous proportions perhaps defying Ministry of Magic classification. In Grindelwald's fuller characterization, Rowling connects him with the quintessential foe of heroic sagas—the dragon—and aligns the forces that oppose him with the legendary phoenix, capable of resurrection from its own ashes. In its third installment, *Secrets of Dumbledore*, the *Fantastic Beasts* series presents a confrontation between phoenix and dragon every bit as momentous as it is in Asian mythology.

Monsters and Monstrosity in the Harry Potter *Series*

Beginning with the narrator's reference to Fluffy as a monster in *Sorcerer's Stone*, the *Harry Potter* series presents readers with numerous dangerous, sometimes lethal creatures, most not invented by Rowling but drawn from medieval bestiaries. These include the basilisk, dragons, giant spiders, and werewolves. Two of these creatures always rank high on lists of common fears: spiders and snakes. One reason the Forbidden Forest is off limits to Hogwarts students is that the acromantula Aragog and his giant spider family who live there constantly need "fresh meat."[7] The basilisk in *Chamber of Secrets* hides by slithering through the Hogwarts plumbing, and although Moaning Myrtle's presence in the girls' bathroom serves as an ongoing reminder of the basilisk's potential to kill, the creature's effects in the second installment all prove reversible: Hermione, Colin Creevy, and others are petrified but later revived. Thus, the basilisk ultimately seems more like a creature of monster film proportions, along the lines of Godzilla, than a realistic beast. This is also true of Aragog, the giant spider raised by Hagrid.

In the Hogwarts textbook *Fantastic Beasts and Where to Find Them*, Newt Scamander includes Ministry of Magic classifications of creatures, sorting them into five categories, which range from "boring" (X) to "Known wizard killer/Impossible to train or domesticate" (XXXXX).[8] Among creatures with a rating of XXXXX are acromantulae (Harry adds several more X's in his copy), basilisks, and dragons. Scamander identifies ten species of dragons, and this prototypical fantasy foe figures prominently in the plots of the first, fourth, and seventh books. This pattern begins with the hatching of Hagrid's pet Norberta *in Sorcerer's Stone*, continues in the first Tri-Wizard Tournament task in *Goblet of Fire*, and recurs in the escape from Gringotts in *Deathly Hallows*.[9] Among the three achievements listed on Albus Dumbledore's chocolate frog card is "his discovery of the twelve uses of dragon's blood."[10] Throughout fantasy literature, the dragon is the most fearsome beast, and from at least the Middle Ages, its defeat has been a stock element in heroic literature, representing domination of the beastly aspect of human nature which, in Christian symbolism, typically represents sin. Probably the best-known example in the Western world is the dragon-slaying by St. George, patron saint of England and Ethiopia.

In the *Harry Potter* series, the dragon's reptilian cousins, snakes, actually pose a greater threat, the two most prominent being Voldemort himself and his companion Nagini. Snakes' predatory nature is also a key feature of Voldemort's character, and he is responsible directly or indirectly for the deaths of about two dozen people. Voldemort also orders Nagini to attack Arthur Weasley, seriously injuring him, and of course he has the goal of killing Harry from the time Harry was a year old.[11] Following his reconstitution at the end of *Goblet of Fire*, Voldemort is described as a human with snakelike features, with red eyes and vertical slits replacing nostrils. He can speak snakes' language, Parseltongue, as can Harry, which is how each accesses the Chamber of Secrets. Voldemort's affinity for Nagini is clear even without Dumbledore's observation that "he is perhaps as fond of her as he can be of anything."[12] Voldemort's affinity for the snake is underscored when Dumbledore explains to Harry the inadvisability of using an animal as a Horcrux due to the risk involved in "confid[ing] a part of your soul to something that can think and move for itself."[13] On September 24, 2018, Rowling announced that the *Fantastic Beasts* films would clarify the transformation of this character from the Maledictus (portrayed by Claudia Kim) to Nagini of the *Harry Potter* series, who can no longer return to human form.[14] This is another reminder, along with the Ministry of Magic's category five creatures, that the effects of some monstrosity cannot be undone.

The true nature of monstrosity in the *Harry Potter* series is evident in the contrast between Voldemort and another character considered by some to be a monster: the werewolf Remus Lupin. Voldemort's quest for immortality makes him an indiscriminate predator; he is driven by entirely egocentric motives. Despite his affection for Nagini, he puts her at risk by making her a Horcrux. Lupin, instead, is willing to die—and ultimately does so—to protect others, not only his wife and young son, but also his students and witches and wizards he doesn't even know.

Moreover, Lupin is willing to do what he can, including enlisting the help of others, to overcome his monstrous attributes and protect others from himself. One reason that Lupin values his teaching position is that it puts him at Hogwarts with a wizard who can brew him Wolfsbane potion: Severus Snape. In addition to drinking the potion, Lupin sequesters himself every full moon to avoid revealing his true status but primarily to prevent himself from victimizing others. The terrible possibilities of such victimization are clear in the character of Fenrir Greyback, Lupin's attacker, a Death Eater who flaunts his appetite for children. Compared to Greyback and to Voldemort, Lupin demonstrates the self-control that ameliorates his monstrous potential.[15] A crucial difference between human monstrosity and the beastly nature of other animals is that human monstrosity such as that of Voldemort and Grindelwald is a choice, and Remus Lupin did not—and would not—choose it.

Dangerous Beasts in the Fantastic Beasts *Series*

With the *Fantastic Beasts* films, Rowling shifts to monsters and monstrosity as the primary subject. Twenty-six creatures appear in *Fantastic Beasts and Where to Find Them* and twenty-eight in *Crimes of Grindelwald*.[16] In the first film, viewers learn that, thanks to a magical extension charm, many of the "beasts" are transported in Newt Scamander's suitcase.[17] Some are enchanting and, at worst, pesky, such as the "gentle, even affectionate ... [but] destructive" niffler, who nicks shiny objects. A bowtruckle, Pickett, often rides in Newt's pocket; while this creature is "intensely shy," according to the *Fantastic Beasts* textbook, it can also use its sharp, pointy appendages to gouge the eyes of anyone trying to steal the wood of its home tree.[18]

Other creatures in Newt's suitcase are more dangerous, such as the Swooping Evil, a butterfly-like creature with spiky wings that Newt carries for self-defense; the Thunderbird, which can create storms while flying; and the Nundu (MoM classification XXXXX), a giant leopard that can destroy whole villages by exhaling disease and that "has never yet been subdued by fewer than a hundred skilled wizards working together."[19] Rowling also nods to the creature lore of the British Isles with her description of the Kelpie, a water demon of Britain and Ireland that can take various forms and thereby tricks its victims into being devoured. Scamander's text suggests that the Loch Ness monster is a Kelpie capable of varying appearances, its malleability thwarting would-be observers.

One "beast" central to the *Fantastic Beasts* series is not mentioned in Newt Scamander's textbook except as the name of that book's publisher: Obscurus.[20] As a condition, the Obscurus develops within a person who cannot express magical powers, often because of social stigma, and the host may internalize this sense of ridicule. A sort of "dark energy," it can cause great harm when released.[21] The person hosting the Obscurus is called an Obscurial; this host's release of magical energy does not appear voluntary but is triggered by strong, usually negative, emotional experience. According to Aberforth Dumbledore, the catalyst for his sister Ariana's Obscurus was an assault on his sister by three Muggle boys, who "got a bit carried away trying to stop the little freak doing [magic]."[22] The combination of shock and revulsion in the trio's reactions to the story make clear that the boys' attack on the six-year-old was severe, perhaps even something taboo, such as a sexual assault: "Hermione's eyes were huge in the firelight; Ron looked slightly sick.... Harry felt a horrible mixture of pity and repulsion; he did not want to hear any more."[23] Whatever happened was enough to provoke Ariana's father, Percival Dumbledore, to retaliate against the boys (violating the Statute of Secrecy) and to cause Aberforth intense pain even recalling the incident decades later. The entire Dumbledore family was irrevocably changed, moving house and creating a rumor "that she was ill."[24] Aberforth says that the incident "destroyed [Ariana].... She was never right again. She wouldn't use magic, but she couldn't get rid of it; it turned inward and drove her mad, it exploded out of her when she couldn't control it, and at times she was strange and dangerous. But mostly she was sweet and scared and harmless."[25] Out of context, this passage could describe either Ariana or Credence. The Obscurus is another example of Rowling's characterizing human psychological trauma in monstrous form (the Dementor, which the author has identified as an emblem of depression, functions similarly in the *Harry Potter* series).[26]

Credence Barebone, who reveals himself as an Obscurial in the first *Fantastic Beasts* film, has come to Gellert Grindelwald's attention in the context of a perplexing prophecy about the pureblood Lestrange family.[27] According to the *Fantastic Beasts: Crimes of Grindelwald* screenplay, this prophecy first appeared sometime before 1927 in a book called *The Predictions of Tycho Dodonus*. The prophecy reads,

> *A son cruelly banished*
> *Despair of the daughter*
> *Return, great avenger*
> *With wings from the water.*[28]

Disguised as Percival Graves, Grindelwald goes to New York to lure Credence from his family with promises of magical training. On the brink of manhood, Credence is losing whatever control he has had over the Obscurus, and in the first film, he (or the Obscurus or some combination) causes the deaths of three people: his sister Chastity, his adoptive mother Mary Lou Barebone, and Senator Henry Shaw. The citywide disturbances caused by Credence's growing inability to control his outbursts alter the plans of Newt Scamander, who has ostensibly come to New York City to return Frank, a Thunderbird, to the American Southwest desert.

According to Leta Lestrange, her brother Corvus was lost at sea after she switched the fussy infant with another baby. When the ship had to be evacuated, Leta, her aunt, and the switched infant—presumably baby Credence—left in a lifeboat, while the real Corvus Lestrange appears to have been lost with the sinking ship. Grindelwald, like many others, has surmised that Credence is the lost Lestrange baby, but *Crimes of Grindelwald* leaves viewers with the sense that his interpretation is a mistake. Grindelwald has associated the Tycho Dodonus prophecy with Credence, just as Voldemort assigned Sybill Trelawney's prophecy to Harry Potter. In the closing seconds of the film, Grindelwald presents Credence with a newly reborn phoenix, calling the chick Credence's "birthright" and whispering that Credence's real name is "Aurelius. Aurelius Dumbledore."[29] The revelation causes Credence's Obscurus to manifest itself again, and its force breaks not only the windows directly before him but also the mountain across the Alpine valley.

When the title of the third *Fantastic Beasts* installment was announced in September 2021, fans pointed to signs that Credence's identity would be one of the "secrets" suggested by that title. Notably, the name does not identify a particular Dumbledore in its phrasing. Knowledge of the Dumbledore family's background provided fans eager for the third installment with two clues that Credence has family traits. The most obvious is the fact that every Dumbledore child's first name begins with "A." The second involves clear hints as early as *Deathly Hallows* that Ariana Dumbledore was also an Obscurial and the likelihood that the condition was a family affliction. Ariana's harboring an Obscurus also explains her family's relocating to protect her and withholding her from Hogwarts and wizarding society in general. By the time it is confirmed in *Secrets of Dumbledore*, the existence of Ariana's Obscurus is no longer much of a secret.

The July 2021 announcement that actor Richard Coyle had been cast as Aberforth Dumbledore was the clearest hint about Aurelius's parentage. Six months later, Amy Hogan argued on MuggleNet that Aberforth's first name, which means "from the river" in Gaelic, is also an important clue, one that could fulfill the Tycho Dodonus prophecy about a "great avenger" returning "with wings from the water."[30] Any association of wings with any Dumbledore means phoenix wings, of course, and the gift of a phoenix is where the paternity conundrum began. Furthermore, much less is known about Aberforth than Albus in *Harry Potter* canon, and in that respect the revelation of a secret son raises fewer questions for readers or viewers. Aberforth would also have no apparent reason for rejecting such a child but *would* have motive for avenging Ariana Dumbledore's death on the man who might have been responsible for it—Gellert Grindelwald. Considering these details, the disclosure of Aberforth as Credence/Aurelius's father in *Secrets of Dumbledore* is less a surprise than a confirmation.

The Sleeping Dragon Wakes

Years before the qilin's appearance in *Secrets of Dumbledore*, the theme of monsters and monstrosity justified Newt Scamander rather than Albus Dumbledore as the *Fantastic Beasts* series' protagonist. In September 2018, Rowling was asked on Twitter why Dumbledore recruited a magizoologist rather than an auror to pursue Grindelwald. She replied that answering this question "would give you the whole plot of the Fantastic Beasts franchise."[31] Michael Walsh offered the theory on *Nerdist* that Newt Scamander was the man for the job because of Grindelwald's nature as a dangerous beast, likely a dragon.[32] Walsh had not yet seen the second *Fantastic Beasts* installment, but that film validated his guess and affirmed that the sleeping dragon had awakened.

The dragon-like nature of Grindelwald's behavior manifests itself in the underground amphitheater during the second film's climax, when he *exhales* his futuristic vision *in a burst of flame*. The vision contains images from the London blitz and the bombing of Hiroshima, and its implication is clear to World War I veteran Jacob Kowalski, who exclaims, "Not another war."[33] The *protego diabolica* charm Grindelwald chooses to ward off the aurors produces flames he can conduct "as though leading an orchestra, the Elder Wand his baton, as the forks of fire strike at AURORS attempting to Disapparate or flee."[34] For his encore, he hurls a ball of fire at Theseus and Newt. (Recall that Albus Dumbledore confesses to Harry that as a youth he had been "inflamed" by Grindelwald's ideas.[35]) Grindelwald's weapon of choice in this second installment of the *Fantastic Beasts* series is fire, and the weapon he covets, the Obscurus, is also conjured through exhalation. Fantasy readers associate exhaled fire with only one sort of monster.

Some dragon imagery is obvious in *Crimes of Grindelwald*, such as the blue flaming serpentine figures Grindelwald conjures in the Paris cemetery. The script says the fire "forms dragon-like creatures intent on annihilation."[36] Shapes of serpents, dragons, and raptors with fangs and claws also appear in *Deathly Hallows* in the Fiendfyre spell in the Room of Requirement. Hermione reminds her friends that this is "cursed fire ... one of the substances that destroy Horcruxes."[37] This diabolical fire incites an atmosphere similar to the Laketonians' panic in *The Hobbit* when the dragon Smaug devours their town in fire. Such flames can be quenched only by special magic, such as the arrow Bard fires at Smaug or the spell that alchemist Nicolas Flamel casts in the cemetery.

Although the association between dragon and flame is more subtle in *Secrets of Dumbledore*, fire remains a favored weapon for Grindelwald and his associates in the film. At the end of his meeting with his old flame in a London restaurant, Grindelwald leaves, appearing to set the place on fire. During the first street rally after the film shifts to Berlin, an Alliance member uses *Incendio,* the fire-making charm, to destroy a banner for Vicêncira Santos, a candidate for Supreme Mugwump. The flaming banner falls, arching vaguely dragon-like in the air. A few minutes later, Newt delivers a message advocating caution from Albus Dumbledore to outgoing Supreme Mugwump Anton Vogel, just as Vogel is about to pardon Grindelwald for his crimes against Muggles. When Vogel asks whether Dumbledore is in Berlin and Scamander shakes his head, Vogel responds, "Of course not. Why leave Hogwarts when the world is burning?"[38] Just before the Walk of the Qilin ceremony, an assistant to outgoing Supreme Mugwump Anton Vogel uses fire to destroy the case Newt Scamander has brought. These uses of fire are all subtle connections with the dragon/phoenix trope.

In both films two and three, other dragon imagery is associated with Grindelwald in veiled hints, such as the wizard's mismatched eyes. This mismatch is very apparent in *Crimes of Grindelwald* and is a point of continuity between Johnny Depp's and Mads Mikkelsen's portrayals of Grindelwald (but more subtle in the more recent film).[39] In dragon lore, vision is the beast's superior sense. According to the *Oxford English Dictionary*, the word *dragon* comes from the Greek δράκων or *dràkon*, meaning "serpent" and derives from the Indo-European root δέρκεσθαι, "to see clearly."[40] The dragon is often characterized as "the one with the (deadly) glance."[41] Notions about the dragon's visual acuity and the inadvisability of looking one in the eye (a characteristic shared with the basilisk) persist as recently as the children's series *How to Train Your Dragon*. Grindelwald's distinctive heterochromia evokes this lore and may foreshadow future developments that feature it.

According to *The Illustrated Signs and Symbols Sourcebook*, dragons' eyesight makes them effective "guardians of treasure and keepers of secrets of some kind, a trait which gives them great wisdom as well as clairvoyant powers."[42] A 2016 Rowling Tweet reinforced this notion of Grindelwald keeping things to himself, revealing that the notorious wizard is an Occlumens, skilled, like Severus Snape, at blocking others' access to his thoughts. This arose in response to a question about why Queenie Goldstein, an obvious Legilimens who has extrasensory access to others' thoughts, cannot detect Grindelwald behind the persona of Percival Graves. Rowling issued a one-word answer: "Occlumency."[43] Perhaps Queenie's skill at legilimency[44] explains Grindelwald's desire to keep her near at the end of *Crimes of Grindelwald*—or perhaps something she reads in his thoughts increases her willingness to go with him. A few scenes in *Secrets of Dumbledore* suggest Queenie's vigilance, but through the third installment, her motives remain unexplained.[45]

Whatever the reason for Queenie's leaving Jacob Kowalski to accompany Grindelwald, Grindelwald has good reason for wanting to guard his thoughts. From about 1926 to 1945, he quietly possesses one of the greatest known wizarding treasures—the Elder Wand. Throughout most of *Crimes of Grindelwald*, he also carries the concealed vial representing his blood troth with Dumbledore, the same vial the niffler snatches in the cemetery scene. In *Secrets of Dumbledore*, Grindelwald's need for privacy of thought primarily concerns his possession of the qilin and plans for its fraudulent use.

Grindelwald also conceals his glimpses of the future for much of *Crimes of Grindelwald*, but his clairvoyance becomes an open topic in *Secrets of Dumbledore* and is discussed among the members of Newt Scamander's team in the train scene just before their arrival in Berlin, when Scamander informs the others that their adversary "has the ability to see snatches of the future."[46] This skill necessitates the team's using a ruse based on the principle of "countersight,"[47] a confusion strategy based on the idea of seven people carrying seven identical cases, with the baby qilin concealed in one of them. While the dragon's ability to "see ahead" is well documented in dragon lore, perhaps it is not surprising that the team representing the phoenix (Dumbledore) is still capable of outwitting its reptilian counterpart. After all, the phoenix has what Katy McDaniel has called "a circular future," a sense of time that is not linear but cyclical.[48] Interestingly, it is the character of Bunty Broadacre, a member of the phoenix team, who points out during the discussion of Grindelwald's clairvoyance that all perspectives, even enhanced ones, are limited: "Nobody knows everything," she whispers in Newt's ear.[49]

In the second film, Grindelwald's ability to see the future is depicted in the World War II–esque visions he shares in the underground amphitheater. His rhetoric is straight out of the Nazi handbook. He begins with the statement, "The moment has come to share my visions of the future that will come if we do not rise up and take our rightful place in the world."⁵⁰ This "vision" reflects Grindelwald's true monstrosity, and his declarations echo the nationalistic German rhetoric during the time of the film's setting, between the two world wars. His signature slogan, "For the greater good," would fit over death camp gates. Described by Rowling in the stage directions as "part demagogue, part rock star," he articulates an exclusionary rhetoric with false modesty.⁵¹ In his recruitment speech, he establishes immediate solidarity with his audience, calling them "My brothers, my sisters, my friends," although opponents are also in the audience.⁵² He stresses his humility and assumes that his listeners share his desire for social change: "You came here today because of a craving and a knowledge that the old ways serve us no longer."⁵³ He denies allegations of prejudice, declaring, "I do not hate Muggles. I do not," but he refers to non-magical people by unflattering nicknames ("Les Non-Magiques. The Muggles. The No-Maj. The Can't Spells").⁵⁴ He claims that his views about these stigmatized groups are mischaracterized.

Like Adolf Hitler, Grindelwald is a skilled orator. He plays word games: Muggles are "not disposable, but of a different disposition."⁵⁵ He proposes to remake the world to his liking, firing up his audience to take decisive action against non-magical humans. Many listeners accept his ideology, convinced by his powerful vision and captivating oratory, including (apparently) Queenie. The appearance of Aurors during the speech serves notice that these remarks will provoke confrontation with the magical authorities. Nagini, unlike Queenie, recognizes the speech for what it is—a call to ethnic cleansing—and tries to hold Credence back. "They're pureblood. They kill the likes of us for sport," she warns him.⁵⁶

The similarities between Grindelwald and Hitler become even more relevant in *The Secrets of Dumbledore*, with its German setting and its central plot involving Grindelwald's candidacy for leader or "Supreme Mugwump" of the International Confederation of Wizards. The main plank in his platform is still ethnic purity; his appeal to Joseph Kama to join his alliance is based on Kama's having descended from a pureblood wizarding family. Grindelwald's determination to be selected leads to perhaps his most vicious act, the slaughter and bewitching of one of the wizarding world's rarest creatures, the qilin. Not only is Grindelwald able to kill this highly magical animal without remorse, but he has also authorized his conspirators to destroy the creature's mother in the act of giving birth in order to steal the baby. It is difficult to imagine a more brutal act.

Rowling has emphasized that despite the array of magical creatures in the films, she is more interested in the beastly nature of human beings than in creatures with hairy coats, fangs, and talons. On her website on November 12, 2018, she answered a question about what sorts of creatures fans could expect to see in the *Fantastic Beasts* series: "What kind of beasts are we talking about here—human or animal?" She wrote,

> [T]here is the metaphorical sense of the beast inside a man, the crude emotions that a manipulative genius like Grindelwald knows how to stoke and use. We're also dealing with the idea of beastly people: that some humans are something less than human. Even where there is great charisma and intelligence, there may be an utter lack of conscience. Finally, I'm exploring the idea of creating beasts, which is to say, othering or dehumanizing our fellow people, as the first step toward cruelty or extermination.[57]

If Voldemort's killing of a unicorn in *Harry Potter and the Sorcerer's Stone* is characterized as an unspeakable act, Grindelwald's slicing the qilin's throat is an inconceivable one, a murder calculated for its perpetrator's personal gain. It suggests magic of the darkest variety, akin to the creation of Horcruxes and is, in a word, beastly.

The association of Grindelwald with the quintessential mythological beast is even more appropriate considering the *Fantastic Beasts* time settings: 1926, 1927, 1932. The quotation "Beware the sleeping dragon, for when she awakes the Earth will shake" is a modern myth of the World War II era ubiquitously attributed to Winston Churchill.[58] The former British prime minister is rumored to have spoken the words as China increased its naval presence north of Australia, suggesting that war involving Indonesia might ensue. But scholars at The Churchill Project of Hillsdale College (Michigan) attest that no such quotation exists in the Churchill canon. Instead, The Churchill Project suggests, it is likely manufactured, probably inspired by Japanese Admiral Yamamoto's warning about "waking a sleeping giant" in the aftermath of the attack on Pearl Harbor on December 7, 1941—except that Yamamoto didn't actually say these words either, according to the Pearl Harbor Visitors Bureau. In fact, the lines are spoken by the actor portraying Yamamoto in the movie *Tora! Tora! Tora!* (1970).[59]

The significance of all this misquoting and misattribution is the dragon's stock position in the universal imagination as the looming danger; the beast so aptly represents peril that no one would question Churchill's or Yamamoto's having said these words, given the fear associated with the build-up to World War II. What is curious is that the dragon has never been a part of the quotation, and yet the mythological beast persists as a metaphor for the coming terror in Rowling's World War II–era storyscape.

Characters in the *Fantastic Beasts* films are easily divided into good guys and bad guys based on their treatment of other creatures, just as that aspect of human nature is a litmus test for distinguishing World War II–era leaders on moral terms. Newt Scamander is the paragon of beastly husbandry, able to endear creatures such as the bowtruckle Pickett and the niffler Teddy to himself while also capable of managing other species toward which the average wizard would likely point a wand and say "Avada kedavra." Newt charms shrieking manticores in the German wizarding prison, Erkstag, with a technique called "limbic mimicry," allowing Theseus and himself to stay alive long enough for Pickett and Teddy to instigate a rescue attempt. The technique "discourages violent engagement," Newt tells Theseus, in a scene that proves the younger brother is perhaps as much a magipsychologist (or charmer?) as a magizoologist.[60] In an abrupt shift to the "tea party" for the Supreme Mugwump candidates occurring simultaneously, the film cuts to the manticores' crustacean cousin: a boiled lobster on a serving platter. This one quick shift encapsulates the dichotomy between soothing beasts and serving them for dinner—or slaughtering them or bewitching them—which is the moral gulf between the series' protagonist and antagonist.

Virtuous Beasts: The Qilin and Phoenix

Like many of the creatures that turn up in the *Harry Potter* and *Fantastic Beasts* series, the qilin is a creature from extant mythology, not Rowling's imagination. In the hiatus between the second and third *Fantastic Beasts* films, Rowling was reading medieval bestiaries, occasionally posting images from them on her website and social media and claiming, in November 2018, to be "immersed" in a Chinese bestiary, the *Shan Hai Jing*.[61] This text, considered a treasure of Chinese culture, probably originates in the fourth century but was not complete until a few centuries later and is a compendium of several authors' work.[62] It has been published in at least three English translations in the twenty-first century.[63] Booksellers' advertisements for the translations often contain the term "fantastic beasts," so one suspects that the film series has jump-started new interest in the concept of bestiaries, generally. A second work of significant influence on Rowling is T.H. White's *The Book of Beasts* (1954), a translation of a twelfth-century Latin source that was "the first and, for a time, the only English translation of a medieval bestiary."[64] The influences of both works on the *Fantastic* Beasts series and, in particular, the relationship between the qilin and phoenix in Chinese mythology, has been well-documented by Beatrice Groves in a series of three blog posts on MuggleNet in April 2022.[65]

The qilin (sometimes spelled K'i-Lin) is also commonly called "the Chinese unicorn," as its most distinctive feature is a fleshy horn protruding from its head. It is one of "the four animals of good omen," as Jorge Luis Borges identifies them in *The Book of Imaginary Beings*.[66] Its most famous appearance in mythology concerns the birth of Confucius, whose pregnant mother was visited by the creature, delivering a prophecy of the coming child's greatness: "Son of the mountain crystal [that is, the essence of water], when the dynasty has fallen, thou shalt rule like a king without royal insignia."[67] Borges calls this event "a version of the annunciation."[68]

The qilin shares with the "Oriental Phoenix," or "Fèng Huáng," the ability to assess human character, distinguishing it from its Western counterpart, which is an emblem of rebirth or resurrection.[69] Says director David Yates, "The Qilin … is able to see into a person's soul and instinctively know the goodness and purity of their heart."[70] In the climax of *Secrets of Dumbledore*, the authentic qilin bows, not to one of the three official candidates for Supreme Mugwump, but to Albus Dumbledore. Only when Dumbledore declines does the creature turn to Brazilian Minister of Magic Vicência Santos (a surname meaning "saints" in Portuguese). Thus, the mythological creature serves to delineate the principal adversaries on moral grounds.

In contrast with the dragon's more bellicose nature, the qilin is so gentle that "It will not tread upon green grass or do harm to any creature," Borges says.[71] Of course, that description of gentleness could as easily apply to Newt Scamander, Dumbledore's favorite magizoologist. Scamander, who is named for a harmless amphibian, studies beasts as a calling; his skill for courting deadly creatures makes him a more suitable candidate for negotiating Grindelwald's monstrosity than an auror, who is more akin to a warrior (although Newt needs aurors like his brother Theseus on his team). The appearance of the qilin in the film series provides the best example to date of the need for Newt's particular expertise. In the opening scene, he serves as midwife at a qilin birth, an event whose auspiciousness is increased by the birth of not one but *two* babies. Although the creature is incredibly rare, Newt knows it well enough to distinguish, in the film's climax, between the false, bewitched qilin and its legitimate twin.

Asian lore concerning the phoenix and dragon also complements the romantic relationship that existed between the young Albus Dumbledore and Gellert Grindelwald. In Chinese mythology, the phoenix is the only worthy counterpart to the dragon. The two are considered equally propitious, and "when they are portrayed together, they have the meaning of pleasing relationships, good luck, and persistent strength."[72] Their co-occurrence is often taken to represent the fullness of *yin* and *yang*, and in Feng Shui they are "the ultimate symbol of love and life as a couple."[73] Placing them together in a home is reputed to ensure harmony. For this reason, they often appear together on imperial decorations.[74] Despite the irrelevance of the traditional gender connotations of *yin* and *yang* to Dumbledore and Grindelwald, they have made a blood troth, and both seem to feel that their promises in the past still constrain their behavior in the present—at least until the blood troth is broken, which also happens in the scene involving the qilin's choice for Supreme Mugwump.

The symbolism of phoenix and dragon leans toward the dragon in *Crimes of Grindelwald* and toward the phoenix in *The Secrets of Dumbledore*. But there can be no mystery about which mythological creature's alliance will ultimately triumph, for moral allegory requires that dragons are slain, and phoenixes always rise again. In the same interview when Rowling called Gellert Grindelwald "the *beast* that was in the back of my mind for nearly ten years," she emphasized the film series' allegorical dimensions, claiming that it is about "the battle between light and dark."[75] Rowling's use of these two mythological creatures to depict that battle continues her tendency (as in the climax of *Deathly Hallows*) to reflect Judeo-Christian theology in a subtle manner. The phoenix stands for rebirth and resurrection, while the dragon's connection to sin and death is entrenched in Judeo-Christian teaching and may even be present in the origin story. In Genesis 3:14, the serpent that tempted Eve is cursed to lose its legs, demonstrating that prior to its role in the Garden of Eden, *it had legs*. Revelation 12:9 depicts Michael and his angels defeating a "great dragon … *that ancient serpent*, who is called the Devil and Satan, the deceiver of the whole world."[76] Again in Revelation 20:2, the dragon is "that ancient serpent." In *Paradise Lost*, John Milton is bolder, depicting the Garden of Eden story as the time "when the Dragon, put to second rout,/Came furious down to be revenged on men," when "our first parents had been warned/The coming of their secret foe, and 'scaped,/Haply so 'scaped his mortal snare."[77] And White affirms in *The Book of Beasts* that "the terms 'dragon' and 'serpent' are interchangeable."[78]

Thus, by the association of this mythological beast with Gellert Grindelwald, Rowling casts him in the background of the *Harry Potter* series and the foreground of the *Fantastic Beasts* series as Albus Dumbledore's tempter and "the deceiver of the whole world," wizard and Muggle alike.[79] The phoenix is light and life, while the dragon is sin and death; its alignment with Satan and death is incorporated in its *Oxford English Dictionary* definitions.[80] Rowling has underscored this alignment with the surname of the character in *Fantastic Beasts and Where to Find Them* who is Grindelwald using a Polyjuice potion: Graves.

Although the *Fantastic Beasts* film series appears unlikely to continue beyond the third film, its fans know that Dumbledore and Grindelwald's pre–*Harry Potter* series storyline has not been fully depicted in the franchise. In the two powerful wizards' confrontation in Bhutan, the Elder Wand did not change hands. Whether filmgoers are likely ever to see the 1945 duel when it finally comes into Dumbledore's possession is a question that even J.K. Rowling herself could not answer, as it is likely a decision for Warner Brothers. If the series does continue, it would be interesting to see what challenge Grindelwald mounts next, having lost the weapon he sought in the first installment (Credence's Obscurus), the boost he acquired in the second (Queenie's legilimency), and his quest for universal power in the third. One wonders if his story arc could include not only occlumency but also the capability to transform himself, animagus-style, into the monstrous form suggested by his beastly nature. Should that occur, the climax of the full *Fantastic Beasts* series could find Newt Scamander facing a dragon, Wiglaf to Dumbledore's Beowulf, in one of the central myths of human narrative. Or perhaps the beastly analogs for Grindelwald and Dumbledore will remain figurative. The elements of the conflict are established. Only time will tell whether the theme grows scales and feathers.

Notes

1. Lana A. Whited, "Here Be Dragons and Phoenixes," *The Quibbler*, MuggleNet (February 8–9, 2019), www.mugglenet.com/2019/02/here-be-dragons-and-phoenixes-part-1/ and https://www.mugglenet.com/2019/02/here-be-dragons-and-phoenixes-part-2/. Some material from these two blog posts is incorporated here with permission from MuggleNet.

2. The Churchill Project, "Sleep of the Saved and Thankful," *The Churchill Project* (Hillsdale College: September 11, 2015), https://winstonchurchill.hillsdale.edu/sleep-of-the-saved-and-thankful-2/. The actual origin of this quotation will be discussed later in this essay.

3. Jorge Luis Borges and Margarita Guerrero, *The Book of Imaginary Beings*, trans. Andrew Hurley, illus. Peter Sís (New York: Penguin, 2006), 202.

4. Katy McDaniel and Emily Strand, hosts, "*Secrets of Dumbledore* and *The Deathly Hallows*," *Potterversity* (podcast), May 23, 2022, www.mugglenet.com/Mugglenet-family/potterversity/. Kudos to Beatrice Groves for predicting the appearance of the qilin in *The Secrets of Dumbledore* in a series of April 2022 blog posts on MuggleNet.

5. AT&T, "Fantastic Beasts: The Crimes of Grindelwald—'A Familiar Magic,'" YouTube, October 16, 2018, 00:1:36, https://www.youtube.com/watch?v=Do2QZsh-EVo. Emphasis added.

6. Travis Prinzi, *Harry Potter and Imagination: The Way Between Two Worlds* (Allentown, PA: Zossima Press, 2009), 79.

7. J.K. Rowling, *Harry Potter and the Chamber of Secrets* (New York: Scholastic, 1999), 279.

8. J.K. Rowling, *Fantastic Beasts and Where to Find Them* (New York: Scholastic, 2013), xxxv.

9. This pattern of repetition in parallel books such as the first, middle, and last is an example of ring composition in the *Harry Potter* series, a narrative strategy discussed extensively by John Granger in works including *Harry Potter as Ring Composition and Ring Cycle: The Magical Structure and Transcendent Meaning of the Hogwarts Saga* (Oklahoma City: Unlocking Press, 2010).

10. J.K. Rowling, *Harry Potter and the Sorcerer's Stone* (New York: Scholastic, 1997), 103. Rowling hints at only a few of these twelve uses of dragon's blood. In *Order of the Phoenix*, Hagrid uses a rare dragon steak to help heal injuries from a giant attack, and in *Half-Blood Prince*, Slughorn uses dragon's blood as part of a ruse to dismiss Dumbledore and Harry by convincing them that he has been attacked by Death Eaters. In *Deathly Hallows*, one of Rita Skeeter's self-proclaimed "scoops" in *The Life and Lies of Albus Dumbledore* is that Dumbledore stole eight of the "uses" from Ivor Dillonsby's notes and came up

with only four on his own. J.K. Rowling, *Harry Potter and the Deathly Hallows* (New York: Scholastic, 2007), 26.

11. Voldemort (or Voldemort by proxy through Nagini) is responsible for the deaths of his grandparents, Tom Riddle, Sr., and Mary Riddle; his father, Thomas Riddle; Myrtle Elizabeth Warren (whose full name was tweeted by Rowling on May 11, 2015), Hepzibah Smith, an Albanian peasant, Bertha Jorkins (by whose death Nagini became a Horcrux), a Muggle tramp, James and Lily Potter, Frank Bryce, Dorcas Meadowes, Charity Burbage, the wandmaker Gregorovitch and a woman working in Gregorovitch's house, Gellert Grindelwald, Peter Pettigrew, and Severus Snape. He also likely killed Amelia Bones, Emmaline Vance, and Bathilda Bagshot. He nearly caused the death of Arthur Weasley by ordering Nagini to attack him. He is also ultimately responsible for Nagini's death by having made her a Horcrux.

12. J.K. Rowling, *Harry Potter and the Half-Blood Prince* (New York: Scholastic, 2005), 506.

13. *Ibid.*

14. "Everything You Need to Know about Nagini," *Wizarding World*, September 24, 2018, https://www.wizardingworld.com/features/everything-you-need-to-know-about-nagini.

For a thorough discussion of the snake-woman trope in the *Harry Potter* and *Fantastic Beasts* series and Rowling's literary sources, see Beatrice Groves's essay "The Snake Woman in *Harry Potter* and *Fantastic Beasts*" in *The Ivory Tower, Harry Potter, and Beyond*, ed. Lana Whited, University of Missouri Press, 2023.

15. For more on how Lupin and Greyback handle their status as werewolves, see Mark-Anthony Lewis's essay in this volume.

16. "A List of Every Beast in 'Fantastic Beasts and Where to Find Them,'" *Higgypop*, April 21, 2017, https://www.higgypop.com/news/list-of-fantastic-beasts/ and "A List of Every Beast in 'Fantastic Beasts: The Crimes of Grindelwald,'" *Higgypop*, March 13, 2019, https://www.higgypop.com/news/list-of-fantastic-beasts-in-crimes-of-grindelwald/.

17. For a full discussion of Rowling's treatment of objects enchanted to appear smaller on the outside than the inside, see Elizabeth Baird Hardy's essay "Muggle Worthy: Deceptive Exteriors and Outsized Interiors in the Wizarding World" in *The Ivory Tower, Harry Potter, and Beyond*, ed. Lana Whited, (University of Missouri Press, 2023).

18. Rowling, *Fantastic Beasts*, 9–10.

19. *Ibid.*, 58.

20. *Ibid.*, xiv.

21. "Magical Abilities That Don't Sound All That Fun," *Wizarding World*, August 16, 2018, https://www.wizardingworld.com/features/magical-abilities-that-do-not-sound-all-that-fun.

22. J.K. Rowling, *Harry Potter and the Deathly Hallows* (New York: Scholastic, 2007), 564.

23. *Ibid.*, 564–65.

24. *Ibid.*

25. *Ibid.*, 564.

26. J.K. Rowling, "J.K. Rowling: The Interview," interview by Ann Treneman, *The Times*, June 20, 2003, https://www.thetimes.co.uk/article/j-k-rowling-the-interview-dshhr7c5fjf.

27. "The Predictions of Tycho Dodonus," Harry Potter Wiki, November 20, 2018, https://harrypotter.fandom.com/wiki/The_Predictions_of_Tycho_Dodonus.

28. J.K. Rowling, *Fantastic Beasts: The Crimes of Grindelwald: The Original Screenplay* (New York: Scholastic, 2018), 227.

29. *Ibid.*, 272.

30. Amy Hogan, "Is the Prophecy in 'Crimes of Grindelwald' Actually About Aberforth Dumbledore?" MuggleNet, January 10, 2022, https://www.mugglenet.com/2022/01/is-the-prophecy-in-crimes-of-grindelwald-actually-about-aberforth-dumbledore/.

31. J.K. Rowling (@jk_rowling), "I could write you an essay in response to this," Tweet, September 25, 2018, 9:54 a.m., https://twitter.com/jk_rowling/status/1044585938590949376?lang=en).

32. Michael Walsh, "Is Grindelwald Himself a 'Fantastic Beast'?" *Nerdist*, September 25, 2018, https://nerdist.com/grindelwald-is-fantastic-beast-theory/.

33. Rowling, *Crimes of Grindelwald*, 251.
34. Ibid., 259.
35. Rowling, *Deathly Hallows*, 761.
36. Rowling, *Crimes of Grindelwald*, 262.
37. Rowling, *Deathly Hallows*, 632, 635.
38. *Fantastic Beasts: The Secrets of Dumbledore*, directed by David Yates (2022; Burbank, CA: Warner Bros.), HBO Max, https://play.hbomax.com/feature/urn:hbo:feature:GYij31wBohZA3MQEAAAKa, 40:15–40:25.
39. Peter Haasch, "Here's How 'Fantastic Beasts: The Secrets of Dumbledore' Deals with Johnny Depp's Absence," *Insider*, April 15, 2022, https://www.insider.com/how-fantastic-beasts-3-replaces-johnny-depp-with-mads-mikkelsen-2022-4.
40. *Oxford English Dictionary, Compact Edition*. Vol. 1, A–O, 1979. s.v. "dragon," n.1.
41. "Dragon," Cryptowiki, January 10, 2019, https://cryptozoology.fandom.com/wiki/Dragon.
42. Adele Nozedar, *The Illustrated Signs and Symbols Sourcebook* (New York: Metro Books, 2010), 197.
43. J.K. Rowling (@jk_rowling), "Occlumency," Tweet, December 15, 2016, 6:35 a.m., https://twitter.com/jk_rowling/status/809361237054201856.
44. "Legilimency," *The Harry Potter Compendium*, harry-potter-compendium.fandom.com/wiki/Legilimency, accessed May 26, 2022. Legilimency is defined in *The Harry Potter Compendium* as "the act of magically navigating through the many layers on a person's mind and correctly interpreting one's findings." This is consistent with Severus Snape's definition of the skill in *Harry Potter and the Order of the Phoenix*.
45. Queenie's willingness to go with Grindelwald at the end of the second film mystifies some viewers. In one scene late in the film, she is depicted drinking tea served to her in a house where Grindelwald is living, raising the possibility of her having ingested a potion. The Imperius Curse has also been suggested by some, and one of my sons asked me after the third film if Queenie is mentally ill. Unfortunately, the third film removed Queenie from Grindelwald's home without explaining why she went there in the first place. This could simply be a loose end (but there aren't many of those in Rowling's works).
46. *Secrets of Dumbledore*, directed by David Yates, 2022; 00:31:00–00:31:05.
47. Ibid., 00:32:08. A similar strategy is used in chapter four, "The Seven Potters," of *Deathly Hallows*.
48. Katy McDaniel, personal correspondence, June 6, 2022.
49. *Secrets of Dumbledore*, directed by David Yates, 2022; 00:35:05–00:35:08.
50. Rowling, *Crimes of Grindelwald*, 249.
51. Ibid., 243.
52. Ibid., 244.
53. Ibid., 245.
54. Ibid.
55. Ibid., 246.
56. Ibid., 240.
57. J.K. Rowling, "Answers to Questions," J.K.Rowling.com, November 12, 2018, https://www.jkrowling.com/opinions/latest-answers-to-frequently-asked-questions/.
58. The Churchill Project, "Sleep of the Saved and Thankful."
59. Mark Lopronto, "Pearl Harbor—Waking the Sleeping Giant," Pearl Harbor, Hawaii, October 30, 2017, pearlharbor.org/pearl-harbor-waking-sleeping-giant/.
60. *Secrets of Dumbledore*, directed by David Yates, 2022; 1:07:59–1:08:04.
61. Beatrice Groves, "An Ancient Chinese Bestiary in 'Fantastic Beasts: The Secrets of Dumbledore': Fantastic Bestiaries and Where to Find Them—Part 2," *Bathilda's Notebook*, MuggleNet, April 6, 2022, https://www.mugglenet.com/2022/04/an-ancient-chinese-bestiary-in-fantastic-beasts-the-secrets-of-dumbledore-fantastic-bestiaries-and-where-to-find-them-part-2/.
62. "Shan Hai Jing," Totally History, accessed June 11, 2022, https://totallyhistory.com/shan-hai-jing/.
63. Anne Birrell, *The Classic of Mountains and Seas* (New York: Penguin, 2001); Richard

66   Ancient Magic

Strassberg, *A Chinese Bestiary: Strange Creatures from the Guideways Through the Mountains and Seas* (Oakland: University of California Press, 2002 and 2008); and Jiankun Sun, Siyu Chen, Howard Goldblatt, *Fantastic Creatures of the Mountains and Seas: A Chinese Classic* (New York: Arcade, 2021).

64. "The Book of Beasts: Being a Translation from a Latin Bestiary of the Twelfth Century," UW-Madison Libraries, accessed June 11, 2022, https://search.library.wisc.edu/digital/APVFA6XOOSG2448C.

65. Beatrice Groves, "'Secrets of Dumbledore' and 'The Book of Beasts': Fantastic Bestiaries and Where to Find Them—Part 1"; "An Ancient Chinese Bestiary in 'Fantastic Beasts: The Secrets of Dumbledore': Fantastic Bestiaries and Where to Find Them—Part 2"; and "The Phoenix and the Qilin in 'Secrets of Dumbledore': Fantastic Bestiaries and Where to Find Them—Part 3," April 5–7, 2022, *Bathilda's Notebook*, MuggleNet, https://www.mugglenet.com/the-quibbler/bathildas-notebook/.

66. Borges, *The Book of Imaginary Beings*, 202.

67. Ibid.

68. Ibid.

69. Anna D'Alessandro, "Fèng Huáng: The Oriental Phoenix and the World's Origin," Discover People/Places, February 9, 2020, discoverplaces.travel/en/feng-huang-the-oriental-phoenix-and-the-worlds-origin/.

70. Palmer Haasch, "All the Creatures That Appear in *Fantastic Beasts: The Secrets of Dumbledore*," *The Insider*, April 21, 2022, https://www.insider.com/creatures-animals-monsters-in-fantastic-beasts-the-secrets-of-dumbledore-2022-4.

71. Borges, *The Book of Imaginary Beings*, 202.

72. D'Alessandro, "Fèng Huáng."

73. "Dragon and Phoenix: Meaning and Symbolism," Dragon Planet, January 28, 2022, dragon-planet.com/dragon-and-phoenix/.

74. "Lords of the Chinese World: The Dragon and Phoenix," ChinaCulture.org, January 10, 2019, http://en.chinaculture.org/chineseway/2014-07/31/content_553822.htm.

75. AT&T, "Fantastic Beasts: The Crimes of Grindelwald—'A Familiar Magic.'"

76. *The New Oxford Annotated Bible*, New Revised Standard Version, Fifth edition. Emphasis mine.

77. John Milton, *Paradise Lost*, University of Pennsylvania School of Arts & Sciences, accessed June 10, 2022, http://knarf.english.upenn.edu/Milton/pl4.html, Book IV, lines 3–8.

78. Quoted in Groves, "'Secrets of Dumbledore' and 'The Book of Beasts.'"

79. Ibid.

80. *Oxford English Dictionary, Compact Edition*, vol. 1, A–O, 1979, s.v. "dragon," n. 4 & 5.

The Real Magic of Christmas in *Harry Potter*

Emily Strand

Even if *Harry Potter*'s Muggle readers have never wielded a wand or attempted to Apparate, many can relate to an important episode in each volume of Harry's story: Christmas. In the 2019 book *Re-Enchanted*, Maria Sachiko Cecire notes that in popular consciousness the Christmas holiday serves as a bridge from the everyday, modern, mundane world to an old-fashioned, wholesome world, brimming with magical possibility.[1] In this way, Christmas possesses the same enchanting power as the Oxford School children's fantasy stories of C.S. Lewis and J.R.R. Tolkien, of which *Harry Potter* is a descendant. Says Cecire, "Christmastime is, like picking up a medievalist children's fantasy novel, an opportunity to set aside the disenchantment associated with rational modernity and slip into an otherworld of magic."[2] Doubling down on bringing the magic, such fantasy stories in the Oxford School often employ Christmas episodes to convey hyper-magical, even religious meaning, such as in Lewis's *The Lion, the Witch, and the Wardrobe*, when Father Christmas arrives with gifts of great responsibility for the Pevensie children in their battle against evil.[3]

Like Christmas in Narnia, Christmas in *Potter*, from *Sorcerer's Stone* to *Deathly Hallows*, carries great significance—especially religious significance. In a story world already teeming with enchantment, *Potter*'s "Christmas moments" subtly point to the literary magic of each book: the internal transformation Harry must make to defeat evil. Ultimately, the Christmas episodes in *Harry Potter* provide episodic glimpses into the particular mode of heroism to which Harry will be called in *Deathly Hallows*—a heroism patterned after the Incarnation of Christ, which embraces the frailty of the human condition for the sake of others and in so doing, triumphs over death.

Harry Potter takes a risk by placing such emphasis on a fundamentally religious holiday, one certainly not celebrated by all readers, especially those of other venerable faith traditions. A Jewish rabbi friend once described what it's like to be Jewish during the Christmas season as a prolonged experience of "FOMO" (fear of missing out) and as a constant, unwelcome reminder that he's different. Christmas's prominence in *Harry Potter* could work to exclude some readers. But Cecire says Christmas has "come to occupy an at least semi-secular identity in Anglo-American culture as a festival of childhood, magic, and nostalgic returns to the past."[4] Beatrice Groves observes that the Christmas episodes in Books One through Six are of a secular variety,[5] featuring holiday activities in which many non–Christians joyfully engage, such as putting up Christmas trees, wearing ugly sweaters (sorry, Mrs. Weasley), and pulling Christmas crackers—festivities which don't require participants to entertain religious beliefs. Rowling's more secular treatment of Christmas in Books One through Six allows the story to be more inclusive, while remaining in continuity with the Oxford School fantasy writers, whose use of Christmas episodes reflects a time when Western, Christian values predominated, without much challenge or critique.

Groves also argues that these more secular trappings of Christmas prepare the reader "for Christmas night in *Deathly Hallows* where the Christian symbolism of the day finally becomes fully present."[6] The books' treatment of Christmas treads a fine line between sacred and secular; by the final Christmas of the series, the story steps firmly to the religious side of that line, for at Christmas in *Harry Potter*, we glimpse the deep and particular religious character of the story. In this sense, the author employs Christmas, existing as it does in both secular and religious contexts, as an entry point for the story's most particularly religious content, climaxing in the Christmas scene in *Deathly Hallows*. Thus the treatment of Christmas in *Harry Potter* is incarnational, like the holiday itself, infusing the sacred into the secular, for the (story) world's transformation and redemption.

Before analyzing this incarnational quality of Christmas in *Harry Potter*, a brief explanation of the meaning of Christmas in the Christian tradition is in order. Evidence exists for Christians celebrating the birth of Christ on December 25 in Rome in as early as 336 AD.[7] The festival celebrated that the ineffable, formless God took human flesh and dwelt among his creation—even became his creation—in the person of Jesus Christ. Brett Salkeld puts it succinctly: "In Jesus, God 'tabernacled' or 'pitched his tent' among us."[8] Thus Jesus himself becomes the true temple—the meeting place between humans and God. Salkeld says this reality eliminates a basic obstacle in humanity's relationship to the divine: "If God is divine, spirit, immaterial, how can we humans, strange mix of matter and spirit that we are, have communion with God?"[9] We cannot leave behind the materiality of our existence, so God joins us in the material world in the most vulnerable human form: as an infant.

It is the beginning of this resolution of the problem of our materiality—our mortality—that Christians celebrate at Christmas, at least in a religious sense. Of course, there are many secular cultural traditions that accompany the Christmas season as well, including bouts of capitalist frenzy and sugary disregard for the preservation of reasonable waistlines. Theologically speaking, however, in the Christian tradition, Christmas is a time for hope and joy and peace, because it commemorates the beginnings of human redemption. Images of the Baby Jesus abound at this time of year, because this child symbolizes human weakness, which God, through Christ, invites to become eternal.

Christmas, from its origins, falls at the winter solstice, the darkest time of the year. Thus light images abound at Christmastime as well, in Christian ritual and hymnody, because the birth of Christ is understood as the metaphorical dawn of salvation, illuminating the darkness of the world so that humanity may navigate this human life with wisdom. But this light imagery has a "dark side," as it were; in the lead-up to Christmas, many Christians observe the season of Advent, acknowledging the darkness of the world in anticipation of the light that comes at Christmas. One eighth-century liturgical text reads, "O Radiant Dawn,/splendor of eternal light, sun of justice:/come and shine on those who dwell in darkness and in the shadow of death."[10] Cecire reports pre–Christian beliefs held "late December as a time when the boundaries between this world and the world of spirits became precariously thin, when evil spirits may be abroad."[11] Christian ritual celebrations of Christmas carry forward these folk beliefs, infusing them with Christian meaning, including stark acknowledgments of the darkness of the world and of death and the longing for a savior who will bring eternal light and life.

These various aspects of Christmas's theological meaning in the Christian tradition come to bear on the holiday's prominence and significance in *Harry Potter*. In the embrace of frailty, the infusion of secular with sacred, in the acknowledgment of darkness and yearning for light, Christmas teaches Harry—and his readers—what it means to be a hero.

Holidays in general feature significantly in *Harry Potter*, and this lends an alluring, festive character to the series. Birthdays, especially Harry's, are often mentioned. In the first half of the series, Halloween serves as the point in the narrative at which the contours of the mystery become apparent to the Trio, or when the villain first shows his hand,[12] such as in Book Four, when on Halloween, Harry's name emerges unexpectedly from the Goblet of Fire. Interestingly, Easter is mentioned in every book but one (*Half-Blood Prince*). Highly significant events occur on or around the Easter holidays in all other volumes, such as the death and burial of Dobby in *Deathly Hallows*. A mention of Easter means the crisis of the plot is near.

But exceptions to the prominence of holidays in *Potter* are also telling. As important a series kick-start as Harry's eleventh birthday is in *Sorcerer's Stone*, his fourteenth and fifteenth birthdays are not depicted. In Books Five, Six, and Seven, Halloween is not depicted either (although in *Deathly Hallows* we get—as Christmas Eve turns to Christmas Day—an extended flashback of the saga's most significant Halloween: the night Voldemort murdered the Potters and Harry received his scar). And while it's true that Easter usually falls just before the crisis of the plot in each book, it receives no more than a passing mention in any of the texts.

Christmas, on the other hand, is a constant. The word itself occurs 234 times in the series,[13] and the holiday is acknowledged in every installment, without exception. This constancy of Christmas could relate to the holiday's significant role in the alchemical symbolism of the series. The pervasive alchemical imagery in *Potter* has been outlined by John Granger, Signe Cohen, and others, but without attention to the place of Christmas therein. Alchemy in literature "parallels the spiritual work necessary for human beings in this life"[14] and forms a spiritual scaffold on which Harry's story is constructed, in each separate volume and throughout the seven-book saga. In each *Potter* story, Christmas plays an essential role in the white or albedo stage, the period of interior purification in the alchemical process. The books consistently flag this stage with the first snowfall of winter, which immediately precedes or directly coincides with Christmas. The enviable fact that Christmas is always a "white Christmas" for Harry not only flags the alchemical stage in each story, but it also further amplifies the hyper-magical space the holiday creates in the narrative, as Cecire notes. Further demonstrating the alchemical function of Christmas, the Christmas episodes in *Potter* always involve an encounter between Harry and his august headmaster, Albus Dumbledore, whom Cohen calls "the primary symbol of the albedo stage in the series."[15] For instance, on Christmas in *Sorcerer's Stone*, Harry receives, as a gift from Hermione, the Chocolate Frog card depicting Dumbledore and sees for the first time Dumbledore's "narrow, loopy writing"[16] in the note that arrives with the "silvery gray"[17] Invisibility Cloak. Along with white, silver also signals the albedo stage of alchemy.[18] Clearly, part of Christmas's function in *Potter* is to bolster the alchemical framework on which the story is carefully cast.

Christmas is more, however, than an alchemical flag in *Potter*. The Christmas scenes in *Sorcerer's Stone* and *Deathly Hallows* have received the most interpretive attention by scholars, but every Christmas episode in *Harry Potter* accomplishes important work, pointing prescriptively to the religious notions that inform Harry's character arc as a heroic figure patterned after Christ. Further, these revealed religious notions express Christian incarnational theology, in which darkness is acknowledged, and despite it, human weakness is embraced as salvific.

Harry's first Christmas at Hogwarts is as cozy and joyful as they come. The first snowfall of the season heralds that Christmas (and the albedo stage of the plot) is near, and "the Weasley twins were punished for bewitching several snowballs so that they followed Quirrell around, bouncing off the back of his turban."[19] More than just hilarious plot foreshadowing, since the whiteness of snow points to purity, this line also foreshadows how pure-hearted, love-filled Harry will throw himself at Quirrelmort in order to defeat him—a fitting means of victory for a child. Even more subtle allusions to Harry's brand of heroism hide in the lush details of Harry's first Hogwarts Christmas. "Festoons of holly and mistletoe"[20] decorate Hogwarts, warding against evil and reminding readers of the associations of Harry's holly wand with Christmas. As classes end for the holiday, Ron teaches Harry to play wizard chess, pointing to the chess game Ron will conduct at book's end, sacrificing himself in humility to allow Harry and Hermione to advance through the protections that guard the Sorcerer's Stone.[21]

On his first Hogwarts Christmas morning, Harry receives proper gifts for the first time, but by far the most precious gift he receives on this or any Christmas is the Invisibility Cloak, accompanied by a note from Dumbledore (although Harry does not yet recognize the writing). Harry's receipt of the Cloak occasions his first of many out-of-bed-at-night-in-the-castle adventures. Cecire contextualizes this particular Christmas adventure within the Oxford School of children's fantasy literature, drawing upon the "Christmas challenge" tradition, paradigmatically depicted in *Sir Gawain and the Green Knight*.[22] Cecire notes more modern works in this school, like *Harry Potter* and Susan Cooper's *The Dark Is Rising* series, reframe this challenge as "a primarily psychological or internal struggle."[23] Cecire describes how this internal challenge plays out in *Potter*, for after Harry enjoys his sumptuous first Hogwarts Christmas, he (aided by his new Cloak) finds the Mirror of Erised, and must come to terms with "the deathly powers beyond human strength,"[24] powers that make what he truly desires—a loving, living family—mere fantasy. After nights of hopeless longing before the Mirror, Harry must be reminded by Dumbledore that "it does not do to dwell on dreams and forget to live."[25] Thus Harry's Christmas is both a cozy celebration of his new home at Hogwarts and also a stark reminder of what he has lost due to the violence of Voldemort, of death itself. This acknowledgment of the cold reality of death also highlights the incarnational character of Christmas in Book One.

But the Cloak itself highlights this incarnational character even more, and in this sense, it had to be given to Harry at Christmas, rather than, as we might have expected, when he first arrived at Hogwarts. In the same breath as his warning to Harry about dwelling on dreams, Dumbledore calls Harry's Cloak "admirable"[26] and encourages him to put it on and get back to bed, as an alternative to dream-dwelling. Cecire notes how this advice rests on popular understandings of the Christmas season, which, despite the opportunities it affords in children's fantasy stories to overcome internal struggles, nevertheless "must come to an end in favor of the business of everyday life."[27] But "everyday life" for Harry, in the wizarding world he now calls home, means a new, heroic identity, characterized by both Christmas and his Cloak. When he first handles the Cloak on Christmas, it is described as "fluid and silvery gray" and "like water woven into material."[28] The baptismal imagery here is apt. Harry does not realize it yet, but this gift from his father James (who sacrificed his life for Harry's), passed through his father-figure Dumbledore (who will do the same), initiates him into a particular type of heroism: one that protects and defends others, using the magic of friendship and humility, rather than violent hubris, to rob death of its power.

Dom Luke Bell, in *Baptizing Harry Potter*, gives a cogent and compelling theological analysis of the Invisibility Cloak, with a long view to the end of the series. Bell explains how themes of power and weakness, humility and strength, operate close to the saga's moral and religious core from its very first chapter, in baby Harry's mysterious defeat of Voldemort: "However, the difference between the first defeat of Voldemort's power and his final defeat is not just the difference between a battle won and war won, it is a difference between defeat by an involuntary and unconscious weakness and defeat by a voluntary and conscious weakness ... we might say it is the difference between Christmas and Easter."[29] To elaborate on Bell's observation, while both Christmas and Easter celebrate Christ, at Christmas, Christians celebrate the *hope and possibility* of the incarnation—the joining of divine and human in Christ. At Easter, believers join with Christ in his ultimate expression of humility and friendship, in consciously choosing weakness and vulnerability, "becoming obedient to death, even death on a cross."[30] But the weakness of God is stronger than human strength.[31] At Christmas, Christians begin learning to view humility as a good, even a divine thing; at Easter, weakness wins.

Harry's signature Cloak is bestowed upon him at Christmas because it points to the key ingredient in his defeat of Voldemort in the end of the series: humility and fellowship, notions at the heart of incarnational theology. Bell says these are the "fundamental values associated with the cloak."[32] In "The Tale of the Three Brothers" in *Deathly Hallows*, the youngest brother's wise choice of hiddenness from death, symbolized by the Cloak, denotes humility and the avoidance of pride, which separates humans from God.[33] Bell points to the ironic relationship between humility and exaltation throughout scripture: that those who humble themselves are honored and lifted up by God. This is no more apparent than in the Gospel accounts of Jesus's humble birth to marginalized people in a marginal space and his ironic exaltation by angels, shepherds, and magi as the savior of humanity.[34] Bell notes that Dumbledore's pride in Harry's choice to keep only the Cloak in *Deathly Hallows* is pride in Harry's spiritual maturity for choosing humility.[35] But the Cloak also points subtly to fellowship. Dumbledore tells Harry in *Deathly Hallows* that the Cloak's true magic is its ability "to protect and shield others as well as its owner."[36] Especially when Harry is young, the Cloak affords him the aid of friends, usually Ron and Hermione, in many of his confrontations with evil. Christmas is the perfect time for Harry to receive this particular gift because, while the Cloak itself does not bring about his triumph, it prefigures and enables the type of heroism that will—just as Christmas prefigures Easter.

The Christmas episode in *Harry Potter and the Chamber of Secrets* works in many of the same ways. First, it is immediately preceded by an incident which reveals one of Harry's most peculiar and important qualities: he is a Parselmouth—one who can communicate with snakes. True to modern Oxford School children's fantasy, this revelation occasions an internal challenge for Harry at Christmastime: is he the "Heir of Slytherin"? Or is he a true Gryffindor? Harry ponders this as he watches the first snow fall outside his window.[37] The next day, that snow has turned into a blizzard, further flagging the purification stage of Harry's alchemical journey. To that end, Albus Dumbledore also makes an important appearance. Harry pays his first visit to the headmaster's office, where his continuing internal struggle—Slytherin or Gryffindor?—prompts him to put the Sorting Hat on his head. It doesn't bring Harry the comfort he hoped for.[38] He must wait until story's end to receive irrefutable confirmation that he is a "true Gryffindor,"[39] as Dumbledore notes, in the form of Gryffindor's sword, which the Sorting Hat provides Harry to defend himself against the Basilisk.

The most noteworthy event of Harry's visit to Dumbledore's office is the introduction of Fawkes the Phoenix, whom Harry meets "on a Burning Day,"[40] when the bird both dies and is reborn. Harry's encounter with Baby Fawkes just before Christmas points to the type of heroism Harry will employ to resolve the story problem—he will go it alone, sacrificing himself to save Ginny, aided only by Dumbledore's "highly *faithful*" pet, whose "tears have healing powers."[41] It also points to Harry's greatest challenge throughout the series: accepting his role as "Dumbledore's man, through and through,"⁴² remaining faithful like Fawkes to Dumbledore's instructions, despite that, in the end of the series, it will mean his own destruction. The death and rebirth of faithful Fawkes right before Christmas hints that if Harry remains faithful, he too will experience a rebirth.

These events occur just before Christmas in *Chamber*; what occurs on the holiday itself is far less cozy than the previous year's celebrations: "Christmas morning dawned, cold and white."⁴³ The Trio use the Polyjuice potion they've been concocting to find out if Malfoy is the Heir of Slytherin (spoiler alert: he is not). This Polyjuice incident showcases the ugly blood purity ideology espoused by some members of the wizarding community. Draco tells a disguised and disgusted Harry and Ron that, 50 years ago, when the Chamber of Secrets was opened, a Muggle-born died, adding with relish, "this time ... I hope it's Granger."⁴⁴ In the darkness of Christmas night, the boys see first-hand the bigotry they are fighting in standing up to Slytherin's heir. The incident also provides a caution in what goes wrong for Hermione, pointing to the potentially dehumanizing effects of going to the side of evil for answers, as they have. With such an approach, one might well end up with whiskers and a tail, or worse. Implied on this "cold, white" Christmas is an alchemical caution to remain pure, for just as in the incarnation of Christ, the promise of salvation lies not in evil places, but in humble ones. The reader is left with the hope and expectation that the Trio's future plans to gain information will rely less on disguising themselves as evil and more on shrouding themselves from it, using Harry's Cloak. Harry is, after all, as Draco mockingly calls him in the episode, "Saint Potter, the Mudbloods' friend."⁴⁵ Like the lofty titles given to the child Jesus at his birth, Harry must grow into this title throughout the saga.

In *Prisoner of Azkaban*, Christmas begins early and is full of incarnational significance. First, Harry receives, as an "Early Christmas present"⁴⁶ from the Weasley twins, a significant and symbolic gift: the Marauder's Map. The map is a useful tool in Harry's particular brand of heroism for, although he first uses the map to sneak out of the castle, its highest purpose in the saga will come in *Deathly Hallows*, when Harry uses it to check on his friends and to safely navigate the castle while hunting the final Horcruxes. Again, as with the gifts the Pevensie children receive to aid their battle against evil in Narnia, Christmas is the right time for Harry to receive the map.

Book Three's Christmas, and especially his receipt of the map, afford Harry the internal challenge associated with the season in Oxford School fantasy. Using it to sneak into Hogsmeade, Harry learns that his father and Sirius Black were friends, that Black is Harry's godfather, and (erroneously) that Black was responsible for his parents' deaths. Harry's other significant gift of the holiday affords a personal challenge: his Firebolt. It is an ambiguous gift; Harry and Ron want to believe it is free of dark magic, but Hermione guesses it was sent by Black (in the end, everyone is right). The broomstick is appropriately given at Christmas because, like the map, Harry will use it or other brooms in his fight against evil, especially as the humble Seeker of Horcruxes in the metaphorical Quidditch game that plays out in the last two books of the series.[47] Finally, Christmas in *Azkaban* has both a Dumbledore encounter (Christmas luncheon is an intimate affair hosted by the headmaster, who wears the silly vulture hat that comes out of Snape's cracker,[48] modeling good-natured humility and fellowship), and it has a shadow side, closing with the confiscation of Harry's new Firebolt by McGonagall, reminding Harry, Ron, and the reader of the ubiquity of evil and danger in the story world—an appropriate message to close the holiday season.

In *Goblet of Fire*, humility is an especial theme of Harry's Hogwarts Christmas, in keeping with Christian incarnational theology which embraces human frailty. The Yule Ball occasions a far more populous Christmas than usual at Hogwarts, giving Harry and Ron a robust audience for age-appropriate lessons in humility resulting from their attempts to secure dates to the ball. Harry is rejected by Cho Chang in favor of his tournament rival, Cedric Diggory[49]; Ron publicly and irrationally invites Fleur Delacour, who is so far out of Ron's league, she doesn't feel it necessary to respond.[50] This humiliation continues for both when, at the ball, Hermione appears on the arm of Victor Krum, the Durmstrang champion,[51] and Harry must lead off the dancing, his date Parvati "steering Harry so forcefully that he felt as though he were a show dog she was putting through its paces."[52] Humiliation is thick on the ground, along with the snow, in Book Four's Christmas. Dumbledore adds to the emphasis on humility in Book Four with a humorous anecdote during dinner about accidentally finding what must be the Room of Requirement.[53] This comment by the headmaster bolsters the theme of humility as a response to Karkaroff boasting to know all the secrets of his school, Durmstrang. Noting the wink Albus gives Harry immediately following,[54] one wonders if Dumbledore isn't intentionally passing Harry a valuable tip about the Room as he takes Karkaroff down a notch.

Goblet embeds one more nod to humility in one of Harry's gifts. The penknife Harry receives this Christmas[55] merits a closer examination for its symbolic meaning, since its material attributes seem redundant; the Alohomora spell works pretty well on locks, and "undoing any knot" doesn't require magic for a sharp knife. Given by his godfather, this gift undoubtedly has spiritual meaning for Harry. Explicit among the earliest and most influential Christian theologians, especially the second-century thinker Irenaeus, was the notion that original sin was reversed through the same course by which it came into the world: two humans. Christ was viewed as a second Adam, one whose obedience reversed Adam's sin of disobedience. This made Mary a second Eve, whose faith in the angel's announcement that she would bear the son of God reverses Eve's sin of desiring the sure knowledge offered by the serpent in Genesis. Irenaeus uses an interesting metaphor to express this: "The knot of Eve's disobedience was untied by Mary's obedience; for what Eve bound by her unbelief, Mary loosed by her faith."[56] Irenaeus emphasizes that, in loosing this knot of evil caused by Eve, humble Mary "became to herself and to the whole human race a cause of salvation."[57] An eighteenth-century Baroque painting by Johann Georg Melchior Schmidtner popularized the image of Mary undoing the knots of sin through her obedience, her foot on the serpent's head. Given the strong associations between Christmas and the humble figure of Mary, Christmas is the right time for Harry to receive a tool that will help him undo knots. For Harry, tied up as he is in Book Four by the "*binding*, magical contract"[58] constituted by whatever evil deception put his name in the Goblet of Fire, Sirius's knife is both a symbolically and spiritually useful gift.

Snowfall, and by association, the Christmas episode with its lessons in humility, comes early in *Order of the Phoenix*, accompanying Harry's and the Weasley twins' lifetime ban from Quidditch by Umbridge.[59] Certainly, the albedo stage of this story, perhaps even of the saga, has begun, when our hero must experience intense purification. The Snitch Harry caught earlier, saving the match from Ron's embarrassing performance as goalkeeper, zooms around the Gryffindor common room in that first-snow scene,[60] as if to say: *the game is not on the pitch anymore, kids—it's real*. After their mortifying Quidditch ban, Harry must prepare to be a different kind of Seeker. Later, Harry finds that Dobby has decorated the Room of Requirement for the final DA session of the year with "a hundred gold baubles" strung from the ceiling, "each showing a picture of Harry's face and bearing the legend HAVE A VERY HARRY CHRISTMAS!"[61] It's yet another humiliation—this one rather on the nose in associating Harry with Jesus, the real-world "reason for the season." The incident points up Harry's savior qualities—his "saving-people thing"[62]—well before Hermione names it near the crisis of the book's plot.

This Christmas also brings signature Oxford School fantasy internal challenges for Harry, especially the ambiguity of his role in the attack on Mr. Weasley and its discovery. The distanced, enigmatic behavior of Albus "Albedo" Dumbledore and Harry's own foreign urge to hurt his headmaster[63] drive home Advent themes of the darkness of the world and its need for a savior as Christmas approaches in *Order of the Phoenix*. The strange test Dumbledore conducts to determine that Harry's and Voldemort's essences are in fact not the same[64] indicates how the crisis at the end of *Order* will be resolved: through Voldemort's essential difference—his inability to possess grief-filled Harry. It also indicates that Harry will survive the saga in the end, because his own loving self-sacrifice for his friends kills the Horcrux within him, allowing his true self to live on.

Christmas itself in *Order* is a bright ray of light shining in a dark story. But not at first; after the attack on Mr. Weasley, Harry experiences a deep low. He feels "dirty, contaminated, as though he were carrying some deadly germ, unworthy to sit … with innocent, clean people whose minds and bodies were free of the taint of Voldemort."[65] He even considers cutting himself off from the wizarding community he has grown to love in order to protect them from himself. When ordered by Dumbledore to stay put through the portrait of Phineas Nigellus Black, Harry struggles to obey. Ironically, even the portrait knows Harry must stop his "adolescent agonizing"[66] and become the pure vessel needed in Dumbledore's plans against Voldemort. As the others put up Christmas decorations, as Sirius sings Christmas carols and the sky outside grows "*whiter*, threatening snow,"[67] Harry retreats further into the House of *Black*, avoiding the purification to which he is called. After Hermione arrives—heroically, by Knight Bus—to open lines of communication for Harry with the others, the Christmas festivities get a lot more joyful, especially for Harry. Sirius is on a high at having company for Christmas, and he leads a transformation of the House of Black from a tarnished, cob-webbed monument of blood purity ideology to a Christmassy oasis of joy; "a great Christmas tree, obtained by Mundungus and decorated with live fairies, blocked Sirius's family tree from view."[68] This detail creates an incarnational juxtaposition, with the values of humility and fellowship, symbolized by the Christmas tree, triumphing in a small yet subversive way over the bigoted elitism of the Black family, represented by their offensive family tree, which had previously "resisted all their attempts to remove it from the wall."[69]

Snow heralds Christmas again in *Half-Blood Prince* and serves up yet another internal challenge for Harry: again, trusting in Dumbledore. Christmas is atypical because Dumbledore himself does not make an appearance. This portends a time when Dumbledore will no longer be physically present in Harry's (or anyone's) life. Harry must learn to trust Dumbledore, even without the luxury of his headmaster's reassuring presence and unflappable confidence to shore up doubt. At issue for Harry this Christmas is Dumbledore's own trust in Snape, after Harry overhears Snape offer to help Malfoy in his nefarious schemes. "'It's Dumbledore's business,'" Lupin tells Harry at the Weasley Christmas Eve. "'Dumbledore trusts Severus, and that ought to be good enough for all of us.'"[70] Lupin then tells Harry of his own work with the werewolves on Dumbledore's behalf, and Lupin's obedience to Dumbledore in the face of this most unpleasant task seems to bolster Harry's own loyalty to his inscrutable headmaster. When Rufus Scrimgeour, Minister of Magic, crashes Christmas lunch, using Percy's painful estrangement from his family to gain an interview with "the Chosen One," Harry becomes a wall of unwavering loyalty to Dumbledore. Scrimgeour, in the snowy grounds of the Burrow on Christmas day, coldly accuses Harry of being a pawn, being "Dumbledore's man through and through,"[71] and Harry is quick to respond in the affirmative. Harry's faith in Dumbledore will be tested again (and again) before the saga concludes, but on Christmas in *Half-Blood Prince*, at least, as he walks the Weasleys' garden with Scrimgeour, Harry sees with clear eyes that his own heroism must conform to Dumbledore's plans, inscrutable though they may be, just as Christ knew, in the garden of Gethsemane, that he must conform his will to the Father's.[72]

It is difficult to overestimate the religious significance of Christmas in *Harry Potter and the Deathly Hallows*. Indeed, as Groves observes, it seems every Christmas has led Harry (and the reader) to this point. It conforms to Cecire's identification of Christmas as a heightened magical space within an already-magical story in that Godric's Hollow, where this Christmas takes place, is a magical village with Muggle inhabitants as well, making it a metaphor for Christmas (or the *Harry Potter* saga) itself, with its deep core of religious meaning that does not exclude secular participation. The pairing of sacred and secular is clear here; in the same sentence, the narrative describes "laughter and pop music" wafting out of a pub door and "a carol start up inside the little church."[73] But Harry and Hermione do not walk toward the pub; they go toward the church, which Groves notes is the only church depicted in the entire saga.[74] The singing coming from it makes "Harry's throat constrict, it reminded him so forcefully of Hogwarts, of Peeves bellowing rude versions of carols from inside suits of armor, of the Great Hall's twelve Christmas trees, of Dumbledore wearing a bonnet he had won in a cracker, of Ron in a hand-knitted sweater."[75] Besides offering a noteworthy linkage of Hogwarts with a church (that real-world "school of magic"[76]), this passage contains carefully chosen allusions to Harry's previous Christmas celebrations that point subtly to the religious themes of the holiday, hidden in secular trappings. Groves says, "As in *Chamber*, the twelve Christmas trees are once again mentioned alongside carols, and it seems possible that the Christian significance of the number (echoing the twelve days of Christmas) is meant to be heard."[77] Dumbledore's habit of not taking himself seriously enough to exclude the wearing of silly bonnets, as well as the hand-knitted quality of Mrs. Weasley's Christmas sweaters, and Ron himself, whom Harry intentionally chose to be friends with over wealthy and arrogant Malfoy in Book One, all point to humility—the value at the heart of the Christian feast celebrating how salvation came to the world through a child.

The church–Hogwarts connection and memories of happy, humble Christmases past do not exhaust the religious content of Christmas in *Hallows*. Granger observes many Nativity images pepper the scene: from Harry and Hermione themselves, "a couple in disguise [traveling] to the man's ancestral home," to the "Holy Family crèche of sorts in the village center,"[78] where a statue featuring baby Harry and his parents stands in memorial to their sacrifice. But these are hidden images; no one notices Harry and Hermione, under the Cloak and disguised as they are, and the Potter crèche changes into a war memorial before Muggle eyes. The virtue of hiddenness or humility, which the incarnation of Christ celebrates, is central here and will remain key to Harry's survival.

This Christmas chiastically echoes the Christmas in Book One by affording Harry encounters with both Dumbledore and his parents, but this time, in memory only. Rowling has said that the New Testament scripture passages Harry reads on the Dumbledore and Potter tombstones in the graveyard in Godric's Hollow "sum up—they almost epitomize the whole series."[79] It is notable that the *only* overt references to Christianity in the seven-book series come at Christmas. But these scripture passages are not just subtle rewards for Rowling's Christian readers; placed at the pivotal moment of the story, they point to *how* our hero will effect the redemption that is his destiny—a destiny the episode emphasizes in its multiple memorials to the Potter family and messages of support, even from strangers, for Harry in his quest.[80] The scripture on the Dumbledore family grave, from Jesus's Sermon on the Mount in Matthew, reads "Where your treasure is, there will your heart be also."[81] In its scriptural context, the passage warns against storing up treasures on earth as a path to happiness, but instead advises storing up treasures in heaven (good deeds, righteousness, etc.). In reference to *Potter*, the passage pits Voldemort's way of living (immortality through murderous Horcruxes) against Harry's (evading death through the Cloak, representing humility), and declares Harry's the godly path. At Christmas, Harry does not understand what the words mean, but later, as he digs Dobby's grave (at Easter), Harry will resolve himself to the pursuit of destroying the Horcruxes, not gaining the other Hallows. This realization in turn comes with understanding for the other scriptural passage, the one on Harry's parents' grave, which he also hears but fails to understand at Christmas: "The last enemy that shall be destroyed is death,"[82] from 1 Corinthians 15:26. Harry realizes, standing in Dobby's grave, that there is no "out" for him, as his brief obsession with the Deathly Hallows had teased. He realizes that, if his own life will be required to fulfill Dumbledore's plan, he's willing to give it. Horcruxes, not Hallows. The last enemy for Harry will be death itself.[83]

But Harry doesn't understand either passage at Christmas; bitterness at the reality of death, especially his parents', inhibits his understanding. The darkness of the world is too real to him on Christmas Eve. Just as he begins to sink into despair, Hermione conjures a wreath of Christmas roses for him to lay at the Potters' grave. Groves identifies the allusion here to Christian devotional stories about the Christmas rose, noting that the appearance of a plant so steeped in Christian symbolism on Christmas night in *Deathly Hallows* is unlikely to be coincidence.[84] Indeed, angelic Hermione's Christmas roses seem to give Harry, like the weeping children in such stories, strength to walk away from the graveyard, "back toward the dark church,"[85] that reminds him of Hogwarts and his own, grim destiny. Soon, he will return to the real Hogwarts, in pursuit of the last of the Horcruxes.

Such glimmers of Christian hope as the church, the scripture, and Christmas roses provide become harder to spot in *Deathly Hallows*' Christmas, but are not absent in what remains of the episode. Harry and Hermione's immediate danger, from the start, makes this Christmas anything but cozy. Even the deep snow on the ground presents a danger.[86] Granger says the darkness and danger of the episode points to the nigredo stage of Harry's alchemical journey, his breaking down completely, and is appropriately depicted on Christmas "because of the darkness of [the] World before the advent of Jesus of Nazareth, the light of the world."[87] Nagini's horrific attack on Harry and Hermione represents "the reason for the incarnation of Christ, namely, the Evil One's dominance in the world before [Christ's] Nativity."[88] The Christian symbolism of the attacking serpent here is apt. Voldemort himself shows up at the close of this terrifying scene, and Denise Roper identifies another Christian allusion in the way the chapter ends—with Voldemort's narrow miss of Harry and Hermione, his resultant scream of rage echoing across "the dark gardens over the church bells ringing in Christmas Day...."[89] Roper points to the English tradition of the "Devil's Knell," in which churches would toll their bells as Christmas Day arrived, a practice that "sprang up around the folk belief that the Devil dies each year at the moment when Christ is born."[90] In this tradition, the bells of Christmas Day announced the Devil's demise, and consistent with Christian incarnational theology, this Christmas moment in *Deathly Hallows* "heralds the beginning of Harry's triumph and serves as a warning to the Dark Lord that his days are numbered."[91]

One final, incarnational note on Christmas in *Deathly Hallows* remains. Harry's holly wand is broken in this horrific attack. Though they both contain phoenix feathers, Harry's wand wood, holly, has always stood in sharp contrast to Voldemort's wand of yew, and the different woods point to Harry's and Voldemort's different approaches to the universal human desire for immortality.[92] Voldemort's yew wand represents toxicity and death, whereas Harry's holly wand points to Christmas and the incarnation, to humility and the embrace of vulnerability. When Harry's holly wand breaks on Christmas, held together only by "one fragile strand of phoenix feather,"[93] it again tests Harry's faith in Dumbledore's approach to the fight against Voldemort. Granger notes, however, that Harry does not throw the broken wand away, but keeps its remnants, which represent his faith, close to his heart.[94] Eventually, Harry will use the deathstick—that Hallow by which he is tempted but knows is not his way—only to repair the holly wand, so he may finally lead the trouble-free,[95] "quiet life"[96] he prefers. Says Luke Bell, the "ordinary life" Harry lived as a young child with the Dursleys protected him from "the spiritual danger of pride";[97] Harry shows humility in longing again for such obscurity (sans the Dursleys, preferably) when his heroic quest is complete.

In a sense, Christmas makes a good metaphor for the *Harry Potter* saga itself, with its deep core of religious meaning that does not exclude secular participation and enjoyment. Throughout the series, Christmas creates a heightened magical space within an already-magical story, offering internal challenges for Harry that help him grow into a particular type of heroism. Consistent appearances by symbolic snow and encounters with Albus Dumbledore signal Harry's alchemical purification, and dark episodes acknowledge, like the season of Advent that precedes Christmas, the darkness of Harry's world and its need for a savior. At Christmas, Harry receives gifts that help him *be* that savior, such as the Invisibility Cloak, the Marauder's Map, Sirius's penknife, even the scripture passages in *Deathly Hallows*, all of which promote humility and fellowship. In short, Christmas in *Harry Potter* possesses the same incarnational qualities as in our Muggle world, buried though they may be under festive, secular trappings. At its core, Christmas in *Harry Potter* teaches Harry—and the reader—the incarnational value of humbly embracing our mortality as the path to salvation.

NOTES

1. Maria Sachiko Cecire, *Re-Enchanted: The Rise of Children's Fantasy Literature in the Twentieth Century* (Minneapolis: University of Minnesota Press, 2019), 129.
2. Ibid., 154.
3. Denise Roper, *The Lord of the Hallows: Christian Symbolism and Themes in J.K. Rowling's Harry Potter* (Denver: Outskirts Press, 2009), 79. Roper also points out that in Tolkien's timeline for his *Lord of the Rings* books, the nine heroes depart from Rivendell to

destroy the ring on December 25, marking the day of Christ's incarnation as the "beginning of the end" of Sauron, Tolkien's Dark Lord.
    4. Cecire, *Re-Enchanted*, 130.
    5. Beatrice Groves, "Carols in Harry Potter and the Myth of the Christmas Rose (Part I)," *The Leaky Cauldron*, December 23, 2018, http://www.the-leaky-cauldron.org/2018/12/23/carols-in-harry-potter-and-the-myth-of-the-christmas-rose-part-1/.
    6. *Ibid*.
    7. Adolph Adam, *The Liturgical Year: Its History and Its Meaning After the Reform of the Liturgy*, trans. Matthew J. O'Connell (Collegeville, MN: The Liturgical Press, 1979), 122. Adam notes that the date corresponds with existing, pre–Christian celebrations but was also a careful calculation of Jesus's birth in relation to his cousin and scriptural forerunner, John the Baptist, thought to have been born at the summer solstice.
    8. Brett Salkeld, "Real Presence and Idolatry," *PrayTell: Worship, Wit and Wisdom*, September 11, 2021, https://www.praytellblog.com/index.php/2021/09/11/real-presence-and-idolatry/.
    9. *Ibid*.
    10. "The O Antiphons of Advent," Prayers, United States Catholic Conference of Bishops, accessed November 9, 2021, https://www.usccb.org/prayers/o-antiphons-advent.
    11. Cicere, *Re-Enchanted*, 137.
    12. hpboy13, "Getting a Clue for Christmas," MuggleNet, December 20, 2018, https://www.mugglenet.com/2018/12/getting-a-clue-for-christmas/?fbclid=-IwAR3Jo6qpTiMsyjoD2m-Ee4G0wBgHxnBMukN-KECqrgy5YTgcRiFuhVGRc70.
    13. Groves, "Carols in Harry Potter and the Myth of the Christmas Rose (Part I)"; Groves cites Nancy Solon Villaluz for this information in *Does Harry Potter Tickle Sleeping Dragons?* (Seattle: Romance Press, 2008).
    14. John Granger, *Looking for God in Harry Potter* (Carol Stream, IL: SaltRiver/Tyndale House, 2006), 38.
    15. Signe Cohen, "The Two Alchemists in Harry Potter," *The Journal of Religion and Popular Culture* 30, no. 3 (Fall 2018): 210. Note the similarities of "albedo" and "Albus."
    16. J.K. Rowling, *Harry Potter and the Sorcerer's Stone* (New York: Scholastic, 1997), 201.
    17. *Ibid*.
    18. Cohen, *The Two Alchemists in Harry Potter*, 209.
    19. Rowling, *Sorcerer's Stone*, 194. This line stands, in the history of literature, as a monument to the rewards of re-reading.
    20. *Ibid*., 196.
    21. *Ibid*., 199. One of the chessmen Harry borrows from Seamus in his Christmas holiday games with Ron foreshadows Ron's sacrifice with his advice to Harry: "Don't send me there, can't you see his knight? Send *him*, we can afford to lose *him*." Later, Ron will remind Harry and Hermione, as he allows himself to be taken, "That's chess.... You've got to make some sacrifices!" *Ibid*., 283.
    22. For more on Arthurian games and *Harry Potter*, see Laurie Beckoff's essay in this volume.
    23. Cecire, *Re-Enchanted*, 166.
    24. *Ibid*.
    25. Rowling, *Sorcerer's Stone*, 214.
    26. *Ibid*.
    27. Cecire, *Re-Enchanted*, 167.
    28. Rowling, *Sorcerer's Stone*, 201.
    29. Luke Bell, *Baptizing Harry Potter: A Christian Reading of J.K. Rowling* (Mahwah, NJ: Hidden Spring, 2010), 93.
    30. Phil. 2:8b, NABRE.
    31. 1 Cor. 1:25, NABRE.
    32. Bell, *Baptizing Harry Potter*, 195.
    33. *Ibid*., 191.
    34. See the second chapters of both Matthew's and Luke's Gospels. Also note that the

name "Quirinius" (clearly the inspiration for Quirrell's first name, Quirinus) appears in the second chapter of Luke, as "governor of Syria" (2:2) at the time of Jesus's birth.

35. Bell, *Baptizing Harry Potter*, 194.
36. J.K. Rowling, *Harry Potter and the Deathly Hallows* (New York: Scholastic, 2007), 716.
37. J.K. Rowling, *Harry Potter and the Chamber of Secrets* (New York: Scholastic, 1999), 197.
38. Ibid., 206.
39. Ibid., 334.
40. Ibid., 207.
41. Ibid., emphasis original. For more on the phoenix's mythic significance, see Lana Whited's essay in this volume.
42. J.K. Rowling, *Harry Potter and the Half-Blood Prince* (New York: Scholastic, 2005), 357. When Harry tells Dumbledore he is indeed his man through and through, Fawkes, from the corner, lets out "a low, soft, musical cry."
43. Rowling, *Chamber of Secrets*, 211.
44. Ibid., 223.
45. Ibid.
46. J.K. Rowling, *Harry Potter and the Prisoner of Azkaban* (New York: Scholastic, 1999), 191.
47. Emily Strand, "The Second War Was Won on the Quidditch Pitch of Hogwarts: Quidditch as a Symbol Set in the Harry Potter Series," in *Harry Potter for Nerds 2*, ed. Kathryn N. McDaniel and Travis Prinzi (Oklahoma City: Unlocking Press, 2015), 115–138.
48. Rowling, *Prisoner of Azkaban*, 228.
49. J.K. Rowling, *Harry Potter and the Goblet of Fire* (New York: Scholastic, 2000), 397.
50. Ibid., 399.
51. Ibid., 414.
52. Ibid., 415.
53. Ibid., 417.
54. Ibid., 418.
55. Ibid., 410.
56. Irenaeus, *Adversus Haereses*, XXII, 4; as quoted in Michael O'Carroll, CSSp, "Mary, Mother of God," in *The New Dictionary of Theology*, ed. Joseph A. Komonchak, Mary Collins and Dermot A. Lane (Collegeville, MN: Liturgical Press, 1987), 638.
57. Ibid.
58. Rowling, *Goblet of Fire*, 256. Emphasis added.
59. J.K. Rowling, *Harry Potter and the Order of the Phoenix* (New York: Scholastic, 2003), 417.
60. Ibid.
61. Ibid., 452.
62. Ibid., 733.
63. Ibid., 474–475.
64. Ibid., 470.
65. Ibid., 492. See Beatrice Groves's essay in this volume for how the notion of uncleanness relates *Harry Potter* to Bram Stoker's *Dracula*.
66. Ibid., 496.
67. Ibid., 497. Emphasis added.
68. Ibid., 501.
69. Ibid., 117.
70. Rowling, *Half-Blood Prince*, 332.
71. Ibid., 348.
72. Matthew 26:39, NABRE.
73. Rowling, *Deathly Hallows*, 323.
74. Groves, "Carols in Harry Potter (Part I)."
75. Rowling, *Deathly Hallows*, 324.
76. Emily Strand, "Harry Potter and the Sacramental Principle," *Worship* 93 (October 2019), 365.

77. Groves, "Carols in Harry Potter (Part I)."
78. John Granger, *The Deathly Hallows Lectures* (Oklahoma City: Zossima Press, 2008), 112.
79. Shawn Adler, "Harry Potter Author J.K. Rowling Opens Up About the Books' Christian Imagery," MTV.com, October 17, 2007, https://www.mtv.com/news/1572107/harry-potter-author-jk-rowling-opens-up-about-books-christian-imagery/.
80. Rowling, *Deathly Hallows*, 332–333.
81. *Ibid.*, 325.
82. *Ibid.*, 328.
83. John Anthony Dunne has noted how this passage from Corinthians represents a tension—that, as Harry notes, it could be construed as a Death Eater idea, to want to destroy death. But Dunne avers, as others have, that Voldemort is a personification of Death in the story, and thus the passage fundamentally refers to the destruction of Voldemort as such. However, Dunne also points out that we see Voldemort (Death) destroyed twice in the saga: once at the beginning, in his Lily-thwarted attempt to kill baby Harry, and finally at the end, when Harry defeats him after having allowed Voldemort to "kill" him. Thus self-sacrifice, Dunne points out, is the paradoxical key to "transcending" death in *Harry Potter*. John Dunne, "The Death of Death in the Death of the Boy Who Lived: the Morality of Mortality in Harry Potter," in *Ravenclaw Reader: The St. Andrews University Harry Potter Conference*, ed. John Patrick Pazdziora and Micah Snell (Oklahoma City: Unlocking Press, 2015), 31–46.
84. Groves, "Carols in *Harry Potter* and the Myth of the Christmas Rose, Part I."
85. Rowling, *Deathly Hallows*, 329.
86. *Ibid.*, 322.
87. Granger, *The Deathly Hallows Lectures*, 112.
88. *Ibid.*
89. Rowling, *Deathly Hallows*, 342.
90. Tanya Gulevich, *The Encyclopedia of Christmas* (Detroit: Omnigraphics, 2000), 183.
91. Denise Roper, "Christmas in *Harry Potter and the Deathly Hallows*," *Phoenix Weasley* blog, December 20, 2010, https://phoenixweasley.wordpress.com/2010/12/20/christmas-in-harry-potter-and-the-deathly-hallows/.
92. Strand, "Harry Potter and the Sacramental Principle," 363.
93. Rowling, *Deathly Hallows*, 348.
94. Granger, *The Deathly Hallows Lectures*, 113. Granger goes on to analyze the Christian content in the episode that immediately follows Christmas in *Deathly Hallows*, noting that, just as the feast of the Baptism of the Lord immediately follows Christmas, so Harry has a post–Christmas baptismal moment when Ron returns to rescue him from drowning in the Forest of Dean, helping him to obtain the sword of Gryffindor, by which the snake Nagini will eventually be defeated. We also learn on p. 383 of *Deathly Hallows* that, early on Christmas morning, Ron hears Hermione's voice coming out of the Deluminator, which allows him to decipher that device's magic and use it to rejoin her and Harry.
95. Rowling, *Deathly Hallows*, 749.
96. Rowling, *Half-Blood Prince*, 350.
97. Bell, *Baptizing Harry Potter*, 179.

Conversation
Ancient Magic

Lana Whited (LW) and Emily Strand (ES) talk with Katy McDaniel (KM) about their essays.

KM: When we think about these images and metaphors in the traditional narratives that not only J.K. Rowling but also the people who are writing the *Fantastic Beasts* films are bringing into [the works], how are they connecting the reader or the viewer into the magical experience and helping us to feel this magic in a real way for ourselves?

LW: For me, I think that's what the dragon and phoenix imagery is all about. To go back to traditions and older sources of magic, you know, one of the oldest conventions in Christian literature is the notion of the dragon as representing the beastly nature of human beings, so that the submission or the slaying of the dragon always represents triumph over that. I think associating the phoenix with this idea of rebirth and resurrection, with the Dumbledore figure and the Dumbledore family, and associating the dragon with Grindelwald and his more self-centered, ambitious form of behaving—for me, that's like the primary way into the moral framework of the story.

ES: Yes, and you know, in my [essay] I think a lot of what I'm trying to convey is that Christmas is this invitation to we Muggle readers to experience that magic [by] drawing upon our own experience. I tried to point out in the [essay] that, Christmas—and [author] Maria Sachiko Cecire seems to agree with this—Christmas is a Christian holiday, obviously, but it has all these secular trappings that do invite non-religious participation in many ways. Even people of other faith traditions can put on an ugly sweater and go to an ugly sweater party. And there are even ugly sweaters at Christmas in *Harry Potter*, which is great.

KM: The numinous ugly sweater! Yes!

ES: The numinous ugly sweater, exactly. But there's just this little bit of magic that happens at this time of year, as the darkness turns to light, that awakens something in all of us, whether we celebrate Christmas in a religious sense or not. And so I do think that the choice of that occasion, to have such important things happen that teach Harry the kind of humility and heroism that he will have to express to resolve the story-problem for the whole series, is a really intentional and really powerful choice on the author's part to invite everyone into the story.

LW: I think also the way the magic is depicted in the [*Fantastic Beasts*] film series focuses a lot on things like curses and very serious forms of magic. But there's a lot of emphasis on charms in [*The Secrets of Dumbledore* (2022)]. The character of Lally, for example, stresses to the Hogwarts students that you need to pay attention in Charms class, because that could be really important. Charms typically have lighter kinds of effects, often reversible. But I think that Newt is a person who is more likely to practice those lighter forms of magic. He has a kind of a characteristic practice of magic that often is the place where humor enters into the film. There's not a better scene than that scene when he does the funny little dance with those creatures, trying to get his brother out. I love that scene the way I love the scenes with the minions in *Despicable Me* [(2010)]. They're just delightful, and they provide levity, but I know our friend Louise Freeman would also say that those lighter scenes provide an important kind of contrast with the more serious moments in the film. But those aspects of magic—the fun part, the part that really brings you joy as a viewer—all of that is still there as well.

KM: Right. And the combination of all of those things together, where you've got the humor, you've got story, you got moral, the dark and the light combined together, and seeing them in close proximity and juxtaposed, I do think is one of the charms of these wizarding world stories. [It] keeps bringing us back for more.

ES: See what she did there with "charms"? It's a double entendre.

KM: [Laughing.] I'm trying! I'm bringing it, Emily, I'm doing my best!

A Question of Character

Padfoot Revelio!
The Life and Love of Sirius Black

Emma Nicholson

Readers experience the *Potter* saga through Harry's eyes. Harry's assumptions and the chronological order in which he receives information heavily influence how we perceive adult characters. They are like the tips of icebergs, floating in Harry's perceptive sea, leading rich lives before he was born and spending much time out of sight while Harry is at Hogwarts.

One such character is the notorious Marauder, Sirius Black. Scholars and fans sometimes see Sirius as reckless and immature. For example, in "Interior/Exterior in the Harry Potter Series: Duality Expressed in Sirius Black and Remus Lupin," Amy Green says Sirius is emotionally stunted.[1] Even the official Wizarding World website starts the article on their favorite Sirius moments with the words "reckless, arrogant, and dare we say it, a bit moody."[2] People seem to aim straight for Padfoot's faults, taking great care to play down his strengths with his lesser traits. But these views replicate the misunderstanding that Harry's limited perception creates about his mysterious godfather.

Rearranging the life of Sirius into a linear story and focusing on smaller clues reveal previously hidden truths about his character. Revisiting the *Harry Potter* books from Black's perspective challenges assumptions we hold about him and enriches our understanding of a man we spend such a tragically short time getting to know. Instead of a character to be admonished with moralistic caveats, we see a man of powerful love and inner strength, who rises above trauma, pain, and circumstance. We can appreciate his humanity, depth, and role as a godfather and understand just how much he adores Harry. Love, a key theme in the *Potter* saga, is not just exemplified by Lily, Harry, or Dumbledore. Sirius is also a true wielder of this powerful magic.

Just Like Your Godfather

Sirius Black was born on November 3, 1959, and spent eleven unhappy years growing up in Grimmauld Place. Padfoot had a patchy childhood, marked by a fierce rebellious streak, confrontation, and rule breaking. However, Sirius's experiences make him a spectacular godfather for Harry; he proves specially equipped to assist a child facing unique challenges, empathetic, and understanding of the Boy Who Lived.

Throughout the books we get comparisons between James and Harry, but Harry's upbringing more closely mirrors his godfather's. Both Sirius and Harry grew up in homes they hated and had bad relationships with their guardians, who clearly favored another child (Regulus/Dudley). They were continuously berated (by Mrs. Black and Mr. Dursley, respectively) and were outliers at home because of their position on the Muggle-wizard divide. Sirius was as un–Blackish as Harry is un–Dursleyish.

Mrs. Black's portrait shows the kind of verbal abuse Sirius suffered in a consistent diatribe. As Sirius explains, his brother Regulus "was younger than me ... and a much better son, as I was constantly reminded."[3] In "The Enduring Pain of Childhood Verbal Abuse," Peg Streep notes, "Verbal abuse and aggression doesn't take place in a vacuum—it poisons the family well and the springs that feed it. Adults who experienced verbal abuse in childhood often tell stories about siblings who joined in and bullied or scapegoated them."[4] This could easily describe both Sirius's life in Grimmauld Place and Harry's life at Privet Drive; Sirius's experience of verbal attacks came not solely from Mrs. Black but likely from the whole family. Kreacher regurgitates words Sirius's parents would have said while they were alive—words that compare Sirius unfavorably with his brother. The house-elf drops an array of them in *Deathly Hallows*:

> "Master Sirius ran away, good riddance, for he was a bad boy and broke my mistress's heart with his lawless ways. But Master Regulus had proper pride; he knew what was due to the name of Black and the dignity of his pure blood. For years he talked of the Dark Lord, who was going to bring the wizards out of hiding to rule the Muggles and the Muggle-borns ... and when he was sixteen years old, Master Regulus joined the Dark Lord. So proud, so proud, so happy to serve...."[5]

Harry and Sirius represented what their households hated. The Black family supported the purification of the wizarding race, which is unsurprising, since Mr. and Mrs. Black were second cousins. Padfoot's parents were a product of the insidious pure-blood habit of marrying within their own family.[6] Sirius was a defiant disappointment to this attitude, and his parent's inbred lineage was likely a point of shame and disgust for him.

Thankfully, unlike Harry, young Padfoot had family members to inspire him. Uncle Alphard Black left him an inheritance, earning him a blast off the family tree.[7] As Mrs. Black's brother,[8] he would have grown up in Grimmauld Place and perhaps empathized with Sirius's plight. Andromeda Tonks, also tapestry-blasted, married a Muggle-born, contrary to the Black family's pure-blood traditions. As Sirius's favorite older cousin, she was probably a big influence on him. Sirius somehow remained grounded despite the toxic environment.

The similarities between Sirius and Harry continue at Hogwarts. Sirius, like Harry, met his best friend on the Hogwarts Express and was sorted into Gryffindor. Sirius decorated his old bedroom to differentiate himself within the household like Hedwig, her cage, and the room's magical messiness differentiate Harry's bedroom from the rest of the house on Privet Drive.[9] Sirius spent holidays at his best friend's house rather than at home, while Harry often stays at The Burrow; Sirius had Snape as a Slytherin enemy like Harry has Malfoy.

Black's determination to be different started on the Hogwarts Express, where he voiced his wish to break the family tradition of being sorted into Slytherin.[10] In contrast, James Potter, his new best friend, had loving parents and a happy home. Harry sees James in Snape's memory on the Hogwarts Express and notes that James has the "indefinable air of being well cared for, even adored."[11] James grew up in a small town and wanted to follow his father's footsteps into Gryffindor. Ironically, this sounds like Ron. The Potters adopted Sirius, like the Weasleys adopt Harry. Black would have been conspicuously aware of his differences to James. He also would have understood how much Harry loved Ron and Hermione as "family."

Sirius chooses the path of love over the bigotry of his upbringing. Like Harry, he stands up for what he knows is right. His defiance is an act of tolerance and acceptance, and Padfoot's rejection of pure-blood doctrine and appreciation of Muggle culture manifest in his decorating:

> The room was spacious and must, once, have been handsome....
> The teenaged Sirius had plastered the walls with so many posters and pictures that little of the walls' silvery-gray silk was visible.... There were several large Gryffindor banners, faded scarlet and gold, just to underline his difference from all the rest of the Slytherin family. There were many pictures of Muggle motorcycles, and also (Harry had to admire Sirius's nerve) several posters of bikini-clad Muggle girls; Harry could tell that they were Muggles because they remained quite stationary within their pictures, faded smiles and glazed eyes frozen on the paper. This was in contrast to the only wizarding photograph on the walls, which was a picture of four Hogwarts students standing arm in arm, laughing at the camera.[12]

No wizard bands, no Quidditch teams. Sirius's magazine tastes were specific: Muggle technology over magic, Muggle women over witches,[13] Gryffindor over Slytherin—everything his parents despised. It's also a clue Sirius may have ventured into the Muggle world as a teenager—*Sports Illustrated: Swimsuit Edition* doesn't come via Owl Post.

His rebellious streak was fostered at school, along with his ego, thanks to his talent, intelligence, and good looks. Even Slughorn laments not collecting Padfoot.[14] Sirius had a cool reputation and sometimes got carried away. Similarly, The Chosen Godson has moments of inflated ego with his fame, Quidditch talent, and good looks (Romilda Vane, anyone?). At least Sirius recognized his propensity for being an "arrogant little berk" later in life.[15]

Harry and Sirius were not model students. Neither became prefect, and both spent time in detention. Harry comes across many of Padfoot's misdeeds and misuses of his power in *Half-Blood Prince* while doing detention himself, forced by Snape to rewrite the detention records of Sirius and James. Harry is unpleasantly surprised by what he reads. McGonagall also describes the double-edged sword of James and Sirius. Noting they were exceptionally bright but ringleaders of their little gang, Minerva wonders whether Hogwarts ever had a bigger pair of troublemakers. This is quite a reputation, only to be challenged by the notorious Weasley twins.[16]

Even though he flouted school rules, Sirius was a *good person* at heart, like his godson. Rosmerta's recollection highlights this: "'Do you know, I still have trouble believing it,' said Madam Rosmerta thoughtfully. 'Of all the people to go over to the Dark Side, Sirius Black was the last I'd have thought.... I mean, I remember him when he was a boy at Hogwarts. If you'd told me then what he was going to become, I'd have said you'd had too much mead.'"[17] Although Black was no angel, people saw his true nature underneath the mischief he managed. Characters who knew him at Hogwarts comment on his love of his friends. He treated James like a brother and was inseparable from his Marauder mates.

He accepted Lupin as a werewolf (without prejudice), becoming an illegal Animagus to support him. He and James even helped Peter with the process so the group could stay together on their adventures. This not only shows the remarkable bond between the group, but the level of talent, determination, and even cognitive control Sirius displayed at a young age to keep command of his "inner beast." Eric Saidel has argued that, in his dog form, Padfoot's mind is influenced by his canine body.[18] Sirius himself notes that when he transforms, his emotions as a dog are less complex.[19] However, he still has enough self-control, even in his fifth year, to (with James) manage a werewolf and influence Lupin's behavior while transformed.

Sirius shared life experiences with Harry, giving the two mutual understanding: starvation, poverty, isolation, his best friends losing faith in him, and an abject dislike of Dementors. Both understood what it was to be an outcast and to be unfairly labeled a traitor, liar, and dark wizard. A case in point is Harry's reaction to the scathing letter from Percy Weasley in *Order of the Phoenix*:

> And with a surge of sympathy for his godfather, Harry thought that Sirius was probably the only person he knew who could really understand how he felt at the moment, because Sirius was in the same situation. Nearly everyone in the Wizarding world thought Sirius a dangerous murderer and a great Voldemort supporter and he had had to live with that knowledge for fourteen years....[20]

Harry shared his feelings and fears with a handful of people, but Padfoot's empathy creates a vast difference in how he responds, and it leads Harry to actively seek his guidance.

In *Goblet of Fire*, Harry considers who to tell about his scar hurting. He figures Hermione would urge him to tell Dumbledore (and meanwhile consult a book). Ron might be bemused, albeit supportive.[21] Eventually, Harry realizes Sirius is the right choice. This is evident in *Order of the Phoenix*, when Harry is stuck at Privet Drive, desperate for news: "Sirius, at least, seemed to understand how Harry was feeling. Admittedly, his letters were just as empty of proper news as Ron and Hermione's, but at least they contained words of caution and consolation instead of tantalizing hints."[22] Sirius empathized because he had similar hardships, and shared experience gave him unique insights into his godson's mind. Black was physically distant from Harry, but he was emotionally close.

The Real House of Black

When Sirius moved away from Grimmauld Place, his life as a young adult started. With his own space and freedom, Black continued to make life choices which showed his love for those close to him and his determination to fight for what was right.

At sixteen Sirius ran away from home and stayed with the Potters, but at seventeen he took his own place and looked after himself with the gold Uncle Alphard left him.[23] Black started his last year at Hogwarts only a month before turning eighteen, so it's likely he acquired his own home while still in his sixth year. All his school holidays during seventh year, and some in sixth year, were spent independent of his biological family. He needed to fend for himself. Despite being "off the leash" in Padfoot's last school years, he was probably responsible. He was financially independent, didn't have a house-elf, and completed his education.

In June 1978, he left Hogwarts and worked for the Order of the Phoenix. He joined Albus Dumbledore in the war against Voldemort, becoming a full member of the Order before he had left his teen years behind him. Moody lists off members of the old Order when he shows Harry the photograph he has kept. Out of twenty-two members, nine died and two were tortured to insanity.[24] The survival rate was poor; standing up against Voldemort was a serious business.[25]

Sirius had only one career in his adult life: fighting as a soldier in a wizarding war. He dedicated his life to the Order and was willing to die to protect those he loved. As he says to Peter, "Lily and James only made you Secret-Keeper because I suggested it. ... I thought it was the perfect plan ... a bluff.... Voldemort would be sure to come after me...."[26] Sirius fully intended to have Voldemort come after him. How many wizards would use themselves as bait for the Dark Lord? In Lily's letter, she says Sirius missed Harry's first birthday because the Order came first. Black was a brave man who held clear priorities and values.

Serving the Order cost Sirius more than Harry's birthday celebration. It destroyed his trust in Remus. Believing Remus to be the spy must have been painful. After all, he'd become an illegal Animagus to support Lupin, and he covered up the fact that Lupin was a werewolf. Katherine Sas has suggested this could be due to latent werewolf prejudice.[27] Green also argues that Padfoot's mistrust may have sprung from Lupin's status as a werewolf or that he overlooked Peter Pettigrew's capacity to carry about the treachery.[28]

However, it is doubtful that any man so solid in his stance on blood lines (or who understood his best friend well enough to know better) would be Lycanthrophobic. Green's second point about overlooking Pettigrew is closer to the mark. Taken one step further, perhaps Sirius mistrusted Remus because the werewolf was clever and capable. Sure, Peter was someone he saw as weak and talentless. Remus, on the other hand, was sensible and smart, and Sirius *respected him*. More than disrespect for Peter, Sirius's conclusion displayed outright admiration of Lupin's capabilities. Moony suspected Padfoot as Voldemort's spy probably for the same reasons: he respected Sirius and everything he could do.

Sirius had James and Lily to rely on, but they were taken from him. Padfoot experienced the shock of seeing their bodies—realizing he had lost his only true family—and the horror of realizing his mistake in trusting Wormtail. He gave up his bike and his godson. He resigned himself to a terrible fate as a fugitive, knowing everyone would think he was Voldemort's spy. Padfoot was abandoned by everyone, despite his dedication to their common fight, despite having always hated dark wizards, and despite the fact that the man they accused him of betraying was his brother. Without so much as a trial under Veritaserum, he was sentenced to lifelong imprisonment in Azkaban.

Azkaban

When the Potters died in 1981, Sirius was sent to prison at the tender age of twenty-two, where he spent twelve years—a third of his lifespan. Much has been said about the effects of Azkaban on Sirius's mental health. Rowling claims the time away from the real world stunted his emotional growth.[29] But when you examine what Azkaban was really like, it's a miracle Sirius wasn't totally insane. If anything, Black surviving the tortures of Azkaban is a testament to his strength. But it may also be proof of his powerful capacity to love.

Fudge says Black was the most highly guarded prisoner, with Dementors outside his cell night and day. Harry describes the Dementors' effect this way: "The cold went deeper than his skin. It was inside his chest, it was inside his very heart...."[30] The gnawing, consistent cold the Dementors produce would have bitten Sirius worse than anyone. Dressed in ragged prison robes, the never-ending hypothermia alone would have been brutal. There were other physical stresses. The darkness the Dementors bring is pitch black, lights vanishing and candles extinguishing in their presence. Prisoner hygiene was also an issue. The *Daily Prophet* photo of Sirius that Stan Shunpike shows Harry reminds him of a vampire.[31] Black had waxy skin, filthy robes, and revolting, matted hair. He was malnourished, thin enough to slip through the prison bars. These were horrible conditions he faced alone.

Unlike most prison systems, solitary confinement in Azkaban seems to be constant, apart from rare official visits. Under the Mandela Rules of the United Nations (UN), such conditions—lack of food and water, continual darkness, and solitary confinement exceeding fifteen days—are all classified as torture.[32] Hagrid was sent to Azkaban in *Chamber of Secrets*. According to Harry, Hagrid's stint was two months,[33] which is four times longer than the UN's limit on solitary confinement. On the other hand, Sirius was incarcerated for around eleven years and seven months. That's 4,230 days, or around 282 times the UN's limit.

The snippets of information we receive about Azkaban describe a prison population driven insane, often to the point of death. Sirius says of Barty Crouch, Jr.'s, death, "He wasn't the only one.... Most go mad in there, and plenty stop eating in the end. They lose the will to live."[34] Hagrid recalls, "Yeh can' really remember who yeh are after a while. An' yeh can' see the point o' livin' at all. I used ter hope I'd jus' die in me sleep...."[35] Allow that to sink in for a moment. In Azkaban, Rubeus Hagrid—happy, tough, loveable Hagrid—lost his sense of self and hoped to die.

Green asserts Sirius was "just barely managing to hold on to his sanity" in Azkaban, but that is not true.[36] Fudge says, "I was shocked at how *normal* Black seemed. He spoke quite rationally to me. It was unnerving."[37] Black had enough strength and presence of mind to slip through the bars of the prison and swim through the freezing North Sea to freedom. In the face of such tremendous hardship, how did Sirius maintain his sanity?

When it was all too much, he transformed into a dog, but this was a short-term coping strategy. Being an Animagus was a *sign* that he had retained some power (a symptom), not the source of his strength (the cause). Hermione asks Sirius how he survived, and he says he doesn't know how he did it but guesses it is because he knew he was innocent. Knowing this fact helped keep him sane and gave him the ability to transform.[38]

However, textual evidence suggests it was not his innocence which helped him retain his sanity and his powers. Hagrid was also innocent. The gamekeeper knew he didn't open the Chamber of Secrets, and yet within two months he had already started to forget who he was. Innocence didn't protect Hagrid from the Dementors or protect Harry when he was attacked. Hagrid and Dumbledore both point out that Dementors care little for innocence. What made Sirius different?

Was it anger? After his betrayal and James and Lily's death, Sirius was determined to track down and kill Peter Pettigrew and seemed to relish the opportunity at the Shrieking Shack to commit the murder for which he was originally imprisoned. Revenge is not a happy thought. Dementors can't take it.[39] Green cites "the desire for revenge against Peter" as one of the factors fueling his escape.[40] But anger and bloodlust cannot fully explain Sirius's escape or Bellatrix would have managed it, along with Barty Crouch, Jr.—probably half of Azkaban held a grudge.[41]

If it wasn't innocence or anger, what was it? The night James and Lily died would have been Sirius's worst memory and likely the one he relived the most under the effect of the Dementors. This memory holds the key to Black's escape. That key was something unique to Sirius in that cold, fiendish place—something most prisoners (as dark wizards) were unlikely to have in their lives, let alone their worst memories. Dumbledore calls it the greatest power there is: love.

Reliving the events in Godric's Hollow over and over meant Sirius mourned for twelve long years. Grieving is an act of love and, as the *Harry Potter* series points out repeatedly, love is powerful. Readers see grief protect Harry from Voldemort's possession in the Ministry of Magic and again when he buries Dobby. Harry reflects, "Grief, it seemed, drove Voldemort out … though Dumbledore, of course, would have said that it was love…."[42] Love can hurt deeply and is not always a happy thought. Yet it is a proven protection against dark magic, as exemplified by Lily Potter. In the wizarding world, lack of love renders people powerless, like Merope Gaunt or Tonks. Love, even in the form of grief, provides protection from dark magic.

Finally, after twelve years of grief's protection, Padfoot's love for Harry gave him the strength to escape. His duty as a godfather called him to action because, as Sirius says, "I had to do something. I was the only one who knew Peter was still alive...."[43] When Black realized Harry was in danger from Wormtail, determination to save the boy he loved most in the world made him unstoppable. He says, "It was as if someone had lit a fire in my head, and the Dementors couldn't destroy it ... it wasn't a happy feeling ... it was an obsession ... but it gave me strength, it cleared my mind."[44] This love, in the form of a desperate need to protect Harry, helped him to do what no other prisoner in wizarding history had done. Sirius's ability to love and to grieve made him the first person to escape Azkaban by the sheer force of his own will.[45]

Dog on the Run

After escaping prison, Sirius spends two years on the run, mostly in ill health and homeless. Yet love keeps him going, driving him to support Harry at every turn, despite the risk to his own safety and freedom.

He lives for a year alone in the Forbidden Forest while he tries to catch Scabbers (and watch Harry play Quidditch), before showing himself at the Shrieking Shack. Then Sirius goes somewhere warm, sending Harry letters with big tropical birds. By the time he breaks into a wizarding home to speak to Harry in a fireplace, he looks better: cleaner, healthier. Unfortunately, the time Sirius spends looking after himself is short. He only lives in the tropics for three months before heading north, spending eight months on the run in the UK until he settles in the Hogsmeade cave. His health declines by the time Harry, Ron, and Hermione visit and discover he has been living off rats.[46]

Black must have been lonely, having little interaction with people and only Buckbeak for company. His social contact during this time is largely confined to letters. We know he writes to Harry and Dumbledore, but it's possible he wrote to Remus, too, as Lupin was the only other person who believed Sirius was innocent and was a close friend. Since it is never discussed in the book, we don't consider the possibility that these two Marauders may have contacted each other during Harry's fourth year, but it seems likely.

Black's homeless state ends with Voldemort's return. At the end of *Goblet of Fire*, Dumbledore issues Sirius instructions to contact the "old crowd": Mundungus, Mrs. Figg, and Remus. Albus says, "Lie low at Lupin's for a while. I will contact you there."[47]

For a short period, Padfoot lives at Moony's, which is the first time in years Sirius lived in a proper home. He had a roof over his head, warmth, comfort, hygiene, food, and most importantly, the affection and company of his best friend.[48] Soon after, the Order of the Phoenix re-forms, and Black returns to Grimmauld Place. But he's trapped there. It's dirty and disheveled and full of awful memories, reinforced by the painting of his screeching mother and Kreacher muttering insults. Sirius is miserable and confined. He is unkind to Kreacher, but being continually reminded that your parents hated you can't have been easy. Sirius says Kreacher was always foul, and potentially the house-elf had been similarly abusive during his childhood. At least at Grimmauld Place, Sirius occasionally has Remus for company, and it is the second time the Marauders live together.

However, while Sirius is trapped because of his fugitive status, Lupin leaves "to do mysterious work for the Order" on a regular basis.[49] Padfoot is unable to help with the war, and on Dumbledore's orders, he remains a talented, full-time soldier who nevertheless sits on the sidelines. Fred Weasley rubs salt in the wound when he confronts Sirius: "'Easy for you to say, stuck here!' bellowed Fred. 'I don't see you risking your neck!' The little color remaining in Sirius's face drained from it. He looked for a moment as though he would quite like to hit Fred…."[50] After his difficult childhood, the first wizarding war, Azkaban, and now being trapped back in Grimmauld Place unable to act, Sirius begins showing signs of emotional distress. It starts with moodiness after Harry's name was cleared at the Ministry hearing. When Nagini bites Arthur Weasley in the Department of Mysteries, it appears Sirius has been up late, drinking alone. Harry notices he is unshaven, still in his day clothes, and smells of stale drink.[51]

Over Christmas his mood improves. Harry can't remember Sirius being happier. He works tirelessly in the run-up to Christmas, cleaning and decorating. Sirius has company and motivation, ensuring everyone (especially Harry) has a good holiday, and supporting the Weasleys in a time of need. Christmas gives him purpose and the opportunity to spend quality time with Harry. It's little wonder he feels so alive again. It's also little wonder the end of Christmas sends him back into a depressed state.

It's ironic that Molly, with a reputation for losing her temper, critiques a traumatized man over his emotional control. No one calls Molly irrational when she screams, even when she's sending Howlers. Did Sirius experience Molly's yelling at her children as a painful reminder of his own mother's behavior? Mrs. Weasley isn't alone in her criticism of Sirius; scholars have also condemned his character. In "Interior/Exterior in the Harry Potter Series," Green litters her essay with admonishing remarks about Black's behavior, asserting that he is reckless and arrogant, endangering to others, casually callous, rash in decision-making, excessively self-important, unable to think through the ramifications of his actions (and thus, guilty of causing James's and Lily's deaths, no less), prone to adolescent cruelty and bouts of rage, and even Lycanthrophobic.[52]

This assessment seems unfairly harsh, but Padfoot does have some shortcomings. Those flaws and mistakes make him relatable and real. Black shows us we are not beautiful *despite* our imperfections, we are beautiful *because of them*. Imperfection makes us wonderfully human, and we all have light and dark inside of us. However, human fallibility is something Harry struggles with. He is judgmental of Dumbledore's past in *Deathly Hallows*, and Snape's worst memory makes him panic about who James Potter really was. Harry seems to see imperfection in a loved one as reason to doubt their true nature, but Black reminds him the world is not split into good people and Death Eaters, and people like James can grow and change.

Padfoot was not a model citizen in Grimmauld Place, but prior to this point, he lived in solitude with no need to exercise etiquette, tact, or emotional control. He's now a frustrated warrior, imprisoned again, craving company and affection. Sirius is moody, but considering the trauma he has suffered, he could be much worse. He doesn't appear to have night terrors, does not lash out angrily at loved ones, or engage in physical abuse. He's not self-harming or obviously battling addiction. Through his turmoil, his primary concern is providing comfort, protection, and a sense of family (which he never had himself) for those he loves.

Evidence that Sirius is a better person than either Molly Weasley or Green suggest shows in his treatment of the man he despises most: Severus Snape. Comprehending the depth of Sirius's hatred for "Snivelly" proves his level of control. Sirius and Snape were enemies at Hogwarts. The prank with Lupin and the bullying in Snape's worst memory were not isolated incidents; harassment was systemic on both sides. Sirius says Snape "never lost an opportunity to curse James, so you couldn't really expect James to take that lying down, could you?"[53] Snape was habitually nasty toward James, Lupin, and anyone else he and his Death Eater pals singled out at Hogwarts. He called Lily, whom he loved, "Mudblood." As a teacher, he continued bullying with vulnerable students: Neville, Harry, Hermione. He forces Lupin out of his job at Hogwarts and sneers at Tonks over her new Patronus. He continually taunts Sirius about being trapped in Grimmauld Place.

Asking Sirius to be kind to Snape is like asking Ron to stop hating Malfoy when Draco bullies Harry. We think of Ron as a loyal and good best friend. We should extend Sirius the same courtesy. Don't forget: Severus wasn't just some awkward loner at Hogwarts. He hung around Voldemort's followers; he wanted to be a Death Eater and chose the dark path.

However, the animosity runs much deeper than bullying or Snape's status as a former Death Eater. The two men mutually blame each other for the death of the Potters. Snape loved Lily, and the entire wizarding community thinks Black betrayed her. Snape reveals his feelings in the Shrieking Shack in *Prisoner of Azkaban* when he says, "Vengeance is very sweet … how I hoped I would be the one to catch you."[54] It's not revenge for a prank Snape desires, but for causing the death of the woman he loved. Even once the Order re-formed, Severus would probably still blame Sirius for Lily's death, because Sirius persuaded the Potters to change to Peter as a Secret Keeper. Likewise, if Black had known Snape overheard the prophecy, he would have been livid (like Harry) and blamed Snape for James's death.

Members of the Order don't understand why Dumbledore trusts Snape and don't appear to know Severus still loved Lily. However, Lupin gives us the first clue the Marauders could have been aware of the complex nature of the James-Lily-Severus triangle at school. Lupin says Snape especially disliked James: "Jealous, I think, of James's talent on the Quidditch field."[55] That little pause ("I think") before Lupin explains the source of Snape's jealousy hints that perhaps he was aware of Snape's deeper feelings for Lily and was shielding Harry from the truth. Having never expressed interest in Quidditch, Snape would not have resented James for his flying abilities. On the other hand, in Snape's memories, we learn the Gryffindors knew Severus was waiting outside the portrait hole to apologize for calling Lily "Mudblood," suggesting they may have known how he felt about her. When Severus confronts Lily about James liking her, there is a point where the intensity of Snape's gaze makes her blush.

Readers can deduce Snape had a crush on Lily from a handful of memories, so it's possible the Marauders reached the same conclusion. They may not have realized Snape still loved her years later, but they might have understood why he was jealous of James. If Sirius knew Snape both fancied Lily and overheard the prophecy, he may have drawn dangerous conclusions from these inferences, perhaps assuming Snively betrayed the Potters in a state of jealousy.

But Snape's worst sin was his mistreatment of Harry: tormenting a child over a father who had been dead for years, failing Harry in Potions, unfairly taking points off him, giving him detention, ejecting him from vital Occlumency lessons. Even Dumbledore acknowledges Snape's continuing hatred of James, telling Harry, "some wounds run too deep for the healing. I thought Professor Snape could overcome his feelings about your father—I was wrong."[56]

Sirius must have been irately conscious of Snape's lingering jealousy. The fight between them in the Grimmauld Place kitchen is a testament to

Padfoot's temper control. Sirius takes several snide hits about not being useful for the Order, and matters only escalate when Snape digs at Harry, saying he is like James and "so arrogant that criticism simply bounces off him."[57] Black tolerates the taunts aimed at himself, only drawing his wand when Severus directs his venom at the Potters.

Sas has noted that Sirius considers the school-yard prank on Snape to be "fair dues" for Snape hoping to get the Marauders expelled.[58] However, Sirius's hardened attitude in the retelling of this story isn't a by-product of his flippancy towards the act itself. Sirius likely knows how terrible it would have been if Snape had met Lupin at the end of that tunnel. What we are hearing in Padfoot's language is an expression of the highly painful emotions that talking about Snape brings up in him. His tone is less reflective of a wish to cause harm to Snape and more of the emotional harm Snape has caused to Sirius and his loved ones.

The quarrel between Sirius and Snape is not a schoolyard grudge. It's a deep and complex animosity over the death of people they both loved dearly—and a boy with his mother's eyes who resembles his father so much that just looking at him brings back painful memories. Knowing this, these conflicts play out as deftly managed by Sirius, even in the face of Snape's goading comments. He shows his commitment to Harry and remarkable strength when faced with a painful past, his enemies, and further confinement.

The Boy Who Loved

When I think of Sirius, I don't think about his pain, flaws, or fleas. I think about his love for Harry. Black is a career soldier, smart and brave. He knows the consequences of standing against Voldemort and is prepared to face death. However, while he may risk his own life, his actions in looking after Harry are far from reckless.

Reckless: the word comes up time after time when people talk about Sirius. Padfoot seems to be the yardstick for recklessness in the collective mind of the fandom.[59] Black's short but sweet role as Harry's godfather provides contradictory evidence. We only see Sirius's godparenting in the fourth and fifth books, but in that limited timeframe we see a steady stream of loving and sensible guardianship.

When Dumbledore asks Harry to recount facing Voldemort in the graveyard of *Goblet of Fire*, he summons Sirius, the one Albus thought Harry needed most. Sirius had written to Harry through the year, advised, encouraged, and supported him, answering every one of Harry's requests for help. He had visited via fireplaces, risking capture by the Ministry.

Sirius lived in a cave and *ate rats* to be near Harry. He wrote daily leading up to the third task, telling Harry to behave and stay safe. Harry makes fun of it, questioning the hypocrisy of Sirius asking him to be a good boy.

During *Order of the Phoenix*, Sirius takes a different but warranted approach. He encourages Harry to start Dumbledore's Army, not caring about Umbridge; it's the Dark Lord who poses the biggest threat to his godson. However, at the start of the book, he cautions Harry, "*Keep your nose clean and everything will be OK.... Be careful and don't do anything rash.*"[60] When Harry faces the Ministry hearing, Sirius maturely advises him not to lose his temper, be polite, and stick to the facts. Black is annoyed Snape is teaching Harry Occlumency, but he is livid when Snape stops teaching him, knowing it is ultimately best for Harry.

Sirius sends Harry several gifts, each purposeful and useful. The Firebolt comes when the Nimbus 2000 breaks. Pigwidgeon arrives with permission for Harry to visit Hogsmeade, solving Harry's and Ron's woes in one go. In *Goblet of Fire*, Padfoot sends Harry a penknife with attachments to unlock any lock and undo any knot.[61] Perhaps Sirius was enabling Harry to sneak out of Privet Drive without alerting the Ministry by unlocking his room door without magic. Sirius (with Lupin) gives Harry a set of books in his fifth year to help with Dumbledore's Army, books with moving color illustrations.[62] Then there's the mirror Harry foolishly neglects, since it was the answer to Harry's communication problems. Even when broken, it continues helping him in the seventh book.

Lastly, in his will, Sirius leaves Harry everything he owns, including Grimmauld Place. He leaves not one scrap to anyone else—not Lupin, the Tonks family, or the Weasleys. Grimmauld Place was a safe haven, allowing Harry to discover the identity of R.A.B., Lily's letter, and Kreacher's secrets. This was the final gift that kept on giving.

Early in *Order of the Phoenix*, when Molly and Sirius argue in the Grimmauld Place kitchen, they're not fighting over what Harry should know. They're arguing over Sirius's fitness as a godfather and his right to make decisions on Harry's behalf. Mrs. Weasley says, "It's not down to you to decide what's good for Harry!"[63] The fight hits a crescendo (thankfully diffused by Remus) when Molly positions herself as Harry's best source of support and goads Sirius by reminding him he's been absent from Harry's life while in Azkaban. Those words hurt Sirius, palpably.[64]

Besides, Molly didn't raise Harry, Petunia did. Mrs. Weasley's times with him were brief and their correspondence limited to Christmas and Easter. She overestimates her position because she underestimates the effort Sirius invested in his relationship with Harry. Sorry, Molly, but even Kreacher could see how close Sirius and Harry had become. Dumbledore tells Harry that when Kreacher left Grimmauld Place, he told Narcissa "that the person Sirius cared most about in the world was you"[65] and that Harry had come to see his godfather as a mixture of father and brother.

Sirius clearly wants to be a part of Harry's life, evidenced by his going to King's Cross as Snuffles. Green says this act is a result of overconfidence,[66] but it is instead a result of his priorities. Padfoot is willing to take risks to live his life with love. He is in the middle of a wizarding war with the most dangerous dark wizard of all time. His godson is marked for death. So what if the Malfoys recognize him! So what if he gets caught! This could be his only chance to do something poor James never had the opportunity to do: see Harry off to Hogwarts.

Padfoot's final act as a godfather reveals the depths of his love and his willingness to make the ultimate sacrifice. Harry comprehends Black's dedication when his godfather disappears through the veil at the Ministry and does not return: "But some part of him realized, even as he fought to break free from Lupin, that Sirius had never kept him waiting before…. Sirius had risked everything, always, to see Harry, to help him."[67] Since Voldemort first threatened the boy, Sirius had accepted the responsibility to protect Harry and to face death. That's why James and Lily chose him as godfather: he loved Harry Potter so much, he was willing to give his life for him.

Many people, faced with Sirius's trauma, would struggle to hold their heads as high. He was a dedicated fighter, loyal friend, devoted godfather, and was willing to sacrifice himself, just like his godson. He was an exceptional wizard and an exceptional person, full of the magic we call love. Padfoot is proof that imperfections don't make you less; they make you richer, more complex, and *beautifully human*.

Finally, a thought for you, the reader. When life seems colder than Azkaban, know that you, too, wield this powerful magic. We can love in the darkest of times, if we only remember to turn on the light in our hearts. Keep loving, and don't let the Muggles get you down.

Notes

1. Amy M. Green, "Interior/Exterior in the Harry Potter Series: Duality Expressed in Sirius Black and Remus Lupin," *Papers on Language & Literature* 44, no. 1 (Winter 2008): 87–108, 95.

2. The Wizarding World Team, "7 of our favourite Sirius Black moments," *Wizarding World*, November 3, 2022, https://www.wizardingworld.com/features/7-of-our-favourite-sirius-black-moments.

3. J.K. Rowling, *Harry Potter and the Order of the Phoenix* (New York: Scholastic, 2003), 112.

4. Peg Streep, "The Enduring Pain of Childhood Verbal Abuse," *Psychology Today*, November 14, 2016, https://www.psychologytoday.com/au/blog/tech-support/201611/the-enduring-pain-childhood-verbal-abuse.

5. J.K. Rowling, *Harry Potter and the Deathly Hallows* (New York: Scholastic, 2007), 193.

6. J.K. Rowling, "The Noble and Most Ancient House of Black," hand-drawn tree Rowling donated to Book Aid International in January of 2006 and auctioned February 22, 2006, https://www.hp-lexicon.org/source/other-canon/bft/. The original image has since been published in *Harry Potter Film Wizardry* and can be seen here: https://i.imgur.com/GbPzUmg.jpg.

7. Rowling, *Order of the Phoenix*, 111.

8. As per the Black family tree, both Sirius' mother, Walburga Black, and his father, Orion Black, had the Black surname when they married. Alphard Black is Walburga Black's younger brother, and it was through this side that the family inheritance was passed down to Sirius. As the oldest sibling, Walburga Black inherited Grimmauld Place, but clearly Alphard also had some of the wealth, which he bequeathed to Sirius. Alphard never married or had children, so it is possible that he rejected the pure-blood doctrine and the practice of inbreeding as Sirius did. His name "solitary one" suggests he made a conscious choice to remain childless and single. Rowling, "The Noble and Most Ancient House of Black."

9. Ibid., 51.

10. Rowling, *Deathly Hallows*, 671.

11. Ibid.

12. Rowling, *Deathly Hallows*, 178–179.

13. Sirius's eye for Muggle girls may have been a manifestation of his distaste for the pure-blood habit of marrying within the family. In addition to encouraging his overt Mugglephilia, the fact that his parents were second cousins may have given him concern that were he to have a child with a witch, this would lead to genetic consequences for any of his offspring (in a macabre echo of Remus fearing to pass on his Lycanthropy to Teddy). Hence, Sirius may have actively (either consciously or unconsciously) sought out Muggle partners to ensure that the risk of inbreeding was mitigated as far as possible.

14. J.K. Rowling, *Harry Potter and the Half-Blood Prince* (New York: Scholastic, 2005), 70.

15. Rowling, *Order of the Phoenix*, 670.

16. J.K. Rowling, *Harry Potter and the Prisoner of Azkaban* (New York: Scholastic, 1999), 204.

17. Ibid., 203.

18. Eric Saidel, "Sirius Black: Man or Dog?" *The Ultimate Harry Potter and Philosophy: Hogwarts for Muggles* (Hoboken: John Wiley & Sons, 2010), 29.

19. Rowling, *Prisoner of Azkaban*, 317.

20. Rowling, *Order of the Phoenix*, 300.

21. J.K. Rowling, *Harry Potter and the Goblet of Fire* (New York: Scholastic, 2000), 21–22.

22. Rowling, *Order of the Phoenix*, 9.

23. Ibid., 111.

24. Ibid., 173–174.

25. Undoubtedly, participating in a wizarding war left as much trauma as any of the other suffering Sirius had endured up to this point—or after it. We see the impacts of war manifest in Mad-Eye Moody (physically and mentally), but we don't often consider how it might have affected some of the other characters.

26. Rowling, *Prisoner of Azkaban*, 369.

27. Katherine Sas, "A Sense of Darker Perspective: How the Marauders Convey Tolkien's 'Impression of Depth' in Prisoner of Azkaban," *Mythlore* 38, no. 1 (Fall/Winter 2019), 171.

28. Green, "Interior/Exterior in the Harry Potter Series," 94.

29. Melissa Anelli and Emerson Spartz, "The Leaky Cauldron and MuggleNet interview Joanne Kathleen Rowling: Part Two," *The Leaky Cauldron*, July 16, 2005, http://www.accio-quote.org/articles/2005/0705-tlc_mugglenet-anelli-2.htm. It could be argued that the psychological signs Sirius displays, such as mood swings, guilt, sadness, irritability,

outbursts of anger, and substance use, actually point towards PTSD and not emotional immaturity. Sirius lacks some of the key signs of emotional immaturity, such as chronic narcissism (thinking you have no faults), lack of self-reflection, lack of guilt or shame, and a disregard for the safety and well-being of others. Rowling perhaps has conflated emotional immaturity and PTSD, as there are some overlapping symptoms.
    30. Rowling, *Prisoner of Azkaban*, 83.
    31. *Ibid*. For more on vampiric imagery and allusions in *Harry Potter*, see Beatrice Groves's essay in this volume.
    32. United Nations, *Standard Minimum Rules for the Treatment of Prisoners (the Nelson Mandela Rules) Rules,* A/RES/70/175 (January 8, 2016), https://undocs.org/A/RES/70/175, 16–17.
    33. Rowling, *Prisoner of Azkaban*, 40.
    34. Rowling, *Goblet of Fire*, 529.
    35. Rowling, *Prisoner of Azkaban*, 221.
    36. Green, "Interior/Exterior in the Harry Potter Series," 94.
    37. Rowling, *Prisoner of Azkaban*, 209.
    38. *Ibid.*, 371.
    39. *Ibid.*
    40. Green, "Interior/Exterior in the Harry Potter Series," 94.
    41. Just because Black *says* innocence and revenge helped him escape doesn't make him correct. He is still giving an opinion. Much of what we know about characters in the *Potter* saga is hearsay, opinion, speculation, and conjecture from the characters themselves. Remember, we are generally looking at life through Harry's lens of what he hears from others, and not at verified, diegetic *fact*. Much like witness testimony in a court trial, we have to question each and every character, even those who are trustworthy, because they are still viewing events from their own perspective; what they know is not always the complete picture.
    42. Rowling, *Deathly Hallows*, 478.
    43. Rowling, *Prisoner of Azkaban*, 371.
    44. *Ibid.*, 372.
    45. Of course, Barty Crouch, Jr., was out of Azkaban before Sirius escaped, but Barty was "sprung" (smuggled out by his parents) and did not escape by his own volition. He needed outside help. Several Death Eaters also fled Azkaban, but like Barty Crouch, Jr., they were also sprung, in this instance by means of a mass jail-break, and did not leave under their own steam either. Sirius was the only one to pull off an actual escape on his own, without any external assistance.
    46. We don't often consider the effects of homelessness and poor physical health on Sirius's mental health, because we figure at least he's better off than he was in Azkaban. But by the time you get to this point, he's endured an abusive childhood, one wizarding war, the loss of loved ones, the torture of Azkaban, exile, and homelessness.
    47. Rowling, *Goblet of Fire*, 713.
    48. While Lupin and Black may have believed each other to be Voldemort's spy, there is a clue that Remus may have still been involved in Sirius's affairs after he was incarcerated: that is, the appearance of Lily's letter in Padfoot's room at Grimmauld Place. According to Sirius's timeline, the letter would have been sent to Sirius while he was living on his own and should not have been at Grimmauld Place at all. The property he lived in alone may have been auctioned off while he was in jail (on the assumption he was never getting out). If that is the case, someone would have had to clear out Sirius's belongings—someone who cared enough to save the letter and return it to him after the Order was re-formed. I suspect Remus. In all probability, the appearance of Lily's letter at the wrong residence is likely to be a plot hole, but I hope fanfic writers will one day do something amazing with it.
    49. Rowling, *Order of the Phoenix*, 118.
    50. *Ibid.*, 477.
    51. *Ibid.*, 475.
    52. Green, "Interior/Exterior in the Harry Potter Series," 94.
    53. Rowling, *Order of the Phoenix*, 671.

54. Rowling, *Prisoner of Azkaban*, 360.
55. Ibid., 357.
56. Rowling, *Order of the Phoenix*, 833.
57. Ibid., 520.
58. Sas, "A Sense of Darker Perspective," 171.
59. Hilary Elizabeth, "Harry Potter: 10 Characters More Reckless Than Sirius Black," *Screenrant*, November 5, 2019, https://screenrant.com/harry-potter-characters-more-reckless-than-sirius-black/.
60. Rowling, *Order of the Phoenix*, 9.
61. Rowling, *Goblet of Fire*, 410. On the Christian significance of this gift, see Emily Strand's essay in this volume.
62. Rowling, *Order of the Phoenix*, 501.
63. Ibid., 88.
64. When you remove all the exposition about Voldemort and Harry's musings from that scene, it clearly boils down to an argument about Sirius's fitness as a godfather. Molly says she's as "good as" Harry's mother and questions who else Harry has to rely on. Even Lupin, though he doesn't want the situation to escalate, clearly takes Black's side on this point. Notably, not a soul steps up to help Molly, not even her own husband. If both Arthur and Remus agree telling Harry information is an acceptable course of action, that speaks to the fact that Sirius is not being reckless here.
65. Ibid., 831.
66. Green, "Interior/Exterior in the Harry Potter Series," 92–97.
67. Rowling, *Order of the Phoenix*, 808.

The Weasley Witches
From Snitches to Stitches to "Not-My-Daughter-You-Bitches"

Louise M. Freeman

Molly and Ginny Weasley exist in a "testosterone zone," outnumbered by men in the family, seven to two. Unsurprisingly, they represent two female archetypes identified by Jungian psychoanalyst Toni Wolff. Ginny begins the series as an awestruck child in *Sorcerer's Stone* and Harry's resident victim-needing-rescue in *Chamber of Secrets*. However, she matures into an archetypal Amazon as she both gains sexual agency and embraces her male aspect or animus. Molly personifies both positive and negative aspects of Wolff's Mother archetype: fertile, nurturing, comforting, and fiercely but sometimes overly protective. At the Battle of Hogwarts, the two women swap roles as Molly defeats Bellatrix LeStrange, and Ginny offers motherly comfort to an injured student. Ginny's and Molly's archetypal complexity is evidence that *Harry Potter*'s women characters, while outnumbered and less prominent than men, are strong, well-developed, and equally important players in the overarching saga.

Toni Wolff and the Feminine Archetypes

In 1934, Toni Wolff, past patient, collaborator, and mistress of Carl Jung, presented an innovative model of the female psyche to the Zürich Psychology Club, over which she presided as president. Wolff's model, which would be published as the 1951 essay *Structural Forms of the Feminine Psyche*, proposed four basic female archetypes, arranged on crossing axes. Two types, Mother and Hetaira (or Lover), are paired on opposite ends of the "personally related" domain. These structural forms prioritize relationships with other individuals: the Mother's children and the

Hetaira's sexual partner. The Amazon and the Medial (or Wise) woman, both of whom relate to wider society more than individuals, reside on the "impersonally related" axis. According to Jungian therapist Peggy Vermeesch, "The Amazon relates first and foremost to the objective cultural values of her time (the collective consciousness), whereas the Medial woman's focus is primarily on any phenomena related to the collective unconscious."[1] Wolff believed that, while women's personalities included aspects of all four structural forms, each has a dominant archetype whose understanding is key to "self-knowledge and self-realization of the modern woman."[2] Archetypes are also useful for analyzing literary characters. In *Harry Potter*, the Amazon and Mother archetypes are best applied respectively to Ginny and Molly Weasley.

"I prefer goal-scoring to Seeking anyway"[3]

Readers have long debated Ginny Weasley's strength and value as a character. While acknowledging her as a "gifted and spirited witch," Gwendolyn Limbach considers Ginny "defined by her relationship to Harry instead of on her own terms and in her own right" and "forced to subjugate her agency in service of Harry's desires."[4] Isabella Goncea and Denise Greenwood claim "Ginny only has a few moments of wisdom and wit until she is pushed aside because Harry wants to protect her from outside dangers."[5] In contrast, Aurélie Lacassagne says, "Ginny is definitively a better wizard than her brothers,"[6] while Jeanne Hoeker LaHaie considers her "brave, smart, nurturing and capable": one of several girls that were "nearly unique in fantasy fiction, which tended to rely almost exclusively on male characters."[7]

Ginny's unusual position in the narrative accounts for the lack of consensus. Sterling Hutchinson, Vivek Datla, and Max Louwerse used computer analysis of the Harry Potter texts to test the hypotheses that (1) social connectedness of characters can be inferred from the proximities of the mentions of their names and (2) the most socially connected characters are mentioned most frequently. The researchers eliminated Ginny from analysis as a data outlier; she had a relatively high number of observed direct relationships (19) but far fewer textual mentions (792) compared to similarly connected characters like Ron (17 relationships, 9144 mentions) and Dumbledore (16 relationships, 3981 mentions).[8] Typically in young adult fiction, the male protagonist's love interest is, if not the second lead character, at least the most prominent female. In *Harry Potter*, Hermione is the female lead. With teenage romances secondary to the Harry, Ron, and Hermione friendship, Ginny's role is necessarily limited.

Ginny changes drastically over the series. In *Sorcerer's Stone*, she does little more than turn up at King's Cross, cling to her mother's hand, whine, and point. Ginny figures prominently in *Chamber of Secrets*, but in the superficially passive role of Gothic maiden rescued from the villain's dungeon by the hero.[9] Laura Măcineanu calls Ginny "a complex character in the series who evolves from being perceived as a damsel in distress to the archetype of the Amazon."[10] Surprisingly, the sobbing child at book's end grows into a popular romantic interest, Quidditch champion, Bat-Bogey hex expert, and student resistance leader.

During her first year at Hogwarts, Ginny feels stigmatized by her family's poverty and her secondhand supplies. Smitten with Harry, she embarrasses herself by sending a singing Valentine. Confiding in her diary, Ginny is possessed by Tom Riddle's soul fragment and used as his pawn, nearly resulting in her death. The trauma of the encounter gives her a connection to Harry shared by no other character. As John Granger argues, Harry himself functions as a type of Gothic heroine, with similarities to both Jane Eyre and *Dracula*'s Mina Harker. Rather than diminishing her as a character, Ginny's endangerment and rescue from the Chamber of Secrets "marks her as Harry's soul mate and fellow Gothic romance heroine."[11]

Unlike in the typical damsel-in-distress tale, Ginny's rescue does not end her story or spark immediate romance with the hero. Instead, Ginny experiences four more books of character growth and two other dating relationships before she wins Harry's heart. While Harry's adventure continues with Ron and Hermione, Ginny is left to mature behind the scenes, with limited presence in the third and fourth books.

Ginny is nearly as absent from *Prisoner of Azkaban* as she was from *Sorcerer's Stone*, with only eighteen mentions. Her most important scene is the Dementor attack on the Hogwarts Express; her reaction is stronger than any other character's, save Harry: trembling and "looking nearly as bad as Harry felt."[12] Ginny's vulnerability, like Harry's, is presumably the result of her trauma with Voldemort. Ginny's only other significant action in Book Three is to repeat a bit of her foolishness from Valentine's Day of *Chamber of Secrets*, by sending Harry a shrilly singing get-well card.

Goblet of Fire is the turning point of the ring-structured series[13]; accordingly, Ginny experiences a significant, though underappreciated, transition at the mid-year Yule Ball. After a two-year unrequited crush, she misses a golden opportunity when Harry and Ron need dates:

> "This is getting stupid. Ginny, you can go with Harry, and I'll just—"
> "I can't," said Ginny... "I'm going with—with Neville. He asked me when Hermione said no, and I thought ... well ... I'm not going to be able to go otherwise, I'm not in fourth year." She looked extremely miserable.[14]

Though brief, this scene is key to Ginny's development. For the first time, she is acknowledged as a potential romantic partner.[15] She is taking Hermione's advice to date others, the better to relax around Harry. Finally, although clearly devastated at her lost opportunity, Ginny never considers dumping Neville.[16] By keeping her word, she demonstrates the moral fortitude necessary to eventually become Harry's love interest.

At the ball, Ginny meets Michael Corner, who becomes her first real boyfriend. Thus, attending the Yule Ball with Neville initiates Ginny's independent sexual agency. Ginny's relationships with Michael, and later Dean Thomas, are consistent with Wolff's Amazon, described as

> independent and self-contained in the positive meaning of the term. She is independent of the male, because her development is not based upon a psychological relationship to him.... Her interest is directed towards objective achievements which she wants to accomplish herself. To be the wife of a distinguished man means nothing to her; she strives to win the laurels herself. The great sportswomen and travellers belong to this category.[17]

Ginny enjoys dating and, to Ron's dismay, snogging, but does not depend on such activities for fulfillment. She ends both relationships because the boy's behavior was unacceptable to her. She chooses her sport over Michael, saying, "He didn't like Gryffindor beating Ravenclaw at Quidditch and got really sulky, so I ditched him."[18] She resents Dean's efforts to help her through the Gryffindor portal. By dating others, strictly on her own terms, Ginny becomes "independent from, and simultaneously irresistible to, Harry."[19] For Harry, Ginny's Amazonian autonomy is at the heart of her attractiveness.

Embracing the Animus in Dumbledore's Army

In an essay footnote, Wolff endorsed the concept of women's "*animus* problem," stating that it "concerns all women in the same way."[20] Emma Jung described this phenomenon in an essay presented to the Zürich Psychology Club in 1931: "A certain sum of masculine spirit has ripened in women's consciousness and must find its place and effectiveness in her personality. To learn to know these factors, to coordinate them so that they can play their part in a meaningful way, is an important part of the *animus* problem."[21] Ginny's psychological growth in Books Five and Six involves embracing her animus and expressing more typically male aspects of her personality. At Christmas in *Order of the Phoenix*, Ginny asserts herself, angrily berating Harry for his self-pity, reminding him coolly of her own possession experience, and assuring Harry that his connection to Voldemort is different. She joins the Quidditch team, initially substituting for

Harry as Seeker, but eventually pursuing her own goals—pun intended—as a Chaser. Her athleticism surprises her rather sexist brothers, who don't understand how she developed her skills, since they had always excluded her from their Quidditch games.

> "She's been breaking into your broom shed in the garden since the age of six and taking each of your brooms out in turn when you weren't looking," said Hermione....
> "Oh," said George, looking mildly impressed. "Well—that'd explain it."[22]

Ginny increasingly identifies with the twins, proving more prankster than prefect. In *Order of the Phoenix,* she joins their celebratory dance at Harry's acquittal and carries on their Umbridge-baiting after they leave Hogwarts. In *Half-Blood Prince,* she co-claims credit for flinging Christmas dinner parsnips at Percy. Her spunk earns respect: "'Size is no guarantee of power,' said George. 'Look at Ginny.... You've never been on the receiving end of one of her Bat-Bogey Hexes, have you?'"[23] Ginny completes her evolution to Amazon by, like Harry, overcoming her early trauma with Voldemort and joining the opposition to his reign, as eager to defeat him as the Trio. Ginny names Harry's student group "Dumbledore's Army" as an alternative to Cho's blander "Defense Association." She understands that Harry's sessions go beyond OWL scores; the members' destiny is combat. Ginny is convincing enough as a student soldier that the twins apparently forget she is underage and bring her to the Battle of Hogwarts.

Ginny's eagerness to fight sparks clashes with Molly. At Grimmauld Place, Ginny begs to learn about Order of the Phoenix activities and, when forbidden, goes "raging and storming at her mother all the way up the stairs."[24] Arguing to remain at the Battle of Hogwarts, Ginny evokes the organizational name that she chose:

> "You're underage!" Mrs. Weasley shouted at her daughter... "I won't permit it! The boys, yes, but you, you've got to go home!"
> "I won't!" Ginny's hair flew as she pulled her arm out of her mother's grip. "I'm in Dumbledore's Army—"
> "A teenagers' gang!"
> "A teenagers' gang that's about to take him on, which no one else has dared to do!" said Fred.[25]

Ginny gets her way. Initially agreeing to remain in the Room of Requirement, she vacates it at first opportunity, running after Tonks to join the battle and ignoring Harry's insistence that she return. Neither Harry's place as her love interest nor his status as the Chosen One stop her from fighting. Far from yielding exclusively to Harry's desires, Ginny embodies the Amazon warrior by continuing to pursue her own aims.

"*Honestly, woman, you call yourself our mother?*"[26]

Molly Weasley is called "the living exemplar of maternal love,"[27] and "the most archetypal motherly character of the series."[28] Wolff describes the Mother positively as "motherly cherishing and nursing, helping, charitable, teaching."[29] Mother archetypes embody fertility; Molly's brood of seven gives her twice as many children as any other mother in the series. A few families, such as the Dumbledores, have three offspring but, of the "Big Seven"[30] most prominent students, five—Harry, Hermione, Neville, Luna, and Draco—are only children.[31]

Despite limited financial resources, Molly "personifies the ideal-type of othermother who takes care of the children of her community,"[32] caring for Hermione at times, along with Harry. Although James Thomas argues that her appearance at the Triwizard Tournament marks her *de facto* adoption of Harry as a seventh son,[33] she begins her mothering at their first King's Cross encounter. Harry is panicked, unable to find Platform Nine and Three-Quarters, when he has a fortuitous encounter with a red-haired family.

> "Now, what's the platform number?" said the boys' mother.
> "Nine and three-quarters!" piped a small girl ... holding her hand. "Mum, can't I go...."
> "You're not old enough, Ginny, now be quiet."[34]

Harry gets the needed information from Mrs. Weasley, but the meeting may not have been coincidental. A pureblood witch who has delivered children to the Hogwarts Express for nine consecutive years is unlikely to suddenly forget the platform number. Either Molly is trying to distract tearful Ginny,[35] or she has noticed the confused child's trunk and owl and speaks intentionally to offer help. While her sons excitedly chatter about the famous scar, and Ginny begs to look, Molly muses, "Poor *dear*—no wonder he was alone, I wondered,"[36] and forbids them to finger-point or query.

Henceforth, Molly treats Harry as family, sending him gifts and hosting him at the Burrow on summers and holidays. She shops for school supplies, feeds him generously, and celebrates his birthday. She worries about his maltreatment at Privet Drive; even while berating her sons for their reckless Ford Anglia rescue, she tells Harry that she and Arthur were making plans to collect him themselves. Standing in for Harry's parents at the Triwizard Tournament, Molly comforts him after the graveyard ordeal: "Mrs. Weasley set the potion down on the bedside cabinet, bent down, and put her arms around Harry. He had no memory of ever being hugged like this, as though by a mother. The full weight of everything he had seen that night seemed to fall in upon him as Mrs. Weasley held him to her."[37] Molly challenges Sirius's authority as godfather when she thinks he is being reckless:

> "Dumbledore must have had his reasons for not wanting Harry to know too much, and speaking as someone who has got Harry's best interests at heart—"
> "He's not your son," said Sirius quietly.
> "He's as good as," said Mrs. Weasley fiercely.[38]

Molly embodies the Mother archetype, instinctively reacting to anyone "in need of protection, in danger, or [who] must be tended, cared for and assisted."[39] The twins tease her with "Honestly, woman, you call yourself our mother?"[40] Both Wolff and the wider wizard community could affirm this statement, without irony or question.

One negative aspect of Wolff's Mother is overprotectiveness. In accordance, Molly occasionally demonstrates "anxious nursing and tutelage of the object when the latter never needed it or no longer needs it, lack of confidence in the latter's strength and independence, and interference with its development."[41] In *Order of the Phoenix*, Molly tries to stop all the students, including adults Fred and George, from hearing news from the Order. In *Deathly Hallows*, though Arthur and Lupin accept the necessity of the Trio's secret mission, Molly does not.

> "You're barely of age, any of you! It's utter nonsense, if Dumbledore needed work doing, he had the whole Order at his command! Harry, you must have misunderstood him. Probably he was telling you something he wanted done, and you took it to mean that he wanted you—"
> "I didn't misunderstand," said Harry flatly. "It's got to be me."[42]

Molly tries to separate the Trio to prevent their planning. Consequently, they are caught off-guard when the Death Eaters attack the wedding. Only Hermione's near-supernatural foresight and magically extended beaded bag prevent disaster. Molly's archetypal protectiveness is admirable, but its excess risks what Wolff calls the worst outcome: "infecting" the mother-figure's charges with her own wants and needs and "thus filling them with a life which is not theirs."[43] If Molly had thwarted the Trio's mission, Harry would not have fulfilled his destiny, and Voldemort might have prevailed.

The Significance of Sweaters

Wolff's Mother "will arrange her outer way of life accordingly ... through motherly professions and activities."[44] One of Molly's annual activities is producing lovingly hand-stitched sweaters. Weasley Christmas jumpers are a tangible symbol of maternal affection. Molly includes Harry in the holiday tradition, creating an ongoing physical representation of her archetypal role. For Harry, after a lifetime of wearing Dudley's cast-offs—including a sweater so ugly that he accidentally used magic to shrink it—the *Sorcerer's Stone* Christmas jumper is the first piece of clothing ever made especially for him and the first gift from a loving maternal figure that he can remember.

Atypically for an eleven-year-old boy, Harry remembers to say thanks at the end of the term. Molly claims it was "nothing," but Weasley sweaters are obviously meaningful symbols of family bonds. In *Half-Blood Prince*, Molly withholds a sweater from prospective daughter-in-law Fleur Delacour, expressing her disapproval of the engagement. In *Order of the Phoenix*, Molly cries when the estranged Percy returns his jumper. When Molly stitches a sweater for Harry that is finer than those for her own children, she displays the motherly power of her nurturing and commitment.

Fred and George, despite their regular conflicts with Molly, appreciate the sweaters' symbolism. They call them "lovely and warm" and insist that Percy wear his.

> "Get it on, Percy, come on, we're all wearing ours, even Harry got one."
>
> "I—don't—want—" said Percy thickly, as the twins forced the sweater over his head, knocking his glasses askew.
>
> "And you're not sitting with the prefects today, either," said George. "Christmas is a time for family."
>
> They frog-marched Percy from the room, his arms pinned to his side by his sweater.[45]

In contrast, Ron's sweater reminds him of his overshadowed status; his gift is always in his least favorite color and lacks the personalized initial that adorns his brothers'.

Subsequent Christmas sweaters renew Molly's living bond with Harry, much as his summer visits to Privet Drive renew Lily's blood protection. The sweaters also relate thematically to each book. Harry wears his *Chamber of Secrets* gift to Christmas dinner and is unbothered by Draco Malfoy's insulting the new garment from the Slytherin table. At the time, Harry was suspected of being the Heir of Slytherin; Malfoy's taunting emphasizes Harry's affiliation with both the Weasleys and Gryffindor. His *Prisoner of Azkaban* sweater is scarlet with a Gryffindor lion, commemorating his rescuing Ginny with the Sword of Gryffindor. The green, dragon-bedecked sweater of *Goblet of Fire* is Molly's commemoration of Harry's victory over the Hungarian Horntail. The *Order of the Phoenix* gift is described only as "the usual hand-knitted jumper,"[46] but at a time when "Umbridge was steadily depriving him of everything that made his life at

Hogwarts worth living,"⁴⁷ the normality of the gift demonstrates Harry's intact Weasley ties. His *Half-Blood Prince* Christmas sweater is decorated with a Golden Snitch after Harry becomes Quidditch captain.

In *Deathly Hallows*, Lily's blood protection has broken, and Harry is isolated from his adoptive family at Christmas. However, in this book the emotional and spiritual significance of the sweaters becomes clear. Christmas Eve finds Harry estranged from Ron, so grieved and discouraged that, at his parents' grave, he wishes he was "sleeping under the snow with them."⁴⁸ As Christmas carols ring, Harry is near tears, remembering "Ron in a hand-knitted sweater."⁴⁹ The situation worsens when Nagini attacks, and Harry's wand is broken. After a narrow escape, Harry is shattered again by reading of Dumbledore's past bigotry. He laments, "All was ashes: How much more could he lose? Ron, Dumbledore, the phoenix wand...."⁵⁰

Recovery begins only after the transition to the Forest of Dean. Harry begins his nightly watch "wearing all the sweaters he owned":⁵¹ presumably, his multiple Weasley jumpers.⁵² After encountering the Silver Doe and the icy pond, Harry strips off his clothes before submerging to retrieve the Sword of Gryffindor. After Ron arrives to rescue Harry, their reconciliation unfolds through the veil of Molly's knitting: "As he dragged sweater after sweater over his head, Harry stared at Ron, half expecting him to have disappeared every time he lost sight of him, and yet he had to be real: He had just dived into the pool, he had saved Harry's life."⁵³ Molly's archetypal motherhood is present in the frigid woods, woven through years' worth of Christmas jumpers. The Horcrux taunts Ron with his deepest fears: Harry usurping not just Hermione's romantic love, but Molly's maternal affection. Although Harry reassures Ron that he loves Hermione platonically, neither speaks of Harry's position as Molly's adopted seventh son, as if the notion that Molly's motherhood could be insufficient to cover both is too absurd to mention. Henceforth, Harry and Ron are genuinely friends who stick closer than brothers, united under common maternal love.

Archetype Inversion at the Battle of Hogwarts

Laura Măcineanu argues that Rowling's female characters are, like those of C.S. Lewis and J.R.R. Tolkien, more complex than immediately apparent because they embody more than one archetype.⁵⁴ This perspective is consistent with Wolff's model, which argues that the integration of multiple archetypes is a necessary part of women's psychological development: "If possible, she will realize the [structural form] which is the most consistent with her nature. By and by, a second form will assert itself from within…. If the gradual integration of the next structural form does not take place, the original one will be exaggerated and turn negative."[55] Furthermore, Wolff proposes that the emerging second archetype will be from a different axis, not the polar opposite of the primary. Peggy Vermeesch explains: "Most women easily integrate a second form: one of the two adjacent forms, meaning on the axis other than the one that contains her dominant form. For example, if Mother is your primary type, it is natural for you to have access to your Amazon or Medial qualities."[56] As adjacent Mother and Amazon archetypes, Ginny and Molly should be able to adopt aspects of the other's dominant form. The Battle of Hogwarts sets the scene for this inversion.

"From worrier to warrior"[57]

Molly's motherly protectiveness manifests as Amazon ferocity as she faces Bellatrix Lestrange. Reviewing *Deathly Hallows*, Karen Coats quips, "It's impossible not to feel satisfied when Molly Weasley turns from worrier to warrior"[58]: in the Hogwarts dining hall, "Molly Weasley's wand slashed and twirled…. Jets of light flew from both wands, the floor around the witches' feet became hot and cracked; both women were fighting to kill."[59] Tison Pugh and David Wallace call this duel the second-most satisfying in the series, as Molly "breaks out of her usual role of tending to the home front and knitting sweaters to kill her murderous adversary while shouting an utterly satisfying expletive":[60] the memorable "NOT MY DAUGHTER, YOU BITCH!"[61] Jeanne Hoeker LaHaie calls this the moment when "Mrs. Weasley's fear and protective instincts for her children reach their apex,"[62] while Sarah Fiona Winters says, "Molly's journey from fussing to fighting proves that the best way to parent a risk-taker like Ginny Weasley is to become a risk-taker oneself."[63]

Perhaps more important than the "satisfying expletive" is what Molly says during the duel, after sweeping not only Ginny, but also Hermione, Luna, and even the invisible Harry to safety: "You—will—never—touch—our—children—again!"[64] Even at the battle's apex, Molly retains her motherly persona. Margaret Mauk says, "Her war cry is not as the mother of Ginny Weasley—'my daughter'—but rather has shifted to that of a universal mother—'our children.'"[65] Molly embodies community motherhood not only through home-cooked meals and hand-knit sweaters, but also through a soldier's willingness to kill. Through Molly's blending of Amazonian power with her Mother archetype, "acts of war are rendered as maternal acts of love."[66]

From Combatant to Comforter

A less memorable but equally important reversal occurs at Harry's final glimpse of Ginny—the last living person he sees before facing death—on his walk to the Forest. Ginny is not fighting but tending someone whose fight is over.

> Someone else was moving not far away, stooping over another prone figure on the ground.... He realized it was Ginny.... She was crouching over a girl who was whispering for her mother.
> "It's all right," Ginny was saying. "It's okay. We're going to get you inside."
> "But I want to go home," whispered the girl. "I don't want to fight anymore!"
> "I know," said Ginny, and her voice broke. "It's going to be all right...."[67]

For the first time, Ginny acts as Molly does, offering care and comfort. Some critics see this shift as a weakening of Ginny's character, reducing her from true soldier to a mere "field nurse tending to the injured."[68] In addition to underestimating the value and bravery of field nurses, this perspective misses the seriousness of this scene for both Harry and Ginny. Although he is tempted to turn back, the sight steels Harry's resolve:

> He wanted to shout out to the night, he wanted Ginny to know that he was there, he wanted her to know where he was going. He wanted to be stopped, to be dragged back, to be sent back home....
> But he was home. Hogwarts was the first and best home he had known....
> With a huge effort, Harry forced himself on.[69]

Readers know nothing about the unnamed girl, except that she is presumably an of-age student who chose to fight Voldemort's forces. Despite her words, Ginny does not attempt to transport the student but simply kneels beside her and holds her hand. Though open to interpretation, this choice could mean that the student is gravely injured, or perhaps already dead. In any case, Ginny is stepping in for the girl's absent mother. The Amazon who seldom cries now chokes up; the imagery recalls Molly's tears over the Boggart-image of her dead family. Just as the threat to children pushed Molly into warrior mode, the horror of battle elicits the maternal caregiver in Ginny.

Compassion and tears do not compromise Ginny's warrior nature, just as Molly's motherhood was not sacrificed to vanquish Bellatrix. Ginny appears next alongside Ron and Hermione, dueling Voldemort himself. By tending the injured student, Ginny integrates a secondary Mother archetype into her primary Amazon, a unifying process indicating growth. Ginny can now empathize with Molly and understand her protective stance. After the battle, as Harry leaves the Great Hall under his Invisibility Cloak, he sees Ginny "sitting with her head on her mother's shoulder."[70]

By incorporating elements of each other's dominant archetype, the Weasley witches have united, both stronger characters who, amid grief, support rather than antagonize each other.

Wolff's archetypes of the mother and the Amazon are useful in understanding Molly and Ginny Weasley and their relationships both to Harry and to each other. Ginny grows from child victim to student warrior, with her attendance at the Yule Ball a subtle but significant turning point in her development. Ginny's increasing identification with her twin brothers shows that she is embracing her animus, developing the independence, courage, and moral strength to become both an important soldier against Voldemort and Harry's love interest. Molly Weasley serves as a surrogate mother for Harry throughout the series. Biological kinship is necessary for the blood charm protection that resides in Harry's skin, but Molly's sweaters are a visible token of manufactured familial bonds. As Harry sheds and replaces his sweaters in the Forest of Dean, they become his "second skin," embodying protective motherly love for the adopted Weasley son. The Battle of Hogwarts offers Molly and Ginny the opportunity to accept elements of the other's dominant archetypes, permanently strengthening both characters and bringing them both comfort and a new emotional closeness.

Notes

1. Peggy Vermeesch, "Toni Wolff's Structural Forms of the Feminine Psyche," Jungian Psychology Space, accessed May 16, 2022, https://www.cgjung.net/espace/jps/articles/peggy-vermeesch/toni-wolff-structural-forms-feminine-psyche/.
2. Toni Wolff, *Structural Forms of the Feminine Psyche*, trans. Paul Watzlawik (Zürich: C.G. Jung Institute, 1956), accessed May 16, 2022, http://ufdcimages.uflib.ufl.edu/AA/00/00/15/82/00001/AA00001582_00001.pdf, 1.
3. J.K. Rowling, *Harry Potter and the Order of the Phoenix* (New York: Scholastic, 2003), 575.
4. Gwendolyn Limbach, "Ginny Weasley: Girl Next Doormat?" in *Terminus: Collected Papers on Harry Potter*, ed. Sharon K. Goetz (Sedalia, CO: Narrate Conferences, 2010), 173.
5. Isabella Goncea and Denise Greenwood, "How Does Male Readership Impact Character Portrayals in Contemporary Young Adult Adventure Novels?" *Journal of Student Research* 10, no. 3 (2021), 8.
6. Aurélie Lacassagne, "Othermothering and Othermothers in the Harry Potter Series," *Journal of the Motherhood Initiative for Research and Community Involvement* 7, no. 1 (2016): 119.
7. Jeanne Hoeker LaHaie, "Mums Are Good: Harry Potter and Traditional Depictions of Women," in *Critical Insights: The Harry Potter Series*, eds. Katherine A. Grimes and Lana A. Whited (Ipswich, MA: Salem Press, 2015), 123.
8. Sterling Hutchinson, Vivek Datla, and Max Louwerse, "Social Networks Are Encoded in Language," *Proceedings of the Annual Meeting of the Cognitive Science Society* 34 (2012): 494-495.
9. Denise Burkhard and Julia Stibane, "Darkness, Danger and Death: Exploring Gothic Places in Harry Potter and the Chamber of Secrets," in *"Harry—Yer a Wizard": Exploring*

J.K. Rowling's Harry Potter Universe, eds. Marion Gymnich, Hanne Birk, and Denise Burkhard (Baden-Baden, Germany: Tectum Verlag, 2017), 68.

10. Laura Măcineanu, "Feminine Hypostases in Epic Fantasy: Tolkien, Lewis, Rowling," *Gender Studies* 14, no. 1 (2015), 78.

11. John Granger, *Harry Potter's Bookshelf* (New York: Berkley Books, 2009), 71. For more on the relationship between Harry Potter and Mina Harker—and *Dracula* in general—see Beatrice Groves's essay in this volume. For more explanation of the Gothic elements of *Harry Potter*, see Amy H. Sturgis's essay.

12. J.K. Rowling, *Harry Potter and the Prisoner of Azkaban* (New York: Scholastic, 1999), 86.

13. John Granger, *Harry Potter as Ring Composition and Ring Cycle* (Oklahoma City: Unlocking Press, 2011), 49.

14. J.K. Rowling, *Harry Potter and the Goblet of Fire* (New York: Scholastic, 2000), 401.

15. It is ironic that the suggestion comes from Ron, given his disapproval of Ginny dating over the next two books and Harry's fear that his pursuing Ginny could doom his friendship with Ron.

16. Few would have blamed her, probably not even Neville.

17. Wolff, *Female Psyche*, 9.

18. Rowling, *Order of the Phoenix*, 866.

19. Beatrice Groves, *Literary Allusion in Harry Potter* (New York: Routledge, 2017), 107, Kindle Edition.

20. Wolff, *Feminine Psyche*, 17.

21. Emma Jung, "On the Nature of the Animus," trans. Cary F. Baynes, in *Animus and Anima: Two Essays* (New York: New York Analytical Psychology Club, 1957), 5.

22. Rowling, *Order of the Phoenix*, 573–574.

23. Ibid., 100.

24. Ibid., 91.

25. Rowling, *Harry Potter and the Deathly Hallows* (New York: Scholastic, 2007), 604.

26. Rowling, *Sorcerer's Stone*, 92.

27. Groves, *Literary Allusion*, 33.

28. Lacassagne, "Othermothering," 116.

29. Wolff, *Feminine Psyche*, 5.

30. Ryan Love, "J.K. Rowling: 'Harry Potter and the Deathly Hallows Part Two is the Best,'" accessed January 29, 2022, https://www.digitalspy.com/movies/a328573/jk-rowling-harry-potter-and-the-deathly-hallows-part-2-is-the-best/.

31. The exceptions are Ron and Ginny Weasley.

32. Lacassagne, "Othermothering," 117.

33. James W. Thomas, *Repotting Harry Potter* (Cheshire, CT: Zossima Press, 2009), 167.

34. J.K. Rowling, *Harry Potter and the Sorcerer's Stone* (New York: Scholastic, 1997), 92.

35. This seems unlikely, given the immediate admonishment to be quiet.

36. Rowling, *Sorcerer's Stone*, 97.

37. Rowling, *Goblet of Fire*, 714.

38. Rowling, *Order of the Phoenix*, 90. For more on this exchange, from Sirius's perspective, see Emma Nicholson's essay in this volume.

39. Wolff, *Feminine Psyche*, 6.

40. Rowling, *Sorcerer's Stone*, 92.

41. Wolff, *Feminine Psyche*, 7.

42. Rowling, *Deathly Hallows*, 88.

43. Wolff, *Feminine Psyche*, 6.

44. Ibid.

45. Rowling, *Sorcerer's Stone*, 203.

46. Rowling, *Order of the Phoenix*, 502.

47. Ibid., 553.

48. Rowling, *Deathly Hallows*, 329.

49. Ibid., 324. For further interpretation of this Christmas scene, see Emily Strand's essay in this volume.

50. *Ibid.*, 360.
51. *Ibid.*, 365.
52. It seems unlikely that Harry would have wasted valuable space in his not-magically-expanded rucksack on Dudley's hand-me-downs.
53. Rowling, *Deathly Hallows*, 371.
54. Măcineanu, "Feminine Hypostases," 69.
55. Wolff, *Female Psyche*, 13.
56. Vermeesch, "Toni Wolff's Structural Forms."
57. Karen Coats, "Harry Potter and the Deathly Hallows," *Bulletin of the Center for Children's Books* 61, no. 2 (October 2007): 109.
58. *Ibid.*
59. Rowling, *Deathly Hallows*, 736.
60. Tison Pugh and David L. Wallace, "A Postscript to 'Heteronormative Heroism and Queering the School Story in J.K. Rowling's Harry Potter Series,'" *Children's Literature Association Quarterly* 33, no. 2 (Summer 2008): 189. According to Pugh and Wallace, the most satisfying duel is Harry's final confrontation with Voldemort.
61. Rowling, *Deathly Hallows*, 736.
62. LaHaie, "Mums Are Good," 132.
63. Sarah Fiona Winters, "Bubble-Wrapped Children and Safe Books for Boys: The Politics of Parenting in Harry Potter," *Children's Literature* 39, no. 1 (2011): 225.
64. Rowling, *Deathly Hallows*, 736.
65. Margaret S. Mauk, "Your Mother Died to Save You," *Mythlore* 36, no. 1 (2017): 123.
66. *Ibid.*, 140.
67. Rowling, *Deathly Hallows*, 696.
68. Limbach, "Girl Next Doormat," 201.
69. Rowling, *Deathly Hallows*, 697.
70. *Ibid.*, 745.

Arthur Weasley and the Misuse of Muggle Artefacts

Kathryn N. McDaniel

Arthur Weasley's flying Ford Anglia has become the iconic symbol of the second book in the *Harry Potter* series, *Chamber of Secrets*. The car appears on the cover of the original Bloomsbury U.K. edition of the book, the 15th anniversary edition, and the illustrated edition by Jim Kay, not to mention it is the featured image on posters for the film adaptation, released in 2002. According to a 2019 Jardine Motors Group survey, cinephiles voted the Ford Anglia scene from the *Chamber of Secrets* film the second-best car scene in film history.[1] On the surface, Mr. Weasley's magical car represents heroic adventure and rescue, as it leads Harry from his imprisonment at Number 4 Privet Drive to the Burrow, the Weasleys' family home. Viewed more closely, however, the car raises troubling questions about cultural intermixing between two segregated communities (magical and Muggle) as well as human creativity in the quest for immortality, both of which are central themes to the entire book series.

A so-called "pure-blood" wizard, Arthur Weasley valiantly tries to breach the Muggle-wizard divide, especially from his position in the Misuse of Muggle Artefacts Department at the Ministry of Magic. But some of his approaches to Muggles, including and especially his bewitched Ford Anglia, are problematic. Wizarding World's article "Why We Love Arthur Weasley So Damn Much" suggests rather glibly that it's ironic that "few are more guilty of dabbling in 'Misuse of Muggle Artefacts' than Weasley himself."[2] Arthur Weasley is thus a useful character through which to think about what is commonly called "cultural appropriation." Understanding where Mr. Weasley's creative tinkering falls within this controversial practice provides a richer understanding of the power relationship between wizards and Muggles and the possibilities for cultural exchange in this fantasy realm. The almost character-like development of the Ford

Anglia itself, however, further points us toward the *Harry Potter* story's views of transhumanism and the human quest for immortality. Arthur's creative but imperfect cultural blending of Muggle technology and wizard magic in the flying Ford Anglia presents a foil for Voldemort's attempts to materially extend his own life through purely magical objects, the Horcruxes. Through this implicit comparison, the *Harry Potter* series highlights the dangers of cultural insularity and "purity" and the power of generative creativity for shaping a lasting legacy.

Mr. Weasley: Father, Inventor, Mugglephile

Readers of the *Harry Potter* series most closely relate to Arthur Weasley as an idealized paternal figure: father of seven, plus sometime stand-in father figure for Harry himself. Affable, wise, responsible, and caring, Mr. Weasley is a model parent and an exemplary member of wizarding society. Although he works hard, he is in essence a family man who listens to his children and values them as individuals. Asked about characters she meant to kill off but didn't, J.K. Rowling mentioned that Mr. Weasley was supposed to die in Book 5, but that she didn't have the heart to go through with it, acknowledging that Arthur Weasley is arguably "the only good father in the whole series."[3]

He also plays an important political role in the books. Mr. Weasley's rejection of pure-blood ideology cues readers not only to the possibility but also the ideal that wizards need not and should not embrace the separatist, racist ideas of Salazar Slytherin, Voldemort, and the Death Eaters. Arthur Weasley's fascination with Muggles reveals an enthusiastic acceptance of the marginalized other in wizarding society, including Muggleborns and so-called "half-bloods" as well as Muggles themselves. His government office in the Misuse of Muggle Artefacts Department—and his own piece of legislation, The Muggle Protection Act—put him in the position to defend Muggles against magical mischief, some of which can be deadly. He champions Muggle protection even though it is a political and career dead-end for him at the Ministry and has perhaps also contributed to the relative impoverishment of his family. Readers often see Mr. Weasley fatigued after a long day of protecting Muggles from bewitched objects. In fact, that's how we first meet Mr. Weasley in *Chamber of Secrets*.

But readers actually meet Mr. Weasley's flying Ford Anglia first. Fred, George, and Ron use the car to literally break Harry out of what has become a Muggle prison at the Dursleys', positioning the car and its drivers as heroes, albeit mischievous ones. Harry hears about Mr. Weasley before actually meeting him. On the drive, or rather, flight to the Burrow, the Weasley boys explain their father's job at the Ministry. Ron says, "It's all to do with bewitching things that are Muggle-made, you know, in case they end up back in a Muggle shop or house." Describing a bewitched tea set that landed in Muggle hands, Ron explains, "It was a nightmare—Dad was working overtime for weeks."[4] Mr. Weasley and the one other person in his department frantically intervene with "Memory Charms and all sorts of stuff to cover it up."[5] Harry immediately notes that Mr. Weasley's bewitching of the car seems contradictory, and Fred laughs, "Yeah. Dad's crazy about everything to do with Muggles; our shed's full of Muggle stuff. He takes it apart, puts spells on it, and puts it back together again. If he raided our house he'd have to put himself under arrest. It drives Mum mad."[6]

Mrs. Weasley is certainly angry at her sons for flying the car: "You could have *died*, you could have been *seen*, you could have lost your father his *job*—," she rages.[7] Death, wizard visibility to Muggles, unemployment—the dangers occur to her in that order of seriousness. When Arthur returns home after a long night of raids that produced only "a few shrinking door keys and a biting kettle," which he characterizes as "Muggle-baiting," Molly confronts him about the car in the shed.[8] She says, "Imagine a wizard buying a rusty old car and telling his wife all he wanted to do with it was take it apart to see how it worked, while *really* he was enchanting it to make it fly."[9] Arthur explains that this would be within the law because "there's a loophole" and "as long as he wasn't intending to fly the car," the car's flight capability would not technically be illegal.[10] "Arthur Weasley," Molly shouts, "you made sure there was a loophole when you wrote that law.... Just so you could carry on tinkering with all that Muggle rubbish in your shed!"[11]

This passage reveals that Mr. Weasley is a defender of Muggles against wizard attacks through appropriated and enchanted Muggle objects, but he is also interested in Muggle objects, especially how they work without magic, and in enchanting Muggle objects himself to enhance them. His position in the Ministry allows him to balance these two potentially competing desires by legislating the intent behind the enchantment. He feels his own intent is innocent, allowing him to escape cognitive dissonance on the matter. Mr. Weasley shows delight at the information that his car made a successful flight (before muttering to them that it was "very wrong indeed").[12] Later, in Diagon Alley, Mr. Weasley engages in a physical brawl with Lucius Malfoy over Muggle rights after Malfoy insults Hermione's Muggle parents. To him, this is all of a piece with his pro–Muggle stance. He likes Muggles and feels a paternalistic call to protect them from wizard mischief—and worse, outright malevolence, which occurs with unfortunate regularity. But he is also fascinated with their technological workarounds that give Muggles power without the use of magic. Muggle technology, in his view, might even aid wizard society if magic were added judiciously to it, for example, to make the car fly, expand the capacity of the car's trunk, and allow it to become invisible ("Not a word to Molly," he tells Harry).[13]

However, Mr. Weasley's eagerness to understand Muggles sometimes comes across as embarrassing or impolite. When he meets Hermione's parents for the first time, his reaction is a bit much. He exclaims, "But you're *Muggles!* ... We must have a drink! What's that you've got there? Oh, you're changing Muggle money. Molly, look!"[14] Mrs. Weasley appears embarrassed by such effusive displays. Arthur misunderstands many aspects of Muggle society and technology—for example, "eckeltricity" and his fascination with "plugs," as well as "escapators" and subway turnstiles, among many others. He might, with a little more research, comprehend these at a deeper level by pursuing Muggle Studies or perhaps even stretching himself to learn electrical engineering. It seems strange that the Weasleys do not have Muggle friends or even many friends who straddle the two worlds.

Some of this is played for laughs with us Muggle readers in the time-honored tradition of showing how someone outside one's own culture might interpret (or misinterpret) certain aspects of it. We're being shown our culture from the outside, in the spirit of Horace Miner's famous anthropological essay "Body Ritual Among the Nacirema," which discussed American practices as if they were foreign.[15] There is something delightful about adult Mr. Weasley making obvious mistakes about the Muggle world and yet showing such appreciation of it at the same time. In a book series that makes us wish we were magical, Arthur encourages us to see the wonders of the technologies we do possess. Things that seem mundane to us like electrical plugs and escalators gain a new shine.

Mr. Weasley fits within the British tradition of the tinkerer who spends hours inventing devices in his workshop. *Xenophobe's Guide to the English* humorously points out this common "type":

> The garden sheds of Britain are abuzz with creativity as men called Ron dream up useful and much-needed devices, such as the perfect egg timer, the self-creasing trouser or a little ladder that hangs over the edge of the bath to let the spider out. An Englishman called Babbage was indulged by his friends while he tinkered endlessly with his "mechanical calculating engines." The result has revolutionized the modern world—computers.[16]

Such inventors may be mere eccentrics but may also, like Charles Babbage, create works of genius. As an inventor of a flying car, Mr. Weasley's clear predecessor in British fiction is Caractacus Potts, the idealized father, dreamer, and engineer in the film *Chitty Chitty Bang Bang*.[17] Caractacus also constructs a magical flying car that heroically saves the day when the family go on a dangerous adventure.[18]

Muggle Technology and Wizard Magic

Unlike Caractacus, though, Arthur creates a flying car by intermingling cultures that exist in a complex power relationship with each other. The situation with the Ford Anglia illustrates some of the problems in the wizard–Muggle divide, in that a lot of Mr. Weasley's misunderstandings come from wizarding world taboos against interacting with Muggles or revealing the magical world to them. Although some scholars have seen magic as a metaphor for technology within the series,[19] the story itself poses them as opposites capable of dividing two cultures. The fusion of Muggle technology with magic can be very dangerous for wizards and Muggles alike, but bear in mind that Molly Weasley's second greatest fear when her sons flew the Ford Anglia (right after the fear they might have died) was that they might have *been seen*. The International Statute of Secrecy, which enforces segregation between the two communities, plays a significant role in making each group "foreign" to the other and limiting cultural exchanges of any kind between them. As Joanna Lipinska has noted, "It is not merely physical danger that prevents wizards from revealing themselves, but rather the fear of losing their identity."[20] Magical people have thus developed their own sense of culture and regulate the borders of their identity so as to distinguish themselves from Muggles. As members of the "Sacred Twenty-Eight" wizard pure-blood families—although reluctant ones who scorn the ideology itself—the Weasleys seem more insulated from the Muggle world than perhaps other families would be.

Mr. Weasley's interests in the nonmagical "other" focus on Muggle technology: how Muggles get around their lack of magic to make life easier and more enjoyable for themselves. Technology is therefore, as a supposed substitute for magic, at the center of wizard–Muggle differences. In the Wizarding World essay on "Technology," Rowling explains that there are indeed wizard legal and cultural prohibitions against the use of Muggle technologies. The essay points out first that magical people have little need for Muggle technology, unless they engage with it "out of slightly condescending curiosity." The Ministry of Magic halted an attempt to create a Wizard Broadcasting Corporation television channel as almost certainly leading to violations of the International Statute of Secrecy. There are cultural restraints on wizards using Muggle technology as well. Rowling writes, "To fill one's house with tumble dryers and telephones would be seen as an admission of magical inadequacy."[21] One key exception was the adoption of a train to transport students to Hogwarts. But the essay on "The Hogwarts Express" notes that this fusion of magic with Muggle technology was incredibly controversial when it was introduced, particularly among pure-blood families who declared it "unsafe, insanitary and demeaning."[22] On the whole, however, wizards like Muggle transportation, with a particular "child-like passion" for cars, even among pure-blood ideologues "who claim never to touch a Muggle artefact and yet are discovered to have a flying Rolls Royce in their garage."[23]

Mr. Weasley is, at least, not alone in his attempts to merge magic with Muggle technology. Magical society, on the other hand, has clear restrictions on this practice and not only (or even primarily) for Muggle protection. When Harry and Ron fly the Ford Anglia to Hogwarts, they nearly get themselves expelled and also get Arthur into a lot of trouble at work, demonstrating the seriousness of this breach. Wizards have both practical and political reasons for the taboos against merging Muggle artefacts with wizard magic.

In terms of the objections, for wizards the main issues are safety and concealment. Arthur's souped-up car works pretty well, especially for a very long flight from King's Cross to Hogwarts. It does eventually flag, though, and this creates a dangerous situation in which Ron's and Harry's safety are in jeopardy. The car engine dies just as they reach Hogwarts grounds. The two boys and Hedwig plummet toward the ground, only saved by crashing into the Whomping Willow, which begins "pummeling every inch of the car it could reach."[24] The car suddenly restarts on its own and speeds "out of reach."[25]

As Molly indicated, safety is only the first priority for wizards when it comes to bewitching Muggle objects. Because the car's invisibility feature fails early in the journey to Hogwarts, the International Statute of Secrecy, which enforces wizard segregation and concealment, is also put at risk. Professor Snape hisses at the boys, "You were seen" and shows them the headline "*FLYING FORD ANGLIA MYSTIFIES MUGGLES.*"[26] This threat to reveal the presence of magical people to Muggles, making witches and wizards vulnerable to persecution or exploitation, is likely why Arthur gets into trouble at work.

The Flying Ford Anglia and Cultural Appropriation

In light of these considerations, the Ministry of Magic is probably unbothered by the prospect that Arthur Weasley's enchantment of the car is an offensive act of cultural appropriation. They would not be offended on behalf of Muggles because so much of their emphasis on the segregation of the two communities stems from fear, arrogance, and contempt. But should readers be concerned about this potential problem? Accusations of cultural appropriation abound in our world—and have certainly been lobbed at Rowling herself—along with justifications for such "cultural borrowing," which Rowling has, in turn, made.[27] The issue of cultural appropriation in general is fraught with emotion and political intensity. As one columnist warned, "No matter your opinion on cultural appropriation, you can be certain that many people think you are wrong."[28] Not all the accusations or the justifications are equally valid. A large part of the debate has to do with nuance, determining where and when cultural borrowing does harm, and understanding cultural fluidity.

Scholars have developed many phrases to describe various acts of creative cultural intertwining, including "cultural exchange" and similarly "cultural engagement," which typically refer to a benign interchange of cultural practices or artefacts.[29] No culture stays static or insular; thus, cultural exchange is part of normal cultural development, and all cultures reflect exchanges from a variety of other cultural contacts that transform them across time and place. Pointing to the value of diversity, the *Harry Potter* series supports such cross-cultural engagement; cooperation among peoples is one of the main strategies for defeating Voldemort. Although Mr. Weasley enjoys such cultural exchanges, the way he goes about tinkering with the Ford Anglia and the charged political context between wizards and Muggles makes questionable the benign nature of this particular exchange.

Cultural appropriation is itself such a broad term that some have suggested using more precise alternatives. For example, some prefer "cultural *mis*appropriation"—since some cultural appropriation may be seen as neutral or even beneficial—though others have suggested abandoning the term "appropriation" altogether.[30] The concept came out of art theory, notably from Kenneth Coutts-Smith who wrote a pivotal essay on the topic in 1974. Examinations like Coutts-Smith's of what he then called "cultural colonialism" referred primarily to the theft of valuable cultural, artistic objects (for example, the so-called Elgin Marbles) or artistic styles (like the European modernists' use of African art). This cultural theft colonially subsumed those works and made them, quite problematically, "western."[31] Philosopher James O. Young has spent much of his career exploring where such acts of appropriation appear innocent, more like cultural exchange, and where they cause harm or extreme offense, which he considers the only significant objections to such appropriations; that is, cultural borrowing is not always "wrong."[32] Historian and cultural theorist George

Lipsitz developed the concept of "strategic anti-essentialism" to refer to a practice whereby a member of a group adopts certain cultural modes of a different, marginalized group in protest against the hegemonic order of which he or she is a part.[33] This is a kind of identity formation that resists the "colonizing" or dominant culture, against what that group considers "essential" to identity, and can be adopted by other similarly marginalized people in society or by those who are part of the dominant culture itself. In these cases, harm comes from misrepresenting the original cultural practice or using it for financial or social gain.

All of these concepts contribute to current definitions of cultural appropriation, the complexity of which is well-captured in Patti Tamara Lenard and Peter Balint's article "What is (the Wrong of) Cultural Appropriation?":

> Cultural appropriation can be defined as the taking of a valuable, yet re-usable or non-exhaustible aspect, of another individual's culture (usually a symbol or practice), for one's own use, where the taker knows what she is doing (or reasonably should know), and where the context of this taking is contested. In other words, in order for an act to be cultural appropriation it must meet four conditions: (1) a taking condition, (2) a value condition, (3) a knowledge or culpable ignorance condition, and (4) a contested context condition.[34]

Lenard and Balint add two "amplifiers" or "complicating factors" that influence the objectionable nature of the cultural appropriation: power inequalities and profit. Arthur Weasley's enchantment of the Ford Anglia fits some but not all of this definition.

Arthur's bewitching of the car meets both the first "taking condition" and second "value condition," since he has the car in his possession, though he appears to have purchased it legitimately, and we know the car has value for both Muggles and wizards. Cars are a very important cultural artefact in modern western society and thus at the center of British Muggle culture. From the wizarding world vantage point, Rowling's "Technology" essay tells us that the Muggle car is especially envied by wizards, who lack a corollary despite their magical abilities. The "knowledge or culpable ignorance" condition is pretty clearly met here, because Mr. Weasley certainly knows what he's doing and the taboo nature of his tinkering. But the fourth condition, that the appropriation is "contested," is not so clear. Although the Ministry of Magic has prohibitions on this appropriation, there is no Muggle outrage about it. However, there's no outrage because Muggles *cannot* know about it due to the Statute of Secrecy. Moreover, it's likely that there were a fair number of memory modification charms carried out on the Muggles mystified by the flying Ford Anglia, which certainly may be interpreted as problematic. What Arthur has done here fits some parts of the definition of cultural appropriation, but the degree and the harm caused to Muggles from this appropriation is questionable.[35]

Lenard and Balint's two amplifiers add an important dimension to this question as well. Mr. Weasley is not making a profit from his car—nor did he ever intend to—and the flying car doesn't meaningfully help his status at all. In fact, it causes him great embarrassment and potential financial ruin. The question of power inequalities is more complex, though, and brings up a very important consideration about the Muggle and magical worlds: which one is dominant? If Mr. Weasley is part of a marginalized, minority community, his cultural merging of magic with Muggle technology might be viewed as an act of counter-cultural fusion that potentially undermines Muggle hegemony. Magical people are after all in the minority, a historically oppressed group who went into seclusion because of that oppression. On the other hand, magic is a significant source of power that potentially allows the wizarding world to oppress Muggles, as readers see when Voldemort takes over the Ministry of Magic: "Magic Is Might."[36] Mr. Weasley would definitely not want to contribute to the oppression of Muggles and continues to be their defender even when that puts him and his family in grave danger. He becomes a core member of the Order of the Phoenix, working secretly against the Death-Eater, wizard-supremacist ministry. After Nagini attacks him in the Ministry of Magic in Book 5, Arthur insists on using Muggle stitches as part of his treatment, which shows a consistent desire to honor Muggle medical technology even when his life is on the line.

Although there are parts of Mr. Weasley's bewitching of the Ford Anglia that put his tinkering in the realm of cultural appropriation, his misuse of Muggle artefacts does not exacerbate an obvious power imbalance, steal or otherwise profit from a marginalized people, or provoke offense or outrage from the Muggle community. It is perhaps something a little less innocent than mere cultural exchange, but he himself may be correct that the intent matters. Meaning no harm, making no profit, and acting out of curiosity and respect, Arthur is not misappropriating a foreign culture so much as he is clumsy in his explorations. Beyond inoffensive, however, in the end his tinkering may also be benevolent. His expression of Mugglephilia matches best the idea of strategic anti-essentialism. "Pure-blooded" Mr. Weasley is making a kind of low-key, personal identity statement against the anti–Muggle prejudice common within the pure-blood wizard community. His tinkering attempts to surmount the "us versus them" thinking at the core of wizarding identity. His admiration for Muggle technology, embodied in the Ford Anglia, and his creative intermixing of it with his own magic constitute a manner of honoring the foreign culture most commonly depicted as inferior and a threat to his own.

Extending Life: Parenthood and Transhumanism

Yet another danger posed by this cultural fusion may be exactly what Arthur had warned Ginny about and reinforced at the end of *Chamber of Secrets*: that the object has developed a mind of its own. At the end of the book, Mr. Weasley cautions, "Never trust anything that can think for itself *if you can't see where it keeps its brain*."[37] In this instance, he is talking about Tom Riddle's diary, which we later know had been transformed into a Horcrux, a magical object containing part of Voldemort's soul. Yet this admonition could also apply to the flying Ford Anglia. Showing independent agency and even personality, the car unceremoniously spits out Ron and Harry after its assault from the Whomping Willow and trundles off to a life in the wilderness of the Forbidden Forest:

> Then, dented, scratched, and steaming, the car rumbled off into the darkness, its red lights blazing angrily.
> "Come back!" Ron yelled after it, brandishing his broken wand. "Dad'll kill me!"
> But the car disappeared from view with one last snort from its exhaust.[38]

A combination of "fine four-fendered friend"[39] and Frankenstein's monster, the car is left to develop its consciousness in the absence of its creator and in social exile. At the end of the book, the car reappears when Aragog and his band of carnivorous spiders attempt to kill Harry and Ron in the Forbidden Forest. Whether the Ford Anglia will be loyal, in the spirit of Chitty Chitty Bang Bang, or murderously vengeful, like the creature in *Frankenstein*, is in some doubt, as the car was quite disgusted with Ron and Harry after the Whomping Willow incident.

Surprisingly, without having been summoned, the car rides to their rescue in the Forbidden Forest, mimicking the heroic liberation that started off the book, now enacted under its own initiative. The Ford Anglia thus embodies the role of deus ex machina, which translates as "god from the machine," a literary term referring to the sudden arrival of a character who resolves a seemingly unresolvable situation at its crisis point. At the critical moment, the Ford Anglia makes a dramatic reappearance: "Mr. Weasley's car was thundering down the slope, headlights glaring, its horn screeching, knocking spiders aside; several were thrown onto their backs, their endless legs waving in the air. The car screeched to a halt in front of Harry and Ron and the doors flew open."[40] Once Harry, Ron, and Fang climb aboard, it charges boldly through the forest, heedless of all damage, including losing its side mirror, and delivers the three to the edge of the Forbidden Forest. The Ford Anglia's independent heroism demonstrates its character development, following a courageous yet mischievous and, thus, Weasley-esque path in the end, that proves helpful to Ron and Harry when they most need it. This enchanted machine changes the boys' fate.

Mr. Weasley does not appear to realize that his warning to Ginny about mistrusting freely thinking objects might apply to his own invention; in this moment, he is talking specifically about the Horcrux diary which enabled Ginny's possession by young Tom Riddle and the reopening of the Chamber of Secrets at Hogwarts. Indeed, it is worth comparing Tom Riddle's diary and Voldemort's other object–Horcruxes to Arthur Weasley's flying Ford Anglia. Both cases show a creative attempt at transformation through magic, and both men produce objects that develop their own sentience and power to act. However, the purposes, "purity," and personalities of these "things" prove distinctive.

Voldemort uses dark magic combined with murder to embed pieces of his soul into magical objects like the diary for the purpose of gaining his own immortality. Adhering to the pure-blood ideology, he scorns the notion of intermixing with Muggles in any way. When making Horcruxes, he chooses objects that are emblematic of the magical community and of high status: his own magical diary, the Gaunt family ring, Helga Hufflepuff's cup, Salazar Slytherin's locket, and Rowena Ravenclaw's diadem.[41] He then attempts to extend his own life materially through his magical transformation of these purely wizard objects. In "The Two Alchemists in *Harry Potter*: Voldemort, Harry, and Their Quests for Immortality," Signe Cohen has likened Horcruxes to the alchemical concept of the homunculus, "a tiny artificially created human being" used interchangeably in some literature with the philosopher's stone that grants eternal life.[42] In making his Horcruxes through acts of death, however, Voldemort has rendered himself unnatural, evil, and inhuman. Cohen argues, "Through committing murders and creating horcruxes, Voldemort moors his desire for an abstract immortality in the material world; the horcruxes are Tom Riddle's transgressions made manifest."[43] Voldemort's Horcrux-objects are smaller versions of him or, in the case of the diary, a younger version of him, and share his nastier qualities. The diary version of Tom Riddle uses guile and merciless ambition to seduce and then possess young Ginny Weasley in pursuit of revenge against Harry. The ring bears a curse capable of bringing death even to the great Albus Dumbledore. The locket enervates the wearer and then divides the Trio with lies inciting jealousy.

These artificial creations represent Voldemort's attempts at self-cloning, a kind of transhuman experiment in continuing human life by enmeshing it within a material object. Muggles most commonly attempt to achieve transhumanism through technology, particularly using cryogenics to delay death and then (in a hoped-for future) merging the human mind with computer systems to prevent death entirely.[44] The

Death Eaters attempt something similar through magical means. Through this parallel, the *Harry Potter* series presents transhumanism as not only flawed in concept but morally corrupt.[45] Although there may be some creativity in Voldemort's use of magic,[46] it is not generative in the sense that it does not create new life, nor does it actually extend Voldemort's human life, because he destroys his humanity in the process. Voldemort's contempt for Muggles and other non-wizard beings ultimately extends to all others outside himself; his insularity, both cultural and personal, are the key to his failure.

In contrast, as the quintessential tinkerer, Arthur Weasley seeks to understand Muggle technology and to merge it with magic in a way that produces a cultural blending of the two kinds of power. He does this out of interest in other people and other ways of life. Choosing an iconic Muggle machine, the automobile, he enchants it while retaining its essence and in the process creates something new. It may have a bit of Arthur's heroic personality in it, but it is not a replica or clone of Arthur designed to extend his life. As a fusion of the two societies, it is distinct, an innovation, and it remains a machine without a human soul. This kind of creativity requires connection with others outside the self—in this case, a whole other culture—and thus has a generative quality. Although it may stray into cultural appropriation, it resonates more closely with the practice of strategic anti-essentialism, a protest of wizard insularity and ethnocentrism. Importantly, the product of Arthur's creative invention ultimately becomes uncontrollable and independent; it "thinks for itself." Perhaps like a lot of cultural intermixtures, whether they be foods, rituals, art, or even people, the end result takes on a life of its own beyond what the initial creator can predict or control. The *Harry Potter* series suggests that this is fundamentally a positive development: that cultures and people should not be walled off from each other.

Arthur Weasley's other role as quintessential father figure also points to Rowling's larger theme about immortality achieved not through material life extension, in the transhumanist way of thinking, but through parenthood and the continuation of cultural traditions through the generations. Emily Strand has argued that "parenting in *Potter* … is portrayed as the only viable and wholesome way of satisfying our human desire for immortality."[47] Arthur knows his children are distinct from himself, with their own unique personalities; they are not mere clones and certainly have minds of their own.[48] Moreover, the Tale of the Three Brothers points to the value of enchanted objects passed down through families as a means of preserving heritage, as a legacy, and thus as a means of preserving life—not the life of an individual but that of a family or a people. Material immortality, such as the homunculus cloning sought by Voldemort, is evil and unnatural and leads inevitably to violence, despair, and death.

That which truly survives over time, the *Harry Potter* series contends, is passed down through different people within families and communities, like the Invisibility Cloak and like family bonds. Mr. Weasley's parenthood (as arguably "the only good father in the whole series") as well as his "misuse" of Muggle artefacts identify him as a model for both cross-cultural exploration and for human connection and family legacy over transhuman immortality. The conclusion of the final book underscores the value of Mr. Weasley's route to longevity over Voldemort's. In the series epilogue, in contrast to Harry's pain-free scar, signifying Voldemort's lasting death, Weasley grandchildren proliferate at King's Cross station. Awaiting that technological-magical hybrid, the Hogwarts Express, this next generation of Weasleys are also hybrids, including those who result from intermarriage with a Muggleborn and with a half-blood. No longer so "pure," the Weasleys have instead successfully, joyfully, and enduringly breached the Muggle-wizard divide.

Notes

1. Gayane Kaligan, "Flying Ford Anglia Voted Second-Best Car Scene in Cinema," MuggleNet, December 30, 2019, https://www.mugglenet.com/2019/12/flying-ford-anglia-voted-second-best-car-scene-in-cinema/.
2. "Why We Love Arthur Weasley So Damn Much," *Wizarding World*, August 14, 2017, https://www.wizardingworld.com/features/why-we-love-arthur-weasley-so-damn-much.
3. "The Harry Potter Characters J.K. Rowling Nearly Killed—and the Ones She's Sorry She Did," *Wizarding World*, November 21, 2018, https://www.wizardingworld.com/features/harry-potter-characters-jk-rowling-nearly-killed-and-the-ones-shes-sorry-she-did.
4. J.K. Rowling, *Harry Potter and the Chamber of Secrets* (New York: Scholastic, 1999), 30–31.
5. *Ibid.*, 31.
6. *Ibid.*
7. *Ibid.*, 33.
8. *Ibid.*, 38.
9. *Ibid.*, 39.
10. *Ibid.*
11. *Ibid.*
12. *Ibid.*
13. *Ibid.*, 66.
14. *Ibid.*, 57.
15. Horace Miner, "Body Ritual Among the Nacirema," *American Anthropologist* 58, no. 3 (1956): 503–507. Try reading about the Nacirema in the Mirror of Erised.
16. Antony Miall and David Milsted, *Xenophobe's Guide to the English* (Wiltshire: Xenophobe's Guides, 2015), 19. My thanks to David Martin for this delightful reference.
17. In the original book by Ian Fleming, the character is somewhat different. He is not the car's inventor and is named Pott instead of Potts, but the connection between the film's version of Caractacus Potts and the character of Arthur Weasley seems clear.
18. For further analysis of the inventor literary type and other literary influences on *Chitty Chitty Bang Bang*, see Will McMorran, "From Quixote to Caractacus: Influence,

Intertextuality, and *Chitty Chitty Bang Bang*," *Journal of Popular Culture* 39, no. 5 (2006): 756-779.

19. Joel Hunter, "Technological Anarchism: The Meaning of Magic in Harry Potter," in *Harry Potter for Nerds*, ed. Travis Prinzi, Oklahoma City: Unlocking Press, 2011, 105-134; Michael Ostling, "Harry Potter and the Disenchantment of the World," *Journal of Contemporary Religion* 18, no. 1 (2003): 3-23.

20. Joanna Lipinska, "The Xenophobic World of Wizards: Why Are They Afraid of the 'Other'?" in *Harry Potter's World Wide Influence*, ed. Diana Patterson (Newcastle upon Tyne: Cambridge Scholars, 2009), 117.

21. J.K. Rowling, "Technology," *Wizarding World*, August 10, 2015, https://www.wizardingworld.com/writing-by-jk-rowling/technology.

22. J.K. Rowling, "The Hogwarts Express," *Wizarding World*, August 10, 2015, https://www.wizardingworld.com/writing-by-jk-rowling/the-hogwarts-express.

23. Rowling, "Technology."

24. Rowling, *Chamber of Secrets*, 74-75.

25. Ibid., 75.

26. Ibid., 79.

27. Criticism has focused on Rowling's "History of Magic in North America" essays on *Wizarding World* and the *Fantastic Beasts* film series, though not exclusively. See Amy H. Sturgis, "Hogwarts in America: In *Fantastic Beasts and Where to Find Them* J.K. Rowling Crosses the Atlantic and Makes a Hash of North American History and Culture," *Reason* (December 2016). See also Liana E. Chow, "What the Hell Happened? Voldemort's Snake Is Actually an Asian Woman," *The Harvard Crimson*, October 2, 2018, https://www.thecrimson.com/article/2018/10/2/nagini-asian-woman/#:~:text=To%20complicate%20the%20situation%20even,It%20should%20be.

28. Jia Tolentino, "Lionel Shriver Puts on a Sombrero," *The New Yorker*, September 14, 2016, https://www.newyorker.com/culture/jia-tolentino/lionel-shriver-puts-on-a-sombrero.

29. *What I Hear When You Say: Cultural Appropriation vs. Appreciation*, Viewing Guide, PBS (2017), https://bento.cdn.pbs.org/hostedbento-prod/filer_public/whatihear/9-Cultural_Approp-Viewing_Guide.pdf.

30. Jessica Metcalfe, "Native Americans Know that Cultural Misappropriation is a Land of Darkness," *The Guardian*, May 18, 2012, https://www.theguardian.com/commentisfree/2012/may/18/native-americans-cultural-misappropriation.

31. Kenneth Coutts-Smith, "Cultural Colonialism," *Third Text* 16, no. 1 (2002): 1-14.

32. James O. Young, *Cultural Appropriation and the Arts* (Oxford: Wiley-Blackwell, 2010).

33. George Lipsitz, *Dangerous Crossroads: Popular Music, Postmodernism, and the Poetics of Place* (New York: Verso, 1994), 62-64.

34. Patti Tamera Lenard and Peter Balint, "What Is (the Wrong of) Cultural Appropriation?" *Ethnicities* 20, no. 2, April 1, 2020: 338.

35. Although the series itself portrays memory modification as (mostly) harmless, we should note that modifying Muggle memories poses quite serious ethical dilemmas.

36. J.K. Rowling, *Harry Potter and the Deathly Hallows* (New York: Scholastic, 2007), 242. For more on the wizard-Muggle power dynamic, see Travis Prinzi's essay in this volume.

37. Rowling, *Chamber of Secrets*, 329.

38. Ibid., 75-76.

39. Lyrics from the title song in *Chitty Chitty Bang Bang* call that winged predecessor of Arthur's Ford Anglia a "fine four-fendered friend." *Chitty Chitty Bang Bang*, directed by Ken Hughes (1968; Los Angeles, CA: Warfield Productions/Dramatic Features), DVD.

40. Rowling, *Chamber of Secrets*, 279.

41. Voldemort also makes Horcruxes out of living beings, Nagini and Harry, that pose their own interpretive challenges. For discussion of the dynamics of these Horcruxes, see Erica Maitland Lange, *Harry Potter and the Theory of Things*, MA thesis (Bucknell University, 2012).

42. Signe Cohen, "The Two Alchemists in *Harry Potter*: Voldemort, Harry, and Their

Quests for Immortality," *The Journal of Religion and Popular Culture* 33, no. 3 (Fall 2018): 214.

43. *Ibid.*, 216.

44. Many fascinating books exist on transhumanism, but for two recent and particularly well-written ones, see Mark O'Connell, *To Be a Machine: Adventures Among Cyborgs, Utopians, Hackers, and the Futurists Solving the Modest Problem of Death* (New York: Doubleday, 2017) and Meghan O'Gieblyn, *God, Human, Animal, Machine: Technology, Metaphor, and the Search for Meaning* (New York: Doubleday, 2021).

45. John Dunne makes this convincing argument in "Harry Potter and the Aims of Transhumanism: A Magical Critique of Technological Posthumanity," *Journal of Religion and Popular Culture* 35, no. 2 (August 2023): 55-71.

46. On Rowling's view of creativity, among good wizards and Death Eaters, see Beth Sutton-Ramspeck, "The Ambivalent Portrayal of Creativity in *Harry Potter*," *The Ravenclaw Chronicles*, ed. Corbin Fowler (Newcastle upon Tyne: Cambridge Scholars, 2014), 122–140.

47. Emily Strand, "Parenting Models in the *Potter* Saga and *Cursed Child*: Human and Divine," *Harry Potter, the Ivory Tower, and Beyond*, ed. Lana Whited (Columbia, MO: University of Missouri Press, 2023).

48. Leonie Caldecott points out that Arthur has seven children just as Voldemort has seven Horcruxes. "Cult or Culture? Some Reflections on Rowling, Pullman and the Contemporary Fantasy Scene," *Culture & Libri* 156/157 (2006).

Conversation

A Question of Character

Emma Nicholson (EN), Louise Freeman (LF), and Katy McDaniel (KM) talk with Emily Strand (ES) about their essays.

ES: One of the ideas all of the essays play with—all three of your essays—is the issue of conformity: whether it's to gender expectation, wizarding world laws, or social taboos against intermixing with Muggles. What should readers take away from these characters that you've written about, about where the pressure to conform comes from and how to deal with it?

KM: Well, Arthur is so very, very much a wizard. [Laughs.] He lives this kind of insular life among wizards. But he's not a conformist, interestingly. He doesn't conform to the pure-blood ideology, even as it takes over. And he's always thinking beyond the structures of the life that he knows, even though he doesn't venture out as much as we think he potentially could. Like, he could get to know some Muggles, you know?

ES: Right, he could just, like, walk up the street, like the twins do. You know, like they flirt with that girl in the shop.

KM: Yes, but even from his own really kind of closed off world, he's always thinking: Is what we're doing a good thing? Do I agree with this part of what my society is doing? If I can't change the structure, how can I fight against it, even in underground ways? Think about the way that he stays at the Ministry of Magic, but he's working against Pius Thickness and all that's happening there at the Ministry.

ES: Yes. It's a dangerous thing to do, to be honest.

KM: Yes, right? He stays within, and he is always aware that there are other ways to do and be, and appreciates them though he stays within. Actually, that fits with one of the things I talk about in my [essay]. I talk about different sort of shades or variations of cultural appropriation—the variety of kinds of practices that fit into that. I suggest that what Arthur does is more like "strategic anti-essentialism," which is a mouthful of a word. But it essentially means that you—from within your own position—you try to adopt some of the ways of oppressed people as a way to value and honor them. That is itself is a kind of expression of solidarity. So, he's not at risk of conforming to Muggle ways. He's going to continue to see them as outside. But he's going to use his connections there to express a love of difference and to try to act upon it—structurally even—so that he's actually doing things to resist the conforming pressures of, you know, the way the ministry becomes in Book Five, Six, Seven. Right? So, I think the fact that he's even putting his nonconformity into action is extremely powerful.

ES: Absolutely.

EN: I guess he knows what it's like to be an outlier, right? Because he's poor.

KM: Yes. Absolutely.

ES: Yes. He's poor, and he's quirky. He *is* interested in these Muggles, he can't let that go. He finds them fascinating, and….

KM: The plugs! The plugs are really cool!

ES: The ekeltricity! Right, I know. Louise, how do the Weasley women teach us about conformity and nonconformity?

LF: Well, Molly, of course, I think values conformity. She has her ideas about how things should be, and when things do not go that way, it does not make her happy. You know, she's not happy when Fred and George drop out of school and go open their joke shop. She wants them to go into a more respectable career. She wants Bill to marry a nice British witch, not this part–Veela girl from France who Molly considers very shallow and not worthy of her son, at least at the beginning.

But you know, what I think is neat about Molly is, when she *can* accept things not going according to her vision, when it's clear that, okay, they're succeeding in this. You know, she has that wonderful scene where she reconciles with Fleur after Bill's been injured, and she realizes that—no—I've misjudged this young woman, she's not as shallow and superficial as I thought she was. She still wants to marry Bill after he's disfigured. Once the twins actually are successful in their joke shop, she's willing to go to the joke shop and enjoy the fruits of their success with them.

ES: Accept their lavish gifts!

LF: Accept their lavish gifts! The diamond hat and the necklace and all this type of stuff. And [she] admits, okay, they have a knack for this. And so that is part of her. So I think she, like the typical mother, values conformity to the rules, values following the rules. She doesn't want them forming an illegal defense society. But, you know, she can accept things … when she needs to, and when she sees that—okay, yes—this is the way to go.

KM: I really relate to that, Louise. I'm seeing shades of myself! [Laughing.]

ES: Yes! I think it's actually a really good model, because she kind of relinquishes rather easily.... It only takes a little bit of a sign from Fleur—that she's actually a little bit deeper than she looks and views Bill more deeply than it might appear—for Molly to kind of come along. And you know, she's still nervous about what the twins are doing, but the energy around their business inspires her as well. I think it's a great example for us moms out there that resist the less conformist choices.

LF: Yes. And of course Ginny, her conforming to expectations is I think a major part of her growth.... Again, she kind of bucks the expectations all along, when she's breaking into the shed and stealing the brooms when she's six years old and learning to fly, even though her brothers won't let her do that.... Ginny really embraces that Fred-and-George aspect of her personality as she gets older. She kind of takes over for them. We increasingly see her doing the "he got off!" dance, and stuff like that, and joining in their pranks, joining in their Umbridge-baiting, as she gets older. Like the twins, she's never a prefect, whereas Bill, Charlie, Percy—and Ron even—were. I think she has that certain disregard for the rules, again, that she has in common with Harry, which is important for her.

KM: Yes, and one of the things I think is interesting there is, I wonder about the role of that trauma in *The Chamber of Secrets* in giving her a sense that she's been altered, that she's going to be different. In a way, she's able to make that a strong core of herself—that enables her to even give advice to Harry, with the Half-Blood Prince's chemistry book.

LF: Yes, exactly. She clearly has that long-term effect of this. One of the few things she does in *Prisoner of Azkaban* is when the Dementors come into the Hogwarts Express, her reaction is almost as bad as Harry's. She doesn't faint, but she's shaking. It says she's "looking nearly as bad as Harry felt." And I think that trauma that she has experienced—Voldemort's mind, up close, [sharing] his mind in a way that only Harry has—has left her with that vulnerability to Dementors that is very similar to him. And you know she does tell Harry, "Get over yourself, you're not possessed. I've been possessed, and if you can remember where you are, and you're not waking up covered with bloody chicken feathers, you're not being possessed."

KM: [Laughing.] It's a high bar!

ES: It is, yes. And you said earlier that she was never a prefect, but what's interesting is that she does take upon herself a leadership role in her sixth year, when Harry and the rest are gone. She does take on the leadership role, with Neville, of instigating....

KM: Rebellion!

ES: Yes, rebellion! They try to steal Gryffindor's sword, they're up to all these things with the Carrows, you know, and it's clear that she's not a prefect, because you basically have to be a Death Eater to be a prefect that year. But she is a leader in Dumbledore's Army, still.

LF: Yes, I think that is very important. I've always wished we had more of a glimpse of what actually went on at Hogwarts that year. I would love to see Neville and Ginny and Luna thwarting the Carrows.

KM: Me, too!

ES: That would be a fascinating movie, or book. That would be really fascinating. So Emma, there's got to be lessons about conformity and nonconformity in the character of Sirius. Go!

EN: Absolutely! You're talking about one of the most nonconformist people in the series. His entire family were like this pure-blood, awful, you know, the purification of the wizarding race, all Slytherins. And he just went, nah, don't care. Family hates Muggles? Don't care. I'm going straight for the motorbikes and all the Muggle technology. Family's all in Slytherin? Don't care! Gets on the Hogwarts Express [and says], "I don't want to be sorted into Slytherin." Rules at Hogwarts? Don't care! At every turn, he just doesn't care about what is expected of him, and he just does his own thing. Which I think is a great example for everybody, but particularly for Harry, because, as we know, the Dursleys just try and squash the magic out of him at every turn.

ES: Right.

EN: And I think the lesson in that is two-fold. When we look at the *Fantastic Beasts* movies in particular, we're shown the danger of what can happen if we squash the magic, or the authenticity, out of young people—Credence Barebone develops an Obscurus. We know what happens when you try to suppress people, and that becomes very dark and very destructive, and there's a good chance that they won't survive that. And if you have young people in your life, and they are not conforming to what society expects—so maybe they're LGBTQ, maybe they're neuro-divergent, or in a minority, or maybe they're gifted, or perhaps they're just a little creative and quirky like Luna—for those kids that are trying to grapple with their authenticity, and they're trying to resolve the fact that they're different to what society expects, there's pressure on them, and it can be heavy. They can often end up masking themselves or living a lie, or squashing their identity. And I suggest that everybody be a little bit more like Sirius and embrace authenticity. Acknowledge we all have light and dark and quirkiness inside of us, and let the young Harrys of the world be who they truly are.

KM: Yes, and I love that that's coming from an adult. Right? Because you know, you can see—yes, Luna's quirky, and we could be more like Luna, but you've got an adult who's living it and who's telling you: yes, it's okay. And this is actually a good way to be.

EN: Yes. If you look at Sirius, his relationships, yes, that authenticity: it may cost him some things. So, he refused to bend to society, and as a result, not everybody likes him. But the loving relationships that he does have are built on his authentic self, and therefore they're solid as a rock.

If you're faced with a dilemma, know that: yes, if you be your authentic self, there's a chance that you may lose some things or some people around you in your life. The pain of loss will lessen over time, but regret will always burn hotter. The older that you get, and the less that you live as your authentic self, the more you'll regret it, until you get to the end of your life and say, "wow, I wish I'd been more me!" So, look to Sirius and understand that even as an adult, you can be quirky and different, and just not care.

KM: Yes, and he goes out the way he would have wanted to go out. You know what I mean? That's a life well-lived.

ES: Defending the people he loves, right? Particularly Harry.

EN: Absolutely. And even in that choice, he was nonconformist. Because even Dumbledore was like "oh, we don't want you to do that, keep yourself out of danger." And people didn't understand it. But it was his choice, and it was in line with who he was inside and how he felt in his heart.

ES: And that's how you know he was really a Gryffindor. He had that kind of a nonconformist type of bravery, but it is bravery in the end, I think.

Self and Others

The Problem with Loving Enemies

*Kindness and Oppression
in "The Wizard and the Hopping Pot"*

Travis Prinzi

In Dumbledore's commentary on "The Wizard and the Hopping Pot" in *The Tales of Beedle the Bard*, he explains that anyone who thinks the tale is a cute little moral lesson about kindness is a "nincompoop."[1] He notes that the story has significant political ramifications, because Beedle wrote it while witches and wizards were tortured, killed, and driven into hiding.[2] In other words, the tale contains not just a personal moral but a political one.

Loving one's enemies is one of the more radical teachings of key religious figures such as Jesus and the Buddha. Martin Luther King, Jr., emphasized love for his own enemies while fighting against deep, historical, violent injustice against Black people. Both Beedle and Dumbledore seem to be following the same moral principle. *Harry Potter*, as a worldwide cultural phenomenon, gives a story-form version of this radical moral teaching. The original seven-book series touches on the same theme. In order to defeat Voldemort, Harry doesn't have to *defeat* Voldemort with power; he needs to *understand* Voldemort. In the final battle, Harry offers Voldemort a way out through remorse. Dumbledore's character in particular is stubbornly kind to some of the meanest and cruelest of characters, including Severus Snape, Draco Malfoy, and Dolores Umbridge.

Harry Potter is not the only popular series to build on this theme. On television, the surprise hit *Ted Lasso* (20 Emmy nominations, seven Emmy awards) is built on the same message. In a world marked by frequent lamentations about our intractable political divides, somehow stories about unconditional love and kindness are finding large audiences.

Complexities abound. This essay seeks to explore two difficulties with "The Wizard and the Hopping Pot" as it stands in relationship to the overall *Potter* canon and how it sits as a political commentary written by an author in our own time. Regarding the story's place in the *Potter* canon, Dumbledore's commentary on the story, the opening chapter of *Half-Blood Prince*, Voldemort's plan to rule the Muggle world, and the power of certain spells each call into question who is really "in power" in the world: Muggles or wizards. Regarding the story's moral in political context, messages of love and kindness often ignore political realities, deep-seated power structures, and are used to keep the oppressed silent in the face of injustice. The demand for kindness from the oppressed—particularly from Black Americans in the face of 400 years of racial injustice in the United States—is often no more than a method for people in power to keep those they oppress silent.

Considering Beedle's story along with Dumbledore's commentary helps untangle the complexities of power in the Muggle/wizard dynamic, revealing if and how Beedle's message of love for enemies is enough to dismantle the systemic oppression we find both there and in our own world. While stories of loving one's enemies are important moral tales, it matters who is telling the story and to whom they are telling it.

The Story

The story's basics are simple enough. "The Wizard and the Hopping Pot" appears on the surface as a fairy tale with a moral lesson for children. A kindly old wizard frequently uses his magical abilities to care for the Muggles in the village where he lives. The Muggles have no idea the man is a wizard, and we know from Dumbledore's commentary that this tale is situated in the midst of "persecution of witches and wizards."[3] After the old wizard dies, his son treats the Muggle townsfolk much differently. Instead of helping them with their troubles, he shuts them out and lets their sickness and problems remain. But the father had cast a spell on his old cauldron (the Hopping Pot) which causes it to mimic the woes of the people his son refuses to help. The clattering, banging, crying, whining, groaning, vomiting, warty pot finally wears the young wizard down, and he begins caring for Muggles as his father did, though perhaps not with the same heartfelt motivation.[4]

Dumbledore's Commentary

Dumbledore comments on a variety of topics, including how the story has been censored over the years. While the more amusing censorship is that of Beatrix Bloxam, who tried to make the story sickeningly sweet, the majority of the story's censorship was the result of its political subtext:

> Beedle was somewhat out of step with his times in preaching a message of brotherly love for Muggles. The persecution of witches and wizards was gathering pace all over Europe in the early fifteenth century. Many in the magical community felt, and with good reason, that offering to cast a spell on the Muggle next door's sickly pig was tantamount to volunteering to fetch the firewood for one's own funeral pyre.[5]

The story, popular with children, was later re-written as an anti–Muggle story in which the Hopping Pot defends the Wizard against the cruel attacks of Muggles. As the oppression progressed, any witch or wizard with pro–Muggle sentiments became the subject of scorn in the wizarding world. Beedle's original tale, then, became a magical retelling of the old moral, "Love your enemies." Even if the Muggles in the town were prejudiced against witches and wizards, and even if the young wizard had to hide his own identity in order to avoid burning at the stake, he should remain kind to the Muggles around him.

Love Your Enemies

This moral lesson has a long history in the teachings of some of the world's greatest religious and political figures. In Jesus's famous "Sermon on the Mount" (Matthew), he issued the following teaching:

> You have heard that it was said, "You shall love your neighbor and hate your enemy." But I say to you, Love your enemies and pray for those who persecute you, so that you may be children of your Father in heaven; for he makes his sun rise on the evil and on the good, and sends rain on the righteous and on the unrighteous. For if you love those who love you, what reward do you have? Do not even the tax collectors do the same? And if you greet only your brothers and sisters, what more are you doing than others? Do not even the Gentiles do the same? Be perfect, therefore, as your heavenly Father is perfect.[6]

The Buddha taught the same concepts. Buddhist scholar Robert Thurman illustrates with passages from *The Dhammapada*, the Buddhist scriptures:

> Here in the world, anger is never pacified by anger. It is pacified by love. This is the eternal truth. Some do not realize that we are all heading for death. Those who do realize it will compose their quarrels…. Happy indeed we live, friendly amid the haters. Among men who hate we dwell free from hate…. I call him a charioteer who holds back the arisen anger as though holding back a swerving chariot. Others are only holders of reins.[7]

More recently in history, Martin Luther King, Jr., preached at length on this moral, perhaps most notably in his sermon on the subject, which he preached against doctor's advice while quite ill. He delivered the sermon "Loving Your Enemies" at Dexter Baptist Church on November 17, 1957. In the sermon, he explains that loving one's enemies is not a hyperbole and not a moral to be held only in interpersonal relationships but politically as well. He touches on communism, democracy, Russia, America, colonialism, imperialism, racism, and interpersonal relationships all in this same message. He is unequivocal in his belief that in both the personal and the political realms, those to whom he preached that morning (Black Americans) were called to love their enemies.[8] He urged his listeners with these words:

> Far from being the pious injunction of a utopian dreamer, this command is an absolute necessity for the survival of our civilization. Yes, it is love that will save our world and our civilization, love even for enemies.
>
> Now let me hasten to say that Jesus was very serious when he gave this command; he wasn't playing. He realized that it's hard to love your enemies. He realized that it's difficult to love those persons who seek to defeat you, those persons who say evil things about you. He realized that it was painfully hard, pressingly hard. But he wasn't playing. And we cannot dismiss this passage as just another example of Oriental hyperbole, just a sort of exaggeration to get over the point. This is a basic philosophy of all that we hear coming from the lips of our Master. Because Jesus wasn't playing; because he was serious. We have the Christian and moral responsibility to seek to discover the meaning of these words, and to discover how we can live out this command, and why we should live by this command.[9]

The message of loving one's enemies has been a moral teaching for centuries, even millennia. It is not without its difficulties.

Power in Potter

We begin with the difficulties and complexities present in the wizarding world and in this particular story. Dumbledore is an interesting character to be commenting on the problem of power. He was, we learn in *Deathly Hallows*, tempted by the allure of power during his relationship with Grindelwald. This was no mere passing phase or whim. He wrote at length to Grindelwald about it; he clearly spent time thinking it through. He wrote:

> Your point about Wizard dominance being FOR THE MUGGLES' OWN GOOD—this, I think, is the crucial point. Yes, we have been given power and yes, that power gives us the right to rule, but it also gives us responsibilities

over the ruled.... When we are opposed, as we surely will be, this must be the basis of all our counterarguments. We seize control FOR THE GREATER GOOD. And from this it follows that where we meet resistance, we must use only the force that is necessary and no more.[10]

Dumbledore not only believed wizards should dominate Muggles, but that they should use force when necessary to do so. We are beginning to see more of this history unfold as the *Fantastic Beasts* movies are released. From the first film, Grindelwald is angry that the wizarding world is forced into hiding and intends to change that. In the most recent installment, *The Secrets of Dumbledore*, we learn more about Dumbledore's youthful sharing of Grindelwald's beliefs. In the opening scene, Dumbledore tries to tell Grindelwald that he only followed those beliefs because he was in love with him. Grindelwald responds, "It was you who said we would reshape the world. It was our birthright."[11]

Later in life, Dumbledore realizes his mistake and attempts to change. His refusal of the position of Minister of Magic is rooted in his distrust of his own temptation to power.[12] Yet the way he operates in the battle against Voldemort (and it seems, too, in the previous battle against Grindelwald) is to maintain a pretty significant chunk of power, which he does not share. This power comes in the form of knowledge. No other person, not even Harry or Snape, is made aware of every bit of knowledge that Dumbledore has—not until Harry is dead and visiting Dumbledore in the temporary afterlife holding station at King's Cross.[13] Even in some small details, Dumbledore can occasionally come across as a bully. Consider when he visits the Dursleys in *Half-Blood Prince*.[14] While he attempts an act of kindness by conjuring them some mead, he causes the glasses to continually hit the Dursleys in the head when they refuse to drink. At first, the glasses nudge them "gently," but eventually, they are "knocking quite insistently on the side of Vernon's head."[15] Apparently, he has not entirely given up on using a little force to get Muggles to see his way. Dumbledore is a bit of a contradiction in his views and actions on power, and this perhaps makes him somewhat suspect as a commentator on these themes.

More complicated than that (we are, after all, sometimes inconsistent in how we live out our beliefs) is the seemingly contradictory messaging about just who is in power throughout the *Harry Potter* series. At face value, it seems simple enough. As Dumbledore describes the history in his commentary on our story, Muggle persecution of the magical community "was gathering pace all over Europe in the early fifteenth century."[16] This widespread persecution continued until the International Statute of Secrecy was agreed upon in 1689, and the wizarding world went into hiding. After this, we can argue that the persecution of witches and wizards was not gone, but ongoing; they were pushed underground by Muggle oppression.

148 Self and Others

Details within the story, however, are a bit contradictory. According to Bathilda Bagshot, and also to Dumbledore's footnote, witches and wizards didn't seem to mind the Muggles' attempts at persecuting them. Harry's essay assignment in Chapter One of *Prisoner of Azkaban* highlights the "gentle, tickling sensation" provided by fire interacting with their Flame Freezing Charms—such an enjoyable experience that Wendelin the Weird allowed herself to be caught forty-seven times.[17] This detail alone is not enough to dismiss the persecution as irrelevant; surely a persecuted group finding a way to relieve the burden of oppression does not necessarily mean the power dynamic has flipped, though it raises questions about who holds power.

The first chapter of *Half-Blood Prince*, however, seems to show a wizarding world that is able to control the major affairs of the Muggle world. It seems evident that "The Other Minister," the Minister of Magic, has far more control than the British Prime Minister. Cornelius Fudge calls all the shots in that meeting, and the British Prime Minister is scared, nervous, and entirely at the mercy of whatever is happening in the wizarding world. From the beginning of their conversation, the portrait's introduction of Cornelius Fudge and request for a meeting, the British Prime Minister has no power whatsoever. He doesn't want the meeting, but he doesn't have a choice in the matter.

Not only does the Minister of Magic control the British Prime Minister, but also the president of another country (names of both president and country are left out to demonstrate that it could be any president from any country). It's obvious that when the British Prime Minister uses his expected call from this president as an excuse to dodge a meeting with Fudge, Fudge has someone close to that president who can perform some kind of memory charm: "We shall arrange for the President to forget to call."[18] It appears that the wizarding world has magical agents in key places in governments throughout the world. The amount of control they could exercise is astounding.

The British Prime Minister's entire political career is subject to events in the wizarding world that are out of his control. The war against Voldemort results in the collapse of a bridge, a hurricane, and the murder of Amelia Bones, all of which cause political turmoil. The breeding of Dementors throughout Great Britain was "spreading despair and hopelessness in his voters."[19] When the new Minister of Magic, Rufus Scrimgeour, arrives, he informs the British Prime Minister that his new secretary, Kingsley Shacklebolt, has been placed there by wizards. The Prime Minister protests, "You can't just put your people in my office, I decide who works for me—."[20] But apparently, he is quite wrong about this. And the Junior Minister, it turns out, is under a "poorly performed Imperius Curse" and is quacking at people, causing no little embarrassment.[21]

In Book Seven, the old Fountain of Magical Brethren, a monument to power structures within the wizarding world, has been replaced in the atrium of the Ministry of Magic with one depicting a much different and broader power structure:

> Now a gigantic statue of black stone dominated the scene. It was rather frightening, this vast sculpture of a witch and a wizard sitting on ornately carved thrones, looking down at the Ministry workers toppling out of the fireplaces below them. Engraved in foot-high letters at the base of the statue were the words MAGIC IS MIGHT....
> Harry looked more closely and realized that what he had thought were decoratively carved thrones were actually mounds of carved humans: hundreds and hundreds of naked bodies, men, women, and children, all with rather stupid, ugly faces, twisted and pressed together to support the weight of the handsomely robed wizards.
> "Muggles," whispered Hermione. "In their rightful place."[22]

Here we have the inevitable consequence of the philosophy young Dumbledore espoused in his letter to Grindelwald. Magical power gives wizards the right to rule the Muggles and to put them into their proper place. Wizard domination of the Muggle world is clearly Voldemort's ultimate goal.

Consider also the fact that Arthur Weasley's controversial piece of legislation is called the "Muggle Protection Act," for which Dumbledore is an advocate. If the wizarding world has enough power to truly and unjustly hurt Muggles, so much so that it requires a law to curb, it calls into question who really has the power.[23] This may be a dynamic that breaks down the magic-as-race analogy sometimes present in analyses of the *Harry Potter* series. We can't find a similar situation in our current situation in the U.S., for example. Black and Brown Americans do not have some secret power with which they can control White people. Indeed, the wizarding community can control minds. Nothing would keep them from taking over the world with several well-placed Imperius curses or Confundus charms.

Taking all of this into account, it is tempting to conclude that the ones who truly hold the power are those in the wizarding world, not the Muggles. A few points weigh against this conclusion. In the first place, one major limiting factor for witches and wizards is evident from a simple look at the numbers. While it's possible that the descriptions of magic's power became too strong to support the Muggles-oppress-magic narrative, the magical community seems so incredibly small that, should all the vast Muggle armies of the world be deployed against them, there's no way magic could withstand this force. Hagrid notes, in fact, that the number of magical people to Muggles is so minuscule that "if we hadn't married Muggles we'd've died out."[24] The ability to exercise some influence over the Muggle world, even at higher levels, is a matter of their world's survival.

Additionally, we'd have to conclude that in the 1600s, while the magical community *could have* just overpowered the Muggle world, for some strange reason they were so unwilling to claim that power that they went into hiding and began denying their own identities to their Muggle neighbors. The way that the magical world quickly breaks into its own opposing factions of power demonstrates that they were not of this unanimous self-sacrificial mindset. While there is always a strain of magical people who think magic should rule (Grindelwald, Voldemort, most Malfoys), the majority of the magical community seems to think this folly, not only because morally they *should not*, but logistically and practically because they *could not*.

It is important, when understanding the plight of an oppressed group, not to land on the idea that they want to be in that state. Such justifications have been used for slavery, for the oppression of women, for ongoing economic disparities between groups with and without power. While the story's author may have overplayed her hand in places by making magic look so powerful that the wizarding world could truly dominate, this is ultimately a story of an oppressed group (the magical community) which goes into hiding and then creates its own oppressive hierarchy within that world.

It seems best, then, to see these exercises of magical power as forms of resistance against a much greater power that would not tolerate their presence and would most likely exterminate them, should they become aware once again of the presence of magical people in the world. But these expressions of power are fundamentally forms of resistance from a group of people who have to deny their identities and pretend to be just like the dominant group (Muggles) in order to stay alive.

Old Strategies and Modern Hopping Pots: Uplift Suasion, Beedle, and Ted Lasso

That brings us around to the sticking point for many in fairy tales like "The Wizard and the Hopping Pot." One could easily see the story as a *reinforcement* of the dominant culture's narrative. Beedle writes, "Rather than reveal the true source of his power, he pretended that his potions, charms, and antidotes sprang from the little cauldron he called his lucky cooking pot."[25] As we've seen from Dumbledore's commentary, the context is crucial: Muggles are in control and actively oppress the magical community. In this context, the wizard is only safe if he *pretends not to be what he is*.

Ibram X. Kendi, in his masterful work *Stamped from the Beginning: The Definitive History of Racist Ideas in America*, devotes a chapter to the concept of "uplift suasion." This abolitionist strategy that surfaced in the late eighteenth century "was based on the idea that White people could be persuaded away from their racist ideas if they saw Black people improving their behavior, uplifting themselves from their low station in American society."[26] Kendi notes that this places the entire "burden of race relations" on Black Americans.[27] In other words, these (White) abolitionists believed that, having been stolen from their homeland, subjected to chattel slavery, raped, and mistreated for almost 200 years, if Black Americans could just embrace good behavior, White people would recognize that Black people were equal to them, and racism would end. Kendi explains the obvious problem: "free Blacks were human and humanly flawed," just like the rest of humanity.[28] But only they, as a group, would be kept in slavery for lack of moral perfection.

Herein lies the troubling point of "The Wizard and the Hopping Pot." The kind old wizard seems perfectly content to hide his identity. The problem of uplift suasion, in the case of racism and slavery in the United States, isn't only that Black Americans are human and therefore flawed; it's that the standard of what is "good behavior" is a White standard. In other words, Black people don't only have to "behave" or "be kind" to be accepted; they frequently have to act according to White cultural norms as the standard of what is good behavior. We can see this in examples as simple as grammatical constructs. How White people speak is "good English," but how Black people speak (sometimes these constructs remain from languages their ancestors spoke on the Western shores of Africa!) may be perceived as a sign of low intelligence by White standards. A Black person who speaks like a White person is called "articulate," and this is considered in some way exceptional to the norm. This simple example works its way out on a much greater level in the educational system in the United States, which is largely rooted in a White framework of knowledge.[29]

Likewise, the wizard works out his place in Muggle-dominated society not by acting freely as himself, out in the open, but by pretending to be a Muggle who can cook up good medicine. He has to deny who he truly is in order to be accepted into society. It's even a step further than uplift suasion, because there's no real evidence the wizard has any plans to eventually convince Muggles that wizards are good. He's content to erase everything that is unique about himself in order to survive.

That is, of course, his choice; it is important to remember this is a story by a wizard for the magical community. Perhaps we can ascribe to the old wizard a Christ-like self-denial, and that is probably the best way to read his kindness. He doesn't believe he needs to claim his rights, status, or potential power in order to be happy; he is satisfied in doing good and kind acts even to those who would burn him at the stake. That is his choice, and it seems in line with loving one's enemies. But systemically, it is a major problem to demand an entire people deny their race in order not to be persecuted. That is essentially what uplift suasion was: act like "civilized" White people, and maybe racism will go away.

In the hands of dominant society, however, a story like this becomes a weapon to keep the oppressed silent. People with power use moral commands and stories about kindness to rebuke the anger of the oppressed. Melissa Florer-Bixler sums it up well in her book, *How to Have an Enemy*:

> I've had a front row seat to the damage inflicted by those who utilize the Sermon on the Plain, and its pair in Matthew, as a cudgel to suppress movement work for liberation and the freedom of individuals to escape harmful situations. Jesus' teaching has been deployed to hold women captive to intimate partner abuse and to impede people from reporting sexual assault in the church. It has been weaponized against vulnerable communities who attempt to pull themselves out from under the heel of oppressive power.[30]

Florer-Bixler has pointed this criticism not only at political dynamics and interpersonal relationships but toward stories that ignore political realities.

The wildly popular television show *Ted Lasso* is primarily a story about unswerving kindness in the face of bullies; it also makes frequent references to *Potter*. There have been at least two clear *Harry Potter* references in *Ted Lasso*.[31] We could even make the case that the show is an extended modern retelling of "The Wizard and the Hopping Pot" in some ways.[32] Throughout season one, Coach Lasso can be seen as the kindly old wizard, and his "son" is Jamie Tartt, the young, talented, but exceedingly arrogant and self-serving football star. From a multi-season storyline perspective we can see the same and perhaps even more poignant dynamic in the developing drama between Coach Lasso and Nate Shelley, the kit-man-turned-coach who grows to hate Ted's kindness by the end of season two and to branch out on his own to be the powerful, bully-style coach he wants to be. Thankfully, in season three, Nate promptly makes the kind of turnaround the wizard's son finally makes—and arguably a more genuine one.

Regarding this modern hopping pot rendition, Florer-Bixler points out that while Coach Lasso is able, through relentless kindness, to change British football on the TV screen, the reality of systemic racism in football (and throughout the world) can't be tackled with the same approach:

> "Ted Lasso" is a peek into the world of mostly white men who are untouched by political and social power, whose primary space of psychic navigation in the world is the relational. This is where the show breaks down. The feminist movement taught us that "the political is personal"—our interpersonal struggles are intertwined with our politics because real people's lives are affected by racism, sexism and homophobia. In Ted Lasso's alt world, politics and power barely exist....

Positivity and kindness may break down personal defenses. From time to time, kindness can even be transformative. But soothing tensions can also distract from the work it takes to confront iron-clad systemic power that is inseparable from the personal lives of the people who are crushed by it.[33]

Florer-Bixler correctly notes that "kindness" is demanded *by* those in power *from* those who do not have it. No matter how serious the offense, the oppression, the disregard for entire communities of people, when those downtrodden people speak up, the powerful demand they "be kind" about it.

We see this clearly in the reactions to demonstrations for racial justice. When Colin Kaepernick knelt during the national anthem to protest police brutality against people of color, it was entirely peaceful. But it was not acceptable to those with power. When protestors took to the streets after the death of George Floyd, it did not matter how vastly peaceful those protests were. The press emphasized acts of violence, and the whole movement was essentially disregarded by the powerful for not protesting kindly enough. But the ongoing problem, returning to Kaepernick, is that there simply doesn't seem to be a "kind enough" way to speak up against systemic bullying in the first place.

Narrative Power and Limitations: Who's Telling the Story?

How do we approach a story like Beedle's tale of the kindly, oppressed wizard who seems not only content with his oppression, but finds it his duty to serve his oppressors? To begin with, stories are not necessarily devalued simply because of their lack of attention to political power dynamics. But noting this lack of attention is vitally important for the way a narrative sits in a given culture. To the first point, our hope and goal is toward a world in which political dynamics cannot hold such power and control over people of color, women, LGBTQ+ people,[34] the poor, etc. And I see much that is good and inspiring in portrayals of worlds where kindness, empathy, love, and accountability are all the norm rather than an exception to it.

If "The Wizard and the Hopping Pot" and other similar stories inspire people to be kinder, they have immense value. We need a kinder world. If and when, however, they are weaponized to keep witches and wizards and Black people and Brown people and women and poor and gay and transgender people silent because they are told they need to "be kind," that must be confronted. Both kinds of stories must exist. We need the ones that show just how ugly heteronormative, White, male power structures are, and we need stories that give us a vision for what it might be like if those power structures were dismantled. The *Potter* canon itself has come under criticism for relying on tropes that reinforce rather than dismantle many of the world's oppressive power structures; these are vital conversations to be had regarding such a powerful and popular story.[35]

The interpersonal versus political divide can sometimes be forced where there is no need. In my own theological studies, I've seen fundamentalist and conservative evangelical Christians in the United States relegate all of Jesus's teaching in the Sermon on the Mount to interpersonal matters, leaving room in their belief system for policies that don't fit, such as aggressive military might, torture, an oppressive prison system, greed as a basis for social progress, and the death penalty.

The key question, when it comes to morals and stories about loving one's enemies, is this: who's telling the story, and why? Who's enforcing the moral code? Florer-Bixler notes this observation from Black liberation theologian James Cone, who was often confronted by White people challenging exactly *how* he intended to fight for Black liberation:

> Would Cone encourage Black Christians to turn the other cheek? How could he reconcile Black liberation with Jesus' command to "go the extra mile"? "There are favorite *white* questions," writes Cone, "and it is significant that they are almost always addressed to the oppressed and never to the oppressors." Cone goes on to say that white people are only concerned about violence when violence is enacted upon them.[36]

Indeed, violent response to the oppression of taxation is cast in America's mythology as an ultimate Good; violent response or even non-violent protest against any power structures in White America are quickly met with chiding from those in power that protestors are not acting kindly enough. Kindness and the belief we should love enemies become weapons to silence the oppressed. For example, Martin Luther King, Jr.'s, sermon "Loving Your Enemies" was preached by a Black man to Black people. He was calling on a group of oppressed people not to give up on the way of love, even for their enemies. When, however, White people take that same sermon and use it to silence the protests of Black Americans, the teaching is turned on its head. "Jesus does not call us to enemy-love for the purpose of making miserable people content with their misery," Florer-Bixler writes.[37] People with power would do much better to ask questions of ourselves about how our views of the world have managed to keep so many under our control for so long. It is not loving for us to continue to maintain oppressive power structures as they are. It is not loving to refrain from actively working to dismantle them.

"The Wizard and the Hopping Pot," then, is a story by a wizard for witches and wizards. But we must be very careful, if we're Muggles, about how we use it and learn from it. We can admire the kindness of the old wizard, but we'd better focus our attention on our Muggle brothers and sisters, challenging the world that makes him have to hide in the first place.

King, in sorting out the personal and the political, the individual and the systemic, preaches it like this:

> When the opportunity presents itself for you to defeat your enemy, that is the time which you must not do it. There will come a time, in many instances, when the person who hates you most, the person who has misused you most, the person who has gossiped about you most, the person who has spread false rumors about you most, there will come a time when you will have an opportunity to defeat that person. It might be in terms of a recommendation for a job; it might be in terms of helping that person to make some move in life. That's the time you must do it. That is the meaning of love. In the final analysis, love is not this sentimental something that we talk about. It's not merely an emotional something. Love is creative, understanding goodwill for all men. It is the refusal to defeat any individual. When you rise to the level of love, of its great beauty and power, you seek only to defeat evil systems. Individuals who happen to be caught up in that system, you love, but you seek to defeat the system.[38]

The danger in a story like "The Wizard and the Hopping Pot" is taking away from it the idea that people in power can continue to silence those they oppress by chiding them for not loving their enemies. Importantly, love for enemies does not remove but embraces calling those enemies to account for their actions. Rabbi Sharon Brous writes about the Exodus story:

> Freedom was hard won for the ancient Israelites, coming only after God unleashed 10 formidable plagues on Egypt. The plagues are commonly read as punishments levied against the Egyptian people for the terrible suffering they forced upon the Israelites, but there is another way to interpret God's actions. One medieval rabbi, Sforno, argued that the plagues were actually brought to awaken the conscience of the oppressor, "to increase the chances that Pharaoh would finally see the light and become a genuine penitent." In other words, what God desired was a true change of heart. God wanted Pharaoh and his people to take responsibility for the injustices they committed. Tell the truth. Make amends. Offer reparations. Chart a new course, together with the Israelites.
>
> In this reading, the objective of the redemption story was the liberation of not only the Israelites but also the Egyptians. They needed to be liberated from the morally perverse mind-set that justified their cruelty in the first place. True redemption requires the transformation of the oppressed as well as the oppressors.[39]

Therein lies the key to a story of enemy love—accountability and hope of redemption are vital to it.

The *Harry Potter* stories conclude with this sacrificial enemy-love. Harry lays down his own life, and then in his resurrection and final battle with Voldemort, he offers Voldemort redemption:

> "…before you try to kill me, I'd advise you to think about what you've done…. Think, and try for some remorse, Riddle…."
>
> "It's your last chance," said Harry, "it's all you've got left…. I've seen what you'll be otherwise…. Be a man … try…. Try for some remorse…."⁴⁰

For those with power, the moral call of love is to lay down one's own rights for the benefit of the poor, the oppressed, the downtrodden. The call of love for us all is to love our enemies, hope for their redemption, but hold them accountable for their actions.

Notes

1. J.K. Rowling, *The Tales of Beedle the Bard* (New York: Children's High Level Group, 2007), 11.
2. *Ibid.*, 12.
3. *Ibid.*, 13.
4. For more commentary on the motivation of the son, listen to the discussion I had with Katy McDaniel and Emily Strand on the podcast *Reading, Writing, Rowling* (now *Potterversity*), MuggleNet, episode 43, "The Wizard and the Hopping Plot," June 8, 2020, https://www.mugglenet.com/2020/06/reading-writing-rowling-episode-43-the-wizard-and-the-hopping-plot/.
5. Rowling, *Tales of Beedle the Bard*, 12.
6. Matt. 5:43–48, *New Revised Standard Version*.
7. Robert Thurman, "Where Is the Love in Today's Resistance?" *On Being*, March 18, 2018, produced by Krista Tippett, podcast, https://onbeing.org/blog/robert-thurman-where-is-the-love-in-todays-resistance/.
8. Martin Luther King, Jr., "Loving Your Enemies," Stanford University Martin Luther King, Jr. Research and Education Institute, accessed October 31, 2021, https://kinginstitute.stanford.edu/king-papers/documents/loving-your-enemies-sermon-delivered-dexter-avenue-baptist-church.
9. *Ibid.*
10. J.K. Rowling, *Harry Potter and the Deathly Hallows* (New York: Scholastic, 2007), 357.
11. *Fantastic Beasts: The Secrets of Dumbledore,* directed by David Yates (2022, Burbank, CA: Warner Bros. Pictures, 2022).
12. Rowling, *Deathly Hallows*, 717.
13. For more on how Dumbledore manages knowledge asymmetries throughout the series, see M'Balia Thomas's essay in this volume.
14. Thanks to Katy McDaniel for pointing this example out to me.
15. J.K. Rowling, *Harry Potter and the Half-Blood Prince* (New York: Scholastic, 2005), 49.
16. Rowling, *Tales of Beedle the Bard*, 12.
17. J.K. Rowling, *Harry Potter and the Prisoner of Azkaban* (New York: Scholastic, 2001), 2.
18. Rowling, *Half-Blood Prince*, 3.
19. *Ibid.*, 15.
20. *Ibid.*, 17.
21. *Ibid.*

22. Rowling, *Deathly Hallows*, 241–242.
23. For more on the power dynamic between Muggles and wizards, see Kathryn N. McDaniel's essay in this volume.
24. J.K. Rowling, *Harry Potter and the Chamber of Secrets* (New York: Scholastic Books, 1999), 116.
25. Rowling, *Tales of Beedle the Bard*, 1.
26. Ibram X. Kendi, *Stamped from the Beginning: The Definitive History of Racist Ideas in America* (New York: Bold Type Books, 2016), 124.
27. Ibid.
28. Ibid., 125.
29. See the 1982 study by Shirley Brice Heath, "What No Bedtime Story Means: Narrative Skills at Home and School," *Language in Society* 11, no. 1 (April 1982), pp. 49–76. See also Beverly Daniel Tatum's work, *Why Are All the Black Kids Sitting Together in the Cafeteria?* (New York: Basic Books, 2017).
30. Melissa Florer-Bixler, *How to Have an Enemy* (Harrisonburg: Herald Press, 2021), 92.
31. *Ted Lasso*, season 1, episode 6, "Two Aces," directed by Elliot Hegarty, written by Bill Wrubel, aired September 4, 2020, on Apple TV+ and *Ted Lasso*, season 2, episode 10, "No Weddings and a Funeral," directed by M.J. Delaney, written by Jane Becker, aired September 24, 2021, on Apple TV+.
32. I am not arguing here that Jason Sudeikis created the show based on the fairy tale but, practically speaking, it has extremely similar themes.
33. Melissa Florer-Bixler, "'Ted Lasso' showed how kindness can change UK soccer. Until we saw the real UK soccer," *Religion News Service*, July 20, 2021, https://religionnews.com/2021/07/20/ted-lasso-showed-how-kindness-can-change-uk-soccer-until-we-saw-the-real-uk-soccer/.
34. Consider the television show *Schitt's Creek*. The show traces the woes of a previously rich family that loses everything and has to live in a small, rural, American town—exactly the kind of location where you could and would find homophobia as a norm. Yet David Rose, who is pansexual and whose relationship with another man is a key part of the series, experiences absolutely no homophobia. The entire town is accepting and loving and supportive. The notion that anyone would be homophobic is entirely dismissed. Our response to this could easily be, "Well this isn't realistic at all, and therefore it's not helpful to the fight against homophobia." I agree with the first half of the statement: *Schitt's Creek* is unrealistic and not a good description of the current state of the world. I disagree with the second half; *Schitt's Creek* gives us a vision of what the world could look like without homophobia. That is a vision we need.
35. Rowling herself has become embroiled in controversy over her stance on feminism and transgender rights, and while her beliefs seem to have come long after she wrote *Harry Potter*, she continues to add to the series, and her views should play some role in understanding and critiquing them. See Brent Satterly's chapter in this volume.
36. Florer-Bixler, *How to Have an Enemy*, 92.
37. Ibid., 98.
38. King, "Loving Your Enemies."
39. Sharon Brous, "Imagine a Bible with No Moses, No Story of the Exodus," *New York Times*, April 14, 2022, https://www.nytimes.com/2022/04/14/opinion/passover-exodus-story-redemption.html.
40. Rowling, *Deathly Hallows*, 741.

Uncle Remus's Shack
Tokenism in the Wizarding World

MARK-ANTHONY LEWIS

Harry Potter's first interaction with a magical person is the moment he meets "Rubeus Hagrid, Keeper of Keys and Grounds at Hogwarts"[1] on his eleventh birthday. Upon first sight, Hagrid is a large and menacing figure: bursting through a cabin door on a stormy night, bending steel without a blush, and reducing Harry's abusive uncle to a blubbering mess. But Hagrid is also warm. He has a funny country accent, he has eyes that glint "like black beetles,"[2] and he baked Harry a cake for his birthday. Hagrid's cuddly and domesticated personality subverts the expectations set by his initially savage appearance.

Over the course of the *Harry Potter* series, Harry comes to learn about the minority cultures of the wizarding world through conversations with friendly part-humans like Hagrid the half-giant, Firenze the centaur, Dobby the elf, and Lupin the werewolf. We can call these part-humans tokens because each is separated from the culture they are meant to represent and thrust unceremoniously into the greater magical world dominated by wizards. These gentle, good-natured folk perform a rhetorical balancing act by describing the plight of their people at the hands of wizard supremacists in a way that is both pitiable and non-accusatory. And each is careful to show some sort of reverence to our protagonist.

The discourse surrounding these minority cultures is always framed by the particular perspectives of these token characters. Each character Harry encounters is an outcast from their native culture. But they must also act as a representative of the culture they were cast out from when navigating the wizarding world.

Part-Humans Live in a State of Double-Consciousness

In his 1903 work, *The Souls of Black Folk*, W.E.B. Du Bois, who grew up in a mostly White town in northern Massachusetts, described a phenomenon particular to the American Negro where one is "always looking at one's self through the eyes of others."[3] As Du Bois describes, the Negro "ever feels his twoness,—an American, a Negro; two souls, two thoughts, two unreconciled strivings; two warring ideals in one dark body."[4] Many of the minority folks of the wizarding world describe this concept of twoness quite literally. Centaurs occupy bodies composed of the upper body of a man and the legs and torso of a horse. Werewolves live each month of their lives split between two bodies and two minds: one human, one wolf. Hagrid and Madame Maxime are both genetically half-giant and half-wizard. Elves, goblins, and giants are humanoid in appearance but also distinctly *not* human.

Wizarding legislation and culture refer to many of these people as "part-humans"; the term part-human canonically includes vampires,[5] half-giants,[6] werewolves, merpeople,[7] and centaurs.[8] But it could also include anyone other than pure-blood wizards. British wizarding law frequently leaves anyone not from a pure-blood family with fewer human rights than others.[9] They are human but also not-human—that is, two souls, two unreconciled strivings, two warring ideals in one body.

The Token Is Both a Representative and an Outcast

The Shrieking Shack is where Remus Lupin, the wizard, goes to become Moony the werewolf. Lupin's transition is a painful and torturous process which Hogwarts expects him to undergo completely alone—separated from the rest of the student body, with no werewolf community to teach him, through shared experience, how to make the process more bearable. He is assigned no one to empathize with him, no one to offer commiseration. After he has purged his wolfish ways, Lupin is once again allowed to enter back into the wizarding fold. Lupin's inclusion at Hogwarts School is the token inclusion of a werewolf made possible only to him. There is no indication in the series that anyone other than Lupin has made use of the Shrieking Shack for transformations, and there's nothing to indicate that Professor Snape has brewed the Wolfsbane Potion for anyone other than Professor Lupin. Lupin's inclusion is made possible solely through Dumbledore's sympathy as headmaster.[10]

Remus Lupin's experience at Hogwarts is a classic case of tokenism. Civil rights leaders like Martin Luther King, Jr., defined tokenism as the symbolic representation of change disguising a lack of actual change,[11] and Malcolm X once defined tokenism as "one or two Negroes in a job, or at a lunch counter, so the rest of you will be quiet."[12]

The other part-humans of the *Harry Potter* series occupy the role of token as well. After being freed, Dobby the elf describes to Harry his lonely odyssey looking for work in a wizarding world that has no use for a free elf.[13] His position at Hogwarts is a token exception among elves; even alongside Winky, another freed elf, Dobby is still the only one to make a salary. After his falling out with the centaur herd in *Order of the Phoenix*, Firenze lives in solitude on the ground floor of Hogwarts in a private terrarium tailored specifically for him. His inclusion under the roof of Hogwarts is a token inclusion leaving him segregated from wizards as well as other centaurs. During the events of *Goblet of Fire*, Hagrid must process the trauma of his outing as a half-giant in wizard newspapers without the companionship of the only other half-giant he has ever met, Madame Maxime. Each part-human must cope with their twoness through the eyes of others and never with the empathy of kin.

But the major part-human characters of *Harry Potter* are not only tokens. They are outcasts as well. As a freed elf, Dobby is an outcast among house-elves—his freedom is an uncomfortable subject among the elves of Hogwarts and absolutely shameful in the eyes of Winky. Hagrid is an outcast among giants, having been abandoned by his giantess mother as a baby and living exclusively among wizards since childhood. Hagrid even tells Madame Maxime in *Goblet of Fire* that he's never met another like himself before.[14] Firenze is literally *cast out* by his centaur herd during the events of *Order of the Phoenix* because of his refusal to obey centaur culture and his degrading obedience to wizarding kind. During the events of *Half-Blood Prince*, Lupin reveals that his werewolf fellows deem him untrustworthy, because he bears "the unmistakable signs of having tried to live among wizards."[15] While a token must, by definition, be from an underrepresented or minority category, each of these tokens has also been rejected by their category as well.

In her 1977 paper "Some Effects of Proportions on Group Life," Rosabeth Moss Kanter argues that belonging to a group with skewed demographics can affect the behavior of both minority members of the group as well as majority members. Kanter says members of the group who belong to a minority category "can appropriately be called 'tokens,' because they are often treated as representatives of their category, as symbols rather than individuals."[16]

Though characters like Lupin and Hagrid have found some semblance of a home among wizards, their efforts will never satisfy their need for what Du Bois refers to as "self-consciousness."[17] Their minority positions will not allow them to escape looking upon themselves through the eyes of others—that is to say, filling the role of representatives or symbols rather than self-conscious individuals. Lupin's appeals to the werewolves in *Half-Blood Prince* and Hagrid's appeals to the giants in *Order of the Phoenix* are necessary actions to achieve any kind of self-fulfillment. Kanter also says,

> Use of the term "token" for the minority member rather than "solo," "solitary," or "lone" highlights some special characteristics associated with that position. Tokens are not merely deviant or people who differ from other group members along any one dimension. They are people identified by ascribed characteristics ... or other characteristics that carry with them a set of assumptions about culture, status, and behavior highly salient for majority category members.... They can never be just another member while their category is so rare; they will always be a hyphenated member, as in "woman-engineer" or "male-nurse" or "black-physician."[18]

While Seamus Finnigan may be the only Irish character of the series, part-humans are different in a more socially conspicuous way. Part-humans like werewolves, half-giants, and centaurs can never fully belong to the wizarding community as long as their category is so rare. They can never be fully-expressed people but always diminished caricatures identified by ascribed characteristics within wizarding society. They will always be part-humans—that is, hyphenated members (were-wolves, mer-people, half-giants) of a *wizarding* community rather than full members of a *magical* community.

Yet despite their unwitting roles as representatives, these part-humans are not even accurate representatives due to their roles as outcasts. Lupin is not your typical werewolf. Firenze is not your typical centaur. Hagrid is not your typical giant. Dobby is not your typical house-elf. These characters are outliers—outcasts of the category they represent. And so, their representation will always be a filtered, sanitized representation—that is to say, an easier pill to swallow for the majority category.

Each Token Has a Double

As early as 1962, Martin Luther King, Jr., gave his "Case Against Tokenism" in an op-ed to the *New York Times*.[19] Later, in his book *Why We Can't Wait*, King argued tokenism was a new method of thwarting the dreams and aspirations of Black people. He defined a token as "a symbol ... a keepsake ... a piece of metal used in place of a coin.... But he who sells you the token instead of the coin always retains the power to revoke its worth.... Tokenism is a promise to pay. Democracy ... is payment."[20]

King echoes the rhetoric of union leader A. Philip Randolph who, earlier in 1960, called tokenism a "thin veneer of acceptance masquerading as democracy."[21]

To King, tokenism was not real change. Tokenism was a *symbol* of the hope that change may come soon, a token gesture from those who hold power over the powerless. By this definition, tokenism is not rhetoric that leads to action; it is appeasement designed to effect complacency rather than create change. Though Dumbledore will accept anyone at Hogwarts, "s'long as they've got the talent,"[22] token inclusions like Lupin, Hagrid, Firenze, and Dobby are only a promise to pay. Their inclusion is at best a small step in the right direction. At worst, it is the equivalent of the Fountain of Magical Brethren, a lie meant to appease. A true democracy of all magical peoples is payment.

Though Malcolm X disagreed with King on the subject of integration, he used much of the same rhetoric when describing tokenism. In a 1963 interview, Black journalist Louis Lomax asked Malcolm X his opinion on the gains Negroes had made in recent years. X responded, "What gains? All you have gotten is tokenism."[23] But much worse than that, Malcolm X argued that tokenism's goal was malicious rather than irreverent. In a speech at Michigan State University of the same year, X said:

> Tokenism is hypocrisy. One little student in the University of Mississippi, that's hypocrisy. A handful of students in Little Rock, Arkansas, is hypocrisy. A couple of students going to school in Georgia is hypocrisy. Integration in America is hypocrisy in the rawest form. And the whole world can see it. All this little tokenism that is dangled in front of the Negro and then he's told, "See what we're doing for you, Tom." Why, the whole world can see that this is nothing but hypocrisy.[24]

To Malcolm X, these efforts at tokenism went beyond appeasement. They were symbols of oppression—the exceptions that prove the rule. It is no wonder that, while some part-humans have been accepted into the fold of Dumbledore's attempts at tokenism, others on the outside look in with disgust. While Lupin, Firenze, Dobby, and Hagrid are all outcasts with token inclusion into the wizarding world, each token is presented with a double who challenges their strivings. Fenrir Greyback, Bane the centaur, Winky the house-elf, and Madame Maxime all challenge our primary part-humans by further demonstrating Du Bois's concept of the "double-consciousness" of Black folk.

As Du Bois says, the Negro lives with "a sense of always looking at one's self through the eyes of others, of measuring one's soul by the tape of a world that looks on in amused contempt and pity." So the token assimilates, but the double refuses to "bleach his Negro soul in a flood of white Americanism, for he knows that Negro blood has a message for the world."[25] These two sides of the same consciousness have warring ideals that must be reconciled to become complete. They argue from opposing pulpits, but they seek the same truth. While our token characters have tried to assimilate into the wizarding world to varying degrees (shedding their differences to be included in the majority group), the doubles have rebelled by not only rejecting assimilation but by also accentuating their differences from the majority—and therefore creating trouble for wizards.

Fenrir Greyback and the Werewolf Community

Although Remus Lupin gains acceptance into Hogwarts school to live what he calls the best years of his life, many werewolves are not so lucky. While Lupin lives in relative comfort among wizards, most werewolves "have shunned normal society and live on the margins, stealing—and sometimes killing—to eat."[26] They live underground, "almost literally."[27] But they clearly have community. They have fellowship. And Lupin infiltrates this community as a spy, sarcastically referring to the other werewolves as his "fellows." But as Lupin tells us, "I cannot pretend that my particular brand of reasoned argument is making much headway against Greyback's insistence that we werewolves deserve blood, that we ought to revenge ourselves on normal people."[28] Lupin is a token who bears the signs of trying to identify himself with his oppressors. To Malcolm X, this token Negro was synonymous to a house Negro during times of slavery:

> Whenever that house Negro identified himself, he always identified himself in the same sense that his master identified himself.... His master's pain was his pain. And it hurt him more for his master to be sick than for him to be sick himself.... If someone came to the house Negro and said, "Let's go, let's separate," naturally that Uncle Tom would say, "Go where? What could I do without boss? Where would I live? How would I dress? Who would look out for me?" That's the house Negro.[29]

Malcolm X argued tokenism was the brainwashing of a subjugated person to make them lose identification with their own suffering fellows. The token was persuaded to choose the well-being of their oppressors over kith and kin. Clearly, this is the thinking of many of the werewolves who choose Greyback's path over Lupin's.

During the events of *Half-Blood Prince*, Lupin describes Greyback to Harry as, "perhaps, the most savage werewolf alive today. He regards it as his mission in life to bite and to contaminate as many people as possible; he wants to create enough werewolves to overcome the wizards. Voldemort has promised him prey in return for his services. Greyback specializes in children.... Bite them young, he says, and raise them away from their parents, raise them to hate normal wizards."[30] Lupin is an outcast of werewolf society, but Greyback is a leader and propagator of werewolf society. He lives not only unashamed of his werewolfness but proud, too. Of course, being systematically oppressed does not mean we must forgive the evil deeds of individuals, but it does help explain those deeds and the complex person behind them, because despite his fierce opposition to subjugation by wizards, even Greyback falls under the same trap as Lupin, only on the opposite side of the wizard war. Greyback is himself a token among the Death Eaters who mock and dehumanize werewolves openly and proudly.[31] Greyback is Lupin's equal-opposite, suffering under the same oppression with an opposite strategy to fight it.

Bane and the Centaur Herd

Though readers can look at Lupin and Greyback and declare Lupin's brand of reasoned argument as the saner of the two options, that choice becomes murkier when we look at the doubles of Firenze and Bane. We first met the centaurs in *Sorcerer's Stone*, where their animosity towards each other is immediately on display: "'Firenze!'" Bane yells upon seeing Harry riding on his back. "'What are you doing? You have a human on your back! Have you no shame? Are you a common mule?'"[32]

Bane, as a conservator and devotee of centaur culture, becomes enraged whenever he sees any centaur show submissiveness to humans. As Bane says, "Centaurs are concerned with what has been foretold! It is not our business to run around like donkeys after stray humans in our forest!"[33] Though Bane sometimes comes across as irrationally angry, his frustrations are understandable. As tokens, avoiding assimilation is near impossible. And as Dolores Umbridge begins to indicate in *Order of the Phoenix* before being silenced by Bane, wizards have encroached on protected centaur land in the past and continue to do so in the present. Their oppression is akin to native genocide in America, and Dolores Umbridge is indeed the writer of their destiny while brandishing the weapon of their oppression.

Centaurs are a proud people with their own culture, customs, and intelligence. As a centaur tells Hermione shortly after the incident with Umbridge, "We do not help humans! … We are a race apart and proud to be so."[34] The centaur's words echo those of Malcolm X who said in his 1963 interview at the University of California, Berkeley, "We don't want to be equal with the white man. He is not the criteria or yardstick by which equality is measured. He's not in a position to tell us we are equal. It's not his right."[35] When you belong to the dominant group, it is easy to assume equality means treating everyone as if they belong to the dominant group. But this undermines the inherent values of the minority group. When Umbridge accuses the centaurs of having "near human intelligence," Magorian, the leader of the centaurs, says, "Our intelligence, thankfully, far outstrips your own."[36]

Where Bane and many other centaurs differ from Firenze is that they refuse to integrate with wizards—probably through a fear of assimilation but also through a strong sense of pride in their own way of doing things. To someone like Malcolm X, the problem with Dumbledore, and the reason his efforts fail, is because he is not in a position to provide equality to the part-humans of the magical world. Equality cannot be given; it can only be taken by the part-human community. As Malcolm X says in his Michigan State speech:

> We don't think as Americans anymore. But as a black man. With the mind of a black man, we look beyond America. And we look beyond the interests of the white man. The thinking of this new type of Negro is broad. It's more international. Integration always thinks in terms of an American. But you'll find the masses of black people today think in terms of "black." And this black thinking enables them to see beyond the confines of America, and they look all over the world.[37]

Wizards view the magical community exclusively through the eyes of wizards. They refer to their community as the "wizarding" world. And even when wizards attempt to amplify the voices of part-human magical people, they do so in the language of wizards and with all of the limitations of that language. Their rhetoric is framed with wizards at the center and all other magical peoples revolving around them. But there is a much larger universe of magical folk whose astronomical model does not place wizards at the center. Centaurs see beyond the confines of wizards. They are cosmic in their thinking.

Winky and the Hogwarts House-Elves

While the centaur and werewolf communities rebel against wizard oppression in ways that make the strivings of Lupin and Firenze more difficult, the greater house-elf community makes an outcast of Dobby, not by rejecting the role assigned to them by the dominant group, but by accepting it.

At the beginning of *Goblet of Fire*, while she is still the property of Barty Crouch, Sr., Winky tells Harry, "House-elves is not supposed to have fun, Harry Potter.... House-elves does what they are told."[38] This view is accepted by the broader house-elf community. An unnamed Hogwarts house-elf tells Hermione, to her shock, "house-elves has no right to be unhappy when there is work to be done and masters to be served."[39] Their discomfort with Dobby's freedom is clear. "Freedom is going to Dobby's head, sir," Winky tells Harry. "I says to Dobby, I says, go find yourself a nice family and settle down, Dobby. He is getting up to all sorts of high jinks, sir, what is unbecoming to a house-elf. You goes racketing around like this, Dobby, I says, and next thing I hear you's up in front of the Department for the Regulation and Control of Magical Creatures, like some common goblin."[40]

While Winky and the rest of the Hogwarts house-elves fit into Malcolm X's view of the brainwashed house Negro, characters like Hermione make the mistake of viewing their oppression through the eyes of wizards and attempting to gift them equality, which cannot be done without acknowledging one's own superiority. Winky's perspective may be tainted by the poisonous rhetoric of her subjugated upbringing, but she and the rest of the house-elves cannot be tricked or manipulated into accepting the gift of wizard equality. Their self-consciousness can only come from within the community.

Madame Maxime

Hagrid the half-giant may be the first magical person Harry meets in the series, but we don't meet another half-giant until Madame Maxime in *Goblet of Fire*. Olympe Maxime's introduction is completely opposed to Hagrid's:

> Harry had only ever seen one person as large as this woman in his life, and that was Hagrid.... As she stepped into the light flooding from the entrance hall, she was revealed to have a handsome, olive-skinned face; large, black, liquid-looking eyes; and a rather beaky nose. Her hair was drawn back in a shining knob at the base of her neck. She was dressed from head to foot in black satin, and many magnificent opals gleamed at her throat and on her thick fingers.[41]

Where Hagrid is at first savage and then tame, Madame Maxime is immediately elegant, sophisticated, and severe. Every aspect of her—from her personality, to the way she dresses, to how her students address her—seems to dissuade any suggestion that she comes from giant heritage. When Hagrid suggests that she might, Maxime's response is, "I 'ave nevair been more insulted in my life! 'Alf-giant? Moi? I 'ave—I 'ave big bones!"[42]

In Ezra Edelman's 2016 documentary *O.J.: Made in America*, friends and acquaintances of O.J. Simpson recount O.J.'s complicated relationship with Blackness and race throughout his life. Around late 1967, Black athletes along with civil rights leaders and activists chose to boycott the 1968 Olympic Games with the support of Martin Luther King, Jr., and famous athletes like Jim Brown, Kareem Abdul-Jabbar, and Muhammad Ali. Simpson, who was at the time a famous football star at the University of Southern California, was approached by Dr. Harry Edwards, a leader in the Olympics boycott. But whenever O.J. was publicly asked about his opinion on the boycott or whether he might possibly participate, O.J. waffled and claimed ignorance on the subject.

In private, Edwards recounts trying to persuade O.J. to join the boycott. He says, "O.J. was approached because he was the biggest name in college athletics at that time. He was also a world record holding track star at that time. So here we got two for one.... When I asked him, I said, 'We're trying to get black athletes to understand they have a role in the current Civil Rights Movement.' His response was, 'I'm not black. I'm O.J.'"[43]

Later in the documentary, *New York Times* journalist Robert Lipsyte recounts interviewing O.J. in June of 1969, and O.J. told him a story:

> He was telling me a story about being at a teammate's wedding with his wife sitting at a table of mostly, as he said, Negroes. And he overheard a white woman at the next table say, "Look, there's O.J. sitting with all those niggers!" And I remember, in my naiveté, saying to O.J., "Jee, wow. That must have been terrible for you!" and he said, "No! It was great. Don't you understand? She knew that I wasn't black. She saw me as O.J."[44]

Where Lupin's, Firenze's, and even Dobby's doubles all become even more extreme caricatures of their category, Hagrid's double attempts to persuade others she has, in her eyes, risen above her category. But as Hagrid tells Harry, "There's some who'd ... pretend they just had big bones rather than stand up an' say—I am what I am, an' I'm not ashamed."[45] No matter how much she may try to assimilate, Madame Maxime is who she is, and shame of it will not allow her to escape her largeness.

The Token Is Untrusted by Both Consciousnesses

The ultimate struggle that comes from a double-consciousness is that the strivings of both consciousnesses will inevitably conflict. Their warring ideals will not allow the other to succeed. Fenrir Greyback can put werewolves above all others and play demagogue. Madame Maxime can ignore her giant heritage, drape herself in satin and opals, and stay safe from the public epithets Hagrid endures. One can pick a side and avoid the conflict that comes from playing for both teams. But the tokens don't always get to pick a side.

As Rosabeth Moss Kanter tells us, "Visibility creates performance pressure on the token. Polarization leads to group boundary heightening and isolation of the token. And assimilation results in the token's role entrapment."[46] Merely by being a token, the token is not only caricatured in the eyes of the majority group, but they are also more likely to fulfill the role created for them or else turn against their native category. Tokens may be

> expected to demonstrate loyalty to the dominant group.... Through loyalty tests, the group seeks reassurance that tokens will not turn against them or use any of the information gained through their viewing of the dominants' world to do harm to the group. They get this assurance by asking a token to join or identify with the majority against those others who represent competing membership or reference groups; in short, dominants pressure tokens to turn against members of the latter's own category.[47]

This is why those like Malcolm X saw tokenism as so nefarious. The brainwashing of the token could do damage to the category as a whole. As Malcolm X says in the Michigan State speech, "The house Negro ... wore his master's second-hand clothes ... ate food that his master left on the table ... lived in his master's house—probably in the basement or the attic—but he still lived in the master's house." The house Negro identified with his oppressors and remained loyal to them even above his own well-being, so much so that "it hurt him more for his master to be sick than for him to be sick himself. When the house started burning down, that type of Negro would fight harder to put the master's house out than the master himself would."[48] The token must display loyalty to survive.

Harry Potter, the Champion

While wizards like Harry Potter and Albus Dumbledore do not represent the wizard supremacist ideology expounded by Lord Voldemort or enforced by the Ministry of Magic, they are popular enough figures within the wizarding world that it would be wise for any part-human to display loyalty to one or both of them.

Upon meeting him for the first time in *Chamber of Secrets*, Dobby tells Harry Potter, with tears in his eyes:

> If he knew what he means to us, to the lowly, the enslaved, we dregs of the magical world! Dobby remembers how it was when He-Who-Must-Not-Be-Named was at the height of his powers, sir! We house-elves were treated like vermin, sir! ... But mostly, sir, life has improved for my kind since you triumphed over He-Who-Must-Not-Be-Named. Harry Potter survived, and the Dark Lord's power was broken, and it was a new dawn, sir, and Harry Potter shone like a

beacon of hope for those of us who thought the dark days would never end, sir.[49]

Harry Potter is the champion of the lowly dregs of the magical world. He is a champion to those who he didn't even know existed. He is a champion to those who he hasn't even met in large numbers. And many of the token characters of the series are careful to pay fealty to him. Upon first meeting Harry in *Sorcerer's Stone*, Firenze tells his fellow centaurs, "Do you realize who this is? ... This is the Potter boy."[50] And during his conversation with Harry in *Deathly Hallows*, Griphook the goblin tells Harry, "I remember, Harry Potter. Even amongst goblins, you are very famous."[51] But even these loyalty tests are not enough to quell all doubt. Even with complete and unconditional loyalty, the token is still separate.

Lupin, the Traitor

The inciting incident of the *Harry Potter* series is the death of Lily and James Potter at the hand of Lord Voldemort. Their death is made possible by the betrayal of a spy who turns out to be one of James's closest friends. During the events of *Prisoner of Azkaban*, we find out that shortly before his death, James Potter and the Marauders hatched a secret plan where he, along with Lily and baby Harry, would hide under the protection of a Fidelius Charm. They would let leak that Sirius Black was the Potters' Secret-Keeper, when in actuality Peter Pettigrew was the secret Secret-Keeper.

All but one of the four Marauders were involved in making this plan: Remus Lupin. But why wouldn't Lupin, the only remaining member of this tight-knit group of friends, be in on the secret? "Not if he thought I was the spy.... I assume that's why you didn't tell me, Sirius?"[52] Lupin says in *Prisoner of Azkaban*. Curiously, though Lupin accepts this suspicion, he offers no reason to be suspected. James could not be the spy, because he was the subject of the spying. But Sirius came from a family of open wizard supremacists, and his own brother was a Death Eater. Peter Pettigrew (the actual spy) was ignored out of a sense of his inferiority. But Lupin had no marks against him—other than being a werewolf.

As a token, Lupin made wizards his closest friends, he remained loyal to them, and he sacrificed his own safety in the fight for their causes. Yet, he was still never fully trusted. Despite living among them, wearing their clothes and eating their food—despite fully assimilating into the dominant group—Lupin's differences never faded. He was still a werewolf, and werewolves cannot be trusted. Even through loyalty tests and assimilation, tokens can neither be fully trusted by the dominant group nor by their own category.

The Double-Consciousness Must Be Reconciled

W.E.B. Du Bois describes a longing by the American Negro to "attain self-conscious manhood, to merge his double self into a better and truer self."[53] The American Negro, like a man made into a Horcrux, is a segregated self of warring ideas in one body "whose dogged strength alone keeps it from being torn asunder."[54] These selves apart cannot be wholly true. Lupin and Fenrir, Dobby and Winky, Hagrid and Madame Maxime, Firenze and Bane need to reconcile their strivings, and in this reconciliation

> he wishes neither of the older selves to be lost. He would not Africanize America, for America has too much to teach the world and Africa. He would not bleach his Negro soul in a flood of white Americanism, for he knows that Negro blood has a message for the world. He simply wishes to make it possible for a man to be both a Negro and an American, without being cursed and spit upon by his fellows, without having the doors of Opportunity closed roughly in his face.[55]

As with all impossible things, it is a struggle but not an unworthy struggle. The battle against the ideals of wizard supremacy did not end with the death of Lord Voldemort. As Snape tells his Defense Against the Dark Arts class in *Half-Blood Prince*, "The Dark Arts ... are many, varied, ever-changing, and eternal. Fighting them is like fighting a many-headed monster, which, each time a neck is severed, sprouts a head even fiercer and cleverer than before. You are fighting that which is unfixed, mutating, indestructible."[56] But with each battle, you gain ground and inch a little closer.

By the end of the *Harry Potter* series, all is not yet well. Dobby's unabashed love of freedom was not enough to end house-elf enslavement. Lupin's ever-conflicted self is proof that even his privileged position in wizarding society was wrought with strife. Hagrid was able to make some gains in acceptance of his brother Grawp, but only small gains in terms of giants. And despite Firenze becoming a teacher at Hogwarts, humans will ever be "blinkered and fettered by the limitations of their kind."[57] But that doesn't make the efforts of these token part-humans futile. As Du Bois says, "This, then, is the end of his striving: to be a co-worker in the kingdom of culture, to escape both death and isolation, to husband and use his best powers and his latent genius."[58] While each token fails in one way or another to reconcile their double-consciousness, their striving is not in vain. These tokens have laid the groundwork for others to pick up where they left off. They have breached the boundaries of the kingdom of culture and they have allowed for the latent genius of their successors to awaken.

Notes

1. J.K. Rowling, *Harry Potter and the Sorcerer's Stone* (New York: Scholastic, 1997), 48.
2. *Ibid.*, 47.
3. W.E.B. Du Bois, *The Souls of Black Folk* (New York: Alfred A. Knopf, 1903), 9.
4. *Ibid.*
5. J.K. Rowling, *Harry Potter and the Goblet of Fire* (New York: Scholastic, 2000), 147.
6. *Ibid.*, 439.
7. J.K. Rowling, *Harry Potter and the Order of the Phoenix* (New York: Scholastic, 2003), 302.
8. *Ibid.*, 600.
9. J.K. Rowling, *Harry Potter and the Half-Blood Prince* (New York: Scholastic, 2005), 368.
10. J.K. Rowling, *Harry Potter and the Prisoner of Azkaban* (New York: Scholastic, 1999), 353.
11. Martin Luther King, Jr., *Why We Can't Wait* (Boston: Beacon Press, 1964), 30.
12. Malcolm X, "A Summing-Up: Louis Lomax Interviews Malcolm X," interview by Louis Lomax, *When the Word Is Given. . . .* (Cleveland: World, 1963), 200.
13. Rowling, *Goblet of Fire*, 378.
14. *Ibid.*, 428.
15. Rowling, *Half-Blood Prince*, 334.
16. Rosabeth Moss Kanter, "Some Effects of Proportions on Group Life," *American Journal of Sociology* 82, no. 5 (1977): 966.
17. Du Bois, *Souls of Black Folk*, 9.
18. Kanter, "Some Effects of Proportions," 968.
19. Martin Luther King, Jr., "The Case Against 'Tokenism,'" *New York Times*, August 5, 1962.
20. King, *Why We Can't Wait*, 30.
21. A.H. Raskin, "Negro Labor Unit Founded by 1,000 Will Fight Racial Pejudice but Leader Denies It Will War on A.F.L.-C.I.O.," *New York Times*, May 28, 1960.
22. Rowling, *Goblet of Fire*, 455.
23. X, "A Summing-Up," 200.
24. Malcolm X, "The Race Problem," January 23, 1963, Michigan State University, East Lansing, Michigan, MP3, 0:58:29, https://onthebanks.msu.edu/Object/162-565-2359/malcolm-x-speaks-at-michigan-state-university-1963/.
25. Du Bois, *Souls of Black Folk*, 9.
26. Rowling, *Half-Blood Prince*, 334.
27. *Ibid.*
28. *Ibid.*, 335.
29. X, "The Race Problem," 0:33:22.
30. Rowling, *Half-Blood Prince*, 334–335.
31. J.K. Rowling, *Harry Potter and the Deathly Hallows* (New York: Scholastic, 2007), 10.
32. Rowling, *Sorcerer's Stone*, 257.
33. *Ibid.*
34. Rowling, *Order of the Phoenix*, 756.
35. Malcolm X, "Malcolm X—interview at Berkley (1963)," interview by Herman Blake, University of California Berkeley, October 24, 1963, 29:14, https://archive.org/details/MalcolmXInterviewAtUCBerkeley/.
36. Rowling, *Order of the Phoenix*, 754.
37. X, "The Race Problem," 1:02:40.
38. Rowling, *Goblet of Fire*, 98–99.
39. *Ibid.*, 538.
40. *Ibid.*, 98.
41. *Ibid.*, 243–244.
42. *Ibid.*, 429.

43. *O.J.: Made in America*, directed by Ezra Edelman (2016; ESPN Films) episode 01, 0:28:30.
44. *Ibid.*, 0:35:55.
45. Rowling, *Goblet of Fire*, 455–456.
46. Kanter, "Some Effects of Proportions," 972.
47. *Ibid.*, 978–79.
48. X, "The Race Problem," 0:33:00.
49. J.K. Rowling, *Harry Potter and the Chamber of Secrets* (New York: Scholastic, 1999), 177–178.
50. Rowling, *Philosopher's Stone*, 257.
51. Rowling, *Deathly Hallows*, 486.
52. Rowling, *Prisoner of Azkaban*, 373.
53. Du Bois, *Souls of Black Folk*, 9.
54. *Ibid.*
55. *Ibid.*
56. Rowling, *Half-Blood Prince*, 177.
57. Rowling, *Order of the Phoenix*, 603.
58. Du Bois, *Souls of Black Folk*, 9.

Conversation
Self and Others

Travis Prinzi (TP) and Mark-Anthony Lewis (MAL) talk with Katy McDaniel (KM) and Emily Strand (ES) about their essays.

KM: [Travis and Mark-Anthony], your section of the book is called "Self and Other," and we've been talking a lot about that through our conversation. What difficulties do you two see in our thinking about ourselves in relation to others and the way we see others in relation to ourselves. So just thinking about that "us versus them" dynamic, what are the difficulties there that narrative can overcome?

TP: Well, one of the big things, obviously, about "the Other" is fear of the unknown. The *Harry Potter* series is much about fear of the unknown and the fear of death—what lies beyond that, that's a big theme. But you know, somebody who's different than me is also unknown. And I tend to think of fear as the real opposite of love, rather than hate.

My essay is located in religious and moral teaching, and there's the kind of basic love commands that are given in the New Testament. For example: love God, love your neighbor as yourself, and then love your enemy. There's that challenge that the one person comes up and gives Jesus, and says, "well, who is my neighbor?" And instead of defining the neighbor, Jesus gives a story dismantling the man's prejudice, and showing that even those horrible Samaritan people can be loving neighbors. So, there's overcoming of one's own fear so that you can open your eyes up to see people differently and equally that I think is vital to this whole conversation.

KM: Oh yes, absolutely. Seeing fear at the root of the Otherness and the idea of "them" being separate from "me," for sure. Mark-Anthony, what do you think?

MAL: I agree with Travis, but I think there's another dimension that makes it a little more difficult, in that even if we want to accept others into the umbrella of "us," even then, we have to acknowledge that other people are different and are okay with their differences and want to be different also. Reconciling those two ideas is really difficult, and I don't even know what the solution is to that.

You know, it's like all people, all Earth life is related, right? We're all from the same primordial soup, but we're all different too. And you can't treat a dog like a person and think that you're treating the dog well, because dogs have different needs than people do. And like we talked about earlier, you can't treat all people as if they're White and think that that's doing them a favor. You have to sort of remember that some of those differences are real, and they're not necessarily a bad thing. But being able to reconcile those two ideas that we're all related but we're all different is one of those difficult things that doesn't necessarily come from hate or fear but just from the difficult-ness of being a person. [Laughs.] Right?

ES: [Laughing.] Right.

KM: Oh yeah.

TP: One of the things that just struck me is, we're supposed to identify with Harry throughout the series. Do you know how many times Harry was wrong about his assumptions about ... just about anything? [Laughing.] So, I think just the imaginative experience of being wrong might train me, for example, to be willing to be wrong about things that I've always assumed were the norm, or right, or the right way to do things. Like, I'm a life-long grammar police, realizing that that's the White, western way of speaking, and that's correct. Well, not necessarily!

It's important to be able to be wrong and to say that even this thing I've held onto my whole life as being the way the world is, well that person over there, who's equally as human as me—and probably smarter—sees it completely differently. Taking the time to sit down and question your assumptions, and hear from somebody else, and re-think it is so important.

MAL: The freedom to be wrong, too, is important. Not just acknowledging that you can be wrong but also the freedom to be able to express your wrong-ness and talk it out and figure it out is important, too. Because it's not helpful to just keep it locked up in your head either, because then you'll never be right.

TP: And we live in such a "gotcha!" world, where as soon as you're wrong, somebody is ready to discredit you and say that you're stupid, and I'm the smart one, and there's the fear of that. Yes. The freedom to be wrong—and that being a safe thing to do—is important.

ES: Yes. It's a privilege to be wrong, and to publicly learn, and learn a different way.

KM: Yes. And as I'm thinking about this, I'm also thinking: Mark-Anthony, your essay on tokenism—I mean, it's a real challenge to people who want a world that is more inclusive, and they don't know how to do it except for tokenism. [Laughs.] What you are pointing out throughout the essay are just the tremendous limitations of that. How can we be inclusive without bringing people in as tokens and creating this two-ness problem?

And I do think it has to do with what both of you have been talking about, which is getting rid of the idea that there is one standard that is normal, that is the way everything should be, and everything needs to be blended. I think of the American "melting pot." That was the metaphor when I was growing up in school, was the "melting pot," that we're all supposed to be melted together in what ends up being a kind of WASP [White, Anglo-Saxon, Protestant] soup, I guess.

ES: [ironically] Yum.

MAL: A TV dinner.

KM: [Laughing.] Assimilation under high temperatures. But the metaphor that I guess kids use now is the "salad bowl," where the idea is that everybody's not supposed to end up the same. That there has to be room for all of the differences to play their part and to all be equally valued. So, I think, as you say Mark-Anthony, the challenges of actually achieving that are enormous, and Travis, your point about the structural aspects that we're often even unconscious of, you know it just creates these huge challenges. But what an important thing to do, to be able to think and talk about those through the characters that we find in "just" a fantasy novel like *Harry Potter*.

Playing Potter

It's All Fun and Games Until...
Leisurely and Competitive Pursuits in Harry Potter *and Chivalric Romance*

Laurie Beckoff

Despite the time-consuming activities of Hogwarts classes and regular run-ins with Dark wizards, Harry Potter still manages to fit recreational activities into his busy schedule. He is, after all, a child, and he deserves a bit of playtime, whether it's a casual game of wizard chess in the Gryffindor common room or a high-flying Quidditch match. Considering the well-noted medieval influence on the wizarding world, it is also thematically fitting for Harry to have a chance to engage in play. Even King Arthur's Knights of the Round Table, who are similarly occupied with quests, battles, and other adventures in a world of myth, magic, and monsters, entertain themselves with various forms of play, ranging from polite merriment to intense competition.

In his 1938 book *Homo Ludens*, Johan Huizinga defines play as a "voluntary activity," as opposed to one undertaken by necessity or for survival, that is separate from ordinary life in that it is clearly pretend and for fun rather than for profit.[1] It has boundaries of time and place, rules, and order.[2] At the same time, he notes that the "contrast between play and seriousness is always fluid" and that despite play being an "interlude in our daily lives," play takes on social and cultural significance that makes it "an integral part of life."[3] In both chivalric romance and *Harry Potter*, play tends to be positioned as secondary to the main plot and in the characters' lives. Heroes have important work to do and only so much time and energy to devote to fun, but courtly and wizarding games end up playing important roles in the lives of the characters and forcing their way to the forefront.

Scholars have examined Quidditch as a microcosm of the wizarding world and Harry's journey, but play is not an entirely separate sphere with strictly metaphorical significance.[4] The boundaries between games and narrative are blurred. While it may be argued that Quidditch could be removed from the series without impacting the story, like its reduced film presence, the sport is essential to character and plot development, as are other forms of wizarding play. There are three main dynamics between games and the larger world of the narrative in *Harry Potter* and Arthurian literature: games can prove useful in practical ways, the risks of innocent games can become truly dangerous, and games are impacted by and reflective of external circumstances. These connections demonstrate the function of games as a device for character- and world-building to establish heroic identity and reveal the values and pitfalls of a society, providing a lens through which to view games in our own culture.

Practice Makes Prowess

In playing games, participants have opportunities for social, physical, emotional, and intellectual development. The usefulness of games is clearest in transferable skill sets, but games can also break loose from their constraints and directly impact the outside world.

Identity

Quidditch gives Harry a sense of belonging and provides a gateway into the magical world. Initially, his lack of familiarity with the game reinforces his status as an outsider. Quidditch is introduced as not just a sport but a staple of magical culture, hailed as the greatest and most popular pastime in the wizarding world, seemingly followed by everyone. Draco Malfoy immediately asks Harry if he plays, Hagrid forgets that Harry is not aware of such an obvious fact of life, and Ron Weasley, despite knowing that Harry was raised by Muggles, asks what team he supports. Harry notices that "[e]veryone from wizarding families talked about Quidditch constantly."[5] His discovery of his natural talent at flying boosts his confidence as a newcomer in this strange new world when "in a rush of fierce joy he realized he'd found something he could do without being taught."[6] For the first time since learning the truth about his parents and past, Harry has the chance to be known for something over which he actually has control, for his own accomplishments and talents rather than something that happened to him as a baby. He becomes not merely the Boy Who Lived but the youngest Seeker in a century, an impressive athlete in his own right.

For medieval knights in both history and literature, games similarly offer opportunities to gain a place in courtly society and prove oneself.

Since many of the surviving sources that depict tournaments are chivalric romances, scholars often view historical and fictional portrayals side by side.[7] Both Thomas Malory and Chrétien de Troyes devote a large amount of space to describing tournaments and jousts in detail. Such martial games are so intrinsic to knighthood that they often seem not to be games at all but deeply serious undertakings directly tied to a knight's overall reputation. Victoria Weiss notes that when women began attending tournaments more often in the late thirteenth century, the events became "a much less dangerous, a much more scripted and controlled—and a much more beautiful and regal—way of forging and then reinforcing aristocratic identity."[8] Tournaments put knights on display, and according to Maurice Keen, just participating, no matter the success of one's performance, served as "a demonstration of a man's right to mingle in an elite society, of his social identity."[9] The spectacle, pageantry, and theater of tournaments and jousts simultaneously bolstered their status as both recreational entertainment and a crucial public venue for establishing social standing.

It is unsurprising that *Harry Potter*'s Triwizard Tournament functions comparably because it is a medieval tradition, "first established some seven hundred years ago," placing its invention in the late thirteenth century.[10] Representing their respective schools and nations, each champion has the chance to win the Triwizard Cup, glory for their school, and one thousand Galleons in prize money. This event offers an opportunity for cultural exchange and international magical cooperation, "to further and promote magical understanding," serving a social purpose on both the individual and institutional level.[11] It even comes with its own pageantry in the form of dramatic entrances and the Yule Ball.

Just as young wizards can boost their own and their school's profile through the Triwizard Tournament, knights use tournaments to demonstrate their skills and thereby win worship. Keen calls tournament performance "a step on the scale of chivalrous perfection."[12] William Caxton, printer and editor of Malory's *Le Morte D'Arthur*, advocated for the reintroduction of tournaments in the fifteenth century, arguing that they would "cause gentylemen to resorte to thauncyent customes of chivalry to grete fame and ronomee."[13] Tournaments allow knights in chivalric literature to gain respect and develop a reputation for their abilities even without appearing on an actual battlefield. Just from peacetime games, Arthur's knights "increased so in arms and worship that they passed all their fellows in prowess and noble deeds," and Lancelot especially stands out because "in all tournaments and jousts and deeds of arms, both for life and death, he passed all other knights," whereby he "increased so marvellously in worship, and in honour."[14] Gareth wants to joust with Lancelot because he knows that facing a knight of such renown will truly challenge his own prowess as well as boost his reputation.

In the fourteenth-century poem *Sir Gawain and the Green Knight*, Gawain, who like Gareth has yet to earn glory, accepts the Green Knight's "game" of allowing a knight to cut off his head and receive a blow in kind the following year, claiming that he is the least valuable member of the court whose death would be the smallest loss, significant only for being Arthur's nephew. Weiss notes that Arthur's laughter following the Green Knight's departure successfully restores cheer to the court because nobles understood games both "as a serious declaration of their status and worth, and paradoxically, as the kind of diversionary, inconsequential activity that working classes understood play to be."[15] The game is simultaneously a critical test of Gawain's knighthood and a recreational source of entertainment. Reflecting Huizinga's idea about the fluidity of seriousness and play, Arthurian and wizarding games toe the line between gravity and amusement.

Physical and Strategic Abilities

Games provide a way for wizards and knights to refine abilities that they need for more serious undertakings. K.S. Whetter notes that martial games do this by "utilising and honing the skills used in war."[16] Keen writes that tournaments "were undeniably good training for war" and posits that they may have been developed specifically for that reason, though their origin is not certain.[17] It is no coincidence that the knights who perform well in tournaments, such as Lancelot, also tend to be fearsome fighters who are formidable in battle. Reminiscent of medieval tournaments, the Triwizard Tournament tasks are intended to test the champions to prove their skills and strategy: "their magical prowess—their daring—their powers of deduction—and ... their ability to cope with danger."[18] Harry indeed ends up learning a great deal of useful magic in preparing for the tournament. His need to summon his broomstick for the first task is the motivation he needs to finally master the Summoning Charm he has been learning, without success, in class.

Elizabeth A. Galway argues that Quidditch, particularly playing Seeker, prepares Harry for his battle against Voldemort.[19] His flying ability is often useful outside of Quidditch matches. On a broom, Harry catches a flying key to proceed toward the Sorcerer's Stone, retrieves the golden egg from a Hungarian Horntail dragon in the Triwizard Tournament, and escapes Fiendfyre in the Room of Requirement. Even on foot, his Quidditch skills are useful, such as when he dodges Voldemort's curse "with the reflexes born of his Quidditch training."[20] When Harry finally defeats

Voldemort, he catches the Elder Wand "with the unerring skill of the Seeker," displaying his talent in the game at a critical moment.[21]

Emotional and Psychological Impact

Quidditch also has emotional and psychological advantages for Harry. As someone who leads a rather stressful life, Harry benefits from having an activity that takes his mind off the threats often lingering overhead. He enjoys having Quidditch practice not only because he likes the sport itself but because he "found that he had fewer nightmares when he was tired out after training."[22] When the season is suspended to allow for the Triwizard Tournament, he "wished he still had Quidditch to distract him; nothing worked so well on a troubled mind as a good, hard training session."[23] Quidditch is often an effective method of stress relief for Harry.

It is Quidditch that motivates Harry to learn how to defend himself against Dementors. Although he is indeed deeply disturbed by how the creatures cause him to hear his mother's voice just before her death and then faint, only when this intrudes on his ability to play a sport does he decide he needs to take action. The concern he expresses to Professor Lupin is "But if the dementors come to another Quidditch match, I need to be able to fight them."[24] He repeatedly reminds Lupin and himself that being unable to cope with Dementors threatens his chances at winning the Quidditch Cup.[25] There are clearly other reasons that Harry wishes to ward off Dementors, but Quidditch serves as an incentive, giving him a specific goal and a deadline by which to accomplish it.

Quidditch is even how Harry motivates himself to face Voldemort and make the ultimate sacrifice. Conceptualizing his journey as a game helps him to make peace with his situation and enables his self-sacrifice. As he enters the Forbidden Forest to meet his death, he thinks to himself, "The long game was ended, the Snitch had been caught, it was time to leave the air...."[26] The significance of Quidditch is literalized in the Golden Snitch, which holds the Resurrection Stone to ease Harry's passing so that the Horcrux inside him can be destroyed and Voldemort can be defeated at last.

Gawain likewise develops emotionally and psychologically through games. His journey advances not prowess but internal growth, testing his piety, virtue, and honesty. His first game is witnessed by the entire court, but the second is much more private, when the lord of the castle proposes that he and Gawain exchange whatever they gain during the day. The lady of the castle repeatedly tries to seduce him—on the first two days, he gives her husband the kisses she gave him, but on the third, he keeps the green girdle with protective powers, hoping to survive the Green Knight's blow.

In Weiss's view, Gawain "takes as deadly earnest what the Green Knight insists on calling game; he then regards as frivolous, gratuitous game what the host and his wife clearly know to be the most serious challenge to Gawain's very being."[27] Gawain is accustomed to knightly games that are played in front of an audience, reward violence, and offer a chance to win glory. As Quidditch drives Harry to confront his fears, Gawain's bargain with the lord requires him to look inside and consider his values, his shortcomings, and the contradictions of chivalry itself as he attempts to navigate temptation while maintaining his honor, thus "exposing the code of chivalry as games played out in public performance, unconnected in any real way to a moral code which demands something more than attention to public behavior."[28] Harry's and Gawain's psyches are molded by games just as much as their skills and reputations are.

Chess

In addition to physical games like Quidditch and tournaments, the wizarding world and chivalric romance have a more cerebral game in common: chess. Wizard chess is played similarly to the non-magical version, with the exception that the pieces move by themselves when directed. Harry sees wizard chess as being "a lot like directing troops in battle," which is effectively what Ron must do later when facing McGonagall's enlarged chess set guarding the Sorcerer's Stone.[29] Suddenly Ron's hobby, seemingly less useful than Hermione's resourcefulness or Harry's knack for flying, becomes essential in a very literal way, requiring Ron's specific skill set and knowledge of the game. As well as showcasing his advanced chess ability, the challenge also allows Ron to take the lead and play the hero in a way that is rare for him as Harry's best friend. Furthermore, the chess match demonstrates his willingness to put his own safety on the line and sacrifice himself for his friends and their mission, his bravery emphasized by his playing as a knight.

Chess, particularly of the magical variety, provides opportunities for characterization in several Arthurian romances as well. Jenny Adams notes that in multiple medieval texts, "chess is decidedly not isolated from the real world but instead furnishes a means to reimagine a social order, forge a relationship between two players, and/or teach lessons to those who watch."[30] In the thirteenth-century Middle Dutch *Roman van Walewein*, Gawain goes on a quest to obtain a flying chessboard for King Arthur, who promises that the successful knight will become his heir, indicating "his understanding of the game as means of self-definition."[31] When Gawain and his lover are attacked by a mob in Chrétien de Troyes's twelfth-century *The Story of the Grail*, he uses an ordinary chessboard as a shield and throws the pieces at the attackers, which "literalizes the game's symbolic violence."[32] Adams contends that his misuse of an intellectual game as an unsuccessful tool of violence indicates his need for further education.[33] In a later continuation of the story, the thirteenth-century *Didot Perceval*, chess takes on a more central and magical role as Perceval loses three matches to pieces that move by themselves, much like McGonagall's enchanted chessmen. Angry at his defeat, he prepares to throw the pieces out a window. The game becomes part of his growth and education as he realizes why he fails where he should succeed. According to Adams, the shifting of chess to "a game of abstraction rather than a physical tool" indicates a developing view of it as being connected to "reason, self-governance, and intellectual development" rather than just violence.[34]

In the Prose *Lancelot*, also written in the thirteenth century, Lancelot likewise plays against magically moving chess pieces, but unlike Perceval, he wins, breaking a magic spell that caused a group of knights and ladies to abandon their lives to sing and dance in perpetuity. Witnesses declare his victory as evidence of his sense and prowess, saying that he will never be defeated in battle just as he was not beaten by the chessboard. Kristin Juel argues that Lancelot's success in the game is reflective of his choice to resist temptation, "choosing the path of reason over the path of the senses."[35] Chess consistently signals significant character growth in both *Harry Potter* and chivalric romance, often tied to wisdom, skill, and leadership.

The Most Dangerous Game

While games can serve practical functions, they can also have negative social, psychological, and physical effects. Ron is extremely susceptible to suffering from nerves and self-doubt based on his Quidditch performance. Hermione points out that Quidditch "creates all this bad feeling and tension between the Houses," and unlike players, her "happiness doesn't depend on Ron's goalkeeping ability."[36] Although games supposedly offer a break from engaging in bloody battles or fighting Dark wizards, they can pose serious threats. A bit of rough play resulting in mild to moderate injuries is presented as comparatively harmless next to activities where lives and entire societies are at stake. This false sense of safety can allow play violence to get out of hand.

In the wizarding world, most injuries, especially non-magical ones, can be treated easily. Broken bones are barely cause for concern. Medicine is far less advanced in the medieval world, but knights are portrayed as tough and capable of withstanding a few blows—and they sometimes have magical aid in protection or healing. Harry is initially struck by the dangerous nature of Quidditch, which other wizards treat rather flippantly. He wonders whether Bludgers have ever killed anyone, to which Oliver Wood responds, "Never at Hogwarts. We've had a couple of broken jaws but nothing worse than that."[37] Broken jaws are still worrisome, and Wood's reply indicates that Bludgers have indeed caused deaths elsewhere. While he insists that Harry need not worry about them as Seeker, Harry maintains, "[U]nless they crack my head open," which one does five years later.[38] As Harry reads more about Quidditch, he learns that "although people rarely died playing Quidditch, referees had been known to vanish and turn up months later in the Sahara Desert."[39] None of the potential risks is enough to stop him from wanting to play. Even more casual wizarding games come with a certain amount of danger. Exploding Snap, while unlikely to do any serious damage, involves cards blowing up. Gobstones shoot a disgusting liquid at the losing side. Wizard chess is safe enough on a regular board, but McGonagall's life-size version proves more dangerous as Ron is knocked unconscious during the game. Wizarding gamers can expect to be singed, splattered, and struck.

It is only when Hogwarts hosts the Triwizard Tournament that a game poses the potential of mortal peril. Dumbledore explains that the tournament began as "a friendly competition" that was "generally agreed to be a most excellent way of establishing ties between young witches and wizards of different nationalities—until, that is, the death toll mounted so high that the tournament was discontinued," and only reinstated with an age restriction.[40] The students are fairly unbothered by this, and even Harry, who is accustomed to regular near-death experiences, is "far more interested in hearing about the tournament than worrying about deaths that had happened hundreds of years ago."[41] When Harry's name comes out of the Goblet of Fire, however, his primary reaction is one of panic. The prevailing theory about why someone would put his name in the Goblet is that the dangerous tournament would be an easy cover for killing him. Barty Crouch, Jr., disguised as Mad-Eye Moody, posits, "Maybe someone's hoping Potter is going to die for it."[42] Sirius Black surmises, "I can't help thinking the tournament would be a very good way to attack you and make it look like an accident."[43] After witnessing Harry narrowly escape a dragon in the first task, Ron exclaims, "Harry, ... whoever put your name in that goblet—I—I reckon they're trying to do you in!"[44]

The tournament causes Harry a level of stress far beyond a typical game, even one as potentially dangerous as Quidditch: "He had never suffered nerves like these; they were way beyond anything he had experienced before a Quidditch match."[45] Despite his history of daring exploits, Harry sees facing a dragon, even in a supposedly controlled environment, as a terrifying trial rather than an exciting adventure. His main goal is not winning or avoiding embarrassment but staying alive. It is reflective of the expected dangers of the tournament that Harry naively assumes that hostages not rescued from the second task will be left to drown. He ends up endangering himself because he takes the game too seriously. While his friends shake their heads at his mistake, and Harry feels ridiculous afterward, it speaks volumes about what Harry has seen of the wizarding world at large and the tournament thus far that he expects success or death.

This blend of entertainment, competition, and mortal peril is characteristic of tournaments in chivalric romance. Although early medieval tournaments were nearly indistinguishable from actual war, Robert R. Hellenga observes that the typical fifteenth-century tournament was "more of a social event than a martial exercise," requiring blunted weapons and including feasting, dancing, and other festivities.[46] Hellenga concludes that Malory's tournaments are somewhere in between, primarily influenced by the more vicious tournaments of his earlier sources but somewhat tempered by modern traditions. In his analysis of warfare and combat in *Le Morte D'Arthur*, K.S. Whetter includes tournaments and friendly jousts alongside outright battle. Knights can expect to be unhorsed at the very least and are liable to be grievously wounded and even slain. Lancelot breaks four knights' backs and one's thigh in a single tournament and "by malfortune struck Sir Tristram on the side a deep wound nigh to the death" in another.[47] Sir Darras has three sons killed in one tournament.[48] The contradictory nature of jousts as both game and war is reflected in their presence at wedding celebrations. Three days of jousts are part of the revels, games, and minstrelsy accompanying the marriage of Sir Gareth and Dame Lyonesse. However, Dame Lyonesse requests "that none that were wedded should joust at the feast," alluding to the high injury and mortality rate.[49]

The line between war and play in Arthurian society is often blurred. Weiss writes that "confusion between the play world and the real world was a prominent feature of chivalry as it was practiced among the nobility in the late middle ages."[50] This confusion can result in games becoming all-absorbing, both emotionally and physically, and legitimately dangerous. In addition to the inherently violent nature of such activities, knights can also get carried away, as Gareth does in a friendly joust with Lancelot, who reminds him, "[F]ight not so sore, your quarrel and mine is not so great but we may leave off."[51] Arthur also halts a tournament when the knights become "wroth out of wit."[52] These confrontations are meant to be tests of prowess and mettle but can quickly become fights to the death.

The Green Knight's game, however, appears to guarantee death from the start, although it is repeatedly presented as a form of play. The word "game" and variations of it appear seventeen times in the poem.[53] Despite the horrifying sight of the Green Knight picking up and speaking from his own removed head, both Arthur and Gawain laugh after he departs, reveling in the marvel and entertainment of what they have witnessed, even though Arthur has misgivings. When Gawain sets off to uphold his bargain, the court bewails the loss of such a noble knight, all but certain that he is going to his death for a mere Christmas game.[54] Carl Grey Martin argues that the Green Knight's game, although seemingly quite different from a tournament or joust, similarly "represent[s] militarism to its practitioners and devotees as an intrinsically valuable, amicable, creative activity, obfuscating its immanent destructiveness, its capacity to fatally alter human bodies."[55] Serious injury and even death are acceptable risks in knightly games, and the court only laments this game's deadly potential because of the setting, magic, and the fact that Gawain does not seem to have a fighting chance.

One aspect of certain wizarding and chivalric games that makes them so dangerous is the requirement to follow through, no matter how risky they become. Dumbledore warns that the Triwizard Tournament "is not to be entered into lightly," as any selected champion "is obliged to see the tournament through to the end" once they have created a "binding, magical contract" by placing their name in the Goblet of Fire.[56] While Gawain does not technically have such a contract, his word is his bond as a knight. He is beholden to the code of chivalry, and the Green Knight warns that if Gawain fails to uphold his end of the bargain, he will be called "recreant," or coward, an insult to his character he simply cannot accept.[57] Gawain repeatedly insists that he must make his meeting, saying that he is "as eager to fall dead as fail of mine errand."[58] To show himself to be a man of his word, Gawain is obliged to abide by the rules to which he agreed and play the game to its supposedly fatal conclusion; not to do so would indicate a lack of honor. Harry and Gawain are both unable to withdraw from their respective games, even when their lives are on the line.

Influence and Interference

Just as games can have an impact beyond the playing field or tabletop, games themselves do not exist in a pure, undiluted vacuum, free from the conflicts and pressures of the outside world. Quidditch can never be a fully fair sport when players ride on broomsticks of different qualities that vary widely in affordability. The obsession with Harry's extremely expensive Firebolt, including frequent remarks about how Gryffindor's rivals cannot compete on inferior brooms, is proof that the broomstick plays a disproportionate role in the game. Players of higher socioeconomic status have an unfair advantage—a fact that Lucius Malfoy exploits by using his wealth to purchase top-of-the-line broomsticks for the Slytherin team, thus securing his son a place on it.

Quidditch comes with a certain amount of danger, but the major perils Harry faces and injuries he sustains playing Quidditch are results of external factors intruding on the game rather than regular gameplay. During his first match, he is almost thrown from his broom due not to another player but to Professor Quirrell's jinx. His arm is broken by a rogue Bludger enchanted by Dobby the house-elf in an attempt to keep Harry away from danger at Hogwarts. Harry falls from his broom in *Prisoner of Azkaban* because of Dementors on the field. When his skull is cracked by a Bludger, it is due to his own substitute teammate's ego and interference that disrupt usual procedures. In a world where there's always someone out to get him, Harry can't catch a break as easily as he can catch a Snitch.

In chivalric and wizarding games, behavior outside a game is suggestive of how participants will conduct themselves during play. Draco Malfoy is a bully both on and off the Quidditch pitch, using the sport as an opportunity to target his rivals' vulnerabilities by insulting Harry and the Weasleys during matches and pretending to be a Dementor to sabotage Harry. Typically heroic Harry "act[s] the hero" and "shows moral fiber" in the second task of the Triwizard Tournament by rescuing Fleur Delacour's sister in addition to his own hostage.[59] Hardworking, honest, and morally upright Cedric Diggory refuses to take the Triwizard Cup for himself when he benefited from Harry's assistance. Noble Sir Lancelot similarly insists that Sir Tristram deserves the tournament prize that Lancelot is awarded because Tristram lasted the longest and only withdrew because Lancelot injured him.[60] Loyal and honorable Sir Gareth switches sides in a tournament to aid Lancelot, earning praise from Arthur, who says that "it is a worshipful knight's deed to help another worshipful knight when he seeth him in a great danger."[61] True colors tend to show themselves in competition, where the pure of heart demonstrate their virtue, while the less upstanding are liable to act dishonorably.

Organizers as well as participants impact gameplay and outcomes. The Triwizard Tournament is bound to be a disaster, considering the state of the government and officials organizing it. Moody's imposter tells Harry that "[c]heating's a traditional part of the Triwizard Tournament and always has been."[62] The corruption and incompetence of the Ministry of Magic are laid bare in its handling of the tournament. Ludo Bagman, despite being a Triwizard judge and Head of the Department of Magical Games and Sports, repeatedly tries to offer Harry help because his gambling habit has landed him deep in debt, and he has bet on Harry to win. Barty Crouch, Sr., Head of the Department of International Magical

Cooperation, stops even showing up to judge because he is held hostage as a result of breaking his Death Eater son out of prison.

The Ministry's disarray only makes it easier for the tournament to be used as part of a plot to return Voldemort to full strength. As dangerous as the tournament is without external meddling, it surpasses its expected hazards, involving attacks on participants and a champion's death. The mishandling of the tournament foreshadows the mismanagement of a much larger issue, as the Ministry shows itself to be wholly unprepared and unwilling to grapple with Voldemort's return. It is unsurprising that an institution unable to protect students in a school sporting event would also fail to support and defend Harry against the Dark wizard who murdered his parents and seeks to kill him. A Ministry that cannot even be trusted to oversee a game surely cannot be relied on during a crisis.

Like the use of the Triwizard Tournament to bring Voldemort back and kill Harry, knightly games can also be manipulated for nefarious purposes, such as pursuing personal vendettas. One such tournament is held by King Bagdemagus and Sir Galahault in *Le Morte D'Arthur* specifically with "the intent to slay Launcelot, or else utterly destroy him and shame him."[63] The Green Knight's game is a scheme devised by King Arthur's half-sister, the enchantress Morgan le Fay, who wanted to test the "the great renown of the Round Table," and "to have grieved Guinevere and got her to die" of fright at the sight of the monstrous knight speaking from his own decapitated head.[64] Less hostile intentions can also influence games, like when Guinevere wants Lancelot to lose a tournament in Chrétien's *The Knight of the Cart* to prove his love for her. In both *Potter* and chivalric romance, personalities, grudges, agendas, politics, and pre-existing relationships do not vanish once gameplay begins.

Conclusion: The Game Is Afoot

By providing opportunities for characters to grow and learn, posing deadly threats, and exposing the principles and failings of institutions and individuals, the supposedly diversionary activities of *Harry Potter* and chivalric literature prove themselves hardly to be diversions from the plot at all. Tournaments, Quidditch, and chess are vehicles for many forms of personal development, but those helpful games can also be harmful when the play world and the real world bleed into each other.

While most modern Muggle forms of play aren't quite as intense as wizarding or Arthurian games, we can still learn from these examples in how we approach our own games, from Dungeons & Dragons to contact sports. Firstly, we should be cautious of dismissing play as unimportant.

Games can be hugely significant in both positive and negative ways, allowing for growth and inclusion or reinforcing inequality and insecurity. Secondly, without proper precautions, friendly competition can become unsafe. Finally, what players and organizers bring into games with them can make or break a game and change the stakes entirely.

Although Huizinga acknowledges that play is an essential and meaningful part of life, his definition indicates that it should first and foremost be fun. Harry has very little fun during the Triwizard Tournament and thinks that the third task is "unlikely to be any fun at all."[65] Tournaments are such a crucial and violent knightly activity that they rarely seem enjoyable. While keeping in mind the potential risks and advantages, we should never lose sight of the primary purpose of playing games and partaking in any form of leisure: to have a good time.

Notes

1. Johan Huizinga, *Homo Ludens: A Study of the Play-Element in Culture* (Abingdon: Routledge, 2002), 7–8, 13.
2. Ibid., 9–10.
3. Ibid., 8–9.
4. See William R. Hunter, "It's All About the Snitch: Quidditch as a Metaphor," in *The Ravenclaw Chronicles: Reflections from Edinboro*, ed. Corbin Fowler (Newcastle upon Tyne: Cambridge Scholars, 2014), 161–71; Emily Strand, "The Second War Was Won on the Quidditch Pitch of Hogwarts: Quidditch as a Symbol Set in the *Harry Potter* Narrative," in *Harry Potter for Nerds II*, ed. Kathryn N. McDaniel and Travis Prinzi (Oklahoma City: Unlocking Press, 2015), 115–38.
5. J.K. Rowling, *Harry Potter and the Sorcerer's Stone* (New York: Scholastic, 1998), 144.
6. Ibid., 148.
7. Maurice Keen, *Chivalry* (New Haven: Yale University Press, 1984), 83.
8. Victoria Weiss, "The Play World and the Real World: Chivalry in *Sir Gawain and the Green Knight*," *Philological Quarterly* 72 (1993): 407–8, Gale Literature Resource Center.
9. Keen, *Chivalry*, 90.
10. J.K. Rowling, *Harry Potter and the Goblet of Fire* (New York: Scholastic, 2000), 187.
11. Ibid., 723.
12. Keen, *Chivalry*, 100.
13. Translation: "cause gentlemen to resort to the ancient customs of chivalry to great fame and renown." Stephen H. Hardy, "The Medieval Tournament: A Functional Sport of the Upper Class," *Journal of Sport History* 1, no. 2 (1974): 91.
14. Thomas Malory, *Le Morte D'Arthur Volume I and II*, ed. Janet Cowen (London: Penguin Classics, 2004), VI.1. References are to book and chapter numbers.
15. Weiss, "The Play World and the Real World," 404.
16. K.S. Whetter, "Warfare and Combat in *Le Morte Darthur*," in *Writing War: Medieval Literary Responses to Warfare*, ed. Corinne Saunders, Francoise Le Saux, and Neil Thomas (Cambridge: Boydell & Brewer, 2004), 169.
17. Keen, *Chivalry*, 88.
18. Rowling, *Goblet of Fire*, 255.
19. Elizabeth A. Galway, "Reminders of Rugby in the Halls of Hogwarts: The Insidious Influence of the School Story Genre on the Works of J.K. Rowling," *Children's Literature Association Quarterly* 37, no. 1 (2012): 73.
20. Rowling, *Goblet of Fire*, 662.

21. J.K. Rowling, *Harry Potter and the Deathly Hallows* (New York: Scholastic, 2007), 744.
22. Rowling, *Sorcerer's Stone*, 216.
23. Rowling, *Goblet of Fire*, 230.
24. J.K. Rowling, *Harry Potter and the Prisoner of Azkaban* (New York: Scholastic, 1999), 189.
25. *Ibid.*, 239, 243.
26. Rowling, *Deathly Hallows*, 698.
27. Weiss, "The Play World and the Real World," 417.
28. *Ibid.*, 415.
29. Rowling, *Sorcerer's Stone*, 199.
30. Jenny Adams, "Colonizing the Otherworld in *Walewein*," in *Games and Gaming in Medieval Literature*, ed. Serina Patterson (New York: Palgrave Macmillan, 2015), 128.
31. *Ibid.*, 130.
32. Jenny Adams, "Medieval Chess, Perceval's Education, and a Dialectic of Misogyny," in *Chess in the Middle Ages and Early Modern Age: A Fundamental Thought Paradigm of the Premodern World*, ed. Daniel E. O'Sullivan (Berlin: De Gruyter, 2012), 123.
33. *Ibid.*, 123, 132.
34. *Ibid.*, 115, 114.
35. Kristin Juel, "Chess, Love, and the Rhetoric of Distraction in Medieval French Narrative," *Romance Philology* 64, no. 1 (2010): 93.
36. J.K. Rowling, *Harry Potter and the Order of the Phoenix* (New York: Scholastic, 2003), 574–75.
37. Rowling, *Sorcerer's Stone*, 169.
38. *Ibid.*, 169.
39. *Ibid.*, 181.
40. Rowling, *Goblet of Fire*, 187.
41. *Ibid.*
42. *Ibid.*, 279.
43. *Ibid.*, 334.
44. *Ibid.*, 358.
45. *Ibid.*, 313.
46. Robert R. Hellenga, "The Tournaments in Malory's *Morte Darthur*," *Forum for Modern Language Studies* 10, no. 1 (1974): 69–70.
47. Malory, *Le Morte*, VI.7, IX.33.
48. *Ibid.*, IX.36.
49. *Ibid.*, VII.35.
50. Weiss, "The Play World and the Real World," 407.
51. Malory, *Le Morte*, VII.4.
52. *Ibid.*, I.11.
53. Martin Stevens, "Laughter and Game in *Sir Gawain and the Green Knight*," *Speculum* 47, no. 1 (1972): 67.
54. Larry D. Benson, ed., *Sir Gawain and the Green Knight: A Close Verse Translation* (Morgantown: West Virginia University Press, 2012), 674–83. References are to line numbers.
55. Carl Grey Martin, "The Cipher of Chivalry: Violence as Courtly Play in the World of *Sir Gawain and the Green Knight*," *The Chaucer Review* 43, no. 3 (2009): 316.
56. Rowling, *Goblet of Fire*, 256.
57. Benson, *Sir Gawain and the Green Knight*, 456.
58. *Ibid.*, 1067.
59. Rowling, *Goblet of Fire*, 503, 507.
60. Malory, *Le Morte*, IX.33–34.
61. *Ibid.*, XVIII.24.
62. Rowling, *Goblet of Fire*, 343.
63. Malory, *Le Morte*, X.50.
64. Benson, *Sir Gawain and the Green Knight*, 2458, 2460.
65. Rowling, *Goblet of Fire*, 551.

Gamifying the *Harry Potter* Studies Classroom

Tison Pugh

"While you are at Hogwarts, your triumphs will earn your house points, while any rule-breaking will lose house points. At the end of the year, the house with the most points is awarded the house cup, a great honor," declares Professor Minerva McGonagall in *Harry Potter and the Sorcerer's Stone*.[1] Her words illuminate one of Rowling's key themes—the competitive nature of children's games, as evident in the ways in which Quidditch matches register Harry's evolution as a heroic protagonist—while also tacitly pointing to the benefits of introducing playful, gaming, and ludic elements into a variety of classroom environments. After all, if a pedagogical practice is adopted at Hogwarts, shouldn't we Muggle teachers consider its utility for our institutions?

At the University of Central Florida, I teach ENL 3378, Harry Potter Studies, an upper-level English literature course focusing on Rowling's series of seven novels and the literary traditions that influenced their themes and genres. One version of the course is designed for a large enrollment class of a hundred students, mostly English majors; the other is designed for a small enrollment class of twenty students in UCF's Burnett Honors College, representing a wide array of majors. For both versions of the course, students participate in a re-creation of Rowling's House Cup Competition and vie in teams for victory over their classmates. This essay discusses the pedagogical benefits of such a ludic learning structure and offers practical advice for incorporating a wide variety of brainstorming activities and other such classroom exercises, loosely disguised as games, that are designed to enhance students' critical thinking and analytical skills. T. Keith Edmunds and Sharon Lauricella define ludic pedagogy as "a teaching philosophy that embraces the importance of fun, play, playfulness, and humor—without sacrificing academic or intellectual rigor."[2]

This phrasing aptly captures my objectives with the *Harry Potter* Studies course. All pedagogical approaches entail unintended liabilities as well, and potential pitfalls of this ludic curriculum will also be discussed, as well as ways to mitigate their effects.

A ludic approach to teaching *Harry Potter* accords well with the prominent attention given to games throughout the series. Hogwarts students play a range of games, including Wizard Chess ("exactly like Muggle chess except that the figures were alive"[3]), Gobstones ("a wizarding game rather like marbles, in which the stones squirt a nasty-smelling liquid into the other player's face when they lose a point"[4]), and of course, Quidditch, the wizarding sport in which Harry excels and through which various house rivalries are expressed over the course of the school year. On the whole, these games offer Harry and readers a diversion from the cataclysmic struggle against Voldemort for the future of the wizarding and Muggle worlds, and Rowling employs them effectively to lighten the series' tone. In a similar vein, while I hope that students do not view my class as a "cataclysmic struggle," the serious nature of their academic endeavors are counterbalanced and lightened by the class's ludic elements. More so, as various scholars have demonstrated, games offer a hermeneutic for better understanding the complexity both of Rowling's texts and of readers' engagements with them.[5]

Along with the rise both of video games in popular culture and of game studies as an academic discipline, proponents of ludic education fervently endorse the potential for games to revolutionize learning. At its core, gamification entails incorporating ludic structures into otherwise non-ludic activities. Jennifer Grouling and colleagues define it within an academic setting as "the process of applying game principles to non-game settings in order to increase engagement"; they further observe that gamification "can involve such practices as using leaderboards, point rewards, achievements, and badges."[6] Some scholars warn that the processes of gamification are often misused, abused, or exploited to deceive those entrapped in a game that, for whatever reason, they are compelled or coerced to play—an apt assessment of the power dynamics involved whenever instructors insist students play a game. Patrick Jagoda further notes that gamification "has been condemned ... for adopting only the least artistic aspects of contemporary digital games—their repetitive grinding, achievement-based operant conditioning, and dopamine-fueled goal orientation"; he demonstrates as well that the practices of gamification often "perpetuate ... hierarchy under the guise of games that are fun, interactive and productive of extrinsic rewards."[7] As Ian Bogost declaims in his justly famous essay "Gamification Is Bullshit," "The rhetorical power of the word 'gamification' is enormous, and it does precisely what the bullshitters want: it takes games—a mysterious, magical, powerful medium that has captured the attention of millions of people—and it makes them accessible in the context of contemporary business."[8] Gamification risks trivializing education, and educators of all disciplines should not shy away from the fact that our fields present numerous intellectual challenges: writing an essay, or solving a quadratic equation, or playing one of Beethoven's sonatas. Students will often struggle to achieve these skills, and in many ways, there is no substitute for the grind and toil of learning. Games can significantly enhance classroom instruction, yet instructors should reflect deeply on their goals and learning objectives before gamifying activities for their students.

Gamifying my *Harry Potter* Studies course does not overwrite its learning objectives, which, as explained on the course syllabus, are as follows: "This course allows students to spend time with a magical wizarding world not merely to enjoy the rich pleasures of these texts but also to practice their critical thinking, communication, and writing skills. Effective critical thinking, communication, and writing skills are integral to success in virtually every discipline, both in college and beyond, and practicing them is essential for laying the groundwork for future success." The strength, utility, and versatility of the English major arises in the many ways in which it challenges and deepens students' thinking, as their classes encourage them to question words on a page and to theorize how words construct meanings for them and others, and to examine the variability of meaning that the same words can communicate. The English major hones students' critical thinking skills, the summum bonum of a liberal arts education, which Ian Bruce summarizes as such: "when expressing critical thinking, writers (or speakers) communicate evaluative judgments on some aspect of their particular area of specialist activity according to the values and standards of the discipline, profession, or area of activity within which the evaluation occurs. In Western societies, critical thinking is usually regarded as a central element of engagement with any field of specialist human activity."[9] Critical thinking stands as the paramount goal of most English literature courses, and this skill set presents a challenge both to the students developing their critical thinking skills and to the instructors teaching them. Learning difficult new skills is not an easy task, and critical thinking is not a game, but the House Cup Challenges of Harry Potter Studies create an effective framework for delivering these lessons.

"Fun" does not stand as the goal or learning objective of any of my courses; I do not object, however, if it is an unintended side-effect, and I incorporate a light ludic superstructure to most of my classes, in which student teams compete over the semester in a series of activities. Generally speaking, the *Harry Potter* Studies class is structured similarly to my other regularly taught courses, including Chaucer, The Legend and Literature of King Arthur, and Literary Gaming. For the most part, students in these classes are assigned both a primary text for each session and a weekly critical reading related to the specific sub-themes addressed during those respective sessions. They write three essays over the course of the semester, due at the end of the fifth, tenth, and fifteenth weeks. The first two essays are relatively short (approximately 1500 words); the third essay requires secondary sources and a deeper argument of approximately 2500 to 3000 words. Most class meetings feature a brief quiz to ensure that students have completed the assigned reading. Such a rudimentary class structure surely matches many other literature courses offered at colleges and universities across the globe.

The course syllabus of *Harry Potter* Studies is available to students online prior to our first class, and so the game begins even before we meet. As Dumbledore explains to Tom Riddle as he prepares to enroll at Hogwarts, "All new wizards must accept that, in entering our world, they abide by our laws"[10]—an apropos statement of the necessity that students adhere to the requirements outlined in a course syllabus. The *Harry Potter* Studies syllabus alerts students to the House Cup Challenges they will be playing throughout the course and outlines its protocols in general terms:

> Each house competes for the glories of the House Cup, and all students of the winning house receive ten bonus points—cumulative points, not percentage points—for their final grade. Other fantastic prizes are possible as well....
>
> Points can be earned in numerous ways, all at the discretion of the professor. Answering a question with particular insight, wit, or clarity, and otherwise contributing to the class's atmosphere of pleasureful erudition will likely earn house points. Sadly, points can be lost as well—and these losses affect not merely the student who incurs the penalty but his or her house as well. Some infractions that result in the loss of house points include coming to class without the required text, using cell phones or texting, or a student not sitting in the proper common room. This list of points and penalties is by no means exhaustive, and the professor reserves the right to reward or penalize houses as he sees fit.

My hope is that the above statement piques students' interest in the class, and it should be noted that the description, while technically accurate and generally matching the tenor of the Hogwarts House Cup Competition, does not wholly reflect the reality of the game. Foremost, I only very, very rarely penalize a house and deduct previously earned points, as such a practice invariably punishes some students for the infractions or misbehavior of others. In complementary contrast, I only very rarely award house points for a question answered "with particular insight, wit, or clarity," as doing so disrupts the flow of a lecture or a class discussion because I have to jot down which student earned them, to which house they belong, and how many points they won. Indeed, it feels somewhat rude to award house points to one student for a particularly insightful answer and then merely to say "thank you for your contribution" to the next students who share their viewpoints. As will soon become apparent, the House Cup Challenges that the students play in class—their primary opportunity to win points for their team—are all pre-planned affairs.

During the first moments of the first day of class, students are sorted into their houses, in a similar, although less magical, fashion as the fictional students of Hogwarts. Without access to the fantastic whimsy of a sentient hat, I instead employ the equally mysterious workings of fortune, as each student draws a color-coded index card from a replica of the Sorting Hat: red for Gryffindor, green for Slytherin, yellow for Hufflepuff, and blue for Ravenclaw. Students then join their teammates in rows pre-assigned for their houses. What to do, however, if students feel they were incorrectly sorted? Rowling's novels allow for the possibility of mis-sorting, with the Sorting Hat admitting that some students present vexing taxonomical challenges. Moreover, as Professor McGonagall states, "Your house will be something like your family within Hogwarts,"[11] and it is likely that some students enrolled in the course with a friend or two, and thus would prefer to join them on the same team. Given these conditions, I allow students the opportunity to enter another house. Five minutes of class time are allotted during which they must find a current member of their prospective house who will agree to join their soon-to-be-former house. The students then switch sorting cards and join their new houses. To ensure that the teams will remain roughly equal in size, I stress that no sorting cards can be created or destroyed in this process.

After the teams are formed, and following some preliminary information about the course's learning objectives and syllabus, the class is ready for its first House Cup Challenge. Each House Cup Challenge is introduced with a time limit for the activity, the number of points to be awarded, and whether one team or multiple teams can win the points. For example, the objective of the semester's first House Cup Challenge is simply for students to learn one another's names, and it is announced on the PowerPoint slide that the challenge lasts five minutes, that it is worth twenty points, and that, in this instance, multiple teams can win the points. The prompt reads as follows: "Successful houses share bonds of friendship, loyalty, and respect, which is impossible without knowing one another's names and being able to greet one another prior to each class. Introduce yourselves to your house mates. House members selected randomly will introduce their house mates to the class. The house that remembers the most names will win the points." Of course, this is simply an "ice-breaker" exercise rebranded as a "House Cup Challenge," but it effectively introduces students to one another and to the ludic structure of the course.

Although I teach both a large section of *Harry Potter* Studies with one hundred students and a small section with twenty students, the House Cup Challenges unfold much the same manner in both classes, with two key exceptions, both of which must be addressed at the beginning of the semester. To keep the sizes of the teams manageable, the 100-student class requires two additional houses: the Dumbledores and the House-elves. Twenty-five students per house is simply too large and unmanageable for all students to have sufficient opportunity to participate. Also parallel to the structures of Hogwarts' houses, each team of the large-section class must select a Prefect as their leader. The Prefects provide me with a point of contact for each house, and they typically report back to the class for their team following a given session's House Cup Challenge. To allow a variety of students the opportunity to serve in this leadership position, teams are allowed to select new Prefects every five weeks, although they often choose to continue with their current leader. Prefects, however, are generally unnecessary for the small-enrollment classes. A group of five undergraduate students should be able to function effectively without someone specifically designated as its leader.

In the following pages I discuss some key examples of the House Cup Challenges that I have created for the *Harry Potter* Studies class, and this essay's appendix provides a skeletal overview of class topics and corresponding games. All of the challenges can nonetheless be subdivided into two overarching categories: those for which students brainstorm lists and those for which they briefly define or apply a key critical concept or narrative theme. The former can be evaluated objectively; the latter, like essays, requires more subjective evaluation. Typically, I allow a shorter amount of time for brainstorming activities, usually between five and seven minutes, whereas the exercises in which students define or apply critical concepts are usually allotted between eight and ten minutes. As much as possible, each House Cup Challenge is followed up with the teams sharing the results of their collaboration and the class as a whole discussing its implications for more deeply understanding the *Harry Potter* novels.

For an example of a brainstorming House Cup Challenge, in one class we discuss the influence of fairy tales on Rowling's novels, and the prompt (7 minutes, 10 points, 1 winner) simply asks, "How is *Harry Potter* like a fairy tale? How many direct parallels can you draw between the *Harry Potter* novels and specific fairy tales?" Students generate long lists of possibilities, including Hermione as a Cinderella figure at the Yule Ball, Hagrid performing a narrative function similar to Cinderella's fairy godmother, and the golden egg of the Triwizard Tournament as reminiscent of Jack's objective in "Jack and the Beanstalk." After discussing these and as many other relevant examples as possible, students are better prepared to examine the influence of fairy tales beyond these allusions and to see the ways in which fairy tales influence Rowling's narrative structures, particularly in her use of "The Tale of the Three Brothers" and the legends of the Deathly Hallows to guide the closing chapters of her epic tale.

Brainstorming lists can also be used to introduce more challenging topics, including literary theories. For instance, one day of class is dedicated to applying queer theory to Rowling's novels, and so I introduce students to two of its key concepts: erotic triangles and open secrets. Erotic triangles involve two or more characters (typically of the same sex) romantically pursuing a third character (typically of the other sex); queer theory has demonstrated that, in many instances, erotic triangles cloak the latent attraction between the two characters of the same sex that is expressed as an antagonistic tension. Open secrets arise when a given community jointly but tacitly recognizes an unwelcome truth; however, by never discussing this secret, they need never act upon it. The relevance of open secrets to queer theory arises in the homophobic possibility that a family might accept a queer relative on the unstated condition that this person's queerness is never mentioned, even as everyone silently knows the truth. The first House Cup Challenge on queer theory (5 minutes, 10 points, 1 winner) instructs, "List as many erotic triangles—from literature, television, film, etc.—as you can"; the follow-up queer-theory House Cup Challenge (also 5 minutes, 10 points, 1 winner) similarly instructs, "List as many open secrets—from literature, television, film, etc.—as you can."

Following a quick overview of examples from other media generated by the teams, we then turn to the ways in which these concepts function in the *Harry Potter* novels. For example, Viktor Krum incorrectly presumes that he is ensnared in an erotic triangle with Harry over their joint admiration for Hermione, and Harry positively assesses his own masculinity after learning of Viktor's jealousy: "He couldn't quite believe he was having this conversation with Viktor Krum, the famous International Quidditch player. It was as though the eighteen-year-old Krum thought he, Harry, was an equal—a real rival."[12] Another excellent example of the dynamics of the erotic triangle occurs when Harry kisses Ginny for the first time while simultaneously negotiating his friendship with Ron: "Harry's eyes sought Ron. At last he found him … wearing an expression appropriate to having been clubbed over the head.... [T]hey looked at each other, then Ron gave a tiny jerk of the head that Harry understood to mean, *Well—if you must.*"[13] We then discuss open secrets, a passing example of which occurs when Harry asks Ron, "Are all your family wizards?" to which Ron replies, "Er—yes, I think so.... I think Mom's got a second cousin who's an accountant, but we never talk about him."[14] In the carnivalesque space of children's literature, the Weasleys never speak of this accountant, illustrating the comic tensions between the normative and the non-normative as the reader learns of the differences between the wizarding and Muggle worlds. Additional examples of open secrets include Squibs, Hagrid's status as a half-giant, and Dumbledore's homosexuality, all of which effectively prepare students to examine more closely the ways in which gender and sexuality are depicted in the *Harry Potter* novels.

The second primary type of House Cup Challenge, in which students briefly define or apply a key critical concept or narrative theme, typically requires a little more class time and is accordingly awarded a few more house points. When we are attempting to negotiate the vast web of contradictions and ironies that constitute the field of children's literature—a corpus typically written by adults who must envision the type of children who would want to read their fictions, with the additional caveat that many adults consider themselves avid devotees of the genre—students are given the following House Cup Challenge (10 minutes, 15 points, 1 winner): "Houses must define the term 'children's literature.' Write down your definition; of course, use complete sentences and correct grammar." Similarly, when we are discussing cinematic adaptations of the *Harry Potter* novels, the House Cup Challenge (8 minutes, 10 points each, potentially 2 winners) asks them, "Other than a *Harry Potter* film, what do you think are the best and worst film adaptations ever made? Use one of Nel's theories of adaptation to justify your answer.[15] One house will win for 'best adaptation' and one will win for 'worst adaptation.' The same house can win both parts of this Double House Cup Challenge." Lively class discussions usually ensue, particularly when the same movies are selected by different teams as the best and the worst adaptations—a fate particularly common for the *Twilight* franchise. This House Cup Challenge assists students in voicing their criteria for determining whether a particular film adaptation effectively or ineffectively captures the spirit and themes of its source text. As a whole, the House Cup Challenges for which students briefly define or apply a key critical concept or narrative theme encourage them not to rehearse the viewpoints of others but to develop their own unique criteria for evaluating a key aspect of literary narrative.

For the most part, the brainstorming exercises pose questions with answers that are objectively right or wrong, and thus evaluating them and awarding the winning points requires little grading time and generates little controversy. When updating the scoreboard during the subsequent class, I congratulate the winning house with a brief acknowledgment of the reason for their victory (e.g., "Congratulations to Slytherin, who triumphed in the fairy-tale House Cup Challenge by listing an astonishing sixteen connections between *Harry Potter* and fairy tales"). For more subjective House Cup Challenges, I often allow the students to select the winning team, which thus exculpates me from any accusations of favoritism. Students are encouraged to vote for the house that they truly believe best responded to the day's Challenge, not simply for their own house; it is apparent that at least a majority of students follow this request because it is extraordinarily rare that the votes indicate that all of the houses have tied. Occasionally I may disagree with the class's selection of the winning team, but the class's judgments are never overruled (although I might compliment and discuss the answers proffered by a losing house). To maintain students' interest in the game, the scoreboard is updated for each class, which allows them to track their accomplishments in relation to their classmates. Owing to the randomly generated teams, most competitions run neck-and-neck over the course of the semester. However, if a team appears to be running away with the tournament at any point, I award runner-up points for daily challenges so that scores do not become overwhelmingly lopsided.

With a slight blush I confess that a day of class is dedicated to playing Quidditch, now known as Quadball[16]—an activity for which very little pedagogical defense can be mounted, other than my belief that the loss of a single hour of instruction in favor of a purely pleasurable experience boosts students' awareness and appreciation that education can be thoroughly enjoyable. Not a Quadball player myself, I turn to the UCF Quadball Team to teach the rules and to referee the matches; they use this class period as an opportunity to recruit new players. Students play as many matches as possible during the class session, and each winning house is awarded fifteen House Cup points. As with Rowling's Quidditch, catching the Snitch ends the game, but because the winning team does not necessarily need to catch the Snitch, five House Cup points are also awarded to the team that accomplishes this objective. Quadball is a contact sport, and so instructions for class play stress that "Rough play—body slamming, tackling, dressing as Dementors—can result in severe penalties to the offending house. (Do not be an overaggressive Beater!)" Finally, not all students enjoy sports, and so playing Quadball is not required; at the same time, students who elect not to play the game can still participate actively in the class event by supporting their teammates. These students are instructed, "Everyone need not play, but everyone should participate. Bring umbrellas for shade, cold water for the players, cheerlead for your team!"

The final lecture of the semester addresses the intersection of the *Harry Potter* novels and the traditions of literary sentimentalism,[17] but the final House Cup Challenge is announced during the previous class:

The Neville Longbottom Awards for Meritorious Achievement in the Field of Merit.[18] If compelled to choose my single favorite moment from the approximately 4000 pages of the *Harry Potter* novels, I would, without hesitation, select the conclusion of *Harry Potter and the Sorcerer's Stone* when Neville, following the more obviously heroic achievements of Harry, Hermione, and Ron, contributes powerfully to Gryffindor's victory in the House Cup Competition. As Dumbledore acknowledges: "There are all kinds of courage.... It takes a great deal of bravery to stand up to our enemies, but just as much to stand up to our friends. I therefore award ten points to Mr. Neville Longbottom."[19] In the spirit of Neville's apotheosis into heroism, The Neville Longbottom Awards for Meritorious Achievement in the Field of Merit seek to recognize students for personal successes beyond the purview of the classroom. Here is the (lengthy) prompt for this final House Cup Challenge:

> What have you or your house accomplished that should be recognized with a Neville Longbottom Award for Meritorious Achievement in the Field of Merit (NLAMAFM)? Have you won a college, university, or other major award? Did you go above and beyond for the benefit of your house or of others? Should a new spell be named in honor of your Herculean achievements in a field? All houses may nominate their house and/or their members for up to four NLAMAFMs that they truly believe they merit. The Professor will assess these nominations and assign points—or not—as he sees fit. Nominations must be emailed to the Professor by noon tomorrow. Nominations must be in the form of PowerPoint slides featuring a photo of the nominee(s).

Five points maximum are awarded for each NLAMAFM, and thus twenty points total are possible for each team. I typically award five points to each nomination, as it seems a bit dour to inform some students that their NLAMAFM efforts fall short of expectations. Given these conditions, frequently the NLAMAFM Awards simply add twenty points to each team's score—and thus do not consequentially affect the final outcome of the game. For the most part, we know our students in their role as students in our classes but do not know much about their nonacademic experiences, and the NLAMAFM Awards offer insights about the depth and richness of their lives, as past winners have raised thousands of dollars for charity, gained entry into prestigious graduate programs, won international scholarships, and so much more. Every now and then, however, something surprises even me, such as when the Hufflepuff team nominated only three students for the NLAMAFM Awards, even though a fourth student—the Hufflepuff Prefect—had reconstituted UCF's Harry Potter Club over the course of the semester. In an oddly appropriate Hufflepuff manner, the Hufflepuffs demurred the victory at hand.

After playing this game throughout an entire semester, striving to outwit and outplay their classmates through stunning feats of intellectual daring and acumen, what glories await the winning team? As with so many games, the thrill of victory should be sufficient in itself, particularly because the prizes awarded are of rather paltry value. Each member of the winning team receives ten bonus points, but given the high number of points for the many quizzes, assignments, exams, and essays assigned throughout a fifteen-week semester, only rarely do these points significantly raise a grade. A signed certificate is also bestowed—"This Certificate Documents That [Student Name] Has Triumphed in the House Cup Challenge of *Harry Potter* Studies"—which I urge the winners to display prominently on their refrigerators for at least a week. As a native Louisianian, I often have a virtual treasure trove of Mardi Gras beads in a seldom-opened drawer in the back of my house, and students of the winning team are bedecked with these gawdy plastic necklaces. (Mardi Gras, a carnival, is thematically related to the carnivalesque inversions of children's literature—an admittedly tenuous connection, but a connection nonetheless.) Finally, I can usually scrounge up the necessary funds from a campus source for the winning team to celebrate with an ice-cream social.

It is well beyond my personal expertise to theorize the psychological phenomena that students experience while playing these House Cup Challenges, and the following observation may simply reflect my overactive imagination, but during several semesters it has appeared that the houses begin to adopt the personalities accorded them in the *Harry Potter* novels. The Slytherins seem ambitious, perhaps even a tad underhandedly so, whereas the Ravenclaws appear confident (even smug?) in their intellectual acumen. The Hufflepuffs display an affable and industrious quality, while the Gryffindors apparently presume they will triumph in the competition and thus, like Harry, simply await destiny to carry them to their predetermined victory. Unlike Harry, however, Gryffindors often lose the House Cup Challenge of *Harry Potter* Studies.

And finally, one important theme *not* to emulate from the *Harry Potter* novels: do not play favorites with students, as Professors McGonagall and Dumbledore do for Harry! Rules are forever bent or broken in his favor, such as when Professor McGonagall places him on the Gryffindor Quidditch team, despite the fact that this is clearly prohibited: "I shall speak to Professor Dumbledore and see if we can't bend the first-year rule. Heaven knows, we need a better team than last year."[20] In a similar scene, Dumbledore recants his rules rather than enforcing them and punishing Harry and Ron: "I seem to remember telling you both that I would have to expel you if you broke any more school rules.... Which goes to show that the best of us must sometimes eat our words."[21] For a classroom game to be effective, instructors must be neither a McGonagall nor a Dumbledore;

they must not elevate any potential Harrys of the class; and they must oversee as fair a game as possible.

Most instructors who have taught over the last twenty years or more have likely noticed that their students are nowadays less likely to talk to one another before class than in years prior due to the ubiquity of smartphones and related technology. Many students engage with their phones rather than with their classmates in the adjacent desks. If gamifying my *Harry Potter* Studies course and other classes contributes little other to the classroom environment than an engaged buzz of conversation prior to class, it has accomplished a great deal already. If games can make our classrooms more enjoyable spaces without detracting from the lessons at hand, as I believe they do through this series of House Cup Challenges, then let the games begin.

Appendix

Class Topics and House Cup Challenges

The following list of class topics and House Cup Challenges by necessity omits the preparatory lectures and discussions that prepare students to respond to these prompts effectively. This skeletal guide can nonetheless provide ideas for instructors to adapt for their unique pedagogical objectives.

CLASS 1 INTRODUCTION

This class's icebreaker activity is addressed in the body of the essay.

CLASS 2 CHILDREN'S LITERATURE

This topic is addressed in the body of the essay.

CLASS 3 FILM ADAPTATION

This topic is addressed in the body of the essay.

CLASS 4 MYTHIC HERO

Brainstorm Harry Potter's similarities to the following mythic heroes: Moses, King Arthur, Superman, and Luke Skywalker.[22]

CLASS 5 ROWLING'S BIOGRAPHY

No House Cup Challenge for this class.

CLASS 6 CARNIVALESQUE

List as many carnivalesque moments, scenes, and encounters in the *Harry Potter* series as possible, but only that occur up to today's reading.

Class 7 Postcolonial and Critical Race Theories
Prove that Harry Potter is racially White. You must find *textual evidence* to support this claim. (It is unfair to use the search feature on an e-reader.) If you can prove that Harry is White, how does Rowling's presentation of his Whiteness differ from her presentation of Black characters' Blackness?

Class 8 Humor, Part 1
List as many specific examples as possible of each of these types of humor:

- dark / gallows / morbid
- highbrow / epigrammatic / witty
- hyperbolic / exaggerated
- juvenile / sophomoric / immature
- deadpan / dry
- slapstick
- ironic
- satirical

Class 9 Gender
Assess the following characters—Harry Potter, Hermione, Ron, Dumbledore, Hagrid, Draco, Voldemort, McGonagall, Snape, Sirius Black, and Dobby—according to Rowling's portrayal of their gender. Which stereotypically masculine, stereotypically feminine, and gender-neutral characteristics do they evince? From this analysis, write a summary statement addressing Rowling's depiction of gender in the series as a whole.

Class 10 Mystery
The introduction to this House Cup Challenge—a mystery in itself—is too long to summarize.

Class 11 Children's Literature and the Theme of Children's Innocence

> Challenge 1: When does innocence end? Brainstorm as many answers as you like.
>
> Challenge 2: In one sentence of no more than twenty-five words, define the importance of children's innocence as a theme for Rowling's *Harry Potter* novels.

Class 12 Queer Theory
This topic is addressed in the body of the essay.

Class 13 Fandom
Which house has the single most dedicated *Harry Potter* fan? Each

house can nominate one member for the *Harry Potter* Biggest Fan Award. Nominees must explain to the entire class why they are deserving of this award. The class will vote on the winner of these points.

Class 14 Close Reading

As the example of "Remus Lupin" demonstrates, many of Rowling's character names merit deep readings. List as many *Harry Potter* characters as possible with the meanings behind their names.

Class 15 Social Class

Assign each of the following characters—Harry Potter, Albus Dumbledore, the Dursleys, Dobby, Professor McGonagall, Sirius Black, the Malfoys, Dolores Umbridge, and Hagrid—one of the following social/economic classes: enslaved beings, poor, working class/"blue collar," middle to upper middle class, and wealthy/aristocratic. Consider as well if any contradiction complicates the character's membership in this social class and explain how a specific aspect of their character or storyline complicates our understanding of their social class.

Class 16 Semiotics

For as many *Harry Potter* characters as possible other than Harry himself (and his lightning scar), determine what sign/symbol best represents them semiotically.

Class 17 Bildungsroman and the School Story

In many ways Harry's heroic journey—the novels' narrative arc—overshadows Harry's personal evolution into adulthood—the novels' emotional arc. For the most part, Harry's heroic journey is easy to trace: triumphs in Quidditch, leading his classmates in Defense Against the Dark Arts lessons, victories over Voldemort, and so on. Find *specific* moments in the texts that document Harry's emotional—not heroic—maturation. (Do not go further than today's reading.)

Class 18 Literary Characters

The class plays a bingo game in which various character types are called, which students must match to characters listed on their bingo cards. Students must be prepared to defend their alignment of the character types with the *Harry Potter* characters to win the game.

Class 19 Religion & Ethics

In rounds, one house competes against another in debating an ethical dilemma. (Most of these ethical dilemmas are well known in philosophical circles, such as the trolley problem, and are simply repopulated with characters from the *Harry Potter* novels.)

CLASS 20 FANTASY

Harry Potter is primarily a portal quest fantasy, but how do the elements of intrusive, liminal, and immersive fantasy also come into play? List as many elements of the portal-quest, intrusive, liminal, and immersive fantasy as you can.[23]

CLASS 21 LITERARY STYLE

> Challenge 1: Pick the single worst *narrated* sentence in *Harry Potter* (as far as we have read). *The sentence should not be dialogue.* What makes this sentence disappointing? What is wrong with its style?
>
> Challenge 2: Pick the two best lines of dialogue in *Harry Potter* (as far as we have read)—one representing demotic, the other hieratic, style. What makes these lines of dialogue exceptional? What gives them style?

CLASS 22 HUMOR, PART 2

We will watch a collection of comic scenes from the *Harry Potter* films.[24] Assign each scene as reflecting a particular theory of humor: relief, cognition, superiority, community. Which theory of comedy is most relevant to the *Harry Potter* films?

- Then, brainstorm examples of relief-, cognition-, superiority-, and community-based humor in the *Harry Potter* novels.
- Which theory of comedy is most relevant to the *Harry Potter* novels? Write a sentence of no more than thirty words distinguishing between the books' and the films' uses of humor. How does humor function differently between the novels and their adaptations?

CLASS 23 FAIRY TALES

This topic is addressed in the body of the essay.

CLASS 24 GAMES AND GAME STUDIES

Instead of a standard-format House Cup Challenge, students are given five minutes of class time to discuss their strategies for the upcoming Quadball match.

CLASS 25 QUIDDITCH

The houses compete in the class's Quadball Tournament!

Class 26 New Media

Wizarding World, the official Harry Potter website, advertises its appeal largely on the fact that J.K. Rowling offers new writing about *Harry Potter* and its extensive cast of characters. Terry Flew, however, would point out that many aspects of this website reflect its recombinant aspects.[25] List as many recombinant features of Wizarding World as you can.

Class 27 Theme Parks

By applying Gustav Freytag's theories of narrative structure to a theme-park ride, nominate one ride that best combines *story* (characters and actions) with both *narrative structure* (e.g., exposition, climax) and *ride structure*.[26]

Class 28 Sentimentalism

As discussed in the body of this essay, the final class of the semester divulges both the results of the Neville Longbottom Award for Meritorious Achievement in the Field of Merit and the final victors of the class's House Cup Challenges.

Notes

1. J.K. Rowling, *Harry Potter and the Sorcerer's Stone* (New York: Scholastic, 1997), 114.
2. T. Keith Edmunds and Sharon Lauricella, "Ludic Pedagogy: Schooling Our Students in Fun," *Faculty Focus* April 23, 2021, https://www.facultyfocus.com/articles/philosophy-of-teaching/ludic-pedagogy-schooling-our-students-in-fun. Numerous scholars have theorized pedagogical strategies relevant to the *Harry Potter* novels, such as the essayists in Valerie Estelle Frankel's *Teaching with Harry Potter: Essays on Classroom Wizardry from Elementary School to College* (Jefferson, NC: McFarland, 2013).
3. Rowling, *Sorcerer's Stone*, 199.
4. J.K. Rowling, *Harry Potter and the Prisoner of Azkaban* (New York: Scholastic, 1999), 50.
5. Scholars analyzing the *Harry Potter* phenomenon through ludic and gaming hermeneutics include Jessica Seymour, "Hunting the Stag in Harry Potter's Games," *Interdisciplinary Literary Studies* 19, no. 4 (2017): 441–60; Anne Hiebert Alton, "Playing the Genre Game: Generic Fusions of the *Harry Potter* Series," *Critical Perspectives on Harry Potter*, 2nd ed., ed. Elizabeth Heilman (New York: Routledge, 2008), 199–223; and Lisa S. Brenner, ed., *Playing Harry Potter: Essays and Interviews on Fandom and Performance* (Jefferson, NC: McFarland, 2015).
6. Jennifer Grouling, Stephanie Hedge, Alyssa Schweigert, and Eva Grouling Snider, "Questing through Class: Gamification in the Professional Writing Classroom," *Computer Games and Technical Communication: Critical Methods and Applications at the Intersection*, ed. Jennifer DeWinter and Ryan Moeller (Farnham, Surrey: Ashgate, 2014), 265–266. See also Lee Sheldon, *The Multiplayer Classroom: Designing Coursework as a Game* (Boston: Cengage, 2012).
7. Patrick Jagoda, "Gamification and Other Forms of Play," *boundary 2* 40, no. 2 (2013): 115, 143.

8. Ian Bogost, "Gamification Is Bullshit," *The Atlantic*, August 9, 2011, https://www.theatlantic.com/technology/archive/2011/08/gamification-is-bullshit/243338/.
   9. Ian Bruce, *Expressing Critical Thinking through Disciplinary Texts: Insights from Five Genre Studies* (London: Bloomsbury Academic, 2020), 2.
   10. J.K. Rowling, *Harry Potter and the Half-Blood Prince* (New York: Scholastic, 2005), 273.
   11. Rowling, *Sorcerer's Stone*, 114.
   12. J.K. Rowling, *Harry Potter and the Goblet of Fire* (New York: Scholastic, 2000), 553.
   13. Rowling, *Half-Blood Prince*, 534.
   14. Rowling, *Sorcerer's Stone*, 99. For more on the importance of secrets in the *Fantastic Beasts* series, see Lana Whited's essay in this volume.
   15. The critical reading assigned prior to this House Cup Challenge is Philip Nel, "Lost in Translation? *Harry Potter*, from Page to Screen," *Critical Perspectives on Harry Potter*, ed. Elizabeth Heilman (New York: Routledge, 2009), 275-90.
   16. Following Rowling's recent transphobic statements, U.S. Quidditch and Major League Quidditch have announced that they would rename their sport "Quadball" to distance their sport from its creator.
   17. On this topic, see my "Sobbing Over Severus Snape? Sentimentalism and Emotional Ethics in J. K. Rowling's *Harry Potter* Novels," *The Lion and the Unicorn* 45 (2021): 46–61.
   18. The title of The Neville Longbottom Awards was inspired by the "Brother, Can You Spare Two Dimes?" episode of *The Simpsons*, which features Mr. Burns attempting to dissuade Homer from a lawsuit by awarding him "The Montgomery Burns Award for Outstanding Achievement in the Field of Excellence."
   19. Rowling, *Sorcerer's Stone*, 306.
   20. *Ibid.*, 152.
   21. J.K. Rowling, *Harry Potter and the Chamber of Secrets* (New York: Scholastic, 1998), 331. M'Balia Thomas's essay in this volume explores Dumbledore's statement from a different angle.
   22. By focusing on five male mythic heroes, this House Cup Challenge might initially appear sexist. The follow-up lecture and discussion moves beyond Joseph Campbell's ideas concerning the (male) mythic hero to feminist reconstructions of this tradition. Paired readings from Joseph Campbell's *The Hero with a Thousand Faces* and Maria Tatar's *Heroine with 1001 Faces* encourage students to see the ways in which Harry adheres to a masculinist tradition even as that tradition is often unnecessarily circumscribed as a path for men.
   23. For an analysis of these four structures of fantasy, see Farah Mendlesohn, *Rhetorics of Fantasy* (Middletown, CT: Wesleyan University Press, 2008).
   24. Many online compilations are available; I typically play about half of the scenes from "Funniest Harry Potter Moments," available on YouTube: https://www.youtube.com/watch?v=ZFc0O3YXpV4.
   25. For a definition of recombinant media, see Terry Flew, *New Media: An Introduction* (Oxford: Oxford University Press, 2002), 11.
   26. For Freytag's theories of narrative structure, see Gustav Freytag, *Technique of the Drama: An Exposition of Dramatic Composition and Art*, trans. Elias J. MacEwan, 2nd ed. (1863; Havre, MT: Griggs, 1896).

Conversation
Playing Potter

Laurie Beckoff (LB) and Tison Pugh (TP) talk with Katy McDaniel (KM) and Emily Strand (ES) about their essays.

ES: Laurie and Tison, some people would argue—not me!—but some people would argue that games are really just in the text for comedic effect, or they're there to sort of distract the reader momentarily from more serious themes of the work. But you two both argue differently. Why should we take a serious look at games in literature?

TP: Well, one of the ways I would answer this is focusing on structure. There's a literary theory concept called ludo-narratology (ludo is the game, narratology is narrative structure), and it takes, as its interest, the ways in which games can shape narrative structures. Chaucer's *Canterbury Tales* is a great example of this; it's a collection of stories, but it's also a tale-telling competition. So, there's the ludic element, a game element, to the story. Another great example from medieval literature is *Sir Gawain and the Green Knight*, which focuses on a beheading game. The Green Knight comes into Arthur's court and has a very interesting proposal of a pastime in which they exchange blows.

We can see this in a range of fiction, not just medieval literature. We can see it in films—there was a movie in the 1990s by David Fincher, *The Game* [(1997)], and so that's another good example. But also, David Fincher likes a lot of serial killer movies, like *Seven* [stylized *Se7en* (1995)] and *Zodiac* [(2007)]. Those movies really engage with games, too, the games that you're caught in when other people are playing them. I think a lot of stories can be productively conceived as playing with their readers and audiences. Perhaps even more obviously is video games. Not all video games have a story, but a lot of the better video games do merge the gaming element with a narrative element.

I think games in literature are mutually constitutive in many ways, and it's helpful to consider the ways in which they successfully, or in other ways unsuccessfully, combine. Obviously for *Harry Potter*, the biggest game in the series is Quidditch, which is not just a diversion from the text, but really helps to build the themes. And the House Cup tournament every year—and the Triwizard Tournament, too. So, these games are not just random events that happen in the story, but ways that Rowling is using gaming to develop her characters, to develop plot points, to develop other themes. So, to just say that the games of the *Harry Potter* novels are just a side part of the story—well sure, it's not the focus of defeating Voldemort—but yet then again, there's Voldemort at the end of the Triwizard Tournament. So it's a little more important than maybe we thought at first.

ES: Right.

KM: Yeah!

ES: Laurie, what do you think?

LB: I agree with everything Tison said. I think that games often do a lot of heavy lifting. I always think about how much they're cut out of the *Harry Potter* films and how we miss out on some really essential moments of characterization. I think even when they're used for comic effect, that comic effect is sometimes telling us something about what people in this society find funny, or find entertaining, or find absurd. People have pointed out how ridiculous Quidditch is, and I think that's reflective of a lot of things in the wizarding world that are really, really ridiculous. So I think that paying attention to—especially in fantasy literature—the types of games that people are playing, and how they're playing them, and how spectators react to them, and how players react to them tells us a lot about the sort of world we're dealing with.

I think particularly with Quidditch, I've seen comparisons to it, talking about it being very "British boarding school rugby," and ways in which it's negative in that way, in establishing a certain type of atmosphere. But then on the other hand, [it's] utterly ridiculous, so it's making fun of that. So, I think that there's so much both direct heavy lifting in terms of leading toward the plot, tying into major characterization, as well as the metaphorical significance of [asking]: what is this telling us about these people and this society in which they reside?

KM: Your idea of how it's linked with British boarding school tradition. That comes through in terms of the idea of: What is the society preparing people to be able to do through their games? And Emily, I think about the title of your Quidditch essay in *Harry Potter for Nerds* [2], which was....

ES: "The Second War Was Won on the Quidditch Pitch of Hogwarts."

KM: Yes, making that direct connection to.... Cricket? I think? Right? [Laughing.]

ES: Mmmm ... or rugby? Something that they played at one of the boarding schools.... Eaton?

KM: I'm not very sporty! Yes, Eaton. So that was supposed to train young boys in a particular kind of teamwork and competition and....

ES: Conflict, yes.

KM: Yes, and empire-building.

ES: Yes!

KM: And all those kinds of ideas. And to sort of then say well, okay, like Laurie, you were saying, "what's Quidditch doing, in that regard?" A lot of heavy lifting, as you say.

Teaching, the Hogwarts Way

Dumbledorisms
The Idiosyncratic Style of a Hogwarts Headmaster
M'Balia Thomas

"You know, Minister, I disagree with Dumbledore on many counts ... but you cannot deny he's got style...."
—Phineas Nigellus[1]

As an applied linguist and teacher educator, I find Phineas Nigellus's comment about Albus Dumbledore having style noteworthy. Possessing style is not a quality one readily attributes to teachers. Yet style is a crucial component of how educators are perceived by their students and colleagues—whether they are viewed as "the best ... ever" (Remus Lupin), "dull" (Rubeus Hagrid), or "cold" and "cruel" (Severus Snape).[2] Style reflects an individual's personal touch. It is their repeated and particular way of going about the duties of work and life and in a manner that reflects their evaluation or stance towards the world and the others in it. As such, style is not neutral. In fact, style can be quite moral depending on the stance that underlies the execution of a style in a particular moment of interaction.

An idiosyncratic speech style is associated with Hogwarts Headmaster, Albus Dumbledore—his use of aphorisms. Aphorisms are "short, pithy sentence[s]"[3] that contain "a nugget of pure truth."[4] A typical aphorism shared by Dumbledore can be seen in the headmaster's admonition to Harry to "Always use the proper name for things. Fear of a name increases fear of the thing itself."[5] Aphoristic statements surface in Dumbledore's conversations and speeches with students across the *Harry Potter* series. In fact, aphorisms surface so repeatedly with Dumbledore that they warrant their own neologism, *Dumbledorisms*.[6]

Dumbledorisms carry pedagogical overtones. They tend to surface in interactions when the headmaster has access to information that another—often younger—wizard does not. Instead of directly addressing, naming, or disclosing the knowledge or information he holds, the headmaster deploys an aphorism in a manner that serves to circumnavigate the asymmetry in knowledge between himself and another. While this strategy allows Dumbledore to manage teachable moments, it holds moral and ethical implications for how he is viewed by characters and readers. This style perhaps is one of the primary reasons that fans across Potterdom accuse Dumbledore of engaging in "[s]ecrets and lies,"[7] as does the headmaster's brother, Aberforth.

While the failure to share knowledge or to take another into "full and uncensored confidence"[8] has been cited as an unethical aspect of Dumbledore's interactions with others, this essay offers an alternative position. Rather than revealing dishonesty and moral ineptitude, Dumbledorisms reflect the headmaster's evaluative stance towards the pedagogical and relational difficulties he experiences as an educator—such as how to navigate issues of access, rights and authority, and responsibilities with respect to possessing knowledge that others do not. Positing that Dumbledorisms are an idiosyncratic style whose stance allows the headmaster to navigate these challenges stirs empathy for a fellow educator and the moral, ethical, and relational challenges of teaching.

Style ... and Stance

Style resides within our everyday speech—how we talk, the things we say, and even how we write. In literature, markers of style surface in the ways an author gives their characters a recognizably unique voice that distinguishes them from other characters. Style may be signaled in a literary work through repeated turns of phrases, such as spells ("expelliarmus") that signal to others that "it's [us], it's the real one"[9]; use of regional varieties or grammatically marked forms ("It's polite, see? Yeh walk toward him, and yeh bow, an' yeh wait. If he bows back, yeh're allowed ter touch him. If he doesn' bow, then get away from him sharpish, 'cause those talons hurt"[10]); and verbs, adverbs, or prepositional phrases used to report a character's speech ("said Dumbledore with a note of amusement"[11]).

Style can be taken up in ways that signal a character's evaluative stance towards the world and events around them. This stance is conveyed through expressions that are evaluative ("Harry. *Nasty*, common name, if you ask me"[12]), epistemic ("*It is my belief* ... that we are all facing dark and difficult times"[13]), and affective ("*I am afraid* so"[14]). Stance is also communicated through the claims made while "explaining, evaluating, arguing, or agreeing,"[15] for such claims tend to draw upon words, labels, and rhetorical strategies that encode attitudes, emotions, judgments, beliefs, and degrees of certainty toward some speech, event, or interactions.

In literature, as in everyday speech and writing, style and stance may come together to create a memorable style, such as Dolores Umbridge's oppressive interjections ("hem hem"), Minerva McGonagall's use of honorifics to express her displeasure ("Mr. Potter"), and Severus Snape's rhetoric of offensive and impolite name-calling in his interactions with students ("dunderheads," "easy prey," "fools"). Moreover, these stylistic turns of phrase communicate evaluative stances that "influence the way in which characters' words are interpreted by readers, which can in turn affect the way they form impressions of characters in [the readers'] minds."[16] One literary stylistic turn of phrase that also expresses evaluative stance is the aphorism.

Aphorisms as Style and Stance

Aphorisms are a literary and rhetorical style that are similar to proverbs ("[g]enerally accepted truths") and maxims ("pithy moral instruction").[17] However, aphorisms distinguish themselves from these forms through their philosophical ways of evoking knowledge and knowing. From the medical wisdom espoused in Hippocrates's *Aphorisms*[18] to the philosophical guidance of Lao Tzu's *Tao Te Ching*,[19] aphorisms embed their wisdom in expressions designed to (1) "educate" and "inform," (2) provide ethical and moral guidance, and (3) redirect and alter perceptions.[20] Their compactness renders their knowledge readily transmittable in oral and written form away from their contextualized place of origin, across genres, space, and time. Their "aesthetic linguistic quality ... [makes them] memorable."[21]

Aphorisms are the vehicles through which wisdom, knowledge, and ways of understanding are shared within communities and cultures. As individual and collected sayings, aphorisms offer a particular way of looking at and evaluating the world. Therefore, the presence of an aphorism in talk is meaningful, as this literary device will be taken up in a particular moment, time, and space and with a specific other. Further, its deployment is as a reflection of the evaluative position the speaker has adopted in alignment with or against a statement, idea, person, or situation.[22]

Aphorisms in Harry Potter

Aphorisms appear throughout the *Harry Potter* series. They are most often delivered by Albus Dumbledore, headmaster of Hogwarts School of Witchcraft and Wizardry. Dumbledore regularly offers up aphorisms—though not to everyone equally. While Dumbledore may chide his colleagues ("Really, Hagrid, if you are holding out for universal popularity, I'm afraid you will be in this cabin for a very long time"[23]), it is to the school's students that he routinely offers aphorisms as tokens of wisdom, pragmatic guidance, and pedagogical reflection.

One of the first aphorisms to surface in the series appears in *Harry Potter and the Sorcerer's Stone*:

> *Ah, music.... A magic beyond all we do here.*[24]

Dumbledore delivers this pedagogically reflective aphorism in the Great Hall during his start-of-term announcements and following a rendition of the Hogwarts school song.

In fact, Dumbledore both begins and ends Harry Potter's first year at Hogwarts with aphorisms. Similar to the aphorism that opened the school year, the closing one is shared in the Great Hall and during end-of-term announcements. The aphorism is delivered as both a justification for awarding house points to and in recognition of the courage displayed by fellow Gryffindor and Harry Potter roommate, Neville Longbottom:

> *There are all kinds of courage. It takes a great deal of bravery to stand up to our enemies, but just as much to stand up to our friends.*[25]

With this aphorism, Dumbledore offers Hogwarts students pragmatic guidance, a deeper understanding of courage, and insight into the values privileged by the headmaster.

Despite these two public displays of aphorisms, Dumbledore more readily deploys aphorisms in intimate interactions with students and most often with the series' protagonist, Harry Potter:

> *It is our choices, Harry, that show what we truly are, far more than our abilities.*[26]

In this conversational interaction, Dumbledore deploys an aphorism not only to impart wisdom to Harry, but also to perform a distinct pragmatic function—to reassure the younger wizard that despite almost having been sorted into Slytherin House and speaking Parseltongue, he is indeed "very different from Tom Riddle," the given name of the series' antagonist, Voldemort.[27]

By pragmatic function, I refer to the phenomenon that the meaning of Dumbledore's aphorisms are "derived not from the formal properties of words and constructions, but from the way in which utterances are used and how they relate to the context in which they are uttered."[28] For example, when Dumbledore confronts Harry about his repeated and unauthorized visits to the Mirror of Erised, a wizarding artifact that shows the "deepest, most desperate desire of our hearts,"[29] the headmaster is sensitive to the needs of 11-year-old Harry. Rather than explicitly reprimand him, Dumbledore offers Harry the following aphoristic remark:

> It does not do to dwell on dreams and forget to live....[30]

This remark allows Dumbledore to avoid issuing a direct warning against the dangers of the magical artifact and instead to offer the young wizard sage advice couched in concise, polite, and indirect linguistic form.

In addition to a pragmatic function, Dumbledore's use of aphorisms plays a pedagogical role. The headmaster deploys aphorisms in teachable moments, often when students are in need of information, wisdom, or guidance. Thus, when Dumbledore catches Harry delving into the Pensieve of his personal memories, he introduces Harry to the magical artifact, but also employs an aphorism to offer a gentle, pedagogical rebuff:

> Curiosity is not a sin.... But we should exercise caution with our curiosity.[31]

Through the deployment of this aphorism, Dumbledore acknowledges Harry's legitimate curiosity, and he provides pedagogical limits. In doing so, the headmaster reinforces his role as educator and headmaster.

The pedagogical function that Dumbledore's aphorisms play with students continues even after the headmaster's death through his bequest to Hermione Granger of his copy of *The Tales of Beedle the Bard*. While not expressly a collection of aphorisms, the stories about magical and non-magical beings embody the wisdom of wizarding culture. In fact, the passing on of such wisdom is evident in Professor Dumbledore's annotated notes to "The Warlock's Hairy Heart"[32]—the tale of a wizard who in desiring to avoid love carves out his heart and locks it away for decades. When the warlock eventually goes to retrieve his heart, he finds that it has shriveled and grown hair. In Dumbledore's annotated notes on the story, the headmaster cites Adalbert Waffling's first Fundamental Law of Magic:

> Tamper with the deepest mysteries—the course of life, the essence of self—only if prepared for consequences of the most extreme and dangerous kind.[33]

With its wizarding wisdom, pragmatic guidance, and pedagogical reflection, this law reads like an aphorism.

Ultimately, in looking across the array of aphorisms uttered by Dumbledore, a pattern emerges. The function, occasion, and content of these aphorisms suggest that Dumbledore's use of aphorisms tends to co-occur in interactional encounters where the headmaster has access to knowledge, experience, or information that another does not. In these instances, Dumbledore deploys this literary and rhetorical style as a stance towards the knowledge asymmetry. Dumbledore adopts this stance so repeatedly in conversations and speeches with Hogwarts students that this act of delivering an aphorism in these interactional moments warrants a name attributable to its source, *Dumbledorisms*.

Dumbledorisms

The stance-laden nature of this idiosyncratic style is reflected in a Dumbledorism's grammatical structure. Like Adalbert Waffling's first Fundamental Law of Magic, Dumbledorisms can take the structural form of a scientific principle, algebraic equation ("z" = "x"+ "y"), or mathematical theorem ("if ... then")—as seen in the following:

> *The truth.... It is a beautiful and terrible thing, and should therefore be treated with great caution.*[34]

Through this algebraic-like formula, the abstract concepts of "truth," "beautiful," and "terrible" are presented as finalizable (knowable) concepts through which the headmaster passes on seemingly objective ("should") but context-absent and impersonal wisdom to Harry.

Dumbledorisms also take the structural form of an imperative. An imperative is a grammatical form that expresses an instructive, almost authoritative "you should"[35] stance. This authoritative stance distinguishes Dumbledorisms from mere evaluative commentary. Readers encounter evaluative commentary in the opening scene of *Harry Potter and the Sorcerer's Stone*. While waiting outside number 4 Privet Drive for the recently orphaned Harry to be delivered to his Muggle relatives, Professor McGonagall reflects on recent events that left Harry orphaned. Repeatedly, she avoids direct use of the name of the perpetrator of these events, Lord Voldemort, to which Dumbledore replies, "My dear Professor, surely a sensible person like yourself can call him by his name? All this 'You-Know-Who' nonsense—for eleven years I have been trying to persuade people to call him by his proper name: Voldemort."[36]

Whereas Dumbledore's comment to McGonagall has more of a chiding nature—his response is filled with honorifics ("my dear Professor") and hedges ("surely")—he makes a similar statement to Harry that is grammatically quite different. His words to Harry are structured as an imperative and delivered with the force of an authoritative, directive, and instructive stance:

> *Call him Voldemort, Harry. Always use the proper name for things. Fear of a name increases fear of the thing itself.*[37]

In contrast to his statement to McGonagall, the headmaster's address to Harry includes an imperative ("call him"), an epistemic adverb of certainty ("always"), and a concluding aphorism ("Fear of a name increases fear of the thing itself").

While the structural forms of Dumbledorisms are revealing, so too are the spaces and places where these forms are shared. Dumbledorisms are most often delivered in safe places that are physically difficult to access—Hogwarts castle, Dumbledore's office, and even Madam Pomfrey's hospital wing, which is where Dumbledore delivers the following aphorism to Harry:

> To the well-organized mind, death is but the next great adventure.[38]

The deployment of aphorisms in difficult-to-access spaces offers a metaphor for the type of knowledge being shared—"a moral, affective, and aesthetic way of knowing"[39] that is born from the challenges of personal, practical, and embodied lived experiences. This metaphorical relationship between aphorisms and space of sharing is most clearly expressed when the headmaster deploys a Dumbledorism in his conversation with Harry in the most difficult space of all to access, the afterlife:

> [T]he true master does not seek to run away from Death. He accepts that he must die, and understands that there are far, far worse things in the living world than dying.[40]

In these hard-to-reach spaces, like the afterlife, deeply embodied, personal, and practical knowledge is shared with the younger wizard through a final Dumbledorism.

Despite reflecting personal, practical, and embodied knowledge, these stories are delivered in a stripped down, depersonalized, and objective grammatical style. As a result, they ring more like the "universa[l] and taken-for-grante[d]"[41] rules or even sacred stories. Sacred stories consist of knowledge drawn from outside the classroom that are "read[ied] and package[ed]"[42] and told in impersonal forms (like aphorisms) where they are funneled "into the school system for the purpose of altering teachers' and children's classroom lives."[43]

> [T]he trouble is, humans do have a knack of choosing precisely those things that are worst for them.[44]

These depersonalized grammatical structures sometimes resemble reflection-on-action.[45] Reflection-on-action describes an individual's reflexive engagement with past action, experience, and knowledge—such as that suggested by the following Dumbledorism:

> Strange how nearsighted being invisible can make you.[46]

This Dumbledorism is delivered to Harry who, in his haste to get to the Mirror of Erised, walks "straight past"[47] the headmaster. Dumbledore admits, "I don't need a cloak to become invisible,"[48] giving the impression through his comment on invisibility that he is speaking from personal experience.

At other times, Dumbledorisms depict reflection-in-action. This type of reflection highlights the breadth or depth of knowledge that is revealed in the moment of displaying "our intelligent action."[49] Dumbledorisms that depict reflection-in-action express a temporal "now" kind of knowledge, as seen in the following Dumbledorism which appears in *Harry Potter and the Chamber of Secrets*:

> [T]he best of us must sometimes eat our words.[50]

Dumbledore draws upon his signature style of deploying an aphorism in a teachable moment. Despite a previous warning that Harry and Ron would be expelled if they broke further school rules (following the Whomping Willow incident), Dumbledore "smilingly" acknowledges to them both that they would not be expelled from Hogwarts. Instead, they would "receive Special Awards for Services to the School"[51] for their parts in saving Ginny Weasley, Gilderoy Lockhart, and all of Hogwarts from the opening of the Chamber of Secrets.

A second Dumbledorism depicting reflection-in-action also surfaces in *Harry Potter and the Order of the Phoenix*. In the privacy of his office, Dumbledore explains to Harry his past (in)actions in sharing information with him, stating: "For I see now that what I have done, and not done with regard to you, bears all the hallmarks of the failings of age."[52] In this instructive moment, Dumbledore seems to adopt a reflective stance towards his actions, especially the impact of these (in)actions on Harry, through the following aphoristic remark:

> *Youth cannot know how age thinks and feels. But old men are guilty if they forget what it was to be young....*[53]

Given the nature of this revelation, this Dumbledorism feels like reflection-in-action. The headmaster applies "knowing-in-action" to the surprise and unexpected circumstance of having finally arrived at the point of having to reveal to Harry important information, as well as the dilemma that kept him from revealing the information previously.

A third Dumbledorism depicting reflection-in-action occurs in conversation between the headmaster and Harry in King's Cross Station. In this space of suspended time, Dumbledore actively reflects on Harry's decision to refrain from pursuing Hallows, in contrast to Dumbledore's own pursuits in this area. As though settling some long unanswered question for himself, Dumbledore remarks on how differently he and Harry have handled the responsibility of knowing about and having access to the power of the Deathly Hallows:

> [P]erhaps those who are best suited to power are those who have never sought it. Those who, like you, have leadership thrust upon them, and take up the mantle because they must, and find to their own surprise that they wear it well.[54]

The "perhaps" suggests reflection, thinking—in the moment and in a way that shares embodied, personal, and practical wisdom.

In all, the headmaster's idiosyncratic style of deploying Dumbledorisms in his interactions with students allows him to share the accumulated wisdom and information he has acquired. Dumbledorisms share this knowledge through grammatical structures that are decontextualized, are void of personal and emotional elements, and obscure the process of coming to know that marks the Dumbledorisms' coming to be. While the process of coming to know is not explicitly expressed in a Dumbledorism, its narrative content hints at its existence. That content also hints at the stance the headmaster holds towards the knowledge he possesses that the individual with whom the Dumbledorism has been shared does not hold. Arguably, this stance reflects the headmaster's relational attempts to manage his roles as headmaster and educator given the knowledge and information he possesses.

The Relational Work of Dumbledorisms

While Dumbledorisms are deployed in moments where knowledge asymmetries exist between the headmaster and another, the deployment of a Dumbledorism is also a relational or face-saving move that allows the headmaster to manage the conversational interactions in which the need for this style arises.

Support for this position is provided in the final chapter of *Harry Potter and The Order of the Phoenix*, "The Lost Prophecy." Following Sirius Black's death at the Ministry of Magic and Voldemort's corporeal return to the wizarding world, Dumbledore meets with Harry in his office. In the safety of his office, the headmaster discloses knowledge he previously withheld from Harry along with several rationales for withholding this information. The rationales include themes of (1) access (what one assumes another knows and is ready and able to know, as well as the certainty of the information to be shared[55]), (2) rights and authority ("to tell, inform, assert or assess knowledge"[56]), and (3) responsibilities (and obligations) to the knowledge held.[57]

These rationales reflect not only the character's stance but also an authorial stance towards knowledge and information—as the series itself withholds knowledge and information from readers in ways that influence both characters' and readers' impressions of Albus Dumbledore as wizard and headmaster.

Access

In "The Lost Prophecy," access to what another is ready and able to know is suggested as rationale for Dumbledore withholding information he possesses. In fact, access—who has it and who does not—is a recurring theme across the series. For example, readers are given authorial access into Harry's inner emotional world and pain, and thus it is easy to align with Harry as readers get a side-along view of his pain, suffering, and fight to survive. Access to Harry's experiences "obligate[s] others to join … in their evaluation, to affirm the nature of the experience and its meaning, and to affiliate with the stance of the experiencer toward them. These obligations are moral obligations that, if fulfilled, will create moments of empathic communication."[58] This access provides readers with knowledge about Harry that the headmaster does not have.

Thus, while readers and Harry's closest friends have access to the protagonist's personal pain and experiences, Dumbledore has only second-hand access to Harry's emotional life and views him as one who is "too young, much too young."[59] As a result, Dumbledore's decisions do not reflect an empathetic engagement with Harry's inner emotional world but a sympathetic one based on the headmaster's own experiences. This position is suggested by Dumbledore when he reveals to Harry that in "[seeing] a shadow of [Voldemort] stir behind your eyes … I was trying, in distancing myself from you, to protect you. An old man's mistake…."[60]

Not until Dumbledore witnesses first-hand Voldemort's attack on Harry in the Ministry of Magic does the headmaster deem Harry "ready" and provide access to information he has been withholding from the younger wizard. Unsurprisingly, Dumbledore marks this turning point with an aphorism:

> *Age is foolish and forgetful when it underestimates youth.*[61]

From this point forward, Dumbledore (mostly) ceases with his use of aphorisms with Harry and instead engages with Harry on a more equal knowledge playing field.

Rights and Authority

Also in "The Lost Prophecy," rights and authority to knowledge surface as themes in Dumbledore's (in)actions around the knowledge he possesses. In particular, he implies these themes as they relate to his "priority … to keep [Harry] alive,"[62] his desire not to see him suffer, and the decisions that he has made over time to ensure his protection. Even Harry recognizes rights and authority as rules by which Dumbledore operates, when he presumes that Dumbledore let him pursue Quirrell in his first year at Hogwarts because "[i]t's almost like he thought I had the right to face Voldemort if I could...."[63]

However, while readers are often concerned with Harry's right to know and be told information, this right is not always considered with respect to Dumbledore's authority to tell. This conflict of rights and authority surfaces often, most notably when Dumbledore attempts to leave bequests to Harry, Ron, and Hermione in his will. Dumbledore leaves them items that, while personal to them, are rather impersonal objects. In Harry not receiving the sword of Gryffindor, we see the ways in which the boundaries between Dumbledore's rights and authority are unsteady, complicated, shifting, and contested. Thus, while Dumbledore may desire to do a thing, his rights and authority to carry out an action are limited, complicating his ability to carry out his desired action.

The issue of rights and authority also surfaces in moments where the headmaster holds information or knowledge that another does not and where he has a mostly professional—and therefore socially limited—authority to divulge this information to another. For example, when Harry encounters Dumbledore in King's Cross, Dumbledore, who has been deceased for almost a year, draws upon his knowledge, wisdom, and authority as deceased to provide Harry with guidance. Harry at this point is truly and legally orphaned—he has no parents, no guardians, no one to guide him. In the face of the disfigured Voldemort baby creature, Dumbledore shares the following guiding words:

> Do not pity the dead, Harry. Pity the living, and, above all, those who live without love.[64]

In this moment Dumbledore assumes the right and authority to speak about the dead and the living as one who has had the experience of being both.

Responsibilities

Finally, responsibilities, in terms of duty and obligation to self and other, is a recurring theme surrounding Dumbledore's (in)actions around the knowledge he possesses. This theme surfaces in "The Lost Prophecy," as well as across the series. Dumbledore's personal and professional responsibilities are often complicated by circumstances beyond his control. These circumstances historically have thrust him in the role of paternal figure, altering the natural order of responsibilities he holds to individuals over whom he may not have natural or legal rights. We see this with Dumbledore's brother and sister and later in Dumbledore's relationship to Harry, for it is Dumbledore who decides that living with the Dursleys is "the best place for [Harry],"[65] a decision that leads to "years of isolation and misery"[66]:

> *The consequences of our actions are always so complicated, so diverse, that predicting the future is a very difficult business indeed.*[67]

Yet, the theme of responsibility also extends to information Dumbledore possesses and the expectation that he has a responsibility to share this information, especially if it concerns another. With Dumbledorisms, the headmaster mediates the uncertain relational boundaries and the sharing of information in such cases. The deployment of a Dumbledorism is a knowledge stance that serves to make knowledge accessible to those who are not the headmaster's legal responsibility to care for, but who are his professional charges. The Ministry's attempt to cover up the role Lord Voldemort played in the death of Cedric Diggory creates such a situation. In his address to the entire school body, Dumbledore interjects an aphoristic statement between divulging that Cedric Diggory died at the hands of Lord Voldemort and that Harry was present and witnessed this tragic event:

> *It is my belief ... that the truth is generally preferable to lies.*[68]

Similarly, Dumbledore wrestles with whether he can and when he should share knowledge with Harry that the latter does not possess. Dumbledore recognizes he has a responsibility to Harry with respect to what he knows; however, not until the fifth book, *Harry Potter and the Order of the Phoenix*, does Dumbledore share his struggle with this responsibility. So, in addition to age (access) as well as rights and authority being factors, Dumbledore addresses this unspoken expectation of responsibility by explaining that he cares more for Harry's happiness "than his knowing the truth."[69]

Following this series of revelations, Dumbledore engages with Harry in a much more straightforward manner. Dumbledore includes Harry in the knowledge-building process. He gives him access, rights and authority, and responsibility in his life and the connection he shares with Voldemort. In fact, fewer aphorisms surface in the series after *Order of the Phoenix*, until Dumbledore's death and reappearance in King's Cross Station.

Conclusion

Phineas Nigellus is right: Dumbledore does have style. In fact, Dumbledore possesses an idiosyncratic style that involves deploying aphorisms in conversations with others, which he executes habitually across the series. Moreover, this pedagogical style harbors Dumbledore's evaluative stance toward knowledge or information he holds, and it reflects his attempts to manage uncertainties about the access, rights and authority, and responsibilities surrounding this knowledge in relation to another.

Dumbledore's style has important implications for readerly perceptions of his character. The stance that underlies this style reflects an alignment or disalignment with the implied or stated wants or needs of the other. Thus, in deploying a Dumbledorism, the reader is aware—consciously or not—that what is reflected in the act is an evaluation of other (including the reader) with respect to this knowledge and a (dis)alignment with the other. For some readers, this stance and its failure to align with the other—the series' beloved protagonist, Harry—does not pay off.

Nonetheless, this evaluation of Dumbledore's (in)actions must consider the headmaster's rights and authority, responsibilities, and access to information. This evaluation must also consider Dumbledore's aphoristic claim that the truth is generally preferable to lies and that perhaps the headmaster deploys aphorisms in his interactions with students as a way to manage the teacherly uncertainty of his rights, authority, responsibilities, and access in operating for the greater good.

Notes

1. J.K. Rowling, *Harry Potter and the Order of the Phoenix* (New York: Scholastic, 2003), 623.
2. M'Balia Thomas, Alisa LaDean Russell, and Hannah V. Warren, "The Good, the Bad, and the Ugly of Pedagogy in Harry Potter: An Inquiry Into the Personal Practical Knowledge of Remus Lupin, Rubeus Hagrid, and Severus Snape," *The Clearing House* 91, no. 4–5 (2018): 188–190.
3. "aphorism, n." *Oxford English Dictionary Online*, accessed March 11, 2022, https://www.oed.com/view/Entry/9141?rskey=3SsATT&result=1.
4. Virginia Woolf, *A Room of One's Own* (London: Flamingo, 1994), 80.
5. J.K. Rowling, *Harry Potter and the Sorcerer's Stone* (New York: Scholastic, 1997), 298.
6. I am eternally grateful to my fellow *Harry Potter* scholar Raphael Carneiro for sharing with me this gem of a term, Dumbledorisms.
7. J.K. Rowling, *Harry Potter and the Deathly Hallows* (New York: Scholastic, 2007), 562.
8. Alicia Willson-Metzger, "The Life and Lies of Albus Dumbledore: The ethics of information sharing and concealment in the Harry Potter Novels," in *Harry Potter's World Wide Influence*, ed. Diana Patterson (Newcastle upon Tyne: Cambridge Scholars, 2009), 293. For more on Dumbledore's secrets, see Lana Whited's and Travis Prinzi's essays in this volume.
9. Rowling, *Deathly Hallows*, 59.
10. J.K. Rowling, *Harry Potter and the Prisoner of Azkaban* (New York: Scholastic, 1999), 114.
11. P. Ruano San Segundo, "A Corpus-Stylistic Approach to Dickens' Use of Speech Verbs: Beyond Mere Reporting," *Language and Literature*, 25, no. 2 (2016): 113.

12. Rowling, *Sorcerer's Stone*, 7. Emphasis added.
13. J.K. Rowling, *Harry Potter and the Goblet of Fire* (New York: Scholastic, 2000), 723–724. Emphasis added.
14. Rowling, *Order of the Phoenix*, 842. Emphasis added.
15. Sam Kirkham, "Personal Style and Epistemic Stance in Classroom Discussion," *Language and Literature* 20, no. 3 (2011): 203.
16. San Segundo, "A Corpus-Stylistic Approach to Dickens' Use of Speech Verbs," 115.
17. Andrew Hui, *A Theory of the Aphorism: From Confucius to Twitter* (Princeton: Princeton University Press, 2019), 4.
18. Hippocrates, *The Aphorisms of Hippocrates* (London: British Library, 2010).
19. Michael LaFargue, "Interpreting the Aphorisms in the Tao Te Ching," *Journal of Chinese Religions* 18, no. 1 (1990): 25–43.
20. David Levine and Alan Bleakley, "Maximising Medicine Through Aphorisms," *Medical Education* 46 (2012): 157.
21. *Ibid.*, 155.
22. Alexandra Jaffe, *Stance: Sociolinguistic Perspectives* (Oxford: Oxford University Press, 2009).
23. J.K. Rowling, *Harry Potter and the Goblet of Fire* (New York: Scholastic, 2000), 454.
24. Rowling, *Sorcerer's Stone*, 128.
25. *Ibid.*, 306.
26. J.K. Rowling, *Harry Potter and the Chamber of Secrets* (New York: Scholastic, 1998), 333.
27. *Ibid.*
28. Geoffrey Leech and Mick Short, *Style in Fiction: A Linguistic Introduction to English Fictional Prose*, 2nd Edition (New York: Routledge, 2013), 290.
29. Rowling, *Sorcerer's Stone*, 214.
30. *Ibid.*
31. Rowling, *Goblet of Fire*, 598.
32. J.K. Rowling, *The Tales of Beedle the Bard* (New York: Lumos, 2008).
33. *Ibid.*, 59.
34. Rowling, *Sorcerer's Stone*, 298.
35. Xu Yueting and Yongcan Liu, "Teacher Assessment Knowledge and Practice: A Narrative Inquiry of a Chinese College EFL Teacher's Experience," *TESOL Quarterly* 43, no. 3 (2009), 505.
36. Rowling, *Sorcerer's Stone*, 11.
37. *Ibid.*, 298.
38. *Ibid.*, 297.
39. F. Michael Connelly and D. Jean Clandinin, *Teachers as Curriculum Planners: Narratives of Experience* (New York: Teachers College Press, 1988), 59.
40. Rowling, *Deathly Hallows*, 720–721.
41. Clandinin and Connelly, *Teachers' Professional Knowledge Landscape*, 8.
42. *Ibid.*, 9, referencing Schwab, 1962.
43. *Ibid.*, 25.
44. Rowling, *Sorcerer's Stone*, 297.
45. Donald Schön, *Educating the Reflective Practitioner: Toward a New Design for Teaching and Learning in the Professions* (San Francisco: Jossey-Bass, 1987).
46. Rowling, *Sorcerer's Stone*, 213.
47. *Ibid.*, 212.
48. *Ibid.*, 213.
49. Schön, *Educating the Reflective Practitioner*, 25.
50. Rowling, *Chamber of Secrets*, 331.
51. *Ibid.*, 331.
52. Rowling, *Order of the Phoenix*, 826.
53. *Ibid.*
54. Rowling, *Deathly Hallows*, 718.
55. Tonya Stivers, Lorenza Mondada and Jakob Steensig, *The Morality of Knowledge in*

Conversation, Studies in Interactional Sociolinguistics (Cambridge: Cambridge University Press, 2011), 9–17.
  56. Ibid., 13.
  57. Ibid.
  58. John Heritage, "Territories of Knowledge, Territories of Experience: Empathic Moments in Interaction," in *The Morality of Knowledge in Conversation, Studies in Interactional Sociolinguistics,* ed. Tanya Stivers, Lorenza Mondada, and Jacob Steensig (Cambridge: Cambridge University Press, 2011), 160.
  59. Rowling, *Order of the Phoenix,* 828.
  60. Ibid.
  61. Rowling, *Half-Blood Prince,* 564–565.
  62. Rowling, *Order of the Phoenix,* 835.
  63. Rowling, *Sorcerer's Stone,* 302.
  64. Rowling, *Deathly Hallows,* 722.
  65. Rowling, *Sorcerer's Stone,* 13.
  66. Susan Reynolds, "Dumbledore in the Watchtower: Harry Potter as a Neo-Victorian Narrative," *Harry Potter's World Wide Influence,* ed. Diana Patterson (Newcastle upon Tyne: Cambridge Scholars, 2009), 282.
  67. Rowling, *Prisoner of Azkaban,* 426.
  68. Rowling, *Goblet of Fire,* 722.
  69. Rowling, *Order of the Phoenix,* 838.

Hem Hem... I Take Umbridge with Bigotry
Using the Witch-in-Pink to Counter Oppression
BRENT A. SATTERLY

"Filthy half-breeds!"—Dolores J. Umbridge

The Letter of Invitation

Dolores J. Umbridge is a witch. And to her ineffable shame, her mother was a Muggle and her brother a Squib. Secretly loathing her family, Dolores and her father blamed her mother for having a Squib in the family. Thus it was that Dolores uttered her first self-satisfied *hem hem* upon receiving her letter of invitation to attend Hogwarts School of Witchcraft and Wizardry in her eleventh year. As she boarded the Hogwarts Express, she henceforth presented herself as pure-blood—literally and figuratively leaving her family behind.[1]

It is the nature of prejudice to germinate in the soil of family upbringing. The forces of family socialization systemically and developmentally categorize people into social hierarchies; some groups are perceived as better than others.[2] Dolores, loathing her family and loving her supposed purity of blood, wouldn't have it any other way.

We first meet Dolores in the Wizengamot, sitting in judgment of one Harry Potter, who stands accused of violating the Restriction of Underage Sorcery in the presence of a Muggle. Thwarted in his attempts to check the Hogwarts headmaster Albus Dumbledore through such transparently twisted proceedings of England's wizarding judicial body, the Minister of Magic, Cornelius Fudge, sends Umbridge to Hogwarts to sit as a professor, serving as his eyes and ears. The newly minted Professor Umbridge is all too keen to seize the opportunity to expand her power within the institution of Hogwarts.[3]

For any teacher, this witch-in-pink is an excellent personified object lesson of internalized prejudices, systemic corruption, discrimination, and cruelty. And the teacher who is authoring this essay is a drag queen. Please grant me some forbearance, dear Muggles, as I embrace a somewhat *Umbridgesque* narcissistic angle in this essay. I was always taught to write about what you know, so much of this is about me. I am a social worker, a teacher, and a Potterhead ... and when I teach, I am the tool. Class is in session. *Hem hem* ... welcome children ... and come with me as we explore how I take Umbridge with bigotry.

Lessons from the Cupboard Under the Stairs

You see, I was always ... different. For two decades, I learned how to be a good liar. In a world where being a gay sissy boy is met with rejection and violence, I quickly learned how to hide. This was especially important while passing through the daily *in-betweens*, the places and spaces where the adult world vanishes—as if an Invisibility Cloak winked it out of existence. Such *in-betweens* included the playground, the mall, the county fair, the locker room, the walk home, and even gatherings of family and friends. But the illusion of the closet is that it will protect you from the *in-betweens*. In reality, however, it taught me how, like Dolores Umbridge, to internally compartmentalize myself, embrace loneliness and isolation, and deny my very humanity. Such developmentally adaptive survival mechanisms schooled me to resist injustice by embodying authenticity. These lessons from the closet are an important part of my story of Umbridge.

Despite the closet, I was viciously bullied because I transgressed my assigned gender role. As a flaming sissy boy, I had a fabulous green purse, filled with playdough and Weebles. It always brought me comfort in times of stress. My purse allowed me to carry the safety of the other world with me as I traversed the *in-betweens*. It was, and will always be, one of my Deathly Hallows.

In my elementary school-age years, I recall my parents taking me to the circus. After the magical show, we got some cotton candy and I saw it: a shining sword—about the size of Bilbo's Sting. It was plastic, but it was simply magnificent. To my surprise, my parents bought it for me. I beamed, imagining myself fighting off monsters, ghouls, and dark wizards. I even took it to school the next day. At recess, fully armored with my Green Purse and Sting, I ran outside, excited to fight would-be Dementors!

Enter Draco Malfoy, or rather, Billy. He was a large, angry, and probably very abused bully. He saw me, grabbed Sting, and snapped it in half. He cackled and pushed me down, to the laughter of onlookers. I hit the pavement with a resounding thump. Seeing my broken Sting on the ground, tears sprang to my eyes. I wanted to scream. I don't know if I was in childhood shock or if it just ignited a fury inside me that I had never known.

Crawling away from the blade-that-was-broken, I walked over to a pile of small river stones nearby. I emptied my purse of its contents—all my precious security—and filled it with those stones. I weighed its heavy contents in my hands. For the first time, I felt strong. I turned slowly, walked over to Billy ... and with a mighty backswing, I cracked him with my Green Purse and all its rocky power square in the face. Billy fell.

I don't remember much after that. A teacher showed up and the *in-between* winked out. Dumping all but three of the stones, I gathered my Deathly Hallows and held my purse against my tummy. I never saw Billy again. Now ... hear me. Am I advocating violence against the Billies of the world? The answer to that question is an unequivocal *no*. I was just a kid and that is sometimes how kids respond. We are *not* children.

The *in-between* of being bullied and the toxicity of the closet taught me two valuable lessons: (1) caring about justice is courageous and (2) being authentically me, in all my weirdness, geekiness, Queerness, and sissy-ness, is magical. I was slowly empowered to embrace myself—it just took time, because the world is harsh to people who are different, be they Squibs or sissy boys, house-elves or heavy-set girls, an Obscurus or an immigrant, Muggles or people of color. But resisting injustice in an authentic way made me a Gryffindor, an advocate, a professor, a social worker ... and a drag queen named Umbridge.

The Schooling of Harry Potter

Belonging is a basic need. It reflects a longing for solidarity and connection to something greater than self.[4] It is no wonder then that when The Boy Who Lived in the cupboard under the stairs received his invitation to join a magical family, he literally jumped at the chance. What he didn't know, but would soon discover, is that this family, like many, had blood feuds, blood bonds, and a bloody history.

The story of *Harry Potter* so inspired me that I began crafting lessons based in the lore and canon to weave into my curricula. Students responded so well that I developed an elective titled The Spell Craft of Social Work: Harry Potter and Social Justice. My social work students were, as a generation, enthralled and ready for deeper exploration: "Activating Millennial motivation, this cultural phenomenon provides themes, characters, and magical environments exploring identity, human development, trauma, families, oppression, privilege, power structures, groups, and diversity."[5] In this class, I had the opportunity to play with various characters to exemplify such social justice-related themes as intersectionality, power and privilege, and the change agent. The course covered topics ranging from Houses and identity formation to blood-status identity politics to trauma to the authoritarian rise of Voldemort to the Ministry's systemic complicity and corruption to Dumbledore's Army and social movements of resistance.[6] But the overarching theme centered around privilege and oppression.

The Dark Mark of Privilege and Oppression

Oppression and privilege are well-explored in the literature.[7] Based on the work of McIntosh and of Robinson and Howard-Hamilton,[8] Linda L. Black and David Stone's concept of privilege is framed as (1) a special advantage that is neither universal nor common; (2) granted, not earned or brought about by talent or effort; (3) an entitlement connected to rank or status; (4) exerted to benefit the recipient and exclude others; and (5) outside of the awareness of those possessing it. The Malfoys, for example, who hold considerable wealth, pure-blood status, professional standing in the wizarding community, and a sheer lack of insight about the extent of such benefits, embody privilege in all of these respects.

Oppression, then, is an outcome in society where privilege goes "unchecked and unchallenged."[9] It occurs in two modes (force or deprivation) and on three levels along a continuum (primary, secondary, or tertiary). Fred J. Hanna, William P. Talley, and Mary H. Guindon define *oppression as force* as an act that imposes an experience, role, label, or a living environment that harms others physically or psychologically.[10] *Oppression as deprivation* is comparable except that it is the removal of affirming or desirable factors. These modes of oppression, however, occur at various levels along a continuum. Primary oppression, on one end of the continuum, is overt, purposeful, and active (e.g., hate groups, discriminatory hiring practices, etc.). Secondary oppression is where individuals benefit from oppression, although they aren't actively engaged in such practices (e.g., *I don't see color!*). Tertiary oppression, on the other end of the continuum, is where members of oppressed groups seek approval from those in dominant groups by betraying a cause for personal advancement (i.e., selling out), thereby harming members of their own group.[11]

These historical, social, and psychological phenomena of oppression and privilege are covered in my courses, but it is the concept of *social privilege* that really spoke Umbridge to me. Black and Stone define social privilege as any benefit, advantage, entitlement, or power that is bestowed or granted to an individual or group as a result of birthright membership and group identities.[12] These authors note that, unlike other definitions, social privilege may or may not be known by those who hold it. In further characterization, they explain it represents an "exaggerated sense of self-worth, belief in personal superiority, [and a] need to continually oppress others to maintain the status quo."[13] And ... hem hem ... if anyone has ever embodied such a definition, it is Dolores J. Umbridge—and she knows it.

The Privilege of Dolores J. Umbridge

Dolores J. Umbridge, pureblood, glides through the halls of the Ministry of Magic basking in social privilege with an arrogant confidence rarely found in the sister of a Squib. Living in a distorted reality, Dolores believes, with all her pink heart, that she deserves such respect and deference due to her earned status and standing in the wizarding world. Employing such psychological defenses as denial and compartmentalization reinforces and safeguards her fragile sense of superiority while simultaneously limiting her emotional development and mental health.[14] In short, social privilege imbues Dolores with a heartily held belief that she is better than others *just by being her*. Her own sense of superiority, coupled with her, shall we say, uncharitable beliefs about how to treat the non-magical community, reveals a dark mark of hatred all its own, arguably beyond any that Voldemort espoused. Her presentation of self—with pink frills, furbelows, kittens, and smiles—starkly contrasts to the darkness in her heart.[15]

The Pink Potion of Pathological Tribalism[16]

Ever wonder how the witch-in-pink came to embody her sense of superiority, her moral authority, and her sadistic contempt for those less than her? Well, she drank the proverbial Kool-Aid, or rather a pink potion of *pathological groupishness*. Allow me to elucidate. Earlier, I noted that it is *belonging* that drives Harry Potter to fly to Hogwarts when given the opportunity. Ultimately, this means that he longs to become part of an ingroup, which deLaplante describes as a network of people sharing common interests and benefiting from connection and interactions within this network.[17] The concept of groupishness—patterns of behaviors and attitudes adopted by any given ingroup and linked to that ingroup's identity—supports an *us vs. them* mentality; our identities become psychologically connected.[18]

Groupishness is inculcated at Hogwarts from day one for every first year under the Sorting Hat. The four great Houses are, in fact, ingroups with specific characteristics, attitudes, behaviors, and even unwritten expectations that define their House. Our House affiliations frame *us* as good, rational, and worthy, whereas their House affiliations frame *them* as bad, irrational, and unworthy. Gryffindor/Slytherin rivalry, anyone?

It is important to note that groupishness isn't dangerous per se. Healthy competition between ingroups, such as Quidditch matches (when there isn't a rogue Bludger), can stimulate ingroups to strive for excellence. The dangers of such groupishness, however, emerge when two ingredients, polarization and cognitive bias, are combined into a deadly pink pathological potion.[19]

Polarization is the magnitude of the actual or perceived differences between ingroups; note that *perceived* differences here are just as significant as real differences. Framing this on a continuum, low polarization allows for tolerance of different viewpoints and civil disagreements on fundamental principles, whereas high polarization maintains that people holding differing viewpoints are fundamentally, morally, and intellectually flawed: "As polarization increases, common ground decreases."[20] Higher polarization results in the urge to segregate with like-minded people, which naturally leads to a sense of solidarity, unity, and lower polarization in their ingroup. However, this ingroup benefit incites viewing the outgroup as biased, irrational, and untrustworthy: "Ingroup solidarity feeds on outgroup animosity."[21] This animosity stokes the primal emotion of fearing difference, which echoes Dolores's own terror of anything even slightly non-human. Such fear can ultimately result in extreme prejudices and discrimination, including racial profiling, hate crimes, and bigoted legislation (e.g., anti–LGBTQIA+ laws, the Muggle-born Registration Commission, transgender military ban, anti-werewolf measures, etc.).

The second deadly ingredient of our pathological potion is cognitive bias.[22] This psychological phenomenon is a subconscious result of our brains trying to simplify how we process information. Cognitive bias, in short, is a misinterpretation of information that influences rational thought and decision-making.[23] While discussing the array of cognitive biases is beyond the scope of this essay, two are relevant to Dolores Umbridge's character: affect bias and cultural cognition.

Affect bias simply refers to how our feelings drive what we think about something. If we feel good about something, we deem it positive, whereas if we feel bad about something, we frame it as negative. For example, from her upbringing, Dolores emotionally *loathed* Muggle-born folk.

They were bad, useless, and inferior in all aspects. Her feelings drove her cognitive evaluation of them.

Want another example, dear reader? Consider how *you* framed Headmaster Dumbledore versus Professor Umbridge upon first meeting both of these vibrant characters. Socially, how is the archetype of the older, White, wizened, kind man who favors you emotionally framed when compared to the frumpy, middle-aged, unattractive, controlling woman who punishes you? Did your feelings have anything to do with how you viewed them? *Hem hem*.... I suspect so.

Another cognitive bias, cultural cognition, is the inclination to conform beliefs about debated facts (e.g., What causes climate change? Does gun control reduce violent crimes? Do immigrants harm society?) to values that embody our cultural identities and thereby our ingroups.[24] When our beliefs are shaped to correspond with our ingroups, and deeply held values emerge, we can wrap ourselves in an echo chamber of moral superiority, rightness, and authority. This might, for example, give one Dolores Umbridge no moral compunction to prevent her from imposing her rigid values upon all students at Hogwarts and justifying tortuous punishments. After all, "naughty children deserve to be punished."[25]

Pink Systemic Corruption

Pathological groupishness has to occur in some context. In a polarized environment that champions cognitive biases, Dolores represents systemic corruption and oppression. Urie Bronfenbrenner's systems theory, a micro- and a macrosystemic ecological approach to human behavior, frames this for us.[26] Microsystems include interactions with individuals, family, and groups, whereas macrosystems involve communities, organizations, policies, and global perspectives.[27] In systems theory, micro- affects macro- and vice versa. When things change in one system, they change in another. When pathological groupishness, social privilege, and oppression combine in such systems, systemic oppression emerges. So let's look at the various roles Dolores plays to further such oppression, like a pink virus.

Dolores as Senior Undersecretary

Within the Ministry, Senior Undersecretary Umbridge serves as the primary assistant to the Minister for Magic. In her role, she exercises considerable power and authority in his name, which comes easily to her given her psychological predisposition and social privilege. Her own corruption is first evidenced in the Wizengamot when, unbeknownst to the magical judicial body, she sends Dementors after a certain Harry Potter in Little Whinging.

When Fudge, in his increasing fear-based paranoia and anxiety about threats to his power, approaches her to teach at Hogwarts to provide some not-so-secret oversight, she greedily accepts. Her own personal opportunity for redressing what she views as a great wrong in her time at Hogwarts, when she was consistently overlooked for positions of leadership, is too delicious for her to pass up.[28] Indeed, "she relished the chance to return and wield power over those who had not ... given her her due."[29]

Even later, after her disastrous failure at Hogwarts, she resumes her post as Senior Undersecretary despite her abuse of power there, revealing the essential corruption of the Ministry. Under the Dark Lord's puppet Minister, Pius Thicknesse, such corruption is sanctioned when Dolores serves happily as the Head of the Muggle-born Registration Commission, degrading, questioning, and imprisoning "Mudbloods." In fact, some do not survive her torment.[30]

Dolores as Professor

At Hogwarts, we see Dolores's darkness really shine with a pink hue. In the microsystem of the classroom, she employs Lipsky's "discretion" as a frontline interpreter of governmental policy.[31] Like police officers, social workers, Aurors, and lawyers, teachers have *discretion*: that is, the power to interpret governmental macrosystemic policy in the execution of their jobs on a microsystemic level.[32] In this case, Professor Umbridge uses her discretionary magic when dictating Ministry-imposed curriculum in this interchange in her Defense Against the Dark Arts class:

> UMBRIDGE: "Your previous instruction in this subject has been disturbingly uneven. But you'll be pleased to know from now on, you will be following a carefully structured, Ministry-approved course of defensive magic.... You will be learning about defensive spells in a secure, risk-free way."
> HARRY: "Well, what use is that? If we're gonna be attacked, it won't be risk-free."
> UMBRIDGE: "Students will raise their hands when they speak in my class. It is the view of the Ministry that a theoretical knowledge will be sufficient to get you through your examinations, which, after all, is what school is all about!"[33]

Professor Umbridge actually codifies educational policy in her simple decision to not allow students to use magic in her classroom, furthering the Ministry's political ideological agenda (suppression of Critical Race

Theory anyone?). With Ministerial authority and social privilege, she unjustly casts the spell of discretion to not only curb independent critical thinking but also limit student development of magical abilities, making them both more malleable and less of a threat.

I would be remiss if I did not highlight the infamous detention of Harry Potter. When Harry, in the aforementioned Defense Against the Dark Arts lesson, insists that Cedric Diggory died at the hands of Lord Voldemort, Professor Umbridge sees it as an opportunity both to exercise her socially privileged, righteous authority and to punish the Chosen One himself. When Harry sits to do lines in her proper office of kittens and pink frills, he observes, "You haven't given me any ink." Dolores rises, unabashedly knowing full well the bloody outcome to follow, and utters with her toad-like smile the most terrifying line in all of *Harry Potter* canon: "Oh, you won't need any ink."[34] This punishment later becomes standard fare for many naughty children at Hogwarts.

Dolores as Inquisitor

When Fudge's twisted paranoia grants her Inquisitorial powers at Hogwarts, Dolores revels in her newly-sanctioned authority. She not only swiftly employs macrosystemic policy changes (i.e., Educational Decrees) altering the very culture of learning and living at Hogwarts, but she also begins observing and interviewing her colleagues in the classroom. Avidly exercising her powers to ferret out threats to the Minister in the name of curricular revision, educational oversight, and policy reform, High Inquisitor Umbridge terminates those professors deemed unworthy, interrogates and tortures students about untoward activities, and all but banishes the magic of Hogwarts through the power of the pen, policy, and the lust for pathological purity.

Senior Undersecretary, Professor, or High Inquisitor—Dolores Umbridge embodies prejudice, privilege, and systemic oppression in its most insidious form: the unequivocal belief that she is always right *no matter whom it hurts*.

"Dragging" a TERF out of the Closet: A Message from Queen Umbridge

Hem hem.... Hello children. And thank you, Dr. Satterly, for those kind words of welcome. And how lovely to see all your bright happy faces smiling up at me. I'm sure we're all going to be very good friends. Let me share a few words with you today about justice. You see, I too take Umbridge with J.K. Rowling.

J.K. Rowling, the author of our beloved *Harry Potter* series, where we, the fandom, have relished the wizarding world, has betrayed us, and most poignantly, the LGBTQIA+ fandom. As if drinking some Polyjuice Potion rendering her unrecognizable to us, this betrayal took the form of a loathsome assault on transgender people cloaked in twisted feminism, whose adherents are known as Trans-Exclusionary Radical Feminists (TERFs). Her social media activities have supported transgender prejudice, literally de-gendering transgender people. Doubling down under criticism, she subsequently posted a transphobic manifesto clarifying her oppressive beliefs.

It is well known among fandoms that the works of such authors are no longer owned by the author but rather by the fandom. I admire that approach—but it feels too convenient to justify still being a Potterhead despite the author becoming anathema. I admittedly almost snapped my wand in two the day she posted her manifesto, and I am not alone in such despair. How could I support and love my transgender and non-binary siblings and still be a Potterhead? Well, I quickly learned that LGBTQIA+ youth who grew up with Harry Potter were more intensely devastated than I. As a, shall we say, more senior (*hem hem*!) gay, cis-male queen, I don't have the same experience that our younger trans and non-binary fans do. But I felt it my duty to advocate from inside the fandom, where many a trans, non-binary, and Queer Potterhead still found a home at Hogwarts. Matthew Jacobs writes about this phenomenon in *HuffPost*:

> What is "Harry Potter" if not the story of an unwanted outcast who discovers his worth after finding a welcoming community? Many LGBTQ readers who grew up fantasizing about Hogwarts saw queer subtext nestled within Rowling's wizardry, and the author further validated their perspectives by continually supporting gay causes. To see her impugn trans women does not compute with the ... Rowling who once seemed like a fortress of tolerance.[35]

And who better to *Bombarda Maxima* a fortress but Dolores J. Umbridge?

Hem hem is my hallmark, but it is more than it seems. For much of my life, I have heard *hem hem* in the ugly faces of well-intentioned teachers, supervisors, co-workers, preachers, neighbors, even family and friends. *Hem hem* is the wonderful, White, wily way to try to erase being responsible for the hate-filled curses that come out of your mouth. It is the rose-scented poo-poo pourri of bigotry—a literal curse of microaggressions.

- "*Hem hem*, I have Black friends."
- "*Hem hem*, love the sinner, hate the sin."
- "*Hem hem*, you're not *that* depressed. Get over it."
- "*Hem hem*, smile, dear."

- "*Hem hem*, there's only one race, the human race."
- "*Hem hem*, not *all* men."

You get my point. But here's the Horcrux: the only thing missing from Rowling's diatribe is *hem hem*. And I will not let She-Who-Must-Not-Be-Named ruin it all. You may ask, "But Professor, what can we do?" Well, my dears, we must first hold our trans and non-binary Potterheads close, and center their voices. To cisgender fans, reflect deeply on our cisgender privilege; bear witness, listen, acknowledge and validate hurt. Recognize that some will leave the fandom for their own self-care.

And to all of us, I say, remember the magic of a fandom! Lev Grossman describes a fandom as "fans, but ... not silent, couchbound consumers of media. The culture talks to them, and they talk back to the culture in its own language."[36] Such fandom language embodies creating, writing, painting, debating, LARPing, gaming, designing, singing, acting, advocating, voting, and more!

Need an example? Consider Alex L. Combs, who wrote in their *Trans-Affirming Magical Care* fanzine, "We decided to make this zine ... partly ... to do what we always do as marginalized fans—make room for ourselves in the text through fanworks."[37] To illustrate, Maia Kobabe, zine contributor, tells the tale of one non-binary Tonks. After being Sorted, Tonks seeks out their House tower. When they find the two sets of dormitory stairs and wonder which to choose, another staircase unfolds. The castle, in its magic, offers Tonks a third option.[38] How perfect.

Now, let me wind down so Dr. Satterly can continue his pontificating. To my transgender and non-binary Potterhead siblings, Moaning Myrtle and I will be your bathroom buddies.

The Pedagogy of Drag

Having analyzed Dolores's character, social privilege, and pathological groupishness, I want to highlight how I embody the antithesis of her in my classroom with a wig, a wand, and serving face. Drag is more than unconventional entertainment. It's about families—communities of sisters, artists, lovers, and performers—who play with gender, reject convention, and personify RuPaul's axiom of "charisma, uniqueness, nerve, and talent."[39] RuPaul captures this poignantly in an interview in *The Wrap*: "Drag is dangerous. Drag is not politically correct ... you're born naked and the rest is drag. And that's political, it's very punk rock, it's very radical. It's this idea that you are not your body. You are an extension of the power that created the whole universe. That's drag. We are all God in drag.[40] Drag queens are iconic symbols of entertainment and activism[41]:

"The drag queen may have all the ... paraphernalia which society uses to determine femininity, but the result is not feminine at all. Drag is a creatively subversive performance, inviting the audience to question frameworks of gender."[42] They not only display courage by transgressing gender in the face of oppression (i.e., hate crimes, TERF, anti–LGBTQIA+ politics, etc.), they also have historically resisted injustices in social movements (e.g., the Stonewall riots, Queer Pride marches, Black Lives Matter protests, etc.). And as I developed my Harry Potter and Social Justice course, I found the marriage between my Queer passion for teaching, theater, and drag in Dolores. The classroom is a stage and teaching merely "academic drag."[43]

Umbridge Attracts and Unbalances

As I swished across campus in full Umbridge drag, with my pink fur-lined cloak flowing behind me dramatically, I recall encountering a large admissions group of prospective students touring campus. Cracking my large pink fan, I emphatically quoted our university motto *"Hem, hem!* We're all Widener!" as I glided by, cloak flapping in the wind. I'm sure Dolores was the topic of conversation over many a dinner table that evening.

And that is the point. Not only does drag attract, but it also unbalances. In the fullness of drag, my femininity as an out, gay, sissy boy professor comes shining through to my students. You might say that my Queerness is on full, pink-frilled display. Culturally, gay sissy boys are paradoxically both disarming and threatening to a sexist, hypermasculine, heteronormative, and emotionally defended (as psychological defense mechanisms designed to safeguard the ego) student body.[44] That is to say, we are both loved and loathed in United States culture.[45] In this drag-cloaked vein, Professor Umbridge subsequently serves as a siren song or a hinkypunk glow for students. They metaphorically hear the melody of the prefects' bathroom siren or glimpse the hinkypunk luminescence in the Forbidden Forest—and are curiously drawn into the lesson, despite themselves. Such enchanting femininity and conventional drag humor, known as *camp*, defuses these aforementioned defenses.

Camp is a queen's bailiwick to unbalance her audience by embodying Queer stigma and juxtapositions,[46] which pair things that don't appear to go together: "a beauty in love with a beast, an old woman living in a shoe, or a man wearing a dress."[47] For example, Dr. Brent is known as a kind and gentle professor whereas Professor Umbridge is, shall we say, boisterous? I recall Dolores entering her raucous classroom, cracking her pink fan, and announcing, "Good afternoon, you sons-o'-witches! Today, we are going to have a spirited debate about the Muggle-born Registration Commission and current U.S. immigration policies. Please note that I will not tolerate any discourtesy. Indeed, *I WILL HAVE ORDER!*" The class gasped immediately and stilled with a pregnant pause, as if waiting to know what Professor Umbridge would do next.

Such humor, used wisely and with theatrical flair, is an over-the-top parody of U.S. pop culture allusions, light-hearted reads (i.e., roasting someone), or shady witticisms.[48] Camp works emphatically well when skillfully exercised to not only engage students but also lower defenses around sensitive content (e.g., immigration policies). In their article on "Drag Pedagogy," Keenan and Lil Miss Hot Mess note that camp places the brunt of the joke of such social ills on macrosystems, not the individual.[49] They cite Isherwood in Baker's *Drag: A History of Female Impersonation in the Performing Arts*, who said, "You're not making fun of it; you're making fun out of it."[50] Camp subsequently allows a queen to discuss painful topics like oppression and privilege by deconstructing and neutralizing them.[51] But be warned … camp as a pedagogical method is not for the unskilled.[52] Leave it to us queens!

Umbridge Engages and Activates

A social work professor who is a drag queen is nothing if not a storyteller to bring tales of social injustice to life in ways that can, indeed, be heart-wrenching. Dolores is the antithesis of who I am as a social worker. Given the unconventional embodiment of drag, I was immediately activated by this pink wicked witch who was every brutal bully, every dispassionate teacher, every violent adult I ever encountered. I must not tell lies—there were too many. By embodying her, I controlled them.

The naked reality of how bigotry is woven throughout U.S. history and society cannot be denied. Contextually, such content must be delivered in a trauma-informed way.[53] But Professor Umbridge's expertise in illuminating the nature of systemic oppression and the execution of such injustices serves her well in the classroom.

With great aplomb, Dolores recounts historical exemplars of oppression and social privilege in the wizarding and Muggle worlds. She likens how social work, as a field (1) effectively abandoned those infected with HIV or AIDS in the early days of the pandemic[54] to the wizarding world's stigmatizing and social rejection of those afflicted with lycanthropy; (2) was complicit with the imprisoning of Japanese Americans in World War II U.S. Internment Camps[55] to the Muggle-born Registration

Commission's deadly interrogation and imprisonment of wizards and witches; and (3) whitewashed social work history to exclude significant contributions of Black and Indigenous people of color (BIPOC)[56] to the systematic whitewashing of the *Harry Potter* films.[57] Dolores continues in her tutelage, however, exploring connections with contemporary Muggle world examples, such as the Muslim travel and transgender military bans, police brutality, anti–LGBTQIA+ bills, the Dobbs decision, the border wall, voter suppression, and the January 6 insurrection.

Stories that reflect such poignant and unjust realities that matter to students not only engage them in critical thinking and course content but also activate them to do something. Indeed, Professor Umbridge is poignantly aware that students are, in fact, a powerful force for social change, like drag itself, outside of conventional avenues. Dumbledore's Army is no faculty committee or institutionally-funded club; it is a secret student organization designed to learn the spell craft of resistance. Calling upon the history of social work as a field of activism and drag as a movement, Professor Umbridge helps students channel social activism passion into change agent activities such as marches, legislator visits, letter-writing campaigns, and voter registration efforts.

A Curtain Call

A finale is often a dramatic conclusion that neatly ties up loose ends, resolves character conflicts, and allows for the audience to feel a sense of *ahhhh*; the victimized are empowered, the villain gets their due, and justice prevails. Alas, dears, such closure is a romanticized notion. The pursuit of social justice is an ongoing endeavor that requires us to witness the pain of oppression, the unfairness of social privilege, and the magical courage of those who resist in all their authenticity—with or without a wig.

Professor Dolores J. Umbridge is an iconic magical character who has brought me such joy in her utterly nefarious unlikability. Embracing her to exemplify the paradox of social justice while cloaked in the witch-in-pink teaches my students to not only strive for justice but be fully and freely themselves in this pursuit. Now, if you'll excuse me ... *hem, hem....* I've got a show to do.

Notes

1. J.K. Rowling, "Dolores Umbridge," *Wizarding World*, August 10, 2015, https://www.wizardingworld.com/writing-by-jk-rowling/dolores-umbridge.

2. Dominic Abrams and Melanie Killen, "Social Exclusion of Children: Developmental Origins of Prejudice," *Journal of Social Issues* 70, no. 1 (2014): 1–11.

3. J.K. Rowling, *Harry Potter and the Order of the Phoenix* (New York: Scholastic, 2003).

4. Yossi Levi-Belz and William Feigelman, "Pulling Together—The Protective Role of Belongingness for Depression, Suicidal Ideation and Behavior Among Suicide-Bereaved Individuals," *Crisis: The Journal of Crisis Intervention and Suicide Prevention* (2021).

5. Brent Satterly, "*Teaching Note:* The Spell Craft of Social Work: Harry Potter and Social Justice," *Journal of Baccalaureate Social Work* 22, no. 1 (2017): 111.

6. Satterly, "Spell Craft."

7. See especially Linda L. Black and David Stone, "Expanding the Definition of Privilege: The Concept of Social Privilege," *Journal of Multicultural Counseling & Development* 33, no. 4 (2005): 243–255; Betsy Lucal, "Oppression and Privilege: Toward a Relational Conceptualization of Race," *Teaching Sociology* 24, no. 3 (1996): 245–255; Peggy McIntosh, "White and Male Privilege: A Personal Accounting of Coming to See Correspondences Through Work in Women's Studies," in *Race, Class, and Gender: An Anthology*, eds. Margaret L. Andersen and Patricia Hill Collins (Belmont: Wadsworth, 1992), 70–81; Tracy L. Robinson, "The Intersection of Dominant Discourses Across Race, Gender, and Other Identities," *Journal of Counseling & Development* 77, no. 1 (1999): 73–79.

8. Tracy L. Robinson and Mary F. Howard-Hamilton, *The Convergence of Race, Ethnicity, and Gender: Multiple Identities in Counseling* (Upper Saddle River, NJ: Merrill, 2000).

9. Black and Stone, "Definition of Privilege," 245.

10. Fred J. Hanna, William B. Talley, and Mary H. Guindon, "The Power of Perception: Toward a Model of Cultural Oppression and Liberation," *Journal of Counseling & Development* 78, no. 4 (2000): 430–441.

11. Hanna, Talley, and Guindon, "Power of Perception," as cited in Black and Stone, "Definition of Privilege."

12. Black and Stone, "Definition of Privilege."

13. *Ibid.*, 251.

14. *Ibid.*; Robinson, "Dominant Discourses."

15. Rowling, "Dolores Umbridge."

16. Although deLaplante uses "tribe" and "tribalism," I will use "ingroup" and "groupishness," given the problematic nature of the term "tribalism," implying cultural appropriation of Indigenous peoples and reinforcing stereotypic cultural and historical assumptions.

17. Kevin deLaplante, "The Dangers of Tribalism," YouTube, January 19, 2018, video, 11:39, https://www.youtube.com/watch?v=7y-b7f6CK2M.

18. *Ibid.*

19. *Ibid.*

20. *Ibid.*, 6:50.

21. *Ibid.*, 8:19.

22. Kevin deLaplante, "Cognitive Biases, Tribalism and Politics (Part 1 of 3): We Can Value More Than One Kind of Thing," YouTube, December 6, 2018, video, 8:55, https://www.youtube.com/watch?v=2NjOzvM41zM&t=0s.

23. Ruhl, Charlotte, "What Is Cognitive Bias?" Simply Psychology, May 4, 2021, https://www.simplypsychology.org/cognitive-bias.html.

24. The Cultural Cognition Project, "The Cultural Cognition Project at Yale Law School," accessed January 24, 2022, http://www.culturalcognition.net/; deLaplante, "Cognitive Biases."

25. *Harry Potter and the Order of the Phoenix*, directed by David Yates (2007; Burbank, CA: Warner Bros.), Xfinity, https://www.xfinity.com/stream/entity/4950300734241750112, 1:34:46.

26. Urie Bronfenbrenner, "Ecology of the Family as a Context for Human Development: Research Perspectives," *Developmental Psychology* 22, no. 6 (1986): 723–742.

27. Urie Bronfenbrenner, "Toward an Experimental Ecology of Human Development," *American Psychologist* 32, no. 7 (1977): 513–530.

28. Rowling, "Dolores Umbridge."
29. *Ibid.*
30. *Ibid.*
31. Michael Lipsky, *Street-Level Bureaucracy: Dilemmas of the Individual in Public Services* (New York: Russel Sage Foundation, 2010), 1.
32. *Ibid.*
33. *Order of the Phoenix,* directed by David Yates, 2007, 36:12–36:56.
34. *Ibid.*, 39:09.
35. Matthew Jacobs, "Mourning the Ellen DeGeneres and J.K. Rowling We Used to Know," *HuffPost*, August 18, 2020, https://www.huffpost.com/entry/ellen-degeneres-jk-rowling-controversy_n_5f32ba6cc5b6960c066ce48b.
36. Lev Grossman, "The Boy Who Lived Forever," *Time*, July 7, 2011, http://content.time.com/time/arts/article/0,8599,2081784,00.html.
37. Alex L. Combs, et al., *Trans-Affirming Magical Care: A Harry Potter Fanzine* (2020), 33, https://alexlcombs.com/transhp.
38. Maia Kobabe, "Tonk's Tale," *Trans-Affirming Magical Care*, Tumblr (February 22, 2020), https://owlswithfins.tumblr.com/post/190966973608/trans-affirming-magical-care-is-a-40-page.
39. John Mercer, Charlie Sarson, and Jamie Hakim, "Charisma, Uniqueness, Nerve, and Talent: *RuPaul's Drag Race* and the Cultural Politics of Fame," *Celebrity Studies* 11, no. 4 (2020): 383.
40. Tim Molloy, "RuPaul Explains Why 'We Are All God in Drag,'" *TheWrap*, September 14, 2019, https://www.thewrap.com/rupaul-explains-why-we-are-all-god-in-drag.
41. Nathaniel Simmons, "Speaking Like a Queen in RuPaul's Drag Race: Towards a Speech Code of American Drag Queens," *Sexuality & Culture* 18 (2014): 630–648.
42. Az Hakeem, ed., *TRANS: Exploring Gender Identity and Gender Dysphoria* (Newark, UK: Trigger Press, 2018), 57.
43. Charles E. Morris III, "(Self-)Portrait of Prof. R.C.: A Retrospective," *Western Journal of Communication* 74, no. 1 (2010): 34.
44. Harry Thomas, Jr., *Sissy! The Effeminate Paradox in Postwar U.S. Literature and Culture* (Tuscaloosa: University of Alabama Press, 2017), ix.
45. *Ibid.*
46. Michael Broder, "Camping It Up in Ancient Rome: A Queer Take on Catullus 16," *HuffPost*, March 11, 2013, https://www.huffpost.com/entry/ancient-rome-homosexuality_b_2813920; Esther Newton, *Mother Camp: Female Impersonators in America* (Chicago: University of Chicago Press, 1972).
47. Broder, "Camping It Up."
48. Helene A. Shugart and Catherine Egley Waggoner, *Making Camp: Rhetorics of Transgression in U.S. Popular Culture* (Tuscaloosa: University of Alabama Press, 2008), 1.
49. Harper Keenan and Lil Miss Hot Mess, "Drag Pedagogy: The Playful Practice of Queer Imagination in Early Childhood," *Curriculum Inquiry* 50, no. 5 (2020): 440–461.
50. Roger Baker, *Drag: A History of Female Impersonation in the Performing Arts* (New York: New York University Press, 1994), 238.
51. Richard Dyer, *The Culture of Queers* (New York: Routledge, 2005); Uri McMillan, "Nicki-Aesthetics: The Camp Performance of Nicki Minaj," *Women & Performance: A Journal of Feminist Theory* 24, no. 1 (2014): 79–87.
52. Campy humor (e.g., throwing shade) can be effective by engaging and unbalancing an audience—or even managing a heckler. Newton notes that such humor is always sarcastic, but a campy delivery defuses the sting. A skilled teacher can paradoxically push the boundaries of humor while also attending to the learning environment. A teacher using campy humor poorly can offend (or even insult) students, dismiss students' perspectives, or damage the learning environment.
53. For trauma-informed teaching, see Jessica Minahan, "Trauma-Informed Teaching Strategies," *Educational Leadership* 77, no. 2 (2019): 30–35, https://www.ascd.org/el/articles/trauma-informed-teaching-strategies; Jane Elizabeth Sanders, "Teaching

Note—Trauma-Informed Teaching in Social Work Education," *Journal of Social Work Education* 57, no. 1 (2021): 197–204.

54. Elizabeth A. Bowen, "AIDS at 30: Implications for Social Work Education," *Journal of Social Work Education* 49, no. 2 (2013): 265–276.

55. Yoosun Park, "Facilitating Injustice: Tracing the Role of Social Workers in the World War II Internment of Japanese Americans," *Social Service Review* 82, no. 3 (2008): 447–483, https://doi.org/10.1086/592361.

56. Kelechi C. Wright, Kourtney Angela Carr, and Becci A. Akin, "The Whitewashing of Social Work History: How Dismantling Racism in Social Work Education Begins with an Equitable History of the Profession," *Archives in Social Work* 21, no. 2/3 (2021): 274–297.

57. While numerous characters were portrayed as an ambiguous race (e.g., Hermione Granger, Beauxbatons students) in the source text, they were cast with white actors. Lavender Brown, originally cast with a Black actor, was recast with a White actor when the character's screen time increased in later films (Julian Suarez, "Racial Diversity in the Media," Under a Tree, May 7, 2018, https://www.underatree.org/our-blog/2018/5/7/racial-diversity-in-the-media). The United Kingdom is a racially diverse nation. It is highly unusual that the films' student body would be primarily white (Kirsten Easton, "Racial Whitewashing and Harry Potter," *SIU Play Analysis Spring 2015*, February 21, 2015, https://siuplayanalysisspring2015.wordpress.com/2015/02/21/racial-whitewashing-and-harry-potter).

Conversation

Teaching, the Hogwarts Way

M'Balia Thomas (MT) and Brent Satterly (BS) talk with Katy McDaniel (KM) and Emily Strand (ES) about their essays.

ES: Now, sometimes when we think about the teaching in *Harry Potter*, it's kind of—it can be, you know, sort of exaggerated, as Katy and I were discussing, with Professor Binns or even Professor Snape, Professor Umbridge. But you two have really shown how deeply the series has made you think about your own pedagogy. How has the series made you think more deeply about that, and how have you incorporated lessons learned from the Hogwarts teachers? Brent, why don't we start with you?

BS: Sure, thanks. Great question. I'm a social work professor, and I think one of the things that *Harry Potter* helped me really to do is—for lack of a better phrase—embrace my magic as a teacher and a social worker, but also as an out, gay, sissy boy drag queen. Right? All of these things that aren't always conventional in what might be considered modern-day academe, and often which can be targeted by the powers that be, including but not limited to faculty governance processes, tenure committees, all those kinds of things.

But I think one of the things that I learned the most about incorporating lessons learned from Hogwarts teachers was what not to do. I mean, Dumbledore selectively favored students based on identity or houses. Snape: literally his personality infected his pedagogy, how he taught, how he harmed students in a classroom. Slughorn treated students as objects. And, of course, Umbridge—everything she did was punish, exploit, manipulate, lie, torture, all that kind of stuff, for her own ends.

But I will say it's not all bad for Hogwarts professors! One of the things I really liked was Hagrid, who taught me the most important lesson, which was to connect with your students and be humble. My biggest pet peeve for teachers and faculty—I don't care if you're kindergarten or professor emeritus—is faculty arrogance. Right? That I am better than you as a student. And that's just not my style, it's not my thing, philosophically, theoretically, all of that. But at the end of the day, it comes down to the fact that we're in this together, and I want you to succeed, and the best way for me to do that with you is to build relationship with you and get to know who you are, so that you are seen and heard and known. I think those kinds of things are important. McGonagall celebrated the whole student. She saw Harry perform really well, and knew that he would do well in Quidditch. And that happened outside her classroom, not in the classroom. And ultimately, let's just all be like Lupin and actually teach our subject. [Laughs] Right?

KM: [Laughing.] But you know, I can't even tell you how many presentations I've seen about teachers at Hogwarts that absolutely think Hagrid is the worst of the teachers.

ES: Ug!

KM: And I'm so glad to hear you talk about his virtues as a teacher, because I do think he's good, you know? I think that's a real value, and I hadn't encapsulated it in my thinking as humility, but I think that's a great way to think about him.

ES: Mm-hmm. And his willingness to connect with the students. Because you're right, Brent, like you said, there is this problem of elitism among certain professors. It's really very off-putting, and I just wonder if people who complain so much about the students, or put students down for asking what they think are stupid questions, if they aren't just communicating that they're not fulfilled in their role, and if they wouldn't be more fulfilled if they let themselves make a connection with the students, instead of constantly putting up the wall between themselves and the students. Just thinking out loud here.

BS: Yes, I think it's a wonderful framework, when you think students are the most important part of your classroom. Like, that's why we're here....

ES: They're the reason for the season!

BS: Exactly! I'm constantly surprised when faculty seem to experience students as an annoyance, or in the way. And I will say, Hagrid—I mean, he embraced experiential learning like nobody's business. So field education is our signature pedagogy, let's get out in the field and do the work.

ES: M'Balia, what about you? What have you learned and incorporated?

MT: Yes. So much of what you all have said resonates with me, but I think I'll go back a little bit and reference this idea that Brent raised earlier about thinking about *Harry Potter* while he was undergoing tenure, while he was in the tenure track. That was the same experience for me. Tenure can really make you reflective, if you are that kind of person to be reflective. There's a lot about becoming a professor that people don't understand, that's really difficult. You see some of the best and some of the worst traits of humanity, that come from your own department, from across campus. You just see so much of humanity that is unexpected in these teaching situations.

So, as I am going through the process of tenure, and part of my job is to train up future teachers, going back to Hogwarts really made me think about the teachers in the stories in a very different way. It made me have so much compassion for the humanity that is within each of these teachers, even the worst ones, the ones who treat students awfully, like Snape—even Umbridge. I always have a great deal of sympathy for Lupin, you know, as an African American professor working in a predominantly White institution. There's just so much about my own lived experience that I saw in Lupin's life.

Across all of the teachers, I could see my colleagues, people that I knew on campus who, in different ways, were suffering, hurting, trying to understand what it meant to work in an educational space, in higher education, and to do a decent job with all of the pressures that we have. Thinking about my colleagues and teaching in this way really helped me to have more compassion for the humanity of the Hogwarts teachers and in particular for Snape and for Dumbledore.

KM: I think you can really see that in your work and in the [essay] you wrote for us. You are humanizing teachers—like, let's appreciate the difficulty of the situation that somebody in the classroom might be experiencing.

MT: Absolutely. You know, as teachers, we are not allowed to have doubts. We are not allowed to be insecure. We are not allowed to like or dislike. I mean, we can't express the fact that sometimes there are students who you don't resonate with. That there is sometimes animosity on the part of the student toward you and sometimes vice-versa. And so how you, as an individual, deal with the reality and the humanity of teaching can be so complicated.

I think with a character like Snape, when you see the difficult time he has in overcoming his own childhood issues to be kind to a student who has no family—you realize, wow! Human beings are really hurt when they walk into the classroom sometimes. And how can we have compassion for that individual? How can we set up a space where they can heal and be better teachers, better human beings to their colleagues and to the students around them?

KM: Brent, I did see that you were resonating with what M'Balia had to say as well.

BS: Oh yeah. The experience of authenticity is so precious to me. And not like Gollum, "*precioussss*," but like: precious. [Laughing] I am a quintessential geek, obviously.

But I think one of the things that is so powerful is that we don't create time and space for teachers to embrace that humanity. To not know how to handle it when I have a student in my class who openly says, "Well, I think all gay people are going to go to hell." And here I am, as an out gay faculty member. How do I manage that? How do I navigate that? And what do I see as my mission as both a professor and a social worker? Because I'm thinking about all of the future clients that they're going to have—their queer clients, and the people who love queer people—that might work with this potential future social worker. What's incumbent upon me, ethically?

It's one of the ways I think in that context—usually I always remember Umbridge in those moments, because Umbridge would punish. Anybody who spoke like that, Umbridge would just slam them, punish them. My grandma always taught me you get more bees to honey than to vinegar. Even in the face of that kind of pain in the moment in the classroom, when a student says something like that, still, I go back to Hagrid: I need to connect with that student and help them understand the humanness of what it means to be a social worker in this context and pursue social justice. It creates a sense of cognitive and affective dissonance, if you will, because it's the whole notion of Allport's contact theory: the more you build relationships with people who are different from you, it's a heck of a lot harder to hate them. Because you can't just simplify them into this nice, neat category. Humans are complex but also messy.

MT: That's right. And even though, as educators, we really reach out to those students who may say things, or they may reject us, one of the things that I am trying to emphasize to my students is that it is important to be authentic and true to yourself. You don't have to say, in this moment, that you are upset with this student, but you have to understand for yourself when you are upset with a student, or when your students aren't showing you love, and that makes you feel sad, or that makes you feel like an ineffective teacher. I think it is so important that, if you want to survive in this field, you have to be true to yourself. You have to understand how you as an educator are motivated—what is driving you?—so that you can then rectify whatever challenges you face that are in front of you.

That's one of the things I love about Dumbledore. I think, over the course of these seven novels, that you see someone who is wise and who is supposed to be all-knowing, really doubting himself in ways that aren't always obvious. But over the course of the series, you see him coming to understand what he knows and what he doesn't know. And finally, his ability to kind of share that with a student. And to admit to a student what you don't know is really challenging, but it is really and truly the only way to connect and have an authentic relationship. For me, that is one of the biggest take-aways from the *Harry Potter* series.

Before the Dismissal Bell
Closing Thoughts

Kathryn N. McDaniel

The Hogwarts school year begins and ends with important words from the headmaster to the students, and so to you, dear readers, we offer a similar benediction at the conclusion (for now) of your *Potterversity* education. The usual deliverer of these final words, Headmaster Albus Dumbledore, is one of the most quotable characters in the *Harry Potter* series. As M'Balia Thomas's essay demonstrates, this is in large part because of his special way of dispensing nuggets of wisdom that, though context-specific in the moment, turn out to be generalizable life lessons. Thus, it seems fitting to conclude our course in *Harry Potter* Studies with a consideration of two of his most quoted, though perhaps contradictory, Dumbledorisms.

In *Sorcerer's Stone*, Dumbledore cautions Harry at the Mirror of Erised that "It does not do to dwell on dreams and forget to live."[1] He means by this, in the moment, that Harry's fixation on a fantasy connection with the image of his dead parents in the mirror should not consume him; he needs to live life in the present and look to the future. He should not let fantasy nonreality overtake what is real and true and now.

Sometimes *Harry Potter* readers are accused of doing just this: living in a fantasy realm so deeply that it blinds us to the real-world demands around us. We might interpret Dumbledore's advice to mean that we should put aside the wizarding world in order to live in our own reality, clear-eyed with feet on the ground. But the realm of the imagination, as we now know Albus Dumbledore would be the first to understand personally, is exceptionally important for how we live our lives, for helping us to be clear-eyed and grounded.

The essays in this book have hopefully demonstrated how fantasy in general—but particularly the *Harry Potter* fantasy stories—can help us understand the world we live in: its complex political and interpersonal dynamics, its deeply rooted traditions and revolutionary transformations; its demands on us as moral actors. As our *Potterversity* faculty authors have demonstrated, the *Harry Potter* series creates an imaginative gateway through which we can analyze other important literature, religion, colonialism, race relations, gender and sexual identities, and what it means to be human—warts and all—in both our magical and Muggle dimensions. More than an escapist refuge, these stories help us, as the series author has said, "imagine better."[2] Our *Potterversity* scholars have often gained profound personal insights from their interactions with the realm beyond Platform 9¾, and we hope you identify with that experience as well.

And so we will conclude not with Dumbledore's statement against dwelling on dreams from the first book, but with his acknowledgment of the vital importance of the imagination in the final book, *Deathly Hallows*. In the version of King's Cross station that appears out of the white void, (perhaps deceased) Harry asks the (definitely deceased) headmaster about whether that experience is real or purely in his head. Dumbledore replies, "Of course it's happening inside your head, Harry, but why on earth should that mean it's not real?"[3]

Readers: May the wisdom you gain from the Potterverse remind you that, though Muggle, you are also magical, and thereby empower you to create a better reality.

Until next time: Class dismissed!

Notes

1. J.K. Rowling, *Harry Potter and the Sorcerer's Stone* (New York: Scholastic, 1998), 214.
2. J.K. Rowling, "The Fringe Benefits of Failure and the Importance of Imagination" (speech, Harvard University, Cambridge, Massachusetts, June 5, 2008), *The Harvard Gazette*, https://news.harvard.edu/gazette/story/2008/06/text-of-j-k-rowling-speech/.
3. J.K. Rowling, *Harry Potter and the Deathly Hallows* (New York: Scholastic, 2007), 723.

Bibliography

Abdi, Amal. "Meet Dark Academia, the Bookish Fashion Trend That's All Over Tiktok." *Refinery29*, October 7, 2020. https://www.refinery29.com/en-us/2020/10/10079305/dark-academia-aesthetic-tiktok-trend.
Abrams, Dominic, and Melanie Killen. "Social Exclusion of Children: Developmental Origins of Prejudice." *Journal of Social Issues* 70, no. 1 (2014): 1–11.
Adam, Adolph. *The Liturgical Year: Its History and Its Meaning After the Reform of the Liturgy*. Trans. Matthew J. O'Connell. Collegeville, MN: The Liturgical Press, 1979.
Adams, Jenny. "Colonizing the Otherworld in *Walewein*." In *Games and Gaming in Medieval Literature,* ed. Serina Patterson, 127–145. The New Middle Ages. New York: Palgrave Macmillan, 2015.
———. "Medieval Chess, Perceval's Education, and a Dialectic of Misogyny." In *Chess in the Middle Ages and Early Modern Age: A Fundamental Thought Paradigm of the Premodern World,* ed. Daniel E. O'Sullivan, 111–134. Berlin: De Gruyter, 2012.
Adler, Shawn. "Harry Potter Author J.K. Rowling Opens Up About the Books' Christian Imagery." MTV.com, October 17, 2007. https://www.mtv.com/news/1572107/harry-potter-author-jk-rowling-opens-up-about-books-christian-imagery/.
Alton, Anne Hiebert. "Playing the Genre Game: Generic Fusions of the *Harry Potter* Series." *Critical Perspectives on Harry Potter*, 2nd ed., ed. Elizabeth Heilman, 199–223. New York: Routledge, 2008.
Anelli, Melissa, and Emerson Spartz. "The Leaky Cauldron and MuggleNet interview Joanne Kathleen Rowling: Part Two." The Leaky Cauldron, July 16, 2005. http://www.accio-quote.org/articles/2005/0705-tlc_mugglenet-anelli-2.htm.
"aphorism, n." Oxford English Dictionary Online. Accessed March 1, 2022.
Ashley. "The Dark Academia Reading List: 49 Books of Tragedy, Elitism, Secrets, Violence and the Pursuit of Knowledge." *The Infinite Library*, August 18, 2021. https://ashsinfinitelibrary.wordpress.com/2021/08/18/the-dark-academia-reading-list/.
AT&T. "Fantastic Beasts: The Crimes of Grindelwald—A Familiar Magic." YouTube video, 00:1:36, October 16, 2018. https://www.youtube.com/watch?v=Do2QZsh-EVo.
Auerbach, Nina. *Our Vampires, Ourselves*. Chicago: University of Chicago Press, 1995.
Babel: Or the Necessity of Violence: An Arcane History of the Oxford Translators' Revolution. Harper Voyager. Accessed March 23, 2022. https://www.harpervoyagerbooks.com/book/9780063021440/babel/.
Bacon, Simon. "The Transmedia Vampire: From Bram Stoker's *Dracula* to HBO's *True Blood*." In *Words, Worlds, Narratives: Transmedia and Immersion*, ed. Tawnya Ravy and Eric Forcier, 55–75. Leiden: Brill, 2014.
Baker, Roger. *Drag: A History of Female Impersonation in the Performing Arts*. New York: New York University Press, 1994.
Barber, Richard W., trans. *Bestiary: Being an English Version of the Bodleian Library, Oxford M.S. Bodley 764*. London: Folio Society, 1992.
Bateman, Kristen. "Academia Lives—On TikTok." *The New York Times*, June 30, 2020. https://www.nytimes.com/2020/06/30/style/dark-academia-tiktok.html.

Becker, Jane, writer. *Ted Lasso.* Season 2, episode 10, "No Weddings and a Funeral." Directed by M.J. Delaney. Aired September 24, 2021, on Apple TV+.

Bell, Luke. *Baptizing Harry Potter: A Christian Reading of J.K. Rowling.* Mahwah, NJ: Hidden Spring, 2010.

Benson, Larry D., ed. *Sir Gawain and the Green Knight: A Close Verse Translation.* Morgantown: West Virginia University Press, 2012.

Black, Linda L., and David Stone. "Expanding the Definition of Privilege: The Concept of Social Privilege." *Journal of Multicultural Counseling and Development* 33, no. 4 (2005): 243–255.

Blake, Olivie. "Olivie Blake *Is Writing." *Olivie Blake*, June 8, 2020. https://www.olivieblake.com/post/olivie-blake-is-writing.

Bogost, Ian. "Gamification Is Bullshit." *The Atlantic*, August 9, 2011.

Borges, Jorge Luis, with Margarita Guerrero. *The Book of Imaginary Beings.* Published as *El libro de los seres imaginarios*, 1967. Trans. Andrew Hurley. Illustrated by Peter Sís. New York: Penguin, 2006.

Bowen, Elizabeth A. "AIDS at 30: Implications for Social Work Education." *Journal of Social Work Education* 49, no. 2 (2013): 265–276.

Brenner, Lisa S., ed. *Playing Harry Potter: Essays and Interviews on Fandom and Performance.* Jefferson, NC: McFarland, 2015.

Broder, Michael. "Camping It Up in Ancient Rome: A Queer Take on Catullus 16." *HuffPost*, March 11, 2013. https://www.huffpost.com/entry/ancient-rome-homosexuality_b_2813920.

Bronfenbrenner, Urie. "Ecology of the Family as a Context for Human Development: Research Perspectives." *Developmental Psychology* 22, no. 6 (1986): 723–742.

———. "Toward an Experimental Ecology of Human Development." *American Psychologist* 32, no. 7 (1977): 513–530.

Brous, Sharon. "Imagine a Bible with No Moses, No Story of the Exodus." *New York Times*, April 14, 2022. https://www.nytimes.com/2022/04/14/opinion/passover-exodus-story-redemption.html.

Bruce, Ian. *Expressing Critical Thinking through Disciplinary Texts: Insights from Five Genre Studies.* London: Bloomsbury Academic, 2020.

Bueta, Ryan. "Fantastic Beasts 3: Richard Coyle is Aberforth Dumbledore and Sequel Largely Set in Germany: Exclusive." *The Illuminerdi*, July 14, 2021. theilluminerdi.com/2021/07/14/fantastic-beasts-3-richard-coyle/.

Burkhard, Denise, and Julia Stibane. "Darkness, Danger and Death: Exploring Gothic Places in Harry Potter and the Chamber of Secrets." In *"Harry—Yer a Wizard": Exploring J.K. Rowling's Harry Potter Universe*, ed. Marion Gymnich, Hanne Birk, and Denise Burkhard, 61–70. Baden-Baden, German: Tectum Verlag, 2017.

Caldecott, Leonie. "Cult or Culture? Some Reflections on Rowling, Pullman and the Contemporary Fantasy Scene." *Culture & Libri* 156/157 (2006). https://archive.secondspring.co.uk/articles/Leonie%20Caldecott%20on%20Fantasy.pdf.

Chow, Liana E. "What the Hell Happened? Voldemort's Snake is Actually an Asian Woman." *The Harvard Crimson*, October 2, 2018. https://www.thecrimson.com/article/2018/10/2/nagini-asian-woman/.

The Churchill Project. "Sleep of the Saved and Thankful." *The Churchill Project.* Hillsdale College. September 11, 2015. http://winstonchurchill.hillsdale.edu/sleep-of-the-saved-and-thankful-2/.

Clandinin, D. Jean, and F. Michael Connelly. *Teachers' Professional Knowledge Landscape.* New York: Teachers College Press, 1995.

Coats, Karen. "Harry Potter and the Deathly Hallows." *Bulletin of the Center for Children's Books* 61, no. 2 (2007): 109.

Cohen, Signe. "The Two Alchemists in Harry Potter." *The Journal of Religion and Popular Culture* 30:3 (Fall 2018): 206–219.

Combs, Alex L., et al. *Trans-Affirming Magical Care: A Harry Potter Fanzine.* 2020. https://alexlcombs.com/transhp.

Connelly, F. Michael, and D. Jean Clandinin. *Teachers as Curriculum Planners: Narratives of Experience.* New York: Teachers College Press, 1988.

Coutts-Smith, Kenneth. "Cultural Colonialism." *Third Text* 16, no. 1 (2002): 1–14.
Craft, Christopher. "'Kiss Me with Those Red Lips': Gender and Inversion in Bram Stoker's *Dracula*." *Representations* 8 (1984): 107–133.
The Cultural Cognition Project. "The Cultural Cognition Project at Yale Law School." Accessed January 24, 2022. http://www.culturalcognition.net.
D'Alessandro, Anna. "Fèng Huáng: The Oriental Phoenix and the World's Origin." *Discover People/Places*, February 9, 2020. http://discoverplaces.travel/en/feng-huang-the-oriental-phoenix-and-the-worlds-origin/.
Delaney, M.J., dir. *Ted Lasso*. Season 2, episode 10, "No Weddings and a Funeral." Aired September 24, 2021, on Apple TV+.
deLaplante, Kevin. "Cognitive Biases, Tribalism and Politics (Part 1 of 3): We Can Value More Than One Kind of Thing." YouTube. December 6, 2018. Video, 8:55. https://www.youtube.com/watch?v=2NjOzvM41zM&t=0s.
———. "The Dangers of Tribalism." YouTube. January 19, 2018. Video, 11:39. https://www.youtube.com/watch?v=7y-b7f6CK2M.
de Troyes, Chrétien. *Arthurian Romances*. Trans. William W. Kibler and Carleton W. Carroll. London: Penguin, 1991.
"Dragon." *Cryptowiki*. Accessed January 10, 2019. https://cryptozoology.fandom.com/wiki/Dragon.
"Dragon and Phoenix: Meaning and Symbolism." *Dragon Planet*, January 28, 2022. https://dragon-planet.com/dragon-and-phoenix/.
Du Bois, W.E.B. *The Souls of Black Folk*. New York: Alfred A. Knopf, 1903.
Dunne, John. "The Death of Death in the Death of the Boy Who Lived: The Morality of Mortality in Harry Potter." In *Ravenclaw Reader: The St. Andrews University Harry Potter Conference*, ed. John Patrick Pazdziora and Micah Snell, 31–46. Oklahoma City: Unlocking Press, 2015.
———. "Harry Potter and the Aims of Transhumanism: A Magical Critique of Technological Posthumanity." *Journal of Religion and Popular Culture*, 35, no. 2 (August 2023): 55–71.
Dyer, Richard. *The Culture of Queers*. New York: Routledge, 2005.
Easton, Kirsten. "Racial Whitewashing and Harry Potter." *SIU Play Analysis Spring 2015*, February 21, 2015. https://siuplayanalysisspring2015.wordpress.com/2015/02/21/racial-whitewashing-and-harry-potter.
Edelman, Ezra, dir. *O.J.: Made in America*. 2016; Bristol, CT: ESPN Films. WatchESPN, http://www.espn.com/30for30/ojsimpsonmadeinamerica/.
Edmunds, T. Keith, and Sharon Lauricella. "Ludic Pedagogy: Schooling Our Students in Fun." *Faculty Focus* 23, April 2021. https://www.facultyfocus.com/articles/philosophy-of-teaching/ludic-pedagogy-schooling-our-students-in-fun.
Elizabeth, Hilary. "Harry Potter: 10 Characters More Reckless Than Sirius Black." *Screenrant*, November 5, 2019. https://screenrant.com/harry-potter-characters-more-reckless-than-sirius-black/.
"Everything You Need to Know about Nagini." *Wizarding World*, September 24, 2018. www.wizardingworld.com/features/everything-you-need-to-know-about-nagini.
FinnBV. "Villains in Dracula and Harry Potter: More than Just Famous Antagonists?" The Leaky Cauldron. Accessed June 21, 2022. http://www.the-leaky-cauldron.org/features/essays/issue4/villains/.
Flew, Terry. *New Media: An Introduction*. Oxford: Oxford University Press, 2002.
Flood, Alison. "Faridah Àbíké-Íyímídé: the 21-year-old British student with a million-dollar book deal." *The Guardian*, September 8, 2020. https://www.theguardian.com/books/2020/sep/08/faridah-abike-iyimide-british-student-million-dollar-book-deal-ace-of-spades.
Florer-Bixler, Melissa. *How to Have an Enemy: Righteous Anger and the Work of Peace*. Harrisonburg, VA: Herald Press, 2021.
———. "'Ted Lasso' showed how kindness can change UK soccer. Until we saw the real UK soccer." *Religion News Service*, July 20, 2021. https://religionnews.com/2021/07/20/ted-lasso-showed-how-kindness-can-change-uk-soccer-until-we-saw-the-real-uk-soccer/.

Frankel, Valerie Estelle. *Teaching with Harry Potter: Essays on Classroom Wizardry from Elementary School to College.* Jefferson, NC: McFarland, 2013.

Freytag, Gustav. *Technique of the Drama: An Exposition of Dramatic Composition and Art.* Trans. Elias J. MacEwan. 2nd ed. 1863. Havre, MT: Griggs, 1896.

Galway, Elizabeth A. "Reminders of Rugby in the Halls of Hogwarts: The Insidious Influence of the School Story Genre on the Works of J.K. Rowling." *Children's Literature Association Quarterly* 37, no. 1 (2012): 66–85.

Gentry, Amy. "Dark Academia: Your Guide to The New Wave of Post-*Secret History* Campus Thrillers." *CrimeReads*, February 18, 2021. https://crimereads.com/dark-academia-your-guide-to-the-new-wave-of-post-secret-history-campus-thrillers/.

Goncea, Isabella, and Denise Greenwood. "How Does Male Readership Impact Character Portrayals in Contemporary Young Adult Adventure Novels?" *Journal of Student Research* 10, no. 3 (2021): 1–15.

Granger, John. *The Deathly Hallows Lectures.* Oklahoma City: Zossima Press, 2008.

_____. *Harry Potter as Ring Composition and Ring Cycle: The Magical Structure and Transcendent Meaning of the Hogwarts Saga.* Oklahoma City: Unlocking Press, 2010.

_____. *Harry Potter Meets Hamlet and Scrooge.* Allentown, PA: Methodios Press/Lulu, 2009.

_____. *Harry Potter's Bookshelf: The Great Books Behind the Hogwarts Adventures.* New York: Berkley Books, 2009.

_____. *Looking for God in Harry Potter.* Carol Stream, IL: Salt River/Tyndale House, 2006.

Green, Amy M. "Interior/Exterior in the *Harry Potter* Series: Duality Expressed in Sirius Black and Remus Lupin." *Papers on Language & Literature* 44, no. 1 (Winter 2008): 87–108.

Grossman, Lev. "The Boy Who Lived Forever." *Time*, July 7, 2011. http://content.time.com/time/arts/article/0,8599,2081784,00.html.

Grouling, Jennifer, Stephanie Hedge, Alyssa Schweigert, and Eva Grouling Snider. "Questing through Class: Gamification in the Professional Writing Classroom." *Computer Games and Technical Communication: Critical Methods and Applications at the Intersection*, ed. Jennifer DeWinter and Ryan Moeller, 265–82. Farnham, Surrey: Ashgate, 2014.

Groves, Beatrice. "An Ancient Chinese Bestiary in 'Fantastic Beasts: The Secrets of Dumbledore': Fantastic Bestiaries and Where to Find Them—Part 2." *Bathilda's Notebook*, April 6, 2022. MuggleNet. https://www.mugglenet.com/2022/04/an-ancient-chinese-bestiary-in-fantastic-beasts-the-secrets-of-dumbledore-fantastic-bestiaries-and-where-to-find-them-part-2/.

_____. "Carols in Harry Potter and the Myth of the Christmas Rose (Part I)." The Leaky Cauldron, December 23, 2018. http://www.the-leaky-cauldron.org/2018/12/23/carols-in-harry-potter-and-the-myth-of-the-christmas-rose-part-1/.

_____. "Christmas in *Chamber of Secrets,* or why is the crowing of the rooster fatal to the basilisk?" The Leaky Cauldron, December 23, 2019. http://www.the-leaky-cauldron.org/2019/12/23/christmas-in-chamber-of-secrets-or-why-is-the-crowing-of-the-rooster-fatal-to-the-basilisk/.

_____. "Christmas in *Chamber of Secrets,* or why is the crowing of the rooster fatal to the basilisk? Part 2." The Leaky Cauldron, December 24, 2019. http://www.the-leaky-cauldron.org/2019/12/24/christmas-in-chamber-of-secrets-or-why-is-the-crowing-of-the-rooster-fatal-to-the-basilisk-part-2/.

_____. *Literary Allusion in Harry Potter.* London: Routledge, 2017.

_____. "The Phoenix and the Qilin in 'Secrets of Dumbledore': Fantastic Bestiaries and Where to Find Them—Part 3." *Bathilda's Notebook*, April 7, 2022. MuggleNet. https://www.mugglenet.com/2022/04/the-phoenix-and-the-qilin-in-secrets-of-dumbledore-fantastic-bestiaries-and-where-to-find-them-part-3/.

_____. "'Secrets of Dumbledore' and 'The Book of Beasts': Fantastic Bestiaries and Where to Find Them—Part 1." *Bathilda's Notebook*, April 5, 2022. MuggleNet. https://www.mugglenet.com/2022/04/the-secrets-of-dumbledore-and-the-book-of-beasts-fantastic-bestiaries-and-where-to-find-them-part-1/.

_____. "The Snake Woman in Harry Potter and Fantastic Beasts." In *The Ivory Tower,*

Harry Potter, and Beyond, ed. Lana A. Whited. Columbia: University of Missouri Press, 2023.
Gulevich, Tanya. *The Encyclopedia of Christmas*. Detroit: Omnigraphics, 2000.
Gunn, James. "Harry Potter as Schooldays Novel." In *Mapping the World of Harry Potter*, ed. Mercedes Lackey, 145–155. Dallas: BenBella, 2005.
Haasch, Palmer. "All the Creatures That Appear in *Fantastic Beasts: The Secrets of Dumbledore*." *The Insider*, April 21, 2022. www.insider.com/creatures-animals-monsters-in-fantastic-beasts-the-secrets-of-dumbledore-2022-4.
———. "Here's How 'Fantastic Beasts: The Secrets of Dumbledore' Deals with Johnny Depp's Absence." *The Insider*, April 15, 2022. www.insider.com/how-fantastic-beasts-3-replaces-johnny-depp-with-mads-mikkelsen-2022-4.
Hakeem, Az, ed. *TRANS: Exploring Gender Identity and Gender Dysphoria*. Newark, UK: Trigger Press, 2018.
Hall, Susan. "School Ties, House Points, and Quidditch: Hogwarts as a British Boarding School." In *Harry Potter and History*, ed. Nancy R. Reagin, 193–217. Hoboken, NJ: John Wiley & Sons, 2011.
Hanna, Fred J., William B. Talley, and Mary H. Guindon. "The Power of Perception: Toward a Model of Cultural Oppression and Liberation." *Journal of Counseling & Development* 78, no. 4 (2000): 430–441.
Hardy, Elizabeth Baird. "Muggle Worthy: Deceptive Exteriors and Outsized Interiors in the Wizarding World." *The Ivory Tower, Harry Potter, and Beyond*, ed. Lana A. Whited. Columbia: University of Missouri Press, 2023.
Hardy, Stephen H. "The Medieval Tournament: A Functional Sport of the Upper Class." *Journal of Sport History* 1, no. 2 (1974): 91–105.
"The Harry Potter Characters J.K. Rowling Nearly Killed—and the Ones She's Sorry She Did." Wizarding World, November 21, 2018. https://www.wizardingworld.com/features/harry-potter-characters-jk-rowling-nearly-killed-and-the-ones-shes-sorry-she-did.
Hellenga, Robert R. "The Tournaments in Malory's *Morte Darthur*." *Forum for Modern Language Studies* 10, no. 1 (1974): 67–78.
Heritage, John. "Territories of Knowledge, Territories of Experience: Empathic Moments in Interaction." In *The Morality of Knowledge in Conversation: Studies in Interactional Sociolinguistics*, ed. Tanya Stivers, Lorenza Mondada and Jacob Steensig, 159–183. Cambridge: Cambridge University Press, 2011.
Hippocrates. *The Aphorisms of Hippocrates*. London: British Library, Reprint 2010.
Hogan, Amy. "Is the Prophecy in 'Crimes of Grindelwald' Actually About Aberforth Dumbledore?" MuggleNet, January 10, 2022. www.mugglenet.com/2022/01/is-the-prophecy-in-crimes-of-grindelwald-actually-about-aberforth-dumbledore/.
Hogle, Jerrold B. "Introduction: The Gothic in western culture." In *The Cambridge Companion to Gothic Fiction*, ed. Jarrold E. Hogle, 1–20. Cambridge: Cambridge University Press, 2002.
hpboy13. "Getting a Clue for Christmas." MuggleNet, December 20, 2018. https://www.mugglenet.com/2018/12/getting-a-clue-for-christmas/?fbclid=IwAR3Jo6qpTiMsyjoD2m-Ee4G0wBgHxnBMukN-KECqrgy5YTgcRiFuhVGRc70.
Hughes, Ken, dir. *Chitty Chitty Bang Bang*. 1968; Los Angeles, CA: Warfield Productions/ Dramatic Features. DVD.
Hui, Andrew. *A Theory of the Aphorism: From Confucius to Twitter*. Princeton: Princeton University Press, 2019.
Huizinga, Johan. *Homo Ludens: A Study of the Play-Element in Culture*. Abingdon: Routledge, 2002.
Hunter, Joel. "Technological Anarchism: The Meaning of Magic in Harry Potter." In *Harry Potter for Nerds*, ed. Travis Prinzi, 105–134. Oklahoma City: Unlocking Press, 2011.
Hunter, William R. "It's All About the Snitch: Quidditch as a Metaphor." In *The Ravenclaw Chronicles: Reflections from Edinboro*, ed. Corbin Fowler, 161–71. Newcastle upon Tyne: Cambridge Scholars, 2014.
Hutchinson, Sterling, Vivek Datla, and Max Louwerse. "Social Networks Are Encoded in

Language." *Proceedings of the Annual Meeting of the Cognitive Science Society* 34 (2012): 491–496.
"Interview with Sarah Gailey, Author of Magic for Liars." *The Qwillery*, June 3, 2019. https://www.theqwillery.com/2019/06/interview-with-sarah-gailey-author-of.html.
Irenaeus, Adversus Haereses, XXII, 4. Quoted in Michael O'Carroll, CSSp. "Mary, Mother of God." In *The New Dictionary of Theology*, ed. Joseph A. Komonchak, Mary Collins and Dermot A. Lane. Collegeville, MN: Liturgical Press, 1987.
Jacobs, Matthew. "Mourning the Ellen DeGeneres and J.K. Rowling We Used to Know." *HuffPost,* August 18, 2020. https://www.huffpost.com/entry/ellen-degeneres-jk-rowling-controversy_n_5f32ba6cc5b6960c066ce48b.
Jaffe, Alexandra. *Stance: Sociolinguistic Perspectives*. Oxford: Oxford University Press, 2009.
Jagoda, Patrick. "Gamification and Other Forms of Play." *boundary 2* 40, no. 2 (2013): 113–44.
Jaigirdar, Adiba. "What Is Dark Academia and Why Is It So Popular." *Book Riot*, September 9, 2021. https://bookriot.com/what-is-dark-academia/.
Jen. "Interview: Katie Zhao, Author of How We Fall Apart." *Pop! Goes the Reader*, August 17, 2021. https://popgoesthereader.com/interview/interview-katie-zhao-author-of-how-we-fall-apart/.
Jenkins, Henry. "Acafandom and Beyond: Week Two, Part One." June 20, 2011. http://henryjenkins.org/blog/2011/06/acafandom_and_beyond_week_two.html.
Juel, Kristin. "Chess, Love, and the Rhetoric of Distraction in Medieval French Narrative." *Romance Philology* 64, no. 1 (2010): 73–97.
Jung, Emma. "On the Nature of the Animus." Trans. Cary F. Baynes. In *Animus and Anima: Two Essays*, 1–43. New York: New York Analytical Psychology Club, 1957.
Kaligan, Gayane. "Flying Ford Anglia Voted Second-Best Car Scene in Cinema." MuggleNet, December 30, 2019. https://www.mugglenet.com/2019/12/flying-ford-anglia-voted-second-best-car-scene-in-cinema/.
Kanter, Rosabeth Moss. "Some Effects of Proportions on Group Life: Skewed Sex Ratios and Responses to Token Women." *American Journal of Sociology* 82, no. 5 (1977): 965–990.
Keen, Maurice. *Chivalry*. New Haven: Yale University Press, 1984.
Keenan, Harper, and Lil Miss Hot Mess. "Drag Pedagogy: The Playful Practice of Queer Imagination in Early Childhood." *Curriculum Inquiry* 50, no. 5 (2020): 440–461.
Kendi, Ibram X. *Stamped from the Beginning*. New York: Bold Type Books, 2016.
Kenzie and Emily, hosts. "Dark Academia." *Shelf-Involved* (podcast), August 26, 2020. https://podtail.com/en/podcast/shelf-involved-podcast/dark-academia/.
King, Martin Luther, Jr. "Loving Your Enemies." Stanford University Martin Luther King, Jr. Research and Education Institute. Accessed October 31, 2021. https://kinginstitute.stanford.edu/king-papers/documents/loving-your-enemies-sermon-delivered-dexter-avenue-baptist-church.
———. *Why We Can't Wait*. Boston: Beacon Press, 1964.
Kirkham, Sam. "Personal Style and Epistemic Stance in Classroom Discussion." *Language & Literature* 20, no. 3 (2011): 201–217.
Kloves, Steve. "'Harry Potter' Countdown: Steve Kloves on a 'Haunting Moment' in 'Half-Blood Prince.'" Interview with Denise Martin. *Los Angeles Times*, June 17, 2009. herocomplex.latimes.com/uncategorized/countdown-to-harry-potter-and-the-half-blood-prince-steve-kloves-talks-up-the-final-moments-between/.
Kobabe, Maia. "Tonk's Tale." *Trans-Affirming Magical Care*. Tumblr, February 22, 2020. https://owlswithfins.tumblr.com/post/190966973608/trans-affirming-magical-care-is-a-40-page.
Kurian, Vera. "The Dark Pleasures of School-Based Mysteries." *CrimeReads*, September 7, 2021. https://crimereads.com/the-dark-pleasures-of-school-based-mysteries/.
Kwong, Lucas. "Dracula's Apologetics of Progress." *Victorian Literature and Culture* 44 (2016): 111–129.
Lacassagne, Aurélie. "Othermothering and Othermothers in the Harry Potter Series."

Journal of the Motherhood Initiative for Research and Community Involvement 7, no. 1 (2016): 116–125.

LaFargue, Michael. "Interpreting the Aphorisms in the Tao Te Ching." *Journal of Chinese Religions* 18, no. 1 (1990): 25–43.

LaHaie, Jeanne Hoeker. "Mums Are Good: Harry Potter and Traditional Depictions of Women." In *Critical Insights: The Harry Potter Series*, ed. Katherine A. Grimes and Lana A. Whited, 123–45. Ipswich, MA: Salem Press, 2015.

Lange, Erica Maitland. *Harry Potter and the Theory of Things*. MA thesis, Bucknell University, 2012.

Lee, Victoria. "Harry Potter and the Conspiracy of Queers." *Tor.com*, October 14, 2019. https://www.tor.com/2019/10/14/harry-potter-and-the-conspiracy-of-queers-discovering-myself-in-fandom-and-roleplay/.

Leech, Geoffrey, and Mick Short. *Style in Fiction: A Linguistic Introduction to English Fictional Prose*, 2nd edition. New York: Routledge, 2013.

"Legilimency." *The Harry Potter Compendium*. Accessed May 26, 2022. https://harry-potter-compendium.fandom.com/wiki/Legilimency.

Lenard, Patti Tamera, and Peter Balint. "What Is (the Wrong of) Cultural Appropriation?" *Ethnicities* 20, no. 2 (April 1, 2020): 331–352).

Levi-Belz, Yossi, and William Feigelman. "Pulling Together—The Protective Role of Belongingness for Depression, Suicidal Ideation and Behavior Among Suicide-Bereaved Individuals." *Crisis: The Journal of Crisis Intervention and Suicide Prevention* (2021).

Levine, David, and Alan Bleakley. "Maximising Medicine Through Aphorisms." *Medical Education* 46 (2012): 153–162.

Limbach, Gwendolyn. "Ginny Weasley: Girl Next Doormat?" In *Terminus: Collected Papers on Harry Potter*, ed. Sharon K. Goetz, 173–205. Sedalia, CO: Narrate Conferences, 2010.

Lipinska, Joanna. "The Xenophobic World of Wizards: Why are They Afraid of the 'Other'?" *Harry Potter's World Wide Influence*, ed. Diana Patterson, 117–124. Newcastle upon Tyne: Cambridge Scholars, 2009.

Lipsitz, George. *Dangerous Crossroads: Popular Music, Postmodernism, and the Poetics of Place*. New York: Verso, 1994.

Lipsky, Michael. *Street-Level Bureaucracy: Dilemmas of the Individual in Public Services*. New York: Russel Sage Foundation, 2010.

"A List of Every Beast in 'Fantastic Beasts and Where to Find Them.'" *Higgypop*, April 21, 2017. www.higgypop.com/news/list-of-fantastic-beasts/.

"A List of Every Beast in 'Fantastic Beasts: The Crimes of Grindelwald." *Higgypop*, March 13, 2019. www.higgypop.com/news/list-of-fantastic-beasts-in-crimes-of-grindelwald/.

Loproto, Mark. "Pearl Harbor—Waking the Sleeping Giant." Pearl Harbor, Hawaii, October 30, 2017. pearlharbor.org/pearl-harbor-waking-sleeping-giant/.

"Lords of the Chinese World: The Dragon and Phoenix." ChinaCulture.org. Accessed January 10, 2019. http://en.chinaculture.org/chineseway/2014-07/31/content_553822.htm.

Love, Ryan. "J.K. Rowling: 'Harry Potter and the Deathly Hallows Part Two is the Best.'" Digital Spy. Accessed January 29, 2022. https://www.digitalspy.com/movies/a328573/jk-rowling-harry-potter-and-the-deathly-hallows-part-2-is-the-best/.

Lucal, Betsy. "Oppression and Privilege: Toward a Relational Conceptualization of Race." *Teaching Sociology* 24, no. 3 (1996): 245–255.

M. (Maxwell), Daryl. "Interview With an Author: Sarah Gailey." July 11, 2019. https://www.lapl.org/collections-resources/blogs/lapl/interview-author-sarah-gailey.

Măcineanu, Laura. "Feminine Hypostases in Epic Fantasy: Tolkien, Lewis, Rowling." *Gender Studies* 14, no. 1 (2015): 68–82.

"Magical Abilities That Don't Sound All That Fun." Wizarding World, August 16, 2018. http://www.wizardingworld.com/features/magical-abilities-that-do-not-sound-all-that-fun.

Malcolm X. "Interview with Malcolm X UC Berkeley, Oct 11, 1963." Interview by Herman Blake. October 11, 1963. Video, 40:08. https://archive.org/details/MalcolmXInterviewAtUCBerkeley/.

———. "The Race Problem." Recorded at Michigan State University, East Lansing, Michigan,

January 23, 1963. https://onthebanks.msu.edu/Object/162-565-2359/malcolm-x-speaks-at-michigan-state-university-1963/.

———. "A Summing-Up: Louis Lomax Interviews Malcolm X," Interview by Louis Lomax, *When the Word Is Given*. Cleveland: World, 1963.

Malory, Thomas. *Le Morte D'Arthur Volume I* and *II*. Edited by Janet Cowen. London: Penguin Classics, 2004.

Martin, Carl Grey. "The Cipher of Chivalry: Violence as Courtly Play in the World of *Sir Gawain and the Green Knight*." *The Chaucer Review* 43, no. 3 (2009): 311–29.

Mauk, Margaret S. "Your Mother Died to Save You." *Mythlore* 36, no. 1 (2017): 123–142.

May, Whitney S. "'Powers of Their Own Which Mere 'Modernity' Cannot Kill": The Doppelgänger and Temporal Modernist Terror in Dracula." *Gothic Studies* 23.1 (2021): 60–76.

McDaniel, Katy, and Emily Strand, hosts. "Episode 22: *Secrets of Dumbledore* and *The Deathly Hallows*." *Potterversity* (podcast). May 23, 2022. www.mugglenet.com/Mugglenet-family/potterversity/.

McIntosh, Peggy. "White and Male Privilege: A Personal Accounting of Coming to See Correspondences Through Work in Women's Studies." In *Race, Class, and Gender: An Anthology*, ed. Margaret L. Andersen and Patricia Hill Collins, 70–81. Belmont, CA: Wadsworth, 1992.

McMillan, Uri. "Nicki-Aesthetics: The Camp Performance of Nicki Minaj." *Women & Performance: A Journal of Feminist Theory* 24, no. 1 (2014): 79–87.

McMorran, Will. "From Quixote to Caractacus: Influence, Intertextuality, and *Chitty Chitty Bang Bang*." *Journal of Popular Culture* 39, no. 5 (2006): 756–779.

Mendlesohn, Farah. *Rhetorics of Fantasy*. Middletown, CT: Wesleyan University Press, 2008.

Mercer, John, Charlie Sarson, and Jamie Hakim. "Charisma, Uniqueness, Nerve, and Talent: *RuPaul's Drag Race* and the Cultural Politics of Fame." *Celebrity Studies* 11, no. 4 (2020): 383–385.

Metcalfe, Jessica. "Native Americans Know that Cultural Misappropriation is a Land of Darkness." *The Guardian*, May 18, 2012. https://www.theguardian.com/commentisfree/2012/may/18/native-americans-cultural-misappropriation.

Miall, Antony, and David Milsted. *Xenophobe's Guide to the English*. Wiltshire: Xenophobe's Guides, 2015.

Millman, Joyce. "To Sir, with Love." In *Mapping the World of Harry Potter*, ed. Mercedes Lackey, 39–52. Dallas: BenBella, 2005.

Milton, John. *Paradise Lost*. 1674. University of Pennsylvania School of Arts & Sciences. Accessed June 10, 2022. http://knarf.english.upenn.edu/Milton/pl4.html.

Minahan, Jessica. "Trauma-Informed Teaching Strategies." *Educational Leadership* 77, no. 2 (2019): 30–35. https://www.ascd.org/el/articles/trauma-informed-teaching-strategies.

Miner, Horace. "Body Ritual Among the Nacirema." *American Anthropologist* 58, no. 3 (1956): 503–507.

Molloy, Tim. "RuPaul Explains Why 'We Are All God in Drag.'" *TheWrap*, September 14, 2019. https://www.thewrap.com/rupaul-explains-why-we-are-all-god-in-drag.

Morris, Charles E., III. "(Self-)Portrait of Prof. R. C.: A Retrospective." *Western Journal of Communication* 74, no. 1 (2010): 4–42.

"The Mysterious Life and Death of Ariana Dumbledore." *Wizarding World*, December 1, 2016. http://www.wizardingworld.com/features/the-mysterious-life-and-death-of-ariana-dumbledore.

Nel, Philip. "Lost in Translation? *Harry Potter*, from Page to Screen." *Critical Perspectives on Harry Potter*, ed. Elizabeth Heilman, 275–90. New York: Routledge, 2009.

Newton, Esther. *Mother Camp: Female Impersonators in America*. Chicago: University of Chicago Press, 1972.

Nozedar, Adele. *The Illustrated Signs and Symbols Sourcebook*. New York: Metro Books, 2010.

"The O Antiphons of Advent." Prayers, United States Catholic Conference of Bishops. Accessed November 9, 2021. https://www.usccb.org/prayers/o-antiphons-advent.

O'Connell, Mark. *To Be a Machine: Adventures Among Cyborgs, Utopians, Hackers, and the Futurists Solving the Modest Problem of Death*. New York: Doubleday, 2017.

O'Gieblyn, Meghan. *God, Human, Animal, Machine: Technology, Metaphor, and the Search for Meaning*. New York: Doubleday, 2021.

Ostling, Michael. "Harry Potter and the Disenchantment of the World." *Journal of Contemporary Religion* 18, no. 1 (2003): 3–23.

Oziewicz, Marek. "Representations of Eastern Europe in Philip Pullman's His Dark Materials, Jonathan Stroud's The Bartimaeus Trilogy, and J.K. Rowling's Harry Potter Series." *International Research in Children's Literature* 3, no. 1 (July 2010): 1–14.

Park, Yoosun. "Facilitating Injustice: Tracing the Role of Social Workers in the World War II Internment of Japanese Americans." *Social Service Review* 82, no. 3 (2008): 447–483.

Patrick, Bethanne. "The 10 books to read in November." *The Washington Post*, October 30, 2018. https://www.washingtonpost.com/entertainment/books/the-10-books-to-read-in-november/2018/10/30/34d15356-dba3-11e8-b3f0-62607289efee_story.html.

"The Predictions of Tycho Dodonus." Harry Potter Wiki, November 20, 2018. https://harrypotter.fandom.com/wiki/The_Predictions_of_Tycho_Dodonus.

Prinzi, Travis. *Harry Potter and Imagination: The Way Between Two Worlds*. Allentown, PA: Zossima Press, 2009.

Pugh, Tison. "Sobbing Over Severus Snape? Sentimentalism and Emotional Ethics in J.K. Rowling's *Harry Potter* Novels." *The Lion and the Unicorn* 45 (2021): 46–61.

———, and David L. Wallace. "A Postscript to 'Heteronormative Heroism and Queering the School Story in JK Rowling's Harry Potter Series.'" *Children's Literature Association Quarterly* 33, no. 2 (Summer 2008): 188–192.

"Qilin." Britannica. Accessed May 26, 2021. https://www.britannica.com/topic/qilin.

Radford-Watley, Aaron. "This book has sold the most copies." *Fox Business*, June 24, 2020. https://www.foxbusiness.com/lifestyle/this-book-sold-the-most-copies.

Reynolds, Susan. "Dumbledore in the Watchtower: Harry Potter as a Neo-Victorian Narrative." In *Harry Potter's World Wide Influence*, ed. Diana Patterson. Newcastle upon Tyne: Cambridge Scholars, 2009. ProQuest Ebook Central.

Reyvor, Nina. "Dark Academia: A Panel Discussion." Moderated by Molly Odintz of *CrimeReads* and hosted by BookWoman. Live event online, October 7, 2021.

Robinson, Tasha. "The Last Graduate fills the Harry Potter void, and so much more." *Polygon*, September 28, 2021. https://www.polygon.com/22697256/the-last-graduate-naomi-novik-scholomance-series.

Robinson, Tracy L. "The Intersection of Dominant Discourses Across Race, Gender, and Other Identities." *Journal of Counseling & Development* 77, no. 1 (1999): 73–79.

Robinson, Tracy L., and Mary F. Howard-Hamilton. *The Convergence of Race, Ethnicity, and Gender: Multiple Identities in Counseling*. Upper Saddle River, NJ: Merrill, 2000.

Roper, Denise. "Christmas in *Harry Potter and the Deathly Hallows*." Phoenix Weasley (blog), December 20, 2010. https://phoenixweasley.wordpress.com/2010/12/20/christmas-in-harry-potter-and-the-deathly-hallows/.

———. *The Lord of the Hallows: Christian Symbolism and Themes in J.K. Rowling's Harry Potter*. Denver: Outskirts Press, 2009.

Roth, Lane. "Film, Society and Ideas: *Nosferatu* and *Horror of Dracula*." In *Planks of Reason: Essays on the Horror Film*, ed. Barry Keith Grant, 245–54. London: Scarecrow, 1984.

Rowling, J.K. "Answers to Questions." J.K.Rowling.com, November 12, 2018. http://www.jkrowling.com/opinions/latest-answers-to-frequently-asked-questions/.

———. "Dolores Umbridge." *Wizarding World*, August 10, 2015. https://www.wizardingworld.com/writing-by-jk-rowling/dolores-umbridge.

———. *Fantastic Beasts and Where to Find Them: The Original Screenplay*. New York: Scholastic, 2016.

———. *Fantastic Beasts and Where to Find Them*. New York: Scholastic, 2013.

———. *Fantastic Beasts: The Crimes of Grindelwald: The Original Screenplay*. New York: Scholastic, 2018.

———. "The Fringe Benefits of Failure and the Importance of Imagination." Speech,

264 Bibliography

Harvard University, Cambridge, Massachusetts, June 8, 2008. *The Harvard Gazette*. https://news.harvard.edu/gazette/story/2008/06/text-of-j-k-rowling-speech/.
_____. *Harry Potter and the Chamber of Secrets*. New York: Scholastic, 1999.
_____. *Harry Potter and the Deathly Hallows*. New York: Scholastic, 2007.
_____. *Harry Potter and the Goblet of Fire*. New York: Scholastic, 2000.
_____. *Harry Potter and the Half-Blood Prince*. New York: Scholastic, 2005.
_____. *Harry Potter and the Order of the Phoenix*. New York: Scholastic, 2003.
_____. *Harry Potter and the Prisoner of Azkaban*. New York: Scholastic, 1999.
_____. *Harry Potter and the Sorcerer's Stone*. New York: Scholastic, 1998.
_____. "The Hogwarts Express." *Wizarding World*, August 10, 2015. https://www.wizardingworld.com/writing-by-jk-rowling/the-hogwarts-express.
_____. "J.K. Rowling: The Interview." Interview by Ann Treneman. *The Times*, June 20, 2003. http://www.thetimes.co.uk/article/j-k-rowling-the-interview-dshhr7c5fjf.
_____. (@jk_rowling), "I could write you an essay in response to this." *Twitter*, September 25, 2018. https://twitter.com/jk_rowling/status/1044585938590949376?lang=en).
_____. (@jk_rowling), "Occlumency." *Twitter*, December 15, 2016. https://twitter.com/jk_rowling/status/809361237054201856.
_____. Juan Cruz. *El Pais*, February 8, 2008. http://elpais.com/diario/2008/02/08/cultura/1202425201_850215.html.
_____. The Leaky Cauldron and MuggleNet chat. July 16, 2005. http://www.accio-quote.org/articles/2005/0705-tlc_mugglenet-anelli-2.htm.
_____. Meredith Vieira, *Today Show* (NBC), July 26, 2007. http://www.accio-quote.org/articles/2007/0726-today-vieira2.html.
_____. "The Noble and Most Ancient House of Black." Donated to Book Aid International in January of 2006 and auctioned February 22, 2006. https://www.hp-lexicon.org/source/other-canon/bft/.
_____. Pottercast's interview. The Leaky Cauldron, December 23, 2007. http://www.the-leaky-cauldron.org/2007/12/23/transcript-of-part-1-of-pottercast-s-jk-rowling-interview/.
_____. *The Tales of Beedle the Bard*. New York: Children's High Level Group, 2007.
_____. "Technology." *Wizarding World*, August 10, 2015. https://www.wizardingworld.com/writing-by-jk-rowling/technology.
_____. "Vampires." *Wizarding World*, August 10, 2015. https://www.wizardingworld.com/writing-by-jk-rowling/vampires.
_____. "What Was the Name of that Nymph Again? or Greek and Roman Studies Recalled." *Pegasus: Journal of the University of Exeter Department of Classics and Ancient History* 41 (April 1988): 25–27.
_____. World Book Day Chat. March 4, 2004. http://www.accio-quote.org/articles/2004/0304-wbd.htm.
Ruhl, Charlotte. "What Is Cognitive Bias?" *Simply Psychology*, May 4, 2021. https://www.simplypsychology.org/cognitive-bias.html.
Ryland, Jen. "Exploring Dark Academia: A YA and Adult Book List." *Jen Ryland Reviews*, April 17, 2021. https://www.jenryland.com/exploring-dark-academia-a-ya-and-adult-book-list/.
Sachiko Cecire, Maria. *Re-Enchanted: The Rise of Children's Fantasy Literature in the Twentieth Century*. Minneapolis: University of Minnesota Press, 2019.
Saidel, Eric. "Sirius Black: Man or Dog?" *The Ultimate Harry Potter and Philosophy: Hogwarts for Muggles*, ed. William Irwin and Gregory Bassham, 22–34. Hoboken: John Wiley & Sons, 2010.
Salisbury, Joyce E. *The Beast Within: Animals in the Middle Ages*, 2nd edition. London: Routledge, 1994/2011.
Salkeld, Brett. "Real Presence and Idolatry." *PrayTell: Worship, Wit and Wisdom*, September 11, 2021. https://www.praytellblog.com/index.php/2021/09/11/real-presence-and-idolatry/.
San Segundo, P. Ruano. "A Corpus-Stylistic Approach to Dickens' Use of Speech Verbs: Beyond Mere Reporting." *Language and Literature* 25, no. 2 (2016):113–129, 2016.

Sanders, Jane Elizabeth. "Teaching Note—Trauma-Informed Teaching in Social Work Education." *Journal of Social Work Education* 57, no. 1 (2021): 197–204.
Sas, Katherine. "A Sense of Darker Perspective: How the Marauders Convey Tolkien's 'Impression of Depth' in Prisoner of Azkaban." *Mythlore* 38, no. 1 (Fall/Winter 2019): 153–174.
Satterly, Brent. "*Teaching Note:* The Spell Craft of Social Work: Harry Potter and Social Justice." *Journal of Baccalaureate Social Work* 22, no. 1 (2017): 111–126.
Schön, Donald A. *Educating the Reflective Practitioner: Toward a New Design for Teaching and Learning in the Professions.* San Francisco: Jossey-Bass, 1987.
Schwab, Joseph. "The Teaching of Science as Enquiry." In *The Teaching of Science*, ed. J. Schwab and P. Brandwein. Cambridge: Harvard University Press, 1962.
Semel, Paul. "Exclusive Interview: Magic for Liars Author Sarah Gailey." *paulsemel.com*, July 15, 2019. https://paulsemel.com/exclusive-interview-magic-for-liars-author-sarah-gailey/.
Senf, Carol A. "*Dracula*: The Unseen Face in the Mirror." *The Journal of Narrative Technique*, 9, no. 3 (1979): 160–70.
"7 of Our Favourite Sirius Black Moments." *Wizarding World*, November 3, 2022. https://www.wizardingworld.com/features/7-of-our-favourite-sirius-black-moments.
"Severus Snape: Vampire (extended thoughts and articles)." 2014. Accessed February 14, 2023. https://harrypotterfantheories.tumblr.com/post/80720198044/severus-snape-moody-potions-master-forever-in-the.
Seymour, Jessica. "Hunting the Stag in Harry Potter's Games." *Interdisciplinary Literary Studies* 19, no. 4 (2017): 441–60.
"Shan Hai Jing." *Totally History.* Accessed June 11, 2022. https://totallyhistory.com/shan-hai-jing/.
Sheldon, Lee. *The Multiplayer Classroom: Designing Coursework as a Game.* Boston: Cengage, 2012.
Shugart, Helene. A., and Catherine Egley Waggoner. *Making Camp: Rhetorics of Transgression in U.S. Popular Culture.* Tuscaloosa: University of Alabama Press, 2008.
Simmons, Nathaniel. "Speaking Like a Queen in RuPaul's Drag Race: Towards a Speech Code of American Drag Queens." *Sexuality & Culture* 18 (2014): 630–648.
Sorg, Arley. "Diagram and Story: A Conversation with R.F. Kuang." *Clarkesworld Science Fiction & Fantasy Magazine* 170. November 2020. https://clarkesworldmagazine.com/kuang_interview/.
The Stefatron. "Funniest Harry Potter Moments." YouTube. February 12, 2012. Video, 16:51. https://www.youtube.com/watch?v=ZFc0O3YXpV4.
Stevens, Martin. "Laughter and Game in *Sir Gawain and the Green Knight*." *Speculum* 47, no. 1 (1972): 65–78.
Stivers, Tanya, Lorenza Mondada, and Jakob Steensig, eds. *The Morality of Knowledge in Conversation: Studies in Interactional Sociolinguistics.* Cambridge: Cambridge University Press, 2011.
Stoker, Bram. *Dracula.* London: Penguin, 1897/2003.
Stone, Jonathan. *Decadence and Modernism in European and Russian Literature and Culture: Aesthetics and Anxiety in the 1890s.* Cham, Switzerland: Palgrave Macmillan, 2019.
Strand, Emily. "Harry Potter and the Sacramental Principle." *Worship* 93 (October 2019): 345–365.
———. "Parenting Models in the *Potter* Saga and *Cursed Child*: Human and Divine." In *Beyond the Ivory Tower*, ed. Lana A. Whited. Columbia: University of Missouri Press, 2023.
———. "The Second War was Won on the Quidditch Pitch of Hogwarts." In *Harry Potter for Nerds II*, ed. Kathryn N. McDaniel and Travis Prinzi, 115–138. Oklahoma City: Unlocking Press, 2015.
Streep, Peg. "The Enduring Pain of Childhood Verbal Abuse." *Psychology Today,* November 14, 2016. https://www.psychologytoday.com/au/blog/tech-support/201611/the-enduring-pain-childhood-verbal-abuse.
Sturgis, Amy H. "Hogwarts in America: In *Fantastic Beasts and Where to Find Them* J.K.

Rowling Crosses the Atlantic and Makes a Hash of North American History and Culture." *Reason*, December 2016.

Sturgis, Amy H., James Thomas, Travis Prinzi, and John Granger. "Gothic Schoolboy (1)" and "Gothic Schoolboy (2)." In *Harry Potter Smart Talk*, ed. James Thomas, Travis Prinzi, and John Granger. 31–61. Constantia, NY: Unlocking Press, 2010.

Suarez, Julian. "Racial Diversity in the Media." *Under a Tree*, May 7, 2018. https://www.underatree.org/our-blog/2018/5/7/racial-diversity-in-the-media.

Sutton-Ramspeck, Beth. "The Ambivalent Portrayal of Creativity in *Harry Potter*." In *The Ravenclaw Chronicles*, ed. Corbin Fowler, 122–140. Newcastle upon Tyne: Cambridge Scholars, 2014.

Tatum, Beverly Daniel. *Why Are All the Black Kids Sitting Together in the Cafeteria*. New York: Basic Books, 2017.

Thomas, Harry, Jr. *Sissy! The Effeminate Paradox in Postwar US Literature and Culture*. Tuscaloosa: University of Alabama Press, 2017.

Thomas, James W. *Repotting Harry Potter*. Cheshire, CT: Zossima Press, 2009.

Thomas, M'Balia, Alisa LaDean Russell, and Hannah V. Warren. "The Good, the Bad, and the Ugly of Pedagogy in Harry Potter: An Inquiry Into the Personal Practical Knowledge of Remus Lupin, Rubeus Hagrid, and Severus Snape." *The Clearing House* 91, no. 4–5 (2018): 186–92.

Thurman, Robert. "Where Is the Love in Today's Resistance?" Produced by Krista Tippett. *On Being* (podcast). March 18, 2018. https://onbeing.org/blog/robert-thurman-where-is-the-love-in-todays-resistance/.

Tolentino, Jia. "Lionel Shriver Puts on a Sombrero." *The New Yorker*, September 14, 2016. https://www.newyorker.com/culture/jia-tolentino/lionel-shriver-puts-on-a-sombrero.

"Twelve Uses of Dragon's Blood." *The Harry Potter Lexicon*. Edited by Steve VanderArk. March 7, 2022. www.hp-lexicon.org/thing/twelve-uses-of-dragons-blood.

United Nations. *Standard Minimum Rules for the Treatment of Prisoners (the Nelson Mandela Rules)*, A/RES/70/175 (January 8, 2016). https://undocs.org/A/RES/70/175.

Vermeesch, Peggy. "Toni Wolff's Structural Forms of the Feminine Psyche." *Jungian Psychology Space*. Accessed May 16, 2022. https://www.cgjung.net/espace/jps/articles/peggy-vermeesch/toni-wolff-structural-forms-feminine-psyche/.

Waller, Gregory A. *The Living and the Undead: From Stoker's Dracula to Romero's Dawn of the Dead*. Urbana: University of Illinois Press, 1986.

Walsh, Michael. "Is Grindelwald Himself a 'Fantastic Beast'?" *Nerdist*, September 25, 2018. https://nerdist.com/grindelwald-is-fantastic-beast-theory/.

Warner Brothers Pictures. "*Fantastic Beasts: The Secrets of Dumbledore*—Official Trailer." YouTube, December 13, 2021. Video, 2:38. http://www.youtube.com/watch?v=Y9dr2zw-TXQ.

Weiss, Victoria. "The Play World and the Real World: Chivalry in *Sir Gawain and the Green Knight*." *Philological Quarterly* 72 (1993): 403–18. Gale Literature Resource Center.

What I Hear When You Say: Cultural Appropriation vs. Appreciation. Viewing Guide, PBS, 2017. https://bento.cdn.pbs.org/hostedbento-prod/filer_public/whatihear/9-Cultural_Approp-Viewing_Guide.pdf.

Whetter, K.S. "Warfare and Combat in *Le Morte Darthur*." In *Writing War: Medieval Literary Responses to Warfare*, ed. Corinne Saunders, Francoise Le Saux, and Neil Thomas, 169–86. Cambridge: Boydell & Brewer, 2004.

Whited, Lana A. "Here Be Dragons and Phoenixes, Parts 1 and 2." *The Quibbler*, February 8–9, 2019. MuggleNet. https://www.Mugglenet.com/2019/02/here-be-dragons-and-phoenixes-part-1/ and https://www.Mugglenet.com/2019/02/here-be-dragons-and-phoenixes-part-2/.

"Why We Love Arthur Weasley So Damn Much." *Wizarding World*, August 14, 2017. https://www.wizardingworld.com/features/why-we-love-arthur-weasley-so-damn-much.

Willson-Metzger, Alicia. "The Life and Lies of Albus Dumbledore: The Ethics of Information Sharing and Concealment in the Harry Potter Novels." In *Harry Potter's World Wide Influence*, ed. Diana Patterson, 293–304. Newcastle upon Tyne: Cambridge Scholars, 2009.

Winstead, Ashley. "Dark Academia and Debt: University thrillers are the literary subgenre of the student loan crisis." *Salon*, July 31, 2021. https://www.salon.com/2021/07/31/dark-academia-and-debt-university-thrillers-are-the-literary-subgenre-of-the-student-loan-crisis/.

Winters, Sarah Fiona. "Bubble-Wrapped Children and Safe Books for Boys: The Politics of Parenting in Harry Potter." *Children's Literature* 39, no. 1 (2011): 213–233.

Wolff, Toni. *Structural Forms of the Feminine Psyche*. Trans. Paul Watzlawik. Zürich: C.G. Jung Institute, 1956. Accessed May 16, 2022. http://ufdcimages.uflib.ufl.edu/AA/00/00/15/82/00001/AA00001582_00001.pdf.

Woolf, Virginia. *A Room of One's Own*. London: Flamingo, 1994.

Wright, Kelechi C., Kourtney Angela Carr, and Becci A. Akin. "The Whitewashing of Social Work History: How Dismantling Racism in Social Work Education Begins with an Equitable History of the Profession." *Archives in Social Work* 21, no. 2/3 (2021): 274–297.

Wruble, Bill, writer. *Ted Lasso*. Season 1, episode 6, "Two Aces." Directed by Elliot Hegarty. Aired September 4, 2020, on Apple TV+.

Xu, Yueting, and Yongcan Liu. "Teacher Assessment Knowledge and Practice: A Narrative Inquiry of a Chinese College EFL Teacher's Experience." *TESOL Quarterly* 43, no. 3 (2009): 493–513.

Yates, David, dir. *Fantastic Beasts and Where to Find Them*. 2016; Burbank, CA: Warner Bros. HBO Max. https://play.hbomax.com/feature/urn:hbo:feature:GXssTNAEn61VGwwEAAABn.

———. *Fantastic Beasts: The Crimes of Grindelwald*. 2018; Burbank, CA: Warner Bros. HBO Max. https://play.hbomax.com/page/urn:hbo:page:GXN3M3Q6SSMLDwgEAAAN7:type:feature.

———. *Fantastic Beasts: The Secrets of Dumbledore*. 2022; Burbank, CA: Warner Bros. HBO Max. https://play.hbomax.com/feature/urn:hbo:feature:GYij3IwBohZA3MQEAAAKa.

———. *Harry Potter and the Order of the Phoenix*. 2007; Burbank, CA: Warner Bros. Xfinity. https://www.xfinity.com/stream/entity/4950300734241750112.

Young, James O. *Cultural Appropriation and the Arts*. Oxford: Wiley-Blackwell, 2010.

Zirngast, Lisa. "Everything you need to know about the 'Dark Academia Aesthetic' Trend." *L'Officiel*, June 17, 2021. https://www.lofficiel.at/en/pop-culture/dark-academia-aesthetic.

About the Contributors

Laurie **Beckoff** received her M.Sc. in Medieval literatures and cultures from the University of Edinburgh. She serves as campaign manager for MuggleNet.com, created its academic section, produces the *Potterversity* podcast, co-authored *The Unofficial Harry Potter Hogwarts Handbook*, and regularly presents at the Harry Potter Academic Conference at Chestnut Hill College. She works as a digital editor and producer in public engagement with the humanities.

Louise M. **Freeman**, Ph.D., is a behavioral neuroscientist and licensed behavior analyst. Her work on psychology and young adult fiction, including *Harry Potter*, has appeared in a variety of journals and anthologies. She speaks at academic conferences and contributes to blogs and podcasts devoted to the scholarly examination of contemporary young adult novels. A retired professor of psychology from Mary Baldwin University, she now works with special needs children in home and clinic settings.

Beatrice **Groves**, Ph.D., is a research fellow and lecturer in Renaissance English at Trinity College, Oxford. She has published three monographs, including *Literary Allusion in Harry Potter* (Routledge, 2017), and a wide number of articles and book chapters on *Harry Potter*'s allusions to other literary classics. She has a dedicated blog, "Bathilda's Notebook," on MuggleNet, and she regularly contributes to *The Rowling Library Magazine* and *Hogwarts Professor*.

Mark-Anthony **Lewis**, M.A., received his degree in professional writing from the University of Massachusetts–Dartmouth. He has made presentations relating to rhetoric and communication at the Harry Potter Academic Conference and the Southwest Popular/American Culture Association Conference. He has also contributed fiction to *Conjuring Worlds: An Afrofuturist Textbook* and writes on topics related to writing and rhetoric at irregardlessmagazine.com.

Kathryn N. **McDaniel**, Ph.D., is the McCoy Professor of History and chair of the Department of History, Philosophy, Religion, and Gender Studies at Marietta College. A British historian specializing in history and popular culture, she has published and presented on travel literature, historical themes in fantasy fiction, and pedagogy. She is the co-editor of *Harry Potter for Nerds II* (Unlocking Press, 2015) and host of the Potter Studies podcast *Potterversity* on MuggleNet.

Emma **Nicholson** is a business analyst from Sydney, Australia, and technical director for the *Potterversity* podcast, where she has also appeared as a guest. She writes about the *Harry Potter* and *Star Wars* worlds at Archive of Our Own, specializing in constructing timelines to reveal overlooked aspects of both plot and characters. You can contact her on her website *Tragic Gift*, where she blogs about personality development and neurodiversity and hosts the *Positive Disintegration* podcast.

Travis **Prinzi**, M.A., M.S., is a cardiac cartographer, which means he specializes in the physical human heart. But in the remainder of his time, with master's degrees in English education and theology and with some graduate work in marriage and family therapy, he also specializes in the figurative human heart. He has been writing about the *Harry Potter* series since 2006, including a book, volumes of essays, and various contributions to scholarly collections.

Tison **Pugh**, Ph.D., Pegasus Professor of English at the University of Central Florida, is the author or editor of more than twenty books. His work in the field of children's culture includes *Harry Potter and Beyond: On J.K. Rowling's Fantasies and Other Fictions* (University of South Carolina Press, 2020), *The Queer Fantasies of the American Family Sitcom* (Rutgers University Press, 2018), and *Innocence, Heterosexuality, and the Queerness of Children's Literature* (Routledge, 2010).

Brent A. **Satterly**, Ph.D., L.C.S.W., is a professor of social work at Widener University's Center for Social Work Education. As a licensed clinical social worker with 30 years of clinical and teaching experience and co-author of *Sexuality Concepts for Social Workers* (Cognella Academic, 2015), his areas of expertise include human sexuality and social work pedagogies, clinical work with LGBTQIA+ populations, and the use of *Harry Potter* and other fandoms in teaching social justice.

Emily **Strand**, M.A., is the author of two books on Catholicism, the co-editor of three scholarly volumes, an instructor at Mount Carmel College, and co-host of *Potterversity*. She has published several *Harry Potter* essays in anthologies and journals and writes about religion and popular culture on the blog LiturgyandLife.com. She is also a musician, composer, and arranger and, together with her band The Town, creates the music for *Potterversity*.

Amy H. **Sturgis**, Ph.D., teaches at Lenoir-Rhyne University and Signum University. The author of four books and the editor or co-editor of ten, she has published work on *Harry Potter* in numerous anthologies as well as in periodicals and served as guest of honor at Harry Potter–related events including the Generic Magic Festival, Mythmoot, and Mythcon. She has taught undergraduate and graduate courses on *Harry Potter* and Dark Academia.

M'Balia **Thomas**, Ph.D., is an associate professor of English Applied Linguistics in the Department of English at the University of Arizona. As a TESOL teacher educator, she uses the *Harry Potter* novels to illuminate theoretical concepts about teacher knowledge, teaching practices, and desired dispositional stances toward learners of English as an Additional Language (EALs).

Lana A. **Whited**, Ph.D., is a professor of English and director of the Boone Honors Program at Ferrum College. She is editor of *The Ivory Tower and Harry Potter*

(University of Missouri Press, 2002), *Harry Potter,* the Ivory Tower, and Beyond (University of Missouri Press, 2023), as well as volumes in the Critical Insights series on the *Harry Potter* series and the *Hunger Games* trilogy. She is the author of *Murder, In Fact: Disillusionment and Death in the American True Crime Novel* (McFarland, 2020).

Index

Advent 69, 76, 80, 81, 263
albedo 70, 71, 76, 82
alchemy 70
Amazon 4, 107–111, 116–118
Animagus 19, 63, 92, 94, 96
animus 107, 110, 118
aphorisms 5, 215, 217–220, 224, 226–227, 228
archetypes 4, 107–108, 112, 115–116, 118
authority 32, 113, 216, 223–227, 234, 236, 238
Azkaban (prison) 94, 95–97, 98, 102, 103

Bane 162, 164–165, 170
Barebone, Credence 53, 139
barghest(s) 14, 15
bats 19, 20
Bell, Luke 72, 81, 256
bells 80
Black, Alphard 91, 104
Black, Sirius 31, 32, 74, 89–103, 169, 186, 205, 206
Blake, Olivie 36, 41
Brous, Sharon 155
Buddha 143, 145
bullying 29, 32, 99, 100, 153
the Burrow 78, 91, 112, 121, 122

Cecire, Maria Sachiko 67, 85
challenge 2, 63, 71, 73, 74, 75, 77, 162, 173, 174, 182, 184, 195–205, 207–208
Chamber of Secrets 51, 96, 109, 131, 222
Chamber of Secrets 14, 16, 18, 24, 50, 51, 73–74, 95, 107, 109, 114, 121–122, 130–131, 138, 168, 222
Chitty Chitty Bang Bang 124, 130
Christ 67, 68, 69, 71, 72, 74, 76, 78, 79, 80
Christian tradition 68, 69
Christianity 79
Christmas 3–4, 9, 67–81, 85–86, 98, 102, 110, 113–115, 188
Christmas Day 70, 78, 80

Christmas Eve 70, 78, 80, 115
Christmas rose 80, 82
Christmas tree 77
church 16, 78–80, 146, 152
civil rights 159, 167
classroom 5, 12, 31, 193, 195, 197, 199, 202, 203, 204, 221, 228, 237, 238, 240–242, 247–250
cloning 132
Cohen, Signe 70, 82, 131, 134
Coutts-Smith, Kenneth 127
Crouch, Barty, Jr. 95, 96, 105, 186
cultural appropriation 4, 121, 126–129, 132

danger 18, 59, 75, 80, 81, 97, 113, 125, 129, 130, 139, 140, 155, 182, 186, 189
Dark Academia 3, 26–39, 43–45
darkness 12–19, 21, 38, 69, 71, 74, 76, 80, 81, 86, 95, 130, 234, 237
death 2, 15, 17, 18, 19, 22, 28, 31–32, 35, 55, 58, 62, 67, 69–74, 79–81, 95, 96, 99, 100, 101, 103, 109, 123, 131, 133, 145, 153, 154, 169, 170, 181–182, 183, 186–188, 190, 219, 221, 223, 226
Death Eaters 32, 33, 99, 113, 122, 132, 164
Deathly Hallows 80, 199, 222, 231, 232
Deathly Hallows (book) 4, 13, 14, 15, 17, 19, 50, 51, 54, 56, 62, 67–68, 70, 72, 73, 74, 78, 80, 81, 90, 99, 113, 115, 116, 146, 169
December 59, 68, 69
Delacour, Fleur 75, 114, 137–138, 189
Dementors 31, 32, 93, 95–97, 138, 148, 183, 189, 201, 231, 237
Devil's Knell 80
Diggory, Cedric 75, 189, 226, 238
Dobby 4, 10, 44, 70, 76, 96, 158, 160–161, 162, 165–166, 167, 168, 170, 189, 205, 206
double-consciousness 159, 162, 167, 170
Dracula 3, 9–22, 43–44
drag 5, 231–232, 240–243, 247
dragon 3, 49–63, 85, 182, 186
Du Bois, W. E. B. 159, 160, 162, 170

273

Index

Dumbledore, Aberforth 53–55, 216
Dumbledore, Albus 3, 5, 21, 49–51, 55, 56, 61, 62, 70, 73, 75, 76, 81, 93, 97, 101, 131, 168, 206, 215, 217, 223, 230, 253
Dumbledore, Ariana 53–55
Dumbledorism(s) 5, 215–227, 253
Dursleys 81, 122, 139, 147, 206, 226

Easter 69–70, 72–73, 79, 102
empathy 93, 153, 160, 216
Eve 62, 76
evil 3, 9, 11, 16, 17, 20–21, 22, 43–44, 50, 52, 67, 69, 71, 73–76, 80, 131, 133, 145–146, 155, 164

fairy tale(s) 18, 144, 150, 198, 199, 201, 207
family 4, 31, 32, 49, 50, 53–54, 58, 77, 78, 79, 85, 90–91, 93, 94, 99, 102, 107, 112, 114–115, 117, 122, 125, 129, 131–133, 139, 159, 166, 169, 197, 199, 230, 231, 232, 236, 249
Fantastic Beasts: The Crimes of Grindelwald 49–50, 53–54, 55, 56, 57, 62
Fantastic Beasts: The Secrets of Dumbledore 50, 54–58, 61–62, 86, 147
father 4, 53, 55, 67, 72, 74, 91, 100–101, 103, 122–123, 124, 132–133, 144, 145, 230
Fawkes 73–74
fellowship 72–73, 75, 77, 81, 163
Firebolt 75, 102, 188
Firenze 4, 158, 160–161, 162, 164–165, 167, 169, 170
Florer-Bixler, Melissa 152–154
Forbidden Forest 50, 97, 130, 183, 241
Ford, Anglia 4, 112, 121–122, 125, 126–131
Frankenstein 34, 130
Fudge, Cornelius 95, 148, 230, 237, 238
Fundamental Law of Magic 219, 220

Gailey, Sarah 35–36
gamification 194–195
gay 153, 231, 239, 241, 247, 250
Gentry, Amy 34–35, 38, 45
Goblet of Fire 69, 76, 186, 188
Goblet of Fire (book) 14, 51, 75, 93, 97, 101, 102, 109, 114, 160, 165, 166
God 21, 68–69, 72–73, 76, 130, 155, 173, 240
godfather 4, 31, 32, 74, 75, 89, 90, 93, 97, 1011102, 103, 113
Godric's Hollow 16, 78, 79, 96
Goldstein, Queenie 57, 58, 63
Granger, Hermione 14, 17, 22, 32, 49, 50, 53, 56, 70, 73, 74, 75, 77, 78, 79, 80, 91, 93, 96, 97, 99, 108, 109, 111, 112, 113, 115, 116, 117, 149, 164, 166, 184, 185, 186, 199, 202, 205, 219, 225

Granger, John 44, 79–81, 109, 119
Green, Amy 89, 94, 95, 96, 98–99, 103
Greyback, Fenrir 52, 162, 163–164, 167
Grimmauld Place 90–91, 93, 98–100, 102, 111
Grindelwald, Gellert 3, 49, 50, 52, 53–54, 55–59, 61, 62, 85, 146–147, 149, 150
Groves, Beatrice 49, 60, 68, 78, 80
Gryffindor (House) 1, 73, 76, 91–92, 100, 110, 114, 115, 138, 140, 179, 188, 197, 202, 203, 218, 225, 232, 235

half-blood(s) 122, 133, 138
Half-Blood Prince (book) 13, 14, 69, 77, 78, 92, 111, 114, 115, 144, 147, 148, 160, 161, 163, 170
Halloween 69, 70
Harker, Mina 10–11, 17, 18, 21, 43–44, 109
headmaster 5, 49, 70, 73, 75, 77, 78, 159, 215–227, 230, 236, 253–254
hero(es) 3, 10, 14, 18, 19, 22, 37, 69, 76, 79, 109, 122, 179, 184, 189, 204
heroism 67, 71, 72, 73, 74, 78, 81, 88, 130, 202
Hogwarts 3, 5, 9, 21, 30–33, 36, 49, 50, 52, 54, 56, 71–72, 75, 78–79, 80, 86, 89, 91–93, 99, 103, 107, 109, 111, 112, 115, 116, 117, 118, 126, 131, 133, 138, 139, 158, 159, 160, 162, 163, 165–166, 170, 179, 186, 189, 193, 194, 196, 197, 198, 211, 215, 217, 218, 220, 221, 222, 225, 230, 234, 235, 236, 237, 238, 239, 247, 248, 249
Hogwarts Express 91, 109, 112, 126, 133, 138, 139, 230
Hogwarts House Cup Competition 196
holly 71, 81
homunculus 131, 132
hope 1, 16, 38, 69, 72, 74, 80, 95, 153, 155, 156, 162, 169
Horcrux(es) 9, 13–14, 17, 22, 43, 51–52, 56, 59, 74, 75, 79, 80, 122, 130–131, 170, 183, 240
House of Black 77, 93, 104, 264
Hufflepuff (House) 1, 202, 203
humiliation 75, 76
humility 58, 71, 72–73, 75–77, 79, 81, 86, 248

immortality 13, 21, 51, 79, 81, 121–122, 131–133
incarnation 67, 74, 79, 80, 81
injustice 29, 33, 37, 38, 143–144, 155, 231, 232, 241, 242
International Statute of Secrecy 53, 125, 126, 128, 147
Invisibility Cloak 70, 71–74, 79, 81, 117, 133, 222, 231
Irenaeus 76

Jesus 68–69, 74, 76, 79, 80, 143, 145–146, 152, 154, 173
Jung, Carl 4, 107, 108
Jung, Emma 110
justice 3, 69, 153, 232–233, 238, 241, 243, 250

Kanter, Rosabeth Moss 160–161, 168
Kay, Jim 121
Kendi, Ibram X. 150–151
King, Martin Luther, Jr. 143, 146, 154–155, 159, 161–162, 167
King's Cross 103, 109, 112, 126, 133, 147, 222, 225, 226, 254
knowledge 2, 3, 5, 18, 21, 28, 31, 43, 54, 58, 76, 93, 108, 128, 147, 151, 184, 216–217, 219, 221–227, 237
Kurian, Vera 26, 35, 37, 38

Lee, Victoria 37, 38
light 12–13, 15–19, 21–22, 62, 69, 77, 80, 86, 95, 99, 103, 116, 122, 126, 139, 155, 166
Lipsitz, George 127–128
Longbottom, Neville 12, 99, 109–110, 112, 138–139, 202, 208, 218
love 3, 4, 10–11, 22, 43–44, 61, 71, 77, 89, 91, 92, 93, 95, 96–99, 101, 103, 108, 110, 111, 112, 115, 116, 118, 121, 137, 143–147, 153, 154, 155, 156, 170, 173, 190, 219, 225, 241, 250
Lupin, Remus 4, 31, 32, 51, 52, 78, 89, 92, 97–101, 102, 103, 113, 158, 159–161, 162, 163–164, 165, 167, 169–170, 183, 206, 215

Madame Maxime 159, 160, 162, 166–167, 170
magic 1, 2, 3, 10, 12, 31, 32, 33, 35–36, 37, 53, 56, 59, 67, 68, 72, 73, 75, 78, 85–86, 89, 92, 96, 102, 103, 114, 122, 123–126, 129, 131, 132, 139, 149, 150, 179, 182, 185, 188, 218, 237, 238, 240, 247
Malcolm X 160, 162–165, 168
Malfoy, Draco 32, 74, 99, 112, 114, 143, 180, 189, 205, 231
Marauders 31, 89, 92, 97, 98, 100–101, 104, 169
Marauder's Map 74, 81
McGonagall, Minerva 32, 75, 92, 184, 186, 193, 197, 203, 205, 206, 217, 220, 248
mental health 95, 234
Minister of Magic 12, 61, 78, 147, 148, 230, 236–237
Ministry of Magic 10, 33, 44, 50, 51, 96, 98, 121, 122, 123, 125, 126, 128, 129, 136, 137, 149, 168, 189–190, 223, 224, 226, 233, 234, 236, 237

Mirror of Erised 43, 71, 218, 221, 253
monsters 10, 11, 19, 20, 22, 49–50, 51, 52, 53, 55, 170, 179, 231
mother 4, 54, 58, 61, 98, 107–108, 111, 112–113, 116, 117, 118, 137, 160, 230
motherhood 115–118
Mudblood 74, 99, 100, 237
Muggle-born 74, 91, 133, 235, 237, 242
Muggle Protection Act 122, 149
Muggles 1, 4, 33, 53, 56, 58, 62, 67, 78, 79, 81, 85, 90–92, 103, 121–133, 136–137, 139, 144–145, 146–151, 155, 180, 190, 193, 194, 200, 201, 220, 230, 231, 232, 242, 243, 254
mythology, Chinese 60, 61

Nagini 17, 51–52, 58, 80, 98, 115, 129
Narnia 67, 74
Nativity 79, 80
Nigellus, Phineas 77, 215, 226
Nosferatu 18–19
Novik, Naomi 36

Obscurus 53–55, 63, 139, 232
oppression 129, 143–156, 164, 165–166, 233, 236, 238, 241, 242, 243
Order of the Phoenix 17, 98, 111, 129
Order of the Phoenix (book) 11, 18, 21–22, 76, 77, 93, 102, 110–111, 113, 114, 160, 161, 164, 222, 223, 226
Oxford School 67, 68, 71, 73, 74, 76

Padfoot 4, 89–103
parenthood 130–133
part-humans 158, 159–163, 165, 170
pathological groupishness 234–236, 240
pedagogy 193, 240–242, 247–248
Pettigrew, Peter 19, 31, 92, 96–97, 100, 169
Pevensie 67, 74
phoenix 3, 49–50, 54–55, 56–57, 60–63, 73, 81, 85
politics 18, 152, 190, 233, 241
Polyjuice Potion 62, 74, 239
Potter, James 31, 72, 90, 91–92, 94, 96, 99–101, 103, 169
Potter, Lily 10, 31, 89, 94, 96, 99–100, 102, 103, 114–115, 169
Potts, Caractacus 124–125
power dynamic(s) 4, 29, 32, 38, 144, 148, 153, 194
Prisoner of Azkaban 3, 12, 19, 31–32, 74–75, 100, 109, 114, 138, 148, 169, 189
Privet Drive 90, 91, 93, 102, 112, 114, 121, 220
privilege 28, 29, 174, 233–234, 236, 238, 240, 242, 243

276 Index

pure-blood 90–91, 121, 122, 125–126, 129, 131, 136, 139, 159, 230, 233
purification 70, 73, 76, 77, 81, 90, 139

qilin 49, 55, 56, 57, 58–59, 60–63

racism 37, 146, 151, 152
Ravenclaw (House) 1, 110, 197, 203
redemption 68–69, 79, 155–156
religion 206–207, 254
responsibilities 146–147, 216, 223, 225–226, 227
Riddle, Tom 15, 109, 130–131, 162, 196, 218
rights 35, 123, 151, 156, 159, 167, 216, 223, 224–225, 226, 227
Rowling, J.K. 2, 9, 11, 16, 17, 20, 21, 22, 31, 34, 35–37, 38, 44, 49, 50, 51, 52, 53, 55, 57, 58, 60, 62, 68, 79, 85, 95, 122, 125, 127, 194, 205, 208, 238–239
RuPaul 240

salvation 18, 69, 74, 76, 79, 81
Satan 15–17, 19, 62
savior 69, 73, 76–77, 81
Scamander, Newt 3, 49, 50, 52, 53, 54, 55, 56, 57, 59, 60, 61, 63, 86
Scrimgeour, Rufus 9, 20, 78, 148
The Secret History 30, 33
Secret-Keeper 94, 100, 169
Seeker 75, 76, 111, 180, 182, 183, 186
serpent 15, 56, 62, 76, 80
Slytherin (House) 1, 73, 74, 91, 92, 114, 139, 189, 197, 200, 203, 218, 235
Slytherin, Salazar 122, 131
snake 50, 51, 73
Snape, Severus 9, 11–12, 14, 15, 22, 31, 32, 52, 57, 75, 77, 91, 92, 99–101, 102, 126, 143, 147, 159, 170, 205, 215, 217, 247, 249
Snitch 76, 115, 183, 189, 201
snow 71, 73, 75, 76, 77, 80, 81, 115
Sorcerer's Stone 71, 182, 184
Sorcerer's Stone (book) 13, 50, 51, 59, 67, 70, 107, 109, 114, 164, 169, 193, 202, 218, 220, 253
Sorting Hat 73, 197, 235
The Souls of Black Folk 159
stance 215, 216–217, 219, 220, 222, 223, 224, 226, 227
Stoker, Bram 3, 9–22, 44
strategic anti-essentialism 128, 129, 132, 136
Structural Forms of the Feminine Psyche 107
style 5, 40, 207, 215–227, 248
sweater(s) 68, 78–79, 85, 113–115, 116, 118
sword 14, 73, 92, 114, 115, 138, 225, 231

"The Tale of the Three Brothers" 72, 132, 199
The Tales of Beedle the Bard 143, 219
Tartt, Donna 30, 33
Ted Lasso 143, 150–152
TERF 238–241
theology 62, 71, 72, 75, 80
token(ism) 4, 158–170, 174–175
Tonks 91, 96, 99, 102, 111, 240
transhumanism 122, 130–133
trauma 4, 32, 33, 34, 53, 89, 98, 99, 103, 109, 111, 138, 160, 233, 242
Trocar 9

Umbridge, Dolores 5, 6, 32, 76, 102, 111, 114, 138, 143, 164, 206, 217, 230–243

vampire(s) 3, 9–22, 43, 95, 159
Van Helsing 14, 17, 21
Voldemort 4, 9–22, 31, 43, 50, 51–52, 54, 59, 70, 71, 72, 77, 80–81, 93, 94, 96, 97, 99, 101, 103, 109, 110, 111, 113, 117–118, 122, 127, 129, 130–133, 138, 143, 144, 147, 148, 149, 150, 156, 163, 168, 169, 170, 182–183, 190, 194, 205, 206, 211, 218, 220, 223, 224, 225–226, 233, 234, 238
vulnerability 32, 72, 81, 109, 138

weakness 69, 71, 72
Weasley, Arthur 4, 51, 76, 77, 98, 112, 121–133, 136, 149
Weasley, Ginny 4, 9, 13, 18, 73, 107–118, 130, 131, 138, 139, 199, 222
Weasley, Molly 4, 98, 99, 102, 107–118, 123–124, 125, 126, 137–138
Weasley, Ron 14, 22, 32, 49, 53, 71, 73, 74, 75, 76, 78, 79, 91, 93, 97, 99, 102, 108, 109, 110, 114, 115, 117, 122–123, 124, 126, 130–131, 138, 180, 184, 185–186, 199, 202, 203, 205, 222, 225
Weasley twins 12, 71, 74, 76, 92, 113, 114, 137
Westenra, Lucy 10, 13, 14, 17
Winky 160, 162, 165–166, 170
Winstead, Ashley 29, 35, 38
Wizarding War 94, 98, 103
Wizarding World 1–5, 36, 37, 54, 72, 86, 93, 96, 122, 125, 128, 129, 136, 145, 146, 147, 148, 149–150, 158, 159, 160, 161, 162, 163, 165, 168, 170, 179, 180, 184, 185, 187, 194, 195, 200, 211, 223, 234, 239, 242, 253

Young, James O. 127
Yule Ball 75, 109, 110, 118, 181, 198

www.ingramcontent.com/pod-product-compliance
Ingram Content Group UK Ltd.
Pitfield, Milton Keynes, MK11 3LW, UK
UKHW041930140426
5217IPUK00014B/394